Last Things

THE MIDDLE AGES SERIES

Ruth Mazo Karras, General Editor
Edward Peters, Founding Editor

A complete list of books in the series
is available from the publisher.

Last Things

Death and the Apocalypse in the Middle Ages

Edited by
Caroline Walker Bynum
and Paul Freedman

PENN

University of Pennsylvania Press

Philadelphia

10 9 8 7 6 5 4 3 2 1

Published by
University of Pennsylvania Press
Philadelphia, Pennsylvania 19104-4011

Library of Congress Cataloging-in-Publication Data
Last things : death and the Apocalypse in the Middle Ages / edited
by Caroline Walker Bynum and Paul Freedman.
    p.   cm. — (The Middle Ages series)
Includes bibliographical references and index.
ISBN 0-8122-3512-6 (cloth : alk. paper). —
ISBN 0-8122-1702-0 (pbk. : alk. paper)
    1. Eschatology—History of doctrines—Middle Ages, 600–1500.
I. Bynum, Caroline Walker.   II. Freedman, Paul H., 1949–
III. Series.
BT819.5.L37   1999
236′.09′02—dc21   99-34223
                                                            CIP

Frontispiece: Jan van Eyck, *The Last Judgment*.
Metropolitan Museum of Art, Fletcher Fund, 1933 (33.92b).

Contents

Introduction

Caroline Walker Bynum and Paul Freedman

Eschatology comes from the Greek *eschatos*—furthest or last—hence our title, *Last Things*, the term medieval thinkers themselves used for the variety of topics covered in this book.[1] Recent scholarship has tended to treat separately concerns that both medieval intellectuals and ordinary people would have seen as closely linked: death, the afterlife, the end of time (whether terrestrial or beyond earth), and theological anthropology or the theory of the person. In bringing within one set of covers essays on all four topics, it is our contention that none can be understood without the others. The interest in medieval death since the foundational work of Philippe Ariès in the 1960s and 1970s, the older debates over the conflict between resurrection and immortality generated by Oscar Cullman in the 1940s, the flurry of attention to the geography of the afterlife stimulated by Jacques Le Goff's *The Birth of Purgatory* in 1981, the outpouring of research on millennialism and apocalypse produced in reaction to Norman Cohn's *Pursuit of the Millennium* (1957), and recent study of the understanding of the human person stimulated in part by German scholars but carried into more popular discourse by historians such as Simon Tugwell and Caroline Bynum—this large body of literature has even more far-reaching implications when taken together than when considered as separate areas of research.[2] The moment of death, the places of the afterlife to which souls depart (heaven, hell, and purgatory), the final judgment or millennial age that may either be or presage the end of time, and the person, reunited at judgment or in the afterlife, are all "last things." By considering them together, we hope to add to discussions of how eschatological attitudes changed over time, to bring into sharper focus the divergent eschatological assumptions of the Middle Ages and the conflicts or incompatibilities among them, and to raise more explicitly than is sometimes done the question of how eschatological understandings hovered over human experience, inflecting the ways people spoke about values and hopes.

Recent Scholarship

There is no shortage of books and articles on aspects of eschatology. In popular as well as academic circles the medieval period is associated with a passionate atmosphere of fear yet also expectation, a preoccupation with the time of Christ's Second Coming and a restless poring over of natural and political disasters and upheavals for signs of the imminent denouement of sacred history. Current anticipation of the arrival of the new millennium, historiographic debates over how the year 1000 was perceived, and the attention given to medieval social movements with their often millenarian tinge—all these have encouraged study and reflection on the eschatological imagination of the Middle Ages. Perhaps more enduring and disturbing than the effects of the approach of the year 2000 are current obsessions with illness and dying that have prompted study of medieval notions of personal death, of a paradise beyond this life, and of the inspirational and protective presence of angelic beings.

Given the proliferation of works on medieval apocalyptic subjects and on medieval ideas of death, some justification is no doubt required for this collection and its intended place in the context of recent works. Eschatology understood as the significance of imminent future history (that is, as apocalyptic) has been a main subject of historical investigations since Marjorie Reeves's pioneering 1969 volume, *The Influence of Prophecy in the Later Middle Ages*. Much attention has been given to the course and influence of specific movements, especially in relation to calculations of the end and their resonance in popular demands for reform, revolution, or renewal. Such studies include influential accounts of individual prophets and prophecies, notably Bernard McGinn's *The Calabrian Abbot* and Robert Lerner's *The Powers of Prophecy*,[3] and a number of works on the Antichrist, among them Richard Emmerson's *Antichrist in the Middle Ages*.[4] Byzantine apocalyptic sentiment has been dealt with masterfully by Paul Alexander's *The Byzantine Apocalyptic Tradition*.[5] A comprehensive encyclopedia on the entire range of apocalyptic subjects has recently appeared.[6]

In addition to accounts of major symbols and prophets, there has been notable progress in perceiving the importance of anti-apocalyptic sentiment in the era of the barbarian kingdoms and the Carolingian Empire, centuries that used to be regarded as devoid of millenarian expectation. Richard Landes, in an article in the collection *The Use and Abuse of Eschatology in the Middle Ages*, has argued that what seem to be jejune temporal calculations of patristic theologians and monastic annalists in fact involved a continuing discourse against an identifiable moment of apocalypse that had the effect of postponing (and thereby ultimately inflating) expectation by recalculating the age of the world and the arrival of the millennial "seventh day."[7] Derk Visser has asserted the enduring importance of a lesser-known figure of the ninth century, Berengaudus of Ferrières, whose optimistic millenarianism reappears as late as in the iconography of the Van Eyck Ghent Altarpiece.[8] Although the apocalyptic formulations of this era were largely discredited and their influence has been more difficult to discern than that of such major high medieval prophets as Joachim or even eccentric later writers such as Arnau de Vilanova, their formulae and expectations would endure and be reworked well beyond the limits of the Middle Ages.

Recent scholarly interest in the apocalypse has centered on timing, not only of the future but also in relation to the past ages of history, and on the identity of prophesied figures such as the Antichrist, the Whore of Babylon, or the Angelic Pope. The various eschatological movements have also been considered as phenomena in their own right. Indeed, since Norman Cohn's *Pursuit of the Millennium*, scholars have argued about how far—or whether—such movements had their origins and expectations in demands for radical social change. The millennium could be seen not only as the unfolding end of history but also as the arrival of justice for the oppressed and inarticulate. Some recent studies have related demands for the humbling of the mighty and the exaltation of the meek to the Peace Movements and the arrival of the year 1000,[9] the heretics burned at Orléans and Arras in the eleventh century, and to the programs of the Spiritual Franciscans, Hussites, and peasant insurrections of the late Middle Ages.[10] The virulent antisemitism of the late Middle Ages has also been linked to apocalyptic speculation about the enclosed unclean peoples of Gog and Magog.[11]

This emphasis on social history has diminished the tendency to regard medieval apocalyptic movements as purely religious or psychological expressions; hence they become something other than instances of the mystical response or spasmodic irrationality so often attributed to the period. In taking this approach historians have attended to the content of apocalyptic anticipation, implicitly dividing the subject into optimistic accounts of a future utopia and fearful pessimism in anticipation of the plagues and other upheavals foretold by the Book of Revelation.[12] Pessimistic tendencies have been related to the psychological needs and religious anxieties of the Middle Ages while the optimistic versions have been the object of a more sociological analysis.

Although the topic of apocalypticism was previously sometimes equated with the history of specific prophetic movements, literary historians have long treated it as a discernible element in medieval thought generally.[13] Following in this tradition, Richard Emmerson and Ronald Herzman suggest that medieval literary works are pervaded by apocalyptic thinking. Katherine Kerby-Fulton has written on the optimistic apocalyptic background to *Piers Plowman*.[14] Rather than seeing apocalyptic sentiment as the expression of unbearable tensions within society or doctrine, medievalists are now more inclined to find it mingled with this-worldly concerns, a lens through which experience and change were viewed, not simply a breaking apart of the established order. After all, as Guy Lobrichon has pointed out, there are almost placidly orthodox ways of approaching the apocalypse.[15] Orthodox interpretations are not merely attempts to put off or obfuscate chiliastic events but also descriptions of how time and individual experience are permeated with the eternal destiny of humanity.

Along with work devoted to the apocalypse per se, there has recently been an outpouring of scholarly literature on two other aspects of eschatology: the fate of individuals at the moment of what Philippe Ariès called "personal death" and the place, or other world, to which their souls depart after such individual judgment. A number of books on dying, death, and the dead in the Middle Ages have emphasized the ways an increasing focus on an individual's own death as the moment of personal accounting inflected much of life and contributed to what the French historian Jean Delumeau has characterized as a Western "guilt culture," so dominated by fear of damnation that much of life became a series of ritual preparations for dying. The increasing prominence of deathbed demons and of hell in art (our frontispiece provides an example) has been widely analyzed both as an expression of religious anxiety and as a mechanism of social control.[16] From historians such as Frederick Paxton who have emphasized the importance of community in early medieval death rituals to recent scholarly literature on such subjects as tomb sculpture and the dance of Death that emphasizes the individualism of late medieval responses, recent work in art history, archaeology, literature, and history has treated the eschatological significance of death as "last thing."[17]

Similarly there has been great attention in the past decades to the places of the afterlife and the means of access to them. Aron Gurevich and Claude Carozzi have explored voyages to the other world; Alison Morgan, Ernst Benz, and Peter Dinzelbacher, among others, have studied the visions of heaven and hell that figure so prominently in late medieval collections of revelations.[18] As even the popular press has noted, medieval ideas of heaven, hell, and purgatory have recently received much scholarly attention. McDannell and Lang, among others, have studied the medieval image of heaven. Alan Bernstein's *The Formation of Hell* is devoted to the gradual theological emergence of hell and the elaboration of its geography.[19] In his path-breaking book *The Birth of Purgatory*, Jacques Le Goff took the study of the third eschatological place beyond questions concerning its doctrinal origin and justification to examine its effect on how this world was regarded and how the drive toward accumulation of wealth could be reconciled with the possibility of salvation.[20] Barbara Newman has recently taken another step by interpreting purgatory less as a place than as a pool of suffering and underlining the role of women in its development.[21]

The Three Eschatologies

Medieval discussions of "last things" sometimes referred primarily to events (such as the 1000-year reign of the saints, the advent of Antichrist, or the resurrection and Last Judgment) that might come to all humanity in time or at the end of time. In the light of such a *telos*, human society was on pilgrimage, in transit (what Frank Kermode calls the mid-dest), confidently expectant or cowering in fear. Eschatological discussions sometimes, however, had in mind predominantly "last things" for each individual at his or her own moment of death—not only the places to which a soul might go, but also the accounting, the call to reckoning, signified by the end. Hence conceptions of "last things" tended to oscillate along several spectra: from collective to indi- *1, 2,* vidual, from temporal to beyond time or atemporal, from a stress on spirit to *3* a sense of embodied or reembodied self.

Many combinations of emphases were possible. Ends could be within time or just beyond. Hope for a millennial arrival within time could be a radical, even revolutionary critique of existing conditions or a support for existing power or for reform already afoot;[22] it could usher in a golden age on earth or herald the immediate end of the world. Or the end for all could be the Last Judgment that ended time itself, consigning all mortals to heavenly bliss or perpetual damnation.

The end could also be individual, a person's own "hour of death." This personal end could be the moment of immediate decision for the separated soul (condemnation or redemption) or the advent of a period of waiting until judgment came for the reconstituted person at the end or beyond the end of time. Or personal death, although decisive, could nonetheless usher in a period of further transformation or purging (often in a third place, purgatory), which in some sense continued the changeability of life into the hitherto supposedly fixed (after)life beyond time. Given this variety of emphases and possible combinations, we may well ask whether we can find any broad patterns of change in eschatological thinking or behavior over the course of the Middle Ages. To answer this question, it may help to put side by side the various areas of recent scholarship mentioned above.

Work on the topics of death, the afterlife, apocalyptic, and theological anthropology has been concerned—as good historical scholarship always is—with change. Study of medieval attitudes toward death and death rituals has tended to agree in essence if not always in detail with Philippe Ariès's sense of a shift in the central Middle Ages from "tamed death"—a death expected and prepared for, experienced in community—to a "personal death," an understanding of the moment of death as a decisive accounting for an individual self.[23] Study of the afterlife has seen a parallel shift, in the twelfth century, from a twofold eschatological landscape of heaven and hell to an at least partially three-tiered afterlife, including the in-between space and time of purgatory, to which most Christian souls go after "personal death" for a propitiating and cleansing that may (or may not, depending on the prayer-work of those on earth) continue until a far-distant Last Judgment. Work on concepts of the human person has detected in the thirteenth century a shift from emphasis on resurrection of the literal, material body at the end of time to stress on the experience of the separated soul after death, although this scholarship has pointed out that the separated soul was at the same time increasingly imaged as bodily (somatomorphic), and that ordinary piety came to be characterized by both a sense of the significance of physical death and an emphasis on the spiritual value of somatic phenomena, especially suffering.

Partly coinciding with and partly departing from this picture, scholarship on apocalypticism and millennialism (those subjects of eschatology that see the collective end as imminent or ushering in a 1000-year reign of the saints) has tended to see the periods of the early church and of the later Middle Ages as physical and material in their eschatologies, characterized by proliferating visions of a final conflagration of the world but also the advent of a perfect earthly society of justice, plenty, and peace. In the 1970s, scholars viewed the period between Augustine's rejection of apocalyptic thinking in the late fourth century and the reemergence of apocalyptic scenarios in the late twelfth century as a period of "realized eschatology," in which Christ's resurrection or Second Coming was already located in the heart of every devout Christian.[24] Recent work has often seen traces of otherwise effaced popular apocalyptic fervor in the anti-apocalyptic writings of clerics and has emphasized (as does Claudia Papka in our volume in discussing *Piers Plowman*) the way the sense of an ending hovers over all spiritual writing in the Middle Ages.[25]

If we consider this body of scholarship in its interconnectedness, it seems clear then, first, that the twelfth and thirteenth centuries do see basic shifts in eschatological assumptions—shifts that must be understood in historical context—but also that several sets of eschatological attitudes coexist and conflict throughout the western European Middle Ages. We may call these sets of attitudes the eschatology of resurrection, the eschatology of immortality, and the eschatology of apocalypse.

In the 1940s, Oscar Cullman argued that Christian eschatology was based fundamentally in the Hebrew notion of embodied person, not in the Greek (or Platonic) identification of soul with self.[26] Thus the early Christian idea of bodily resurrection, an element of the Christian creed from circa 200, was crucial to hopes of ultimate salvation and significance, whereas the notion that what survives is an immortal spirit, temporarily encased in flesh, is a later and only partially successful grafting from classical culture. Such an effort to sort out ideas according to intellectual precursors alone belongs to a particular stage of twentieth-century historiography in which debates about Christianity versus classical culture or Pauline versus patristic Christianity reflected in part debates between Protestant and Catholic understandings of the early church. Today we tend to locate ideas more historically and are inclined to regard the emphasis on bodily resurrection in the years around 200, as does Carole Straw in her essay, in the context of a need for retribution and triumph associated with the experience of persecution, or as other scholars have recently done, in Greco-Roman as well as Jewish death rites with their emphasis on reassembling bodies for peaceful and respectful burial.[27] Similarly, we are inclined to situate the emergence of an emphasis on a separated soul immediately after death and on a place (or time or kind of experience) for that soul's continuing development both, as Carole Straw and Peter Brown do, in changing circumstances and ideas of political and ecclesial authority and, as Manuele Gragnolati does, in changing sensibilities concerning the person and the significance of suffering. Nonetheless there does seem to be (as Cullman's analysis makes clear) a disjunction and incompatibility throughout medieval texts between an eschatology of resurrection—a sense of last things that focuses significance in the moment at the end of time when the physical body is reconstituted and judged—and an eschatology of immortality—in which the experience of personal death is the moment of judgment, after which the good soul (and it is necessarily the soul that is in question, because the body is moldering in the grave) either gains glorification and beatific vision at once or moves into the experience of growth through suffering known as purgatory.

The disjunction between immortality and resurrection does not, how-

ever, seem to encompass fully the variety of eschatological emphases between
the second and the sixteenth centuries. Scholars today are inclined to pay
greater attention than did those of mid-century to what we can call the eschatology of apocalypse—a stance that assumes the imminent arrival of the
end of the world for all of humanity. Sharing with the eschatology of resurrection an emphasis on the end of time, a sense of the person as embodied,
and a focus on humanity as collective, the eschatology of apocalypse shares
with the eschatology of immortality a sense that what matters is the here and
now, an end that looms as immediate or very soon. Apocalyptic eschatology
contrasts, however, with both the eschatology of resurrection and that of immortality in implying a political payoff. It faces toward society and coerces
the here and now, although it can be reformist as well as radical and does
not necessarily, as scholars in the 1950s argued, recruit the disadvantaged or
the discontented. As the papers of Backman, Hudson, Daniel, Smoller, and
Papka make clear, the eschatology of apocalypse not only gives rise to predictions of the horrors or delights of imminent end, but also sometimes inflects
and deepens literature, such as descriptions of plague or visions of heaven,
hell, and resurrection, that seems originally to arise from traditions with a
much less imminent sense of "last things."

The three eschatologies differ in what the person seems fundamentally
to be and the extent to which his or her fate is individual or collective, in how
and whether time seems to be marching, in where the end is located, in the
extent to which "last things" provide a locus from which the here and now
is reformed, rejected or embraced. Moreover, they are not fully compatible.
Certain problems are obvious. If the moment of personal death determines
whether one goes to heaven or hell, judgment at the end of time, although
required by the Christian creed, may seem superfluous or supernumerary;
furthermore, it is hard to see why the resurrection of the body adds anything,
as Bernard of Clairvaux says it must, to a beatific vision already received by
souls in heaven.[28] If the separated soul works out the payment for sins in
a personal between-time, how will this individual time-calculus square with
the march of ages or days toward either a distant bodily resurrection or an
imminent Antichrist and world conflagration? Won't some souls in purgatory run out of time? If the signs or even the calendar point to an immediate
end of the world for all people, why should the Christian quantify individual
sins and their penalties or endow masses to be said for centuries rather than
gather an army to re-take Jerusalem or execute Christ's persecutors? Or, to
take another example, if relics reside in altars awaiting resurrection, how can

the saints simultaneously petition Christ in heaven? But if they do not so petition, how then can the faithful escape not only final condemnation but also decades or centuries of purgatorial fire?

Theologians and preachers occasionally worried about some of these issues and incompatibilities. But for the most part eschatological thinking and behavior encompassed contradictions fruitfully, if not always easily. It would be quite wrong to see any text explored in this volume as an example of a single eschatology, just as it would be inaccurate to take the nuanced historical changes described by our authors as the replacement of one eschatology by another. Although each element changes meaning and significance over time, bodily resurrection, the experience of separated soul, and the looming of apocalypse are all present in some sense in every text discussed below. For example, Bernard of Clairvaux's heaven, explored by Anna Harrison, might seem a fine-tuned case of an eschatology of immortality if the pressure of resurrection belief did not so deeply influence Bernard's concept of person. The plague literature explored by Laura Smoller maps onto a late-medieval scientific curiosity about wonders an eschatology that is not only apocalyptic but also individualistic and materialist in ways that connect to concerns for immortality and resurrection.

The contradictions and richness of the texts and experiences described in this volume should not disconcert us. As most recent scholarship underscores, religion is not so much doctrine as a way of life. Medieval eschatology was, like life, profoundly inconsistent. Perhaps eschatology is, in the western tradition, the most paradoxical aspect of religiosity. There are religious traditions in which self flows from a spirit world to which it almost effortlessly and seamlessly returns, traditions in which earthly existence is a moment in an eternal dreaming. In such a sensibility, neither individual nor collective death is exactly an end. In contrast, the western religious traditions—Islam, Judaism, and Christianity—are all brooded over by the sense of "last things." A sense of the end, whether soon or distant, individual or collective, contradicts (indeed explodes) itself, for it looks to a moment that gives significance to the course of time by finally denying or erasing (ending) that to which it offers significance. If eschatology is then essentially paradoxical, we should not be surprised to find that the plethora of eschatological writings produced by the western European Middle Ages utilizes and deepens rather than denies or impoverishes its multifold and contradictory traditions.

Because all three eschatologies are found in every era and indeed in every effort to explore and describe "last things," we have not organized the essays presented here as different kinds of eschatology. Rather we have grouped them under three rubrics: "The Significance of Dying and the Afterlife," "Apocalyptic Time," and "The Eschatological Imagination."

Part I focuses on changing concepts of the afterlife and hence of the space and time of personal, individual destiny. Carole Straw and Peter Brown provide complementary descriptions of the emergence of a sense of purgatory out of an earlier spirituality that focused on judgment and resurrection. Manuele Gragnolati describes fourteenth-century notions of heaven and hell, in which heaven is achieved via an experience of suffering that—while not purgatory—functions as such in the poetry studied. The death of the archbishop of Cologne discussed by Jacqueline Jung is not only an instance of personal sanctity via martyrdom parallel to the early eschatological understanding traced by Straw; it also, like the poetry Gragnolati studies, makes suffering the vehicle to the individual's afterlife. Hence the disparate papers in Part I are all in a subtle sense about purgatory or purgation.

Part II treats authors and texts that are apocalyptic in the sense of expecting an imminent end to the world, although Benjamin Hudson's review of Gaelic literature also treats texts that focus on distant resurrection and both E. Randolph Daniel and Laura Smoller suggest that the authors they study are in no simple sense apocalyptic. The essays in Part III address several classic texts and objects that either directly confront or indirectly evoke "last things," both apocalyptic and non-apocalyptic. Although they share definitions of eschatology with the earlier essays, these final papers focus less on what the texts tell us about last things—whether death or heaven or heaven on earth—than on how an awareness of end time inflects the ways people think about and depict self and community. Hence every essay in this collection in some sense reflects all three of the eschatological awarenesses of the European Middle Ages.

The Themes of This Collection

The four papers in Part I concern the transformation worked by death, a future event taking place in a more assuredly proximate time than the apocalypse. Its advent, even in the most placid life, is unmistakable. Apart from the disturbing and often terrifying anticipation, certain issues provoked by the Christian attitudes toward death are discussed in the four essays: the relation between the individual's death and the ultimate disposition meted out by the Last Judgment; the condition of the soul after death in relation to bodily suffering in this world and the future resurrection of the flesh, and the significance of earthly pain and penance for the soul's destiny in the next world. In all these matters, the personal drama of death is to be understood in relation to a progressive unfolding of collective history, divine order, and the eschatological climax that provides the ultimate disposition for individual soul and body.

In the church of the martyrs described by Carole Straw, the winding up of this world and its tawdry affairs seemed near, and so the question of the soul's sensations in the (short) span between personal death and collective resurrection did not directly arise. The expectation of physical torment as a climax to worldly existence corresponded with immediate entry into bliss in its aftermath. That torment was itself an individual glimpse of the end not only because of testing and purgation but also as prologue to an immediate heavenly existence. The earthly body's sensations applied to the martyrs while the resurrected flesh and its sufferings were invoked to dramatize the punishment of the persecutors in the world to come.

The stark extremes of sanctification and punishment in the early church changed first with the embrace by Rome and later with the waning of ancient Christianity. Peter Brown describes a world in which a large category of the partially bad or the worldly but well intentioned had to be dealt with. The existence of such a category and Augustine's rejection of perfectionism meant that the expiation of inadequacy might push against the borders of the afterlife, an afterlife that was itself extended by the retreat of a certain, immediate judgment. The first glimmers of purgatory are visible in considering the disposition of these *non valde mali*, the imperfect but not reprobate, not because of their intrinsic deserts but because of a dialectic of divine mercy and a process of personal satisfaction of spiritual debts. Here again the evolving attitude toward the transformations wrought by death was affected by (and in turn influenced) eschatological assumptions. While the church of the martyrs had little interest in penance and telescoped purgation into the drama of martyrdom, the early medieval church focused more on the painfully slow improvement of the self. God as the righteous judge of the wicked or as the unaccountably merciful figure of the late and post-Roman world gave way to a more careful keeper of a penitential ledger as the apocalypse receded.

The remaining two essays deal with the high Middle Ages and the sufferings of the body before and after death. As in Carole Straw's discussion of martyrdom, so too in Jacqueline Jung's essay, it is atrocious physical suffering before a violent death (here of the archbishop of Cologne) that determines the fate of the soul. In the arguments put forward by Caesarius of Heisterbach, however, martyrdom is not the climax of a pious life but a holy death made necessary by a worldly life. The archbishop, an example of the *non valde mali* but as a powerful rather than a mediocre man, was sanctified by reason of his horrible death, a brief but intense purgation reminiscent of early Christian martyrdom but under the sign of penance rather than triumphant witness—an example of sweeping divine mercy.

Physical suffering was also important to Bonvesin de la Riva, as Manuele Gragnolati argues, but in a form somewhat different from that posited by Caesarius of Heisterbach. Pain in this life is an inevitable accompaniment to the corrupt body whose weakness and rottenness are unmistakable indications of the approach of death. For Bonvesin such weakness is overcome in a very physical heaven. But suffering is a means of salvation itself if we join with the graphically depicted agony of Christ on the cross. In a sense then, an affective *imitatio Christi* is a kind of purgatory. But to Bonvesin the arrival of the end is immediate. As with the early church (but for different reasons), entry into the afterlife brings with it the full impact of divine judgment on the individual.

The articles in Part II concern the best-known aspect of medieval eschatology, the arrival of an apocalyptic end of the world and of time. The end time might be anticipated as a series of disasters, as was commonly the case in the Irish writings studied by Benjamin Hudson. So grim was the prospect of the final judgment that among the special favors for Ireland that St. Patrick was thought to have procured from God was a promise to destroy it seven years before the ultimate ordeal to be suffered by the rest of the world. As Laura Smoller points out, those undergoing the terrifying experience of the Black Death were moved, not surprisingly, to regard the pestilence as more than a natural disaster—part of a movement of catastrophes from East to West indicating that the end time was at hand.

On the other hand, millennial expectation could challenge the exclusive emphasis on divine wrath. An era of exile might also promise a new Exodus from human failure and corruption, according to E. Randolph Daniel's analysis of the prophetic theories of Joachim of Fiore. Clifford Backman shows how Arnau de Vilanova, the renowned physician and apocalyptic theorizer of the late thirteenth and early fourteenth centuries, combined fears of humanity's inadequacy before the impending onslaught of Antichrist with an essentially optimistic exhortation to radical reform and expectation of a time of peace after a sharp period of testing.

In all these instances apocalyptic chronologies were set with a certain precision: the immediate present of the Black Death of 1348–49, Irish fears centered around the arrival of the Feast of John the Baptist in 1096, Joachim's expectations for 1200, and the predicted arrival of Antichrist according to Arnau de Vilanova in about 1365. Beyond precise issues of timing, however, the authors of the articles in Part II consider the interaction of chronology and collective apocalypse with the eschatological view of human life. Hudson notes the Gaelic proclivity for journeys and visions of the next world and a sense of different fates, for the Irish collectively as in St. Patrick's privilege already alluded to, or the special status of St. Ailbe and his followers awaiting the final judgment in penitential rest. Occasionally Ireland itself was thought of as the promised land, thus asserting a form of realized eschatology, the active fulfillment of antecedents to the end of time. In the case of Joachim of Fiore there is a similar sense of realized anticipation, that the era of exile is reaching its climax but the leader of the exodus to salvation, St. Bernard, has already appeared.

Clifford Backman and Laura Smoller explore the confluence of materialistic and miraculous explanations for eschatological phenomena. Backman explains how a doctor and scientist, generally enthusiastic about naturalistic and materialist explanations, nonetheless avoids discussion of bodily reassemblage at the end of time, stressing instead the joy of heaven. Arnau's precision was focused on determining the *when* rather than the *what* of apocalypse. Smoller demonstrates how the plague epidemic was explained by reference to natural causes understood in terms of apocalyptic prophetic traditions. As Smoller points out, place, time, and event all possessed eschatological significance so that the report of the doctors of Paris on the causes of the plague is a series of naturalistic explanations to be read within an eschatological context and set of assumptions. Such a mixture modified and softened stark predictions of the timing of the apocalypse. It was imminent as revealed by measurable signs and prophecy, but its exact timing remained ambiguous and dependent on the unfolding of nature according to divine plan.

The essays in Part III treat in detail some very famous texts and objects and thereby raise large questions about ways of imagining "last things" between the twelfth and fourteenth centuries. Anna Harrison gives an interpretation of Bernard of Clairvaux's sermons for All Saints, some of his most studied sermons. Harvey Stahl relates a gorgeous full-page miniature from a late thirteenth-century Book of Hours to contemporary reliquaries and thus casts light on one of the most important paintings of the Middle Ages, Hubert and Jan van Eyck's *Ghent Altarpiece* of 1432. Claudia Rattazzi Papka poses in a new way the issue of voice in two of the most famous texts of the fourteenth century, Dante's *Commedia* and William Langland's *Piers Plowman*.

Anna Harrison's essay addresses heaven—a goal that lies beyond earth and time, yet can tantalize the yearning soul in this life with a foretaste of blessedness. She argues that Bernard of Clairvaux's heaven is less a community of saints than an individual experience of beatitude, however important community may be as the backdrop against which spiritual growth through suffering and sympathy occurs. Harrison's Bernard is indeed the chimera he understood himself to be; the paradoxes she finds in his view of heaven encapsulate several of the paradoxes of high-medieval eschatology. Harrison shows us a departed soul already tasting union but needing body for final ecstasy. Bernard's heaven, as she interprets it, is one in which consummation both does and does not come at personal death; it is a realm in which the monastic community both is and is not integral, a goal beyond time in which nonetheless we find that which is essential to time — change, development, the growth of desire.

Using late medieval art, Harvey Stahl gives a description and interpretation of heaven quite similar to Harrison's. The afterlife he finds depicted in an early fourteenth-century Book of Hours is a heaven, a heavenly church, and a place of beatific vision available to the faithful (as is Bernard's heaven) before the end of time. Situating this place of blessedness in the context both of Triumph of the Virgin iconography and of reliquaries, Stahl shows how problematic and powerful is the painted embodiedness of the blessed. The fact that both the Book of Hours miniature and the monumental Ghent altarpiece are presented in a reliquary-like frame calls attention to the bodies of the blessed, as do the complex iconographic connections in the miniature to the Bodily Assumption of the Virgin. Yet this heaven, like Bernard's, is no longer clearly located after Apocalypse or Judgment. The blessed place Stahl explores is a heaven outside time, available now — one in which the soul is already body-shaped (somatomorphic).[29] Such depictions of heaven as a place for somatomorphic selves before resurrection and judgment are perhaps the context for understanding the sensibility Clifford Backman sees in Arnau de Vilanova, a sensibility in which intense materialist curiosity nevertheless avoids locating and probing too specifically the eschatological body.

Claudia Rattazzi Papka's essay is infused with a sense of eschatological paradox similar to the paradox Harrison finds in Bernard. Papka treats the *Divine Comedy* and *Piers Plowman* as what she calls "fictions of judgment" — that is, narratives that simultaneously claim access to a transcendent perspective on history and assert their contingent status as human, "made" artifacts (*fictiones*). Through attention specifically to apocalyptic moments in the two poems (moments that claim to announce "last things") and to moments of self-referentiality (moments when the authors reflect on the limits of their knowledge and expression), Papka shows that Dante claims a transcendent voice, transgressing human limits, while Langland's reluctance to make such claims may be related to the much discussed indeterminacy characteristic of his poem. Papka suggests that the contrast between Langland and Dante represents a general turning in the fourteenth century from poetry confident enough to speak the (of course self-consciously constructed) voice of the *eschaton* to a more situated, hesitant, and partial apocalyptic voice. Her readings help us to see that all eschatological texts reflect in some way their status as fictions; hence all must assert, whether consciously or not, their own nature as mediating and contingent, as paradoxical claims to speak in the now of what is beyond time and speech.

The Year 2000

This volume considers the various manifestations of medieval eschatological thinking and so is not directly concerned with possible parallels with contemporary concerns. Some such reflection is unavoidable, nevertheless, in view of the arrival of the year 2000 and the widely credited truism that we live in apocalyptic times. In fact the investigation of medieval ideas of last things shows just how little our era dwells on apocalyptic apprehensions in any meaningful way. It is our contention that the late twentieth century is not apocalyptic, although it may be eschatological in the broad sense we have tried to emphasize here. The year 2000 is an event surrounded by a largely artificially generated excitement and will almost certainly be thrown onto the already massive dust heap of popular culture once it has enjoyed its brief place in the public imagination, to join channeling, oat bran, and the Spice Girls. Its one semi-serious aspect, the threatened "Y2K" computer failure, in fact exemplifies the evanescent quality of the event. Few people expect computer code problems to bring about an end to the world as we know it. Discussion becomes animated only regarding the costs of fixing it or the possible unintended but temporary consequences of missing some needed repairs. It is a *faux* apocalypse and, insofar as it marks any sort of threat, a massively secular one.

Those who really do believe in an imminent apocalypse, like the Branch Davidians or the enthusiasts for comets, are hard to take seriously except in terms of the havoc they, or their suppression, have wreaked. While perhaps more violent than some of their predecessors, they are part of a long chain of apocalyptic hopes that have characterized the fringes of American religious and pseudo-scientific enthusiasm since the nineteenth century and will outlast the turn of the millennium.

The present moment is, if anything, characterized by a *waning* of apocalyptic expectations of both a final conflagration and the arrival of a just society. The underlying assumptions, certainly of most Americans, that things will go on pretty much as they are now except with some newer and slicker technology contrasts dramatically with the real apprehensiveness of the mid-twentieth century or with the more sweeping confidence of Bellamy's *Looking Backward* and other futurologists at the turn of the last century.[30] The danger of some sort of nuclear war is probably greater now than in the 1950s, given the proliferation of weapons and the decentralization of political power in the world, but this threat lacks the immediacy and coherence of Soviet-American confrontations of yore. Nothing remotely approaching the mid-century atmosphere of dread and brinkmanship now exists. Recent pseudo-apocalyptic movies like *Armageddon* or *Deep Impact* end happily with a return to normalcy as opposed to genuinely pessimistic end-of-the-world productions of decades past such as *On the Beach* or *Fail Safe*.

Expectation of a favorable revolutionary transformation of society flourished during much of the twentieth century but died by its close. That change takes place and accelerates is undeniable, but it is no longer widely believed that principles of scientific socialism, or of eugenics, or behaviorism need only be applied to create a utopian order. Nor is it widely believed as was the case a hundred years ago that public life and democracy will expand, that the citizenry will become wiser, or that workers will have a larger share in the management of enterprise. If the "free market" serves as a commonly held current nostrum, its promise is of an expansion very much resembling what already exists.

Where there may be some similarities between the medieval and the contemporary is in terms of eschatology more broadly defined. Many recent manifestations of popular culture express an anxiety over the instability of bodily identity resulting from such things as genetic manipulation, organ transplants, or cloning. Recent examples of the theme of survival in a body transplant and the identity problems engendered by such a form of survival include Lawrence Steinberg, *Memories of Amnesia*, Nancy Weber, *Broken-Hearted*, and Laurel Doud, *This Body*.[31]

Popular culture in recent years has also been particularly obsessed with dying, near-death experience, and survival after death. Elizabeth Kübler-Ross pioneered analysis of dying as a progressive experience in work that after three decades remains very influential.[32] In 1994 Frank J. Tipler attempted to give a proof from modern science of the resurrection of the dead at the end of time, a book that received wide (if temporary) attention.[33]

More significantly for our purposes, death, heaven, and ghosts are now regarded as ways of assessing the significance of a life in a manner seemingly reminiscent of late medieval memento mori literature. Toni Morrison's *Beloved* is among the most impressive examples of use of the theme of supernatural survival to explore the significance of individual life.[34] A number of films such as *Ghost*, *Heaven Can Wait*, or *Truly, Madly, Deeply* concern attempts to influence or remake mortal life after death with comic or pathetic effect.[35] The spate of recent illness memoirs may be simply part of the irresistible, cloying spread of the therapeutic, but it also evokes the medieval idea that a "good death" serves as an emblem of how one has lived.

Here, too, however, as with apocalyptic scenarios, the contemporary take on the eschatological is more sunny than its superficial resemblance to the Middle Ages at first suggests. We imagine death, near-death, or otherworldly journeys, even ghosts, in terms of sweetness and the realization of an essentially good self. Medieval journeys to the other side by and large dwelled more on hell than on heaven. The return of the deceased was not usually very reassuring.[36] We are inclined to congratulate ourselves for facing (or at least talking about) death more frankly than was the case twenty or thirty years ago, but our approaches remain somewhat confused and blandly optimistic.[37] Current preoccupations with dying, near-death experience, or the supernatural are much less shaped and coherent than was the case in an era with a greater everyday familiarity with death and a universally shared doctrine of survival after death. Nonetheless, as the revival of interest in angels demonstrates, our era can't help but mimic and appropriate language and imagery from the Middle Ages even if rendered in an eclectic and doctrineless fashion.

We do feel unease before a future that seems likely to include terrible environmental destruction, the proliferation of world systems that control by mindless technology, a degradation of sensibility, literacy, and attention span, perhaps even that effacement of the human signalled by Heidegger. These are, however, not as vivid or immediate as apprehension of the arrival of Antichrist, or the joining of earthly events with a theologically worked out divine order, or the once dreaded World War III. At the end of the twentieth century we are neither very apocalyptic, nor very eschatological, nor even very scared. Not, perhaps, as much as we ought to be.

PART I

THE SIGNIFICANCE OF DYING AND THE AFTERLIFE

Settling Scores

Eschatology in the Church of the Martyrs

Carole Straw

BENEATH THE ALTAR, the souls of the martyrs[1] cried indignantly for ven-geance.[2] In the "terrible tribunal of [the] savior and master,"[3] persecutors would find "no mercy" from God's exacting justice.[4] From a black abyss, a sulfurous fire blazed ingeniously: it could burn forever, but never consume its victims.[5] The tables would be turned and insults would recoil upon the per-petrators. Martyrs would become triumphant victors, judging the very ones who had pronounced such brutal sentences upon them.[6] Polycarp shook his fist, "Get out of here, godless heathens!"[7] Tied to the stake, he warned, "You threaten me with a temporary fire that is soon extinguished. But you don't know about the judgment that is to come, and the everlasting fire that awaits unbelievers."[8] Perpetua's friends lectured the mob, "stressing the joy they [had] in their suffering," and "warn[ing] them of God's judgment." "You've got us, but God will get you!"[9]

The martyrs would have their satisfaction; scores would be settled. The martyrs' heroic endurance and the perfected life of their resurrection would prove beyond question the doctrine for which they had surrendered their lives. God's wrath would vindicate Christians and confound the obstinate pagans.[10] Apocalyptic judgment was "the prayer of Christians," Tertullian proclaimed. "This will bring shame to nonbelievers; this will bring joy to the angels."[11]

This unsparing world of the martyrs was founded on a strict sense of justice as exact requital, a *lex talionis*, for the Christian universe was governed by reciprocal exchanges designed to achieve balance and equilibrium. For Christians, the Apocalypse would be that critical moment of resolution when good would be rewarded and evil punished. Only after that final reckoning would equity, justice, and harmony prevail, when accounts had been settled and each rendered his due. These conceptions of reciprocity and retribution lay at the heart of the distinctive apocalyptic mentality that characterized the church of the martyrs in this true "age of anxiety" (c. 100–313).[12]

Simply to *be* of this church was to share this apocalyptic mentality. Writers were militant and demanding, impatient of ambiguity and complexity, and wedded to absolutes. Reflection and introspection gave way to instinctive, visceral responses. Revelation and subjective conviction replaced discursive reasoning; violence often succeeded persuasion. The concrete and material prevailed over the abstract and immaterial: heaven and hell, the soul and body of the afterlife were elaborated in terms easily understood by analogy with realities known. People, motivations, and actions tended to be reduced to moralistic types: monster and martyr, cruelty and altruism, tragedy and triumph. So, too, polarities of spirit and flesh were fastidiously antithetical, never approaching harmony and reconciliation. The universe was divided and embittered: the ancient mentality of the vendetta overwhelmed more subtle ideas of justice and moral reform. Extremism, a lack of subtlety, willful disregard of vital distinctions, a tendency to cast events in the worst light possible—all characterized this aggressively defensive style of thought. This apocalyptic mentality was the child (for good or evil) of an agonistic, contest culture.[13]

From a long historical perspective, this mentality is extremely significant. Apocalypticism translated into martyrdom, for it demanded of Christians a willingness to die for Christ at Armageddon. The martyr would remain the supreme ideal, even though later, less literal translations would include monks, crusaders, missionaries, and less august exemplars of self-abnegation. Second, the status of the Christians as a persecuted elect worked to shape the church into a resilient, rigorous, and potentially expansive institution of social and ideological change. Here passivity was transformed into activity: the martyr became the monk, and also the bishop; and even the average Christian, whose sacrificial patience made him a stalwart and obedient member of the body of Christ.[14]

This world without quarter fostered a severe eschatology, for the bitter tensions between Christians and nonbelievers evoked ever more acrimonious and alarming predictions. Eschatology was central to, and inseparable from, the larger political aims of winning credibility and respectability for Christians.[15] Growth of the community seemed impossible without this safety; yet ironically the community flourished the more from the lack of it.[16] But how did one prove the truth of Christianity to win a secure place in society? Early apologists (e.g., Justin, Tatian, Athenagoras, Minucius Felix) had sought toleration and focused on a distant *Parousia* as the "truth test" to earn credibility and justify accommodation for the new sect.[17]

As tensions and persecutions grew more fierce, however, emphases shifted. Capitalizing on their rejection, Christians defined themselves more assertively in opposition to their enemies, be they pagans, Jews, Docetists, or other heretics—and this to their advantage. The "truth test" became martyrdom itself; the apocalypse was now. The martyr ($\mu\acute{\alpha}\rho\tau\upsilon\varsigma$) was the "witness" who testified to the truth; more than that, martyrs came to *prove* the truth actively, for the truth they proved was embodied in the suffering itself, and so was self-evident: tautologous and autogenous. This is how and why the word evolved in meaning from "witness" to "one who suffers for a cause."[18]

Through the *agon* ($\dot{\alpha}\gamma\acute{\omega}\nu$), the trial or ordeal of suffering, martyrs were demonstrating truths, for truth was "real" in being experiential and tangible. If any should be like doubting Thomas, the "evidence of the eyes" was not wanting in "the wounds of God's servants," in the "glory of their scars."[19] Fellow bishops wrote to Cyprian: "What is more glorious . . . than to have proved the truth in public testimony; than by dying, to conquer death which is feared by all?"[20] No scientific method, no canons of evidence existed to discover the truth or elucidate its content. Authority acted, standing behind the beliefs it promoted.

In this late antique world, the *agon* proved the worth of someone by the audience's judgment of his public performance, thus affirming or disputing that witness's testimony. Knowledge was gained by challenges, contrasts, and revelation; trust in itself was not trustworthy: it needed to be tested and tried. "For how can a general prove the valor of his soldiers unless they have an enemy?" Lactantius asked. And since God himself could not be opposed, he instigated adversaries to prove the fidelity and devotion of his servants.[21] "How great was the *proof of faith*" (emphasis added) the Maccabees supplied with their confession and martyrdom in their ordeal, Cyprian praised.[22] Action was proof; seeing was believing.

The *agon* proved truth because it was trial and judgment affording choices and alternative results. Martyrdom was a "crisis" ($\kappa\rho\acute{\iota}\sigma\iota\varsigma$), a time for decision and judgment, like Christ's resolution to align his will with the Father's and accept the cup of his suffering in Gethsemane (Mark 14: 36; Matt. 26: 39; Luke 22: 42).[23] Christians therefore had to choose one way or the other, lest confusion prevail when seeking "to serve two masters" (Matt. 6: 24). Confusion meant uncertainty, instability, and suspicion: the deceitful works of the devil. God, on the other hand, represented clarity, order, constancy, and certainty: truth. Of confession and denial Tertullian wrote: "For where one is, both are. For contraries always go together."[24] Unless put to the test, this mysterious muddle could not be sorted out; the winner would not emerge, truth would not be verified. In the end, truth was what (or who) emerged as victor from the *agon*. This was an ambitious age of fluid authority, where charismatic personalities and impressive actions validated beliefs. A later world would receive truths codified by authorities representing a well-established hierarchy. But the martyrs broached a frontier of auspicious possibilities.

The passions of the martyrs became a still-frame of mediation. They revealed and documented the transcendent truths that arose from the stunning exposition of suffering in the arena. This world and the next had collided; normal boundaries separating distinct realities had dissolved. God and the angels watched their champions, while demons wore the masks of blasphemous persecutors. Living at once with the natural and supernatural, Christians could see what remained veiled to others, which if others saw, they too would surely believe.[25] The martyrs' passions show how and by what processes the carnal was linked and could be elevated to the spiritual world. In this, the very reality of suffering and death provided the equivalent of "scientific" evidence to convince skeptics of realities beyond. Death was the great guarantor, the ineluctable salesman: Christian teachings must be true, for no one would die for a false doctrine or volunteer his or her life without a purpose.[26]

In this logic, just as Christ's resurrection foreshadowed the resurrection of all humanity and the afterlife was anticipated in the martyrs' sacrifice, in a circular way the martyr's sacrifice proved Christ's resurrection: how could martyrs die unless there were really a resurrection?[27] By extension, martyrdom was proof of all Christian truths: the genuine passibility of Christ's flesh, the immortality of the soul, the inevitability of the Last Judgment, and the divine mystery of how Christ's passion could generate the new life of the resurrection.[28] The proof of the pudding was in the making, so to speak. One need not wait until the wrath of the Last Judgment to see Christianity vindicated. One could glimpse truths now in the sacrifices of the martyrs.

The truths revealed were broadly twofold. Every martyrdom was both a private and public, an individual and communal "revelation." Personal identity was connected with communal truth, and communal truth depended on personal valor. Certainly, martyrdom was deeply personal and immediate, an exercise in defining individual authenticity or identity: what *did* it mean to be a "real" Christian? How could one be saved? Yet individual testimony could not be separated from communal concerns. The community validated truth and won adherents through the sacrifice of its members: "The blood of martyrs was seed."[29] Paradoxically, by death the Church gained life. "God permits persecutions," wrote Lactantius, "that the people of God might be increased. Some desire to know what that good is that is so defended even unto death."[30]

Simply by taking a stand and proving beliefs by their deaths, martyrs sharpened even further the boundaries between Christians and nonbelievers. Among members of the body of Christ, hostility to external enemies reenforced the internal sense of fellowship and underscored the need for unwavering obedience to the authority of the bishop.[31] Martyrs both reenacted the sacrifice that was the foundation of Christian doctrine and illustrated the charity that should animate the institutional Church as it grew. All should be as the martyr Stephen: wounded, yet praying for the enemies who persecuted him.[32] Predictably, then, the rising enmity of the pagans correlated with Christian exhortations to bury internal dissensions and be animated by the Holy Spirit.

How did the present troubles relate to the end? Not every writer made an explicit equation of his or her own times with the apocalypse.[33] Perhaps it did not seem necessary. A more accurate index of apocalypticism is simply the liberal use of signal passages and imagery from the Bible such as those from the Apocalypse of John, or the dire predictions of Christ of persecution and catastrophe to befall Jerusalem.[34] These texts present the immediacy of revelation: Christians faced the devil *now* in persecutions, and the Lord was present *now* to help Christians in their trials. If the secular world was polluted with demons,[35] Christians needed to cultivate the purity of their own community all the more vigorously. Sacred and profane worlds could not be mixed. "No one can serve two masters," Tertullian quoted Matthew 6:24. "What fellowship has light with darkness? (see 2 Cor. 6:14). What has life to do with death?"[36]

Loyalties were polarized. No middle ground, neutrality, or ambiguity existed in this world of stark black and white contrasts. "No one extends a welcoming hand to an opponent. No one admits another unless he is a kindred spirit."[37] Lines were drawn and sides taken. This imposed a dreadful urgency to come to one's senses and reaffirm one's true allegiance. "He who is not with me is against me," Christ had said (Luke 11:23).[38] The sharp lines demarcating adversaries were typical of this manner of thinking in general. Rigid dichotomies prevailed.

In this militant mentality, the imagery of conflict and competition further defined one's adversaries. Christians were "soldiers" "fighting in battles" against the devil or "athletes" and "gladiators" "contending" in a "race" or in the "agon" of the "arena."[39] Christians were set in opposition to the devil and his proxies: governors, executioners, and the pagan audience in general. One could choose to please either God or man.[40] In this polarized world, those of merely earthly birth stood in contrast to those recreated in spirit and reborn in Christ. No longer did Christians live in this world; they awaited God's gifts in heaven.[41] So deep was this antagonism that Ignatius of Antioch imagined human beings as being one of "two coins," stamped either with God or the world.[42] Two corporate bodies existed: one of the devil and his members, the other of Christ.

This very opposition to the enemy bonded Christians more closely to each other. Christians came to think of themselves as a persecuted elect, the righteous few hounded cruelly by the world but chosen and beloved of God. "From the beginning, righteousness suffers violence," Tertullian observed; Cyprian and Augustine repeated his judgment. Abel, David, Elias, Jeremias, Esaias, Zacharias, the Maccabees, all suffered.[43] "Precious in the sight of the Lord is the death of his saints" (Ps. 145: 25). This being so, the zealous Tertullian concluded that *all* Christians were called to be martyrs.[44] " 'For thy sake we are slain all the day long. We are regarded as sheep for the slaughter,' " Cyprian quoted the Bible to explain Christians' consecration as offerings to God and their vows or *devotiones* (Rom. 8: 35–36, Ps. 43: 21–22).[45] History proved that Christians had a mission, a divine calling separating and elevating them from the squalor of the profane world. To bear the world's contempt became a badge of honor. Christians might be "bound as sheep," but they belonged to a mighty shepherd. "The shepherd will not desert you, nor can the love and promises of the Lord fail you here or in the next world."[46] To know this could make a vast difference: persecution was a mark of pride, not shame; of God's favor, not his neglect. Indeed, God disciplined his children from love, Lactantius argued. This was one reason why persecutions were permitted.[47]

Urgency, inflexibility, and a passion for the absolute drove Christians in a search for finality: the resolution of antipathies and the restitution of right order. Cyprian and others anticipated and even welcomed the worst: this would be the *agon*, a discernment to sort things out. To be purged like gold in the crucible (cf. Wis 3: 6), to offer the sacrifice of a broken spirit (Ps. 51: 17), to suffer for Christ's sake gained one the crown.[48] In the church of the martyrs, Christians *expected* the hatred of the world. Writers warned Christians to be prepared for affliction, as if there were no alternatives. "Since the world hates a Christian, why do you love that which hates you and not follow Christ who has redeemed and loves you?" Cyprian asked.[49] Christ's words prophesied a war of extermination:[50] "Then they will deliver you up to tribulation and will put you to death, and you will be hated by all nations for my name's sake."[51] Christians had to learn to confess God while expiring in the persecutor's hands. To become coheirs of Christ meant learning to overcome tortures and to love punishments. If Christians were to be hated, they would accept gladly the torments of the enemy to beat them in a contest of wills. "We are strengthened by harshness and destroyed by softness," Tertullian asserted.[52] Others agreed: Christians were strengthened by the scourge;[53] one must get through the contest without flinching.[54]

The trial of martyrdom would discern realities and eliminate the derangement of manifold choices. Singularity meant certainty, and this meant truth and security. Persecution was a winnowing fan separating the wheat from the chaff, the elect from the damned (Matt. 3: 12).[55] The net had been cast indiscriminately, and now those caught would be examined.[56] At last, the sheep would be separated from the goats.[57] Confusion and ambiguity were dangerously unpredictable and unstable; decisions must be final and unconditional. "Persecution [was] a judgment," Tertullian concluded, "and the verdict [was] either approval or condemnation."[58] In this all-or-nothing universe, loyalty must be absolute and unquestioned. Hesitant souls were fodder for the devil.

Martyrs were needed in this hostile world if the Church were to prosper and be "built up." Persecution heightened the urgency of the message, specifying the quintessential characteristics of the Christian. A lukewarm convert was worthless because declaring one's loyalty was the point. To be unwilling to confess was to deny Christ in Tertullian's eyes.[59] Simply to be a Christian was to put oneself on the line. "We are a people willing to die," wrote Tertullian.[60] We thank the executioner when we are sentenced to death.[61] Ignatius thought he would merit the title of authentic Christian only when he was martyred.[62] To Minucius Felix it was a point of honor that Christians could express their free will in undertaking suffering to exhibit loyalty to their master. "How beautiful a spectacle for God, when a Christian measures his strength with pain" when "he esteems his liberty above all things; when he yields to God alone, whose he is."[63]

In a similar vein, Tertullian wrote majestically of demonstrating fidelity through voluntary sacrifice: "I am [Christ's] servant, I alone worship him; for his teaching I am put to death."[64] This willingness to sacrifice one's life made a Christian part of the body of Christ, a corporate member of the Church animated by the Holy Spirit and indwelt by Christ.[65] According to Ignatius, "If we are not in readiness to die into [Christ's] passion, his life is not in us."[66] To seal one's faith with death signified the highest commitment one could make. Unity and cohesion could not be stronger.

To suffer and die joyfully not only marked one as choosing to participate in Christ; such self-sacrifice was also an obligation or duty members owed to imitate their head, "suffering willingly what Christ suffered," for "no servant was better than his master."[67] Whether described as a covenant,[68] a duty to die for the Name (*kiddush ha-shem*),[69] a vow or *devotio*,[70] pledge (*pignus*)[71] or an oath (*sacramentum*),[72] Christians had obligations as God's chosen people especially to repay their redemption. Christ had ransomed Christians from death with his own life. Now Christians were bound to repay the debt. Christ ransomed humanity with his own blood; destined for hell, they were instead purchased for heaven.[73] Cyprian quoted Paul, " 'You are not your own, for you have been bought at a great price. Glorify God and bear him in your body' " (1 Cor. 6: 19–20).[74] Being Christ's body, Christians were obligated to "complete" the "afflictions" in Christ's body (Col. 1: 24) for themselves and for others.[75] Like Christ, martyrs were high priests offering themselves as "blameless sacrifices,"[76] or eucharistic offerings replicating the sacrifice of Christ.[77]

Like all contracts, such covenants, pledges, and vows were reciprocal. Christians repaid the debt they owed Christ for their salvation by bearing witness to his name, but this also gained Christians a reward in return. "So everyone who confesses me before men, I also will confess before my Father who is in heaven," Christ assured his followers (Matt. 10: 32). "The measure you give will be the measure you get back" (Luke 6: 38, Matt. 7: 2, Mark 4: 24).[78] Suffering now for the sake of Christ would insure one's future integrity at the Last Judgment. "We pray that if we suffer the penalty for the sake of our Lord Jesus Christ we shall be saved, for this is the confidence and salvation we shall have at the terrible tribunal of our Savior and Master sitting in judgment over the whole world," Justin replied to the prefect.[79]

In this economy, redactors would even write of martyrs "purchasing" heaven or salvation through their suffering. "Fixing their eyes on the favor of Christ [the martyrs] despised the tortures of this world, in one hour buying an exemption from eternal fire."[80] Following the equity of this universe, greater sufferings would necessarily merit greater rewards.[81] In this universe of retribution, martyrs' deaths and confessions glorified God as forms of loyalty and worship. In return, the martyrs themselves would be confessed; moreover, they would be glorified in the measure of their self-giving.[82] Bearing witness through death won the ultimate reward of being assimilated to Christ's body, and thus glorified in one's own body.[83]

The candid economics of this transaction may strike the modern reader as simplistic, but early Christians continued classical tradition, viewing justice as retributive. Suffering was rewarded with the resurrection in heaven: "we pay out the very things whose benefit we pay to gain, the very things are expended which become profits, the price and the commodity are the same," Tertullian calculated unsentimentally.[84] Universal order meant balance, equilibrium, and reciprocity.[85] Such sublime orderliness was God's providential dispensation.[86] Disorder was by definition diabolical. Apocalypticism arises when this cosmic balance is perceived to be out of order: Christians held this perception; most pagans did not.[87]

Such a rigid and harsh universe might well disturb Christians of a later age. A God of dreadful severity upheld this dichotomous universe, but in that very punctilious exactitude lay mercy as well as justice. Certainly, God was a stern taskmaster who would "exact every last penny"[88] and scrutinize the hidden recesses of one's conscience.[89] This divine judge oversaw the martyrs and demanded excellence and supreme effort. Justly and fittingly, this God was strict precisely because he had been so merciful in his initial creation. In contrast to the Necessity and Destiny of paganism, Christianity meant freedom and hope: liberation from a deterministic fate, illumination instead of ignorance, the conquest of death and all its attendant fears.[90] Despite the severity of God's justice, his mercy still offered a path out of this dangerous universe.

This merciful God had given humanity open opportunities that allowed martyrs (and later monks) to become the astonishing heroes of legend. Reason allowed imitation of the Lord's perfection; a will unfettered by compulsion enabled free choice of the good.[91] Grace and free will worked together: "If you desire to do the good, God stands ready to assist you," Ignatius explained.[92] One's "earnest efforts to imitate God" would gain at last the "likeness," the "similitude to God" that was the goal of creation. God made humanity with the ability to acquire the knowledge and discipline to gain incorruptibility.[93] Balance and synergy interwove divine grace and human will, so that Christians could be divinized.[94] Many Christians optimistically anticipated an ἀποκατάστασις, a restoration, or an ἀνακεφαλαίωσις, recapitulation of all creation.[95] The fundamental goodness and beauty of the first creation would be recaptured.

If so much had been given, much was expected. "The mercy of God consisted in this," wrote one redactor, "that the very ransom [martyrs] believe to be paid by [their] own blood was granted to [them] by God almighty."[96] Christ's body was knit closely with ties of gifts and obligations, grace and free will, freedom and necessity. The most precious and binding exchange, of course, was the gift of self. To express this as gifts of love deemphasized the necessity of fulfilling an obligation, although such a mandate was there and sanctioned by hell if one failed. Instead, gratitude sprang forth: "What can we give God in return for all he has given us?" Origen asks, quoting Psalm 116: 12. His answer: "perfection in martyrdom."[97] Nothing else would demonstrate and return such love.

While love and free choice motivated martyrdom, hell was never out of the martyrs' ken. Despite optimistic hopes for a cosmic restoration, these beliefs did not negate the monumentality of evil. Evil could not be temporized in a "world soaked with blood," where impunity was wrested by "the sheer magnitude of cruelty."[98]

Hell was a negative incentive driving the martyrs to face the *agon*. The typical warning in martyrs' passions was that "hell is worse than any earthly torture."[99] Allusions to hell applied to Christians as well as pagans, for both would undergo the "same death, judgment, and punishment for all mankind."[100] This should have sobered shaky Christians. Like Biblis, martyrs who wavered would come to their senses after recalling the eternal punishment of Gehenna awaiting them. Instantly steeled by fear of the future, they could master any temporal punishment.[101] The afflictions of the flesh were momentary and worked for eternal glory; our sufferings would be less than our rewards, Tertullian argued.[102] Hell put martyrdom into perspective. If martyrs did not fear death, rightly, they feared hell.

The martyrs' hell was not only the common late antique inheritance of Tartarus and Gehenna. More specifically, it was defined a fortiori by the sadistic practices of the Roman court and army. Hell was as physical as heaven was spiritual in this dichotomous thinking of apocalypticism. The lack of spiritual and psychological definitions of hell points again to the *agon*. The martyrs' hell was far from Augustine's anguished separation from the face of God. Discipline was the martyrs' goal, training for the *agon*, and this was above all corporal *ascesis*. Fear of hell built a muscular spirit, capable of withstanding trial and torture.

Fear of hell reinforced adherence to community rules, and in the Church of the martyrs no sympathy was extended to the slothful. Because one had free choice (which did not obviate the need for grace), evil was then deliberate perversion and obstinacy. The Lord had made known his law; no allowance could be conceded to laxity, for this indicated feeble intention. Cyprian believed those who recanted under torture had really failed in will and faith; such cowardice and ignorance were damnable, if not repented.[103] In this universe of competent will and certain knowledge of the good, if fools chose evil, they were obviously responsible. Was that not just? Sinners obstinately rejected all that made Christians Christian: the call to reform and perfection, to die to the world and be reborn in Christ. Tertullian prescribed a strict reading of the law to meet these criteria of perfection: whatever was not expressly permitted was prohibited.[104] One needed to be strict because forgiveness was not won easily.[105] Such puritanical restrictions only reinforced Christians' sense of who they were as "God's people" and the duties they owed to preserve such intimacy with God.

Moral choices reflected loyalties that determined social behavior. Christians were to be different in ways highly visible (and not infrequently annoying) to others. Nonconformity was a virtue. Christian women could not offend God with garish cosmetics, for this revived the odium of Eve, destroyer of God's image.[106] Men could not take oaths to competing secular powers, nor could the dead be ornamented with crowns, for these were reminiscent of pagan practices.[107] Worldly entertainments and spectacles emulated the ancient ritual sacrifices to pagan gods.[108] Mixed marriages were problematic, unless conversions resulted. Ptolemaeus suffered martyrdom because a repudiated spouse wanted revenge.[109] Humility and chastity were proper individually; significantly, these behaviors strengthened social cohesion because the whole community was endangered if these directions of the Holy Spirit were ignored.[110] Each Christian could recognize the other in the uniformity of their behavior.[111]

Persecution had challenged Christians to choose between gods, and this defined sin on a deeper spiritual level. Sin was idolatry, a lèse-majesté, amounting to a disloyalty and dishonor that defied God.[112] Sin was war, and sinners were traitors following the falsifier and deceiver rather than the creator and teacher.[113] Morality became a contest of "corporate cultures." To which body did one choose to belong, that of God or the devil? Entrance was mutually exclusive: standards of "the club" were inflexible, and infringements of the rules were visited harshly. In this agonistic world, honor, authority, and power could not be divided: the winner took all. To God "alone" belonged "all power and glory," just as Christians belonged to Christ, having been ransomed from death and the devil by his sacrifice. More, as the chosen people engaged in a covenant with God, they could not dare to sin, for this was fornication betraying the purity and fidelity owed a spouse.[114]

Sins amounted to flagrant actions threatening to undermine the cohesiveness and credibility of the community because they disregarded the doctrines that defined its character. The danger came from the laxist who could be coopted and assimilated; it came from the nonconformist heretic whose idiosyncratic behavior caused disruption. Sin had to be defined unambiguously, and consequently, bishops struggled to get control over the means of its expurgation. (A dead martyr was an asset, a live confessor a liability!).[115] Two treatises (*De lapsis, De ecclesiae catholicae unitate*) address the disruption caused by penitential practices. The lapsed took advantage of privileges of penance given to confessors, and this undermined the power of the bishop. Centralization and monarchy ensured order and credibility. Only later when the Church reached accommodation with the world would sin become more mysterious, psychological, and complex.[116] Later, the search would be undertaken for a

secure penitence that might offer mercy and hope to the average and very fal-
lible Christian for whom martyrdom would be a heroic legend.[117] When external enemies retreated, internal enemies proliferated. New practices would
then arise to address these new complications, whether they were from the
monk who rejected the world or the bishop who was forced to live in it.

The world of the martyrs was more direct, if equally mysterious. The
community of the martyrs was already living in the next world, having rejected the world wholly to participate in the transcendent life of Christ.
Christ's defeat of death and sin had inaugurated his kingdom already inwardly
and spiritually in the hearts of Christians; this is the message of Paul. "The
promises of the future have been given to us in the resurrection of Christ,"
Clement of Rome wrote.[118] "We look to the heavens and see Christ glorified.
By him the eyes of our heart are open and we have a taste of immortal knowledge."[119] Christians awaited only death, the beginning of that true life when
body and soul would be joined to Christ in heaven. Martyrdom was that passage to heaven, for it guaranteed one entrance to that holy sanctuary, having
been washed clean of sins by a second baptism of blood.[120] Eschatology was
realized with the martyrs. Martyrdom was resurrection, a triumph won, a goal
achieved. Just as suffering and death could be demonstrated and so taken as
proving the truth, Christians extended their argument to assert that the successful *agon* documented the achievement of the goal itself. " 'Today we are
martyrs in heaven. Thanks be to God!' " Nartzalus exulted.[121] Torture was "endured not as a day of martyrdom but of resurrection,"[122] and witnesses were
"happy" that martyrs were "going to such great glory,"[123] being "restored to
heaven and to their hopes."[124] Pionius states, "I am hurrying [to martyrdom]
that I may awake all the more quickly, manifesting the resurrection from the
dead."[125] But what did this "resurrection" of martyrdom really mean?

Fittingly, the passibility of the flesh was to be transformed into impassibility. Tertullian argued that the resurrected flesh would be a "reformation
of our condition, not our nature, by removing all sufferings from it and be-
stowing protections on it." Christians would still have flesh, but it would be
impassible: "Thus our flesh will remain even after the resurrection—so far indeed susceptible of suffering, as it is the flesh, and the same flesh too; but at
the same time impassible, inasmuch as it has been liberated by the Lord for the
very end and purpose of being no longer capable of enduring suffering."[126]

As Christ had united divinity and humanity in his Incarnation and removed death and suffering through his redemptive sacrifice, the glorified
body of the Christian would also be quite unlike the normal human body,
suffering neither the pain of the martyrs' agonies nor the distressing muta-

bility all bodies qua bodies endure. To live like angels was to be free of any bodily necessity—eating, drinking, childbearing, death.[127] Justin Martyr saw the end of life as freedom from feeling (ἐν ἀπαθείᾳ).[128] Christians were to be "immortalized" or "deified" (ἀπαθανατίζεσθαι).[129] "God is spirit," Tertullian asserted, "and he requires that his worshippers be of the same nature."[130] The idea of a perfected body so fascinated early writers that Origen was even thought to have posited that the resurrected body would be a circle, the perfect shape.[131] Glorified flesh would be changed and purged from the damages of sin, and this implied that "normal" flesh was in need of much remediation. The burden of sin was crushing, and radical reversals were needed to restore the flesh. As the first Adam had sinned in the flesh, so the second brought redemption of the flesh through the bruises of his body.[132] If humanity fell through temptations and sins of the flesh, so the discipline of the flesh could compensate for its sins. "Since by man came death, by man came the resurrection of the dead" (1 Cor. 15: 21).[133]

The body was the battered vehicle of a marvelous transformation, for torture and physical suffering conveyed martyrs across the boundary between this world and the next.[134] The body was elevated to the sublime role of uniting humanity to God and to other human beings; it was also the agent of the Christian's transformation to glory: martyrdom was both the moral injunction to imitate Christ and the *telos* of all life: "to attain God" (θεοῦ ἐπιτυχεῖν), to reach "perfection in Christ" (ἀπήρτισμαι ἐν Ἰησοῦ Χριστῷ), in Ignatius's words.[135] In Tertullian's words, "The man who is afraid to suffer cannot belong to him who suffered for us. But the one who does not fear suffering, he will be perfect in love."[136] Spiritually and psychologically, Christians were bound in something of a mystical union with Christ. They "bore in their own bodies the sufferings of Christ's flesh."[137] How then could they ever be separated?

As members of Christ's body, Christians would share Christ's triumph, as they shared his suffering. Sufferers would be bound in a kind of mystical union to Christ and to one another. The members of Christ shared his achievements because they *imitated*, that is, reenacted suffering and death. Action was literal and physical, not merely metaphoric. Therefore martyrs could be said to "share Christ's cup" and "participate" in his sufferings. "Now since it is through the flesh that we suffer with Christ, for it is the property of the flesh to be worn away by suffering, to the same this belongs the recompense which is promised for suffering with Christ," Tertullian wrote.[138] Ignatius explained, "If I shall suffer, then I am a freed-man, delivered by Jesus Christ; and I shall be reborn in him, free."[139] To be glorified in return was perhaps the greatest blessing of martyrdom. Christ was sacrificed; martyrs repaid that sacrifice and through participation gained what Christ had won. Here the language of reciprocity and exchange was especially strong. We are the heirs of God and fellow heirs with Christ, provided we "suffer with him in order that we may also be glorified with him" (cf. Rom. 8: 16–17).[140] In Tertullian's outspoken Montanist economics: "We pay out the very things whose benefit we pay to gain, the very things are expended which become profits, the price and the commodity are the same."[141]

Suffering purified the body from sin so that it might be resurrected in perfection; in it debts were discharged. For this reason, Christians embraced the healing medicine of suffering. By the grace of God, the second trial of Sanctus proved to be "not a torture, but rather a cure."[142] For Tertullian, suffering was necessary to open heaven.[143] The body's very vulnerability had changed from a liability to an asset.

Martyrdom demonstrated various changes to come already in this life, not only in the spiritual regeneration of everyday life brought by Christ's resurrection, but even in the more spectacular manifestations of the life beyond. In a remarkable division, martyrs were in heaven enjoying glory even though their physical bodies remained on earth. Contemporary African bishops wrote Cyprian that they had even gazed upon the triumphant and glorious martyrs abiding with the angels.[144] With a foot in both worlds, martyrs "imitated here what they would be there."[145] "About to reign with God, [martyrs] were already reigning in mind and heart."[146] They took on "the image of God's glory" and became "immortal with him, sharing eternal life through the Word."[147] Their ontological status changed as well. Martyrs were "no longer men but angels."[148] Once God's "servants" (*servi*), they now become his "friends" (*amici*).[149] Most happily, martyrs were offered a glimpse of heavenly secrets while still on earth, reassuring Christians of the truth of Christian doctrine and the value of their own sacrifices.

Martyrdom itself was a winnowing process, for it served to separate the soul from the body. This proved the soul's immortality and its life with Christ in heaven, a triumph demonstrated by Christians' contempt of death.[150] Christians could "despise" death because of their conviction, or rather, their "certain knowledge" of the afterlife.[151] As was typical, the way martyrs faced death and suffering was taken to prove these transcendent truths.[152] Christians argued that willing deaths proved Christ's divinity and triumph over death. "Christ taught us to despise the penalty of death . . . to be convinced that there will be a judgment after death and a reward given by God after the resurrection," Apollonius announced.[153] To die a beautiful death was certain proof that life did not end and God was in charge. As Apollonius explained: because it is "through God that we are what we are," "we make every attempt not to die a coward's death."[154] Pionius died "peacefully and painlessly," giving his soul "in trust to the Father, who had promised to protect all blood and every spirit that has been unjustly condemned."[155] Despising death and torture could be inverted and transformed to enthusiasm for them because death led to glory. Martyrs who embraced death eagerly and joyfully were the rule in the passions.[156] Punishments were not afflictions but sources of joy.[157]

Being "already in heaven" allowed martyrs to dissociate themselves from bodily suffering. When the heart is in God, the body feels no pain. "Where your heart is, there your treasure lies," Tertullian quoted Matthew 6: 21.[158] Simply being indwelt by God meant God would answer for martyrs in their distress; therefore they need not fear arrests or inquisitions.[159] Facing torture, martyrs like Perpetua were "in ecstasy," such that they had no recollection of their grisly ordeals.[160] God would help martyrs bear their pain. Blandina had no fear of suffering in the arena, though she had agonized giving birth. "Now *I* suffer what I suffer. However, then there will be another in me who will suffer for me, since I will also suffer for him."[161] Again, the balance, the "justice" of this world organizes experience into reciprocal exchanges.

In dying, the martyrs revealed hints of the brilliant transformation to come. Christ took over, indwelling the martyrs so that they miraculously shared Christ's impassibility in their own ordeals. Often the martyrs' bodies glowed or shone with dazzling white light, just as Christ's body in his Transfiguration (Mark 9: 2–3 and Matt. 17: 2–3).[162] The garments of Successus "glowed," he "dazzled" bodily eyes with his "angelic brilliance."[163] Suddenly "Christ shone on the face of a brother" "by the grace of the suffering that was to come." Pagans recognized his "election" and dispatched him.[164] Marian and James also "flashed from the approaching passion,"[165] while the Trinity was visible in Fructuosus's face.[166]

Suffering proved that the body transformed could negate physical laws, the most ominous being death itself. Perpetua could rout death, but instead willed it for Christ. "It was as though so great a woman, feared as she was by the unclean spirit, could not be killed unless she herself willed it."[167] Other passions reveal the supernatural resilience and fortitude of the martyrs' bodies in their defiance of death. Papylus exhausted three teams of exactors,[168] while Sanctus "withstood all . . . with extraordinary, superhuman strength."[169] Bodies regained their integrity; indeed, they are augmented and glorified through torture, like Pionius, who retained his purity and dignity,[170] or Sanctulus, who grew straight after being broken with torture.[171] Polycarp's immolation was a Eucharistic sacrifice.[172] In all ways martyrs were magnified through suffering, like Marian, who "through his faith in God, grew as great in body as well as soul."[173] Martyrs demonstrated how very different the physics of the supernatural world were from those of ordinary reality.

The care tendered the deceased bodies of the martyrs further proved their sanctification and connectedness with the world beyond. Their remains became especially important to the Christian community in their battle against critics and skeptics. The persecutors of Lyon cremated the martyrs' bodies and threw them in the Rhône, challenging the Christian God to rescue and resurrect them.[174] Consequently, the essays that dwell on the fragmentation of the body would serve to vindicate God's omnipotence by insisting that every last particle of flesh would be collected for the resurrection. Such arguments would console Christians: the omnipotent God would restore them. Whatever horrors demons and human beings might devise, they were incapable of outmaneuvering the Creator of heaven and earth.

The bodies that remained served useful purposes for the community. Fortunately, Polycarp's body was only cremated, so his ashes could be collected and his anniversary celebrated as a "memorial to those who have already fought the contest and for the training and preparation of those who some day will do the same."[175] The body of Cyprian was exposed to the curiosity of pagans but was secretly rescued by Christians. His blood was caught by napkins, presumably to be used as relics.[176] Fructuosus's ashes shed miracles to increase the faith of believers and set examples for the young. Those who tried to hide them as private possessions were chastened by a vision of the saint himself, who demanded their return to the church.[177] Charity and community must prevail.

Martyrdom taught Christians about the body's perfectibility through passion, and writers exhorted Christians not only to face persecution with fortitude, but also to bear the adversities of everyday life patiently.[178] Such may not have been the most cheerful lessons Christians gained from martyrologies. More joyous were the fresh glimpses of heaven. Martyrs gained spiritual sight; prisons and blindfolds were ineffective to martyrs, for "no darkness [could] impede the vision of a soul that is free (*libera*)."[179] Visions also documented the power of the martyr as mediator between these two worlds. Sometimes martyrs simply fell into trances or saw visions (*uisio*; ὄψις). They might prophesy the future, discern souls, see glimpses of the world beyond, or simply behave eccentrically. Nevertheless, all their activities testified to the truth of Christian teaching about the world beyond, underscoring the reward of the just and the punishment of the profane.

Some brief examples may be given. Perpetua's intimacy with the Lord was enviable, and she was unabashedly ambitious. She could "chat with the Lord" (*fabulari cum Domino*) and request visions.[180] The Lord, moreover, was quite obliging in answering her with visions predicting her victorious passion[181] and her successful intercession for a brother in the underworld. Polycarp foresaw his own immolation in a vision of flaming pillows[182] and amazed the crowd when he faced East and prayed for two hours "full of divine grace."[183] Broader in scope was Marian's prophecy of vengeance: earthquakes, famines, a plague of poisonous flies.[184]

Many of these visions moderns might term "near-death" experiences whose purpose is reassurance and consolation. Illumination was characteristic: heaven was a world of light, and light was life. Victor's vision before his passion is telling: a child "whose face shone with a brilliance beyond description" consoled him with the words, "Have confidence, for I am with you."[185] Facing their passions, some martyrs were encouraged by old friends: Potamiaena appears to Basilides,[186] Agapius visited James,[187] Successus entered Flavian's house in a glowing gown.[188] Some martyrs even had round-trip tickets to shuttle back and forth to earth: Cyprian logged many miles visiting Flavian, Marian, and Montanus to advise them how to tolerate suffering.[189] Polycarp himself appeared to Pionius, the redactor of his passion. (Perhaps the saint could not forbear editorial comments.)[190] Such return visits served to reassure the community of life after death: a protector had preceded them and would show them the way. These divine emissaries could steel confessors for their approaching passion. The impulse of all these visitations from the other world is decidedly activist.

What lay at the end of it all, besides the immutable, reformed, and impassible body?[191] While Hebraic tradition excluded the direct sight of God, Christians were more willing to imagine the face of Christ, if not the Father. Visions tended to be vague: dazzling figures were presumably those of the Lord, although they were not always identified as such. Different was Perpetua, influenced by *The Shepherd of Hermas*. An elderly shepherd offered Perpetua milk. In the same passion, Saturus saw walls of light, a garden and angels, while his aged man had a youthful face.[192] Quartillosa's young man of "remarkable stature" gave everyone generous cups of milk.[193] While the giving of milk probably echoes baptismal rituals and obviously the image of Christ as good shepherd, nevertheless, the maternal overtones of such nurturing should not be ignored.

In a universe of exact measures, the images of Christ as comforter were balanced by those of the Lord as exactor. As one faced passion, courage could be strengthened by remembering that God was also a harsh judge and disciplinarian. Perpetua saw the Lord not only as a good shepherd but as an athletic trainer with a disciplinary rod.[194] James echoes Perpetua's vision, seeing a brilliant giant in an athletic tunic.[195] The Lord was presumably the handsome judge in the shining high tribunal seen by Marian, a role which, like that of the trainer, suggests the demanding standards of *ascesis*.[196]

Glimpses of heaven itself were seldom recorded in detail, with the exception of Perpetua's, which is assumed to reflect Montanist influences. Such scant information teased the audience, but imaginations sometimes could compensate. In early martyrs' passions, it was sufficient to establish that right order would be restored—good rewarded and evil punished. What mattered was the vindication of the corporate Christian community and its beliefs. Indeed, to be too explicit could undermine the trust and expectation that kept the community together. Victor's vision both reveals and conceals truth, a balance that nourishes faith and acknowledges its need. We are moving toward a world in which written records and established authorities would define truths: the very recording of martyrs' passions would be part of the process of authentication.

Now this was the Lord from heaven, and Victor asked him where heaven was.
"It is beyond the world," said the child.
"Show it to me," said Victor.
He said to Victor, "Then where would be your faith?" [197]

Faith was the end, the *telos*, of the martyrs' witness. They died to prove the faith, and their deaths disclosed knowledge of the spectacular transformation awaiting believers. For early Christians, martyrdom was an apocalypse of varied aspect, for that terrifying moment revealed many beautiful truths: the indisputable credibility of Christian doctrine, the hidden bones of the martyrs' invincible courage, the secrets of angelic life to be shared with the elect. Christians lived in a world of contrasts and reciprocities, seeking always the balance, clarity, and resolution that defined a just universe. They could welcome the *agon*, the gruesome and pitiless ordeal, for it would earn a rich reward: a discernment of mysteries; revelations that could only console believers and augment the faith. The sweet truth was earned only through bitter trial.

This rigorous mentality of the church of the martyrs is central not only to understanding this age, but also to the future doctrine of the Church. The most ambitious and radical practices of self-sacrifice would continue to be valued as the most authentic form of Christianity. Historically, the perfectionists would always be deemed to be closer to God and therefore deserving of higher status in the institutional Church and (we might assume) in heaven as well. Those who sought accommodation with the world would be lesser citizens in the kingdom of God, fellow travelers whose allegiance could be easily impeached. This lesson the monks of the desert demonstrated pointedly after the Constantinian revolution, and the lesson was never forgotten.

The eschatology of the church of the martyrs also had a lasting impact. In emphasizing the antithesis of carnal and spiritual, the damned and the elect, writers shaped a particular view of life after death. The resurrection, while it is by definition an affirmation of the flesh, was so only dialectically: through the sufferings of the flesh, martyrs attained glory, just as Christ had been transfigured through suffering to come into his *maiestas* (cf. John 9: 18–36). The dualism of spirit and flesh remains. The joys of heaven as imagined by those in the church of the martyrs (and indeed later) were particularly those of the spirit. Those of the flesh were (and are still) deemed inappropriate. The Christian heaven is not the Moslem heaven of lush gardens, brocaded couches, and nubile virgins with retiring glances.[198] Quite the opposite. Impassability was God's gift to the glorified body, and the body was to enjoy both freedom from the acute sufferings of martyrdom and liberation from the passions and needs of everyday life, which might also be sources of pleasure. For Christians, the flesh could be celebrated only when it ceased to be the flesh they knew.

Eastern and Western traditions would deal differently with this legacy. The Eastern church would come to celebrate divinization ($\theta\epsilon\omega\sigma\iota\varsigma$) as a fundamental doctrine, translating the rigorous demands of the martyrs into a program of divinization through progressive stages of asceticism. Having run the race, the heroic ascetics like abba Pambo and Paul the Hermit could await their crowns. The West, on the other hand, would embark on a different course with Augustine, who would be less optimistic about humanity's spiritual progress, much less its heroism, and more convinced of the severity of God's scrutiny. But Augustine would offer consolations for the fragile and ever-imperfect soul. The remedies of penitence and faith in the infinity of divine mercy could ease the terror of those facing the *iudex tremendus*. Augustine's cry from the *Confessions* (10.35.57), "My one hope is your exceedingly great mercy," would do much to console Christians who could only listen to the heroic feats of martyrs but never repeat them.

A universe polarized between heaven and hell, the saved and the damned, is taken for granted. Isn't this what eschatology means? As historians, we should be wary of the obvious. Origen's vision of the end with the rehabilitation of the devil and the restoration of all creation ($\dot{\alpha}\pi\sigma\kappa\alpha\tau\dot{\alpha}\sigma\tau\alpha\sigma\iota\varsigma$) to prelapsarian goodness offered a startling alternative. Yet Origen's doctrine would be declared heretical. The dialectical tension between spirit and flesh, good and evil, God and the devil proved to be an unassailable foundation of Christian thought. Redemption of humanity, with its sorrows of the flesh, could only be achieved through transformation. The heavenly body shone with a vitality whose brilliance reflected the aching burden of passion and pain the earthly body had once borne.

The Decline of the Empire of God

Amnesty, Penance, and the Afterlife from Late Antiquity to the Middle Ages

Peter Brown

IN THE FIRST DECADE of the sixth century, Jacob, future bishop of Batnae in the region of Sarug, south of Edessa, described in a *memre*, a poetic homily, the manner in which the average parishioner might listen to a sermon:

When the preacher speaks of matters that concern perfection, it leaves him cold; when he tells stories of those who have stood out for their zeal for righteousness, his mind begins to wander. If a sermon starts off on the subject of continence, his head begins to nod; if it goes on to speak of sanctity, he falls asleep. But if the preacher speaks about the forgiveness of sins, then your humble Christian wakes up. This is talk about his own condition; he knows it from the tone. His heart rejoices; he opens his mouth; he waves his hands; he heaps praise on the sermon: for this is on a theme that concerns him.[1]

The Christian churches of late antiquity were full of such persons. Writing in the 420s against the moral perfectionism of the Pelagians, Augustine insisted that the *peccata levia*, the lighter, barely conscious sins of daily life that affected every Christian should not be held to exclude them from the hope of salvation. He wrote to none other than the patriarch Cyril of Alexandria that he had been accused by Pelagians of denying the existence of hellfire. He answered that not every sin led to damnation: "this error must by all means be avoided by which all sinners, if here below they have not lived a life which is entirely without sin, are thought to go to the punishment of eternal fire."[2] Many good Christians sinned through human ignorance and frailty. There would be room, eventually, in heaven for those "who indulge their sexual appetites although within the decorous bonds of matrimony, and not only for the sake of children, but even because they enjoy it. Who put up with insults with less than complete patience . . . Who may even burn, at times, to take revenge . . . Who hold on to what they possess. Who give alms, but not very generously. Who do not grab other people's property, but who do defend their own—although they do it in the bishop's court and not before a secular judge."[3] Such small sins could be atoned for, without recourse to dramatic public penance, by regular, unhistrionic practices—by the daily recitation of the "Forgive us our trespasses" of the Lord's Prayer and by the giving of alms to the poor.[4]

Though reassuringly normal to modern, post-Augustinian eyes, such persons posed an acute problem to the late antique Christian imagination once they died. Augustine considered that their *peccata levia* were caused by a tenacious, subliminal love of "the world" and by habitual, unthinking over-enjoyment of its licit goods.[5] Sins such as those were by definition pervasive and elusive. It was unlikely that they would all have been fully atoned for by the sinner in his or her own lifetime, even by the daily practices that Augustine recommended. Christian souls were faced with unfinished business in the next world.

Thus when, around 420, Augustine came to write an *Enchiridion*, a *Manual of the Christian Faith*, for Laurentius, a layman, he offered a definition of the category of the faithful for whom the traditional prayers offered by the faithful on behalf of the souls of the departed could be considered effective. Prayers were not needed for the *valde boni*—for such persons they were, rather, "thanksgivings." They were of no help to the *valde mali*. But they were effective as "propitiations" for a broad category, which Augustine defined by means of a significantly open-ended *non valde*, a "not very": the *non valde mali*, the "not very bad."[6] In writing in this way, Augustine faced a pastoral and imaginative situation whose consequences have attracted the attention of many of the best modern scholars. In his lucid book, *In hora mortis: l'évolution de la pastorale chrétienne de la mort aux ive et ve siècles*, Eric Rebillard has drawn attention to the transformation of traditional Christian attitudes to sin implied in the "redefinition of penance" in the Christian churches in the West in the course of the fifth century. As Rebillard makes plain, Augustine was not alone in the tendency to "dramatize the temptations of every moment" and to insist on a reshaping of the Christian attitude to sin: "it was no longer a matter of sins [that is, of *crimina*, clearly defined "mortal" sins, such as adultery, murder and perjury] for which the believer must obtain pardon, but, rather, of the confession that one is nothing but a sinner before God."[7] Inevitably, such an attitude gave to the *peccata levia*, the day-to-day sins of the *non valde mali*, a consistency, a pastoral importance, even a diagnostic status (as perpetual symptoms of the weakness and ignorance into which humankind had fallen since the sin of Adam) that they had lacked at a time when "sins" had meant, above all, *crimina*—the sins of the hardened, known sinner that the Church had the unique, indeed miraculous, power to absolve. The Christian church had shocked pagans by the apparent ease with which serious sins seemed to be forgiven in those who joined it. The Christian emphasis on forgiveness seemed to undermine the *disciplina*, the high moral tone, of Roman society.[8] Now the image of the church as a sanctuary in which sinners became saints overnight, through conversion, repentance, and forgiveness, was replaced by a community where all members remained sinners. All Christians were committed to daily preparation for the *hora mortis*, for the moment of their death, through daily recognition of their sinfulness.[9]

But, as Augustine's *Enchiridion* made plain, the story could not be said to end at the moment of death. The prayers of the faithful for the departed were taken to imply that the partially unatoned souls of the *non valde mali* faced further eventualities. Augustine remained characteristically economical in his description of those eventualities. It was enough for him to stress that prayers on behalf of the departed were effective in some way: they obtained "complete remission or, at least, damnation itself becomes [because of them] less intolerable."[10] The Christian imagination went further. The imaginative representations of the fate of the soul as it entered the other world varied greatly from time to time and from region to region. Such representations differed markedly in the degree of risk to which the soul was thought to be exposed. Upper-class Christian epitaphs in Rome, for instance, hinted that all but the most fortunate (that is, of course, the deceased whose virtues were celebrated on such an epitaph) might have to wait somewhat tremulously before being ushered into the sweet light of the presence of Christ, much as one would wait before being introduced into the intimate presence of the emperor.[11] Monks in Syria and Egypt, by contrast, thought in more dramatic terms. On its upward journey to heaven, the departed soul was jostled by ranks of demons, who sought to claim the soul for themselves on the strength of the unatoned sins that each soul still carried with it. Such a "journey of the soul" was thought of as the last stage in the drama of the monk's perpetual battle with sin, now rendered utterly palpable in a world whose terrors were no longer mercifully veiled by the flesh.[12] Even Saint Martin was believed, by those around him, to have been confronted on his deathbed by the Devil. He addressed the Devil, significantly, as *cruenta bestia*, as a "bloodthirsty beast."

The Devil was almost a personification of Death, the last enemy to be over-come in the long, living martyrdom of Martin's life. But the Devil also came as a creditor, entitled to claim his dues, if he could find any in Martin.[13] Looking back on the account at the end of the sixth century, Gregory of Tours stressed that aspect of Martin's deathbed. If even the departing soul of Martin was forced to halt for a moment on its way to heaven to give account of itself to the Devil, then the average Christian had good reason to be anx-ious: "What, therefore, will happen to us sinners, if this wicked faction (*pars iniqua*) wished to have so holy a bishop?"[14] A little later, in the seventh cen-tury, common anxieties about the departure of the soul were taken up and transformed into a series of dramatic narratives. The souls of a privileged few had set out for the other world. At the moment of their apparent death in the course of acute illness, their souls had been taken from their bodies, shown significant sections of the other world, and then returned to life, to recount their experiences for the benefit of the living.[15]

Faced with so many vivid narratives, we should be careful not to endow any one of them with universal validity for all Christians of the age. They were fluctuating and incomplete representations, such as are best described in the words of Claude Lévi-Strauss as the "fabulation of a reality unknown in itself."[16] They were pieced together from many sources to impose imaginative form on a problem that was almost too big to be seen. It is the problem itself that deserves our attention, and not the various imaginative representations that were conjured up from time to time to render it bearable, even thinkable.

Put very briefly: neither in late antiquity nor in the early middle ages should we underestimate the silent pressure exercised on all Christians by the inscrutable anomaly of death. As Eric Rebillard has shown, the fear of death had been dismissed, even repressed, in some early Christian writings. But, with the victory of Augustine over the Pelagians, a current of feeling that was already widespread among Christians was allowed to come to the fore. The fear of death was accepted as an irreducible, even a salutary, aspect of human nature. It could not be dismissed by the believer.[17] Fearful, or simply awe-inspiring, the *hora mortis*, the "hour of death," embraced an entire block of human experience, up to and beyond the moment of death itself.

Hence the care with which Fred Paxton, in his book on *Christianizing Death: The Creation of a Ritual Process in Early Medieval Europe*, chose the term "liminal" to characterize a fundamental aspect of the position of the dead per-son around whom the early medieval ritual of the dead came to be created.[18] Borrowed from van Gennep's study *Rites of Passage*, the term "liminal" con-veys, in neutral language, something of the sense of anomaly, of the weight of conflicting emotional structures, and the sense of danger that surrounded the souls of the *non valde mali* as they left this world for the next. In the Christian imagination, the moment of death was an exact reflection, in miniature, of the terror of the Last Judgment. Theologians might be able to keep the "particular judgment" of the soul, after death, separate in their minds from the general Last Judgment of all resurrected souls and bodies at the end of time. But the fact that both were experienced as moments of intense and perilous "liminality" telescoped the two judgments in the minds of believers. Both caught the individual at a dangerous time, stripped of all customary forms of definition: stripped of the body and of an entire social persona by death; rejoined to a body, but not yet attached to a society at the moment of the resurrection, the human person waited in a state of painful depletion before the throne of Christ. Christ's judgment would decide into which one of the two great societies to which all human beings must eventually belong the person would be incorporated—the society of the saved in heaven or of the damned in hell.

The "liminality" of the departed soul implied that the soul underwent a period of waiting. This period of waiting might be cut short, even canceled, in a glorious manner in the case of the *valde boni*, the saints, who were instantly received into heaven. But it threatened to last for an indefinite period of time for the majority of the faithful, the *non valde mali* as Augustine had defined them. As Paxton has shown so well, the rituals that handled with reverence the "liminal" corpse as it lay among the living communicated a clear religious message that drew attention to the liminal status of the soul after death.

What this useful term does not, of course, include was equally important to late antique and early medieval Christians. The departed soul stood before a God who was anything but liminal. God's sovereign initiative as judge and as source of forgiveness had to be imagined. It was God who would decide how to bring to an end the painfully indecisive state of the average soul. At some time, it was hoped, he would invite the soul into the joy of his presence. That much was known. But in what ways and according to what morally convincing, current notions of justice and mercy on his part, and of amendment on the part of the sinner, could he be imagined as acting, both at the moment of death and, finally, for body and soul alike, on the Last Day?

Forced to think about the unthinkable on this particular issue, Christians of the fifth and sixth centuries tended to fall back on the fixed components of their thought-world. They drew comfort from well-established imaginative structures. But they found that no one imaginative structure could do justice to the full extent of the problem. Each structure reflected significantly different areas of experience. As a result, what is usually presented as the emergence of a doctrine of purgatory in the Latin West may best be seen in terms of the inconclusive juxtaposition of two such structures. One structure placed the greater emphasis on the eventual purgation of the soul after death. The other stressed God's exercise of his sovereign prerogative of mercy. At some time or other—most probably, it was thought, at the Last Day—God's amnesty would wipe clean the slate of human sins, much as an emperor on earth was known to pardon criminals and remit arrears in taxes.

Of these two traditions, the one associated with Augustine and Gregory the Great and the consequences that later ages would draw from their works stressed the purgation of sins by the individual sinner in this life and in the next. Spiritual growth was assumed to be a prolonged and painful process. For that reason alone, it almost certainly took more than a lifetime to become worthy of the presence of God. As Claude Carozzi has seen very clearly, Augustine found himself forced, by the logic of his commitment to the notion of purgation and his deep sense of the perpetual incompleteness of the human soul, to introduce an ambiguous wedge of "duration" into the timeless world of eternity: for him, the souls of the *non valde mali* in the next world were, as it were: "plongées dans une forme de durée."[19] A strongly rooted imaginative tradition gave a major place in this process of purgation to the operation of "fire" of some kind.[20] Ever since the third century, Christians had appealed to the authority of Paul's First Epistle to the Corinthians, 3: 13, 15: "and the fire shall try every man's work of what sort it is . . . If any man's work shall be burned, he shall suffer loss: he himself shall be saved, yet so as by fire" (1 Cor. 3: 13, 15).

For Clement of Alexandria and for Origen, this was a "wise fire," "strong and capable of cleansing evil."[21] For Clement and Origen, and for many others, fire was a symbol not only of God's ability to transform every level of his own creation, but also of the ability of repentant sinners to transform themselves.

In such a view, the responsibility of the sinner for his or her own sins linked final forgiveness to personal transformation. Emphasis on the necessity for the "purgation" of the soul as the sine qua non of entry into the presence of God always looked back across the centuries to the long, austere labor on the self associated with the moral world of the classical philosopher. It is the last transformation, in Christian times, in the long history of the notion of *le souci de soi*, as we have learned to appreciate it from the works of Pierre Hadot and of the late Michel Foucault—that search for exacting, personal transformation that was the hallmark of the classical tradition of philosophical ethics.[22] Even if, for Christian thinkers such as Augustine and Gregory the Great, the process of purification took place under the shadow of God's mercy and depended on his grace at every stage, the center of gravity of the imaginative structure associated with the notion of purification rested heavily on the individual and on his or her ability to take on full responsibility for his or her own healing. In order that this slow process should reach completion, the Christian imagination must not allow itself to toy with the prospect of arbitrary action on the part of God. Forgiveness was always necessary, and forgiveness would come, but no sudden act of amnesty must be thought to be capable of intervening, as it were, to break the rhythm of the soul's slow healing. It is in that aspect that the thought of Augustine and Gregory the Great betrays its deep, classical roots.

That particular feature of the Christian notion of the purification of the Christian soul deserves special emphasis. It is a feature that was strangely homologous with previous thought. The moral world of the classical philosopher had always been characterized by a carefully maintained vacuum of power. Slow and authentic self-transformation, pursued without fear or favor, was the upper-class philosopher's answer to the proximity of overwhelming power. The sage's actions took place in pointed contrast to an ever-present alternative—the exercise of power by a ruler capable of wielding vast authority in a largely unconsidered manner. Unlike the sage, the ruler was as capable of reckless acts of generosity as he was of crushing severity. Neither were morally valid actions. Philosophers did not act in this manner, nor, ideally, did they depend on the good graces of those who did so.[23]

Yet Christianity, like Judaism, had endowed God with just those attributes of infinite power, linked to the sovereign prerogative of mercy, which characterized "the kings of this world."[24] *Clementia* was an all-important imperial prerogative because the act of forgiveness was a stunning suspension on the part of a Roman emperor of an untrammeled power to harm.[25] It was the same with God. The words of the Collect for the twelfth Sunday after Pentecost, in the *Gelasian Sacramentary*, "Deus, qui omnipotentiam tuam parcendo maxime et miserando manifestas,"[26] appeal to a frankly "imperial" virtue in God. It was a virtue still appreciated by those Tudor and Stuart divines who incorporated the same Collect, without change, in the Book of Common Prayer: "O God, who declarest thy almighty power chiefly in showing mercy and pity."[27]

We should not underestimate the constant presence of imperial practice in the minds of late antique Christians, for late Roman practice helped them to frame the question of the forgiveness of unatoned sins beyond the grave. A solution that placed a heavy emphasis upon a relation to the self, favored by

Christian moralists such as Augustine and Gregory the Great, was frequently eclipsed or at least inhibited by a solution posed in terms of relations with power. God's supreme power assumed, on an imperial model, an uncircumscribed reserve of mercy that overshadowed the strict implementation of his justice.

When, for instance, monks and nuns in sixth-century Gaul gathered around the table on which the corpse of their recently deceased companion was laid out for washing, their prayers addressed a bruising paradox: at that very moment, two seemingly irreconcilable natures were being brought face to face—a human soul, released from the body and still "soiled" with the dirt of life in a sinful world, now drew close to the immense purity of God and his angels. Its first, most urgent need was for mercy. It was on the *indulgentia* of God, on his sovereign prerogative of amnesty as emperor of the living and the dead, that the prayers of the mourners placed their principal emphasis. What was asked for was an act of amnesty that came to the "soiled" soul as much from outside its own power to clean itself as did the act of the washing of the soiled, helpless corpse. In the words of the *Sacramentary of Gellone*:

et si de regione tibi contraria . . . contraxit . . . tua pietate ablue indulgendo . . . tu, Deus, inoleta bonitate clementer deleas, pietate indulgeas, oblivioni perpetuum tradas.

And if this soul has contracted stains which come from this mortal region, so contrary to Your own. . . . May your Piety wash them away by showing Indulgence, may You, by the goodness rooted in your nature, annul it with Clemency, that you may remit its debts in an act of amnesty, that You may consign [those debts] to perpetual oblivion.[28]

It is always difficult to translate Merovingian Latin such as that of the *Sacramentary of Gellone*. But we will not go far wrong if we render the sonorous phrases of such a prayer by doing full justice to their heavy "imperial" overtones. Modern students of the liturgy are attracted to *le climat festif et pacifié*, the "festive and peacefully resigned" tone of the ancient liturgies of the dead.[29] Liturgists tend to contrast the tone of such liturgies with the morbid anxieties that characterized the liturgies of the middle ages and to wish for their reinstatement as more authentic early Christian witnesses to the mood appropriate to Christians in the face of death. What it is easy to forget is that these liturgies reflect not so much greater confidence in the love of God as a notion of the absolute power of God, rooted in the most formidably autocratic aspects of the late Roman imperial office. Late Roman Christians found it natural to pray to a God for whom the act of mercy was in itself a declaration of almighty power.

What mattered to these Christians was that this was power that could be moved to mercy. A long-established model of the workings of royal power had set in place a mechanism by which pleas for mercy would be considered. The notion of absolute power and the consequent right to exercise amnesty deliberately left space for a third factor: the presence, near the ruler, of persons whose principal, most publicly acclaimed privilege was the right bestowed on them by the ruler to exercise *parrésia*, "freedom of speech," to forward claims for forgiveness. Christ, in the first instance, was the supreme intercessor for the humanity that he had redeemed with his own blood. But Christ's throne was flanked by created beings—the angels and the saints—whose prayers would be heard. They were authorized by him to plead on behalf of their sinful protégés. They were intercessors. Indeed, they were frankly recognized as *patroni*, "patrons," sufficiently confident of enjoying his friendship to bring before him, with some hope of success, pleas for mercy on behalf of their many far from perfect clients.[30]

Altogether, amnesty was in the air. When he came to write on the Last Judgment in the penultimate book of the *City of God*, Augustine found that he had to deal with a surprisingly wide variety of views on the amnesty of God, "which I have had experience of, expressed in conversations with me."[31] In holding up such views for criticism, Augustine was not reporting only the wishful thinking of woolly minded persons. He was touching the outlines of an imaginative structure endowed with exceptional long-term solidity. What he heard was that, at the Last Judgment, the power of the saints would prevail to obtain forgiveness for all but the worst sinners. For, so the argument went, if the saints had prayed for their persecutors when alive, how much more effective would their prayers be when they stood in the presence of God? At that time, their prayers would no longer be impeded by the frailty of their bodies, and their enemies would lie "prostrate before them, as humble suppliants."[32] What saint could resist such an occasion to show mercy? The amnesty granted by God in answer to the prayers of the saints on their great day of intercession would be wide. It would certainly cover all baptized Catholics who had partaken of the Eucharist and perhaps many others. As for hell itself, its eternity might also be disrupted by God's amnesty. The purifying fire of which Paul had spoken was the fire of hell itself in which sinful Catholics would be immersed for a short time.[33]

Augustine dismissed such views. But they were neither trivial nor isolated. Indeed, variants of such views, and not those of Augustine, were prevalent in the immediate future. Thus, in around 400, the poet Prudentius, who was himself a retired provincial governor, could take for granted when he wrote his *Cathemerinon*, his poem *On the Daily Round*, that every Easter, perhaps even every Sunday, was marked by a spell of remission of punishment for that "population of dark shades" who were confined in hell or (what amounted to much the same thing) in the hell-like prison of the netherworld, where they awaited definitive sentence at the Last Judgment.[34] Such remission was only to be expected. It had worked its way deep into the language of amnesty in a Christian empire. Valentinian I could hardly be called the most gentle of emperors, yet he knew how to celebrate Easter in a manner worthy of his God. In the words of an edict preserved in the *Theodosian Code*: "On account of Easter, which we celebrate from the depths of our heart, We release from confinement all those persons who are bound by criminal charges and who are confined to prison."[35] In the yet more pious Ravenna of the emperor Honorius, prisoners would be released from jail every Sunday to be conducted to the local baths "under trustworthy guard," subject to the supervision of the local bishop.[36]

The issue of periodic respite from punishment in hell raised by Prudentius was in itself somewhat peripheral;[37] it was simply a testing of the outer limits of a solidly established structure of expectations that would last until well into the late sixth century. Thus Gregory of Tours, who died in 594, still thought instinctively in terms of the grand drama of intercession and amnesty. Reticent about so many aspects of himself and his family, Gregory was at his most urgently autobiographical when he thought of himself on the Last Day:

And when, at the Last Judgement, I am to be placed on the left hand, Martin will deign to pick me out from the middle of the goats with his sacred right hand. He will shelter me behind his back. And when, in accordance with the Judge's sentence, I am to be condemned to the infernal flames, he will throw over me that sacred cloak, by which he once covered the King of Glory [by sharing it with Christ in the form of the beggar with whom he had divided his officer's robe] and will gain a reprieve for me, as angels tell the King. . . . "This is the man for whom Saint Martin pleads."[38]

The world of Gregory of Tours was characterized by repeated, dramatic scenes of amnesty. In this respect, the Merovingian state of the sixth century had remained formidably late Roman. Its upper classes found themselves implicated, on a day-to-day basis, in the stark antitheses of justice and forgiveness, abject humiliation and protection that formed the ever-present background to the religious sensibility of Gregory himself. Faced by the King of Heaven, kings knew exactly how to behave. In 561, after a reign of fifteen years, the aging king Chlothar came to the shrine of Saint Martin at Tours: "in front of the tomb . . . he went over all the actions in which he had, perhaps, failed to do what was right. He prayed with much groaning that the blessed confessor should beseech the mercy of the Lord, so that, through Martin's intervention on his behalf, God might cancel the account of those things which he had done wrongly."[39]

The *potentes* of the kingdom were expected to behave in the same manner before their king. Guntram Boso, for instance, was a notoriously tricky member of the newly formed elite of Austrasia. But he was also sufficiently close to the Catholic piety of Gregory to allow himself on one occasion to be persuaded by a soothsayer that he would be Gregory's successor as bishop of Tours.[40] When he fell out of favor with Brunhild, the queen mother, he knew what he should do: "He began to go around the bishops and courtiers. . . . He then pinned his hopes on gaining pardon through bishop Agerich of Verdun, who was god-father to the king . . . stripped of his arms and in fetters, he was brought into the King's presence by the bishop. . . . Falling at the king's feet, he said: *Peccavi* 'I have sinned.' The king ordered him to be raised from the ground and placed him in the hands of the bishop: 'Holy bishop, he is yours.'"[41] And so, once again, Guntram Boso wriggled free. A loyal devotee of Saint Martin,[42] despite his weakness for soothsayers, one suspects that he thought that he might yet do the same on the Last Day.

Gregory wrote as he did because he considered that his contemporaries had become complacent. They had allowed the prospect of the Last Day to slip from their minds. Gregory's careful calculations of time and detailed record of the signs of growing disorder around him were meant to warn those who, unlike himself, were inclined "to expect no longer the approach of the end of the world"—*qui adpropinquantem finem mundi disperant*—and who lived confidently sinful lives as a result.[43] As for Gregory, the throne of Christ at the Last Day and the desperate appeals for amnesty that would be offered to it at that time were a looming presence, rendered perpetually actual to him in his own world by so many sharp, small scenes of patronage, protection, and amnesty.

In other areas of Christian Europe, however, the throne of Christ was not invested with the same heavy associations of sovereign mercy as came naturally to Gregory, as he wrote in the recognizably late Roman society of southern Gaul. In Ireland, in the early 630s, Abbot Fursey fell ill when on a visit to his kin. He experienced a series of visions of the other world that constitute the first continuous narrative of the journey of the soul in the other world in the Latin literature of the middle ages.[44] What is revealing about Fursey's visions is that in these visions the throne of Christ was infinitely distant and that, although God's incalculable reserve of mercy was asserted by the angels who protected Fursey, it was asserted in a manner that implied that such a view did not come naturally.[45] It needed to be defended against more commonsensical views of the working of God's justice.

The Ireland in which Fursey had his visions was a land of virtually no state power. As a result, it was a land without amnesty. Irish kings could be as forceful and as violent as was any Merovingian, but their power remained carefully masked by a "polite political discourse" that saw them still as no more than chieftains surrounded by free clients.[46] Law and order derived from "elaborate norms of conduct . . . and a set of juridical institutions that positively sanctioned adhesion to these norms." While a state like the Merovingian kingdom could impose adherence to these norms by fear of punishment, Irish law "controlled through a system of prevention and frustration of individual autonomy, which limited the social damage any one person could do."[47] Caught in a "system of control embedded in the kinship group," the life of a compatriot of Fursey notably lacked high moments of amnesty granted by a superior power. Such power did not exist, or, if it did, it could not show itself in so starkly "vertical" a manner. Life was controlled horizontally, as it were. It involved the unremitting accumulation and paying-off of obligations: the making of honor payments to "restore the face" of injured neighbors; the offering of mutual sureties (which could include the grim exchange of hostages); the creation of agreements sanctioned by liability to distraint of cattle; innumerable claims from kinsmen, enforced in the last resort by "the horror of a visit by a professional satirist."[48] While Gregory of Tours looked out on what was still a late Roman society, where the daily exercise of power gave imaginative weight to hopes of amnesty on the Last Day, Fursey saw no such thing. What he saw, rather, was a world in which every debt must be paid and every wrong atoned—he saw a world that was a lot more like purgatory.

Hence the deliberately inconclusive nature of Fursey's vision. Part of this comes from the fact that he was a man who had "returned" from the other world, with a message only about its lower reaches. But the emergence of that particular genre in itself implied a view of the world that would have puzzled a contemporary Byzantine reader, as would the many absences in Fursey's account. The throne of God was nowhere to be seen. The escorting angels and the demons acted as if they were in a space of their own. The angels who escorted Fursey were impressive beings, winged creatures blazing with impenetrable light and surrounded by the sound of exquisite singing.[49] But they lacked the brisk confidence of officials sent directly from the throne— instantly recognizable as such, as they would be in Byzantium, by their court dress.[50] Nor did the demons offer their challenge according to the correct forms of Roman administrative law. They did not produce a heavy sheaf of documents to prove their claims for outstanding debts.[51] Instead, the demons lined up against Fursey "in battle array," showering him with arrows and setting up a spine-chilling battle yell.[52] They knew their rights: "If God is just, this man will not enter the kingdom of Heaven. . . . For God has promised that every sin that is not atoned for on earth must be avenged in Heaven."[53] Only the angels who protected Fursey invoked a higher court by saying "Let us be judged before the Lord." For the demons, that was the last straw: "Let us get out of here, for here there are no norms of justice."[54]

More significant still, the fire that, in a late antique imaginative model, usually ringed the throne of God—and so was thought of as the last barrier between the human soul and the all-consuming fire of the presence of God— had lost its association with that throne. Cut loose from the divine presence, the fire acted as if on its own, guarding the threshold between this life and the next: "It searches out each one according to their merits. . . . For just as the body burns through unlawful desire, so the soul will burn as the lawful, due penalty [of each vice]."[55]

Fursey's *Visions* may seem exotic to us, but they were not a purely local document. They were written down in northern Gaul. They circulated precisely among the new elites of Francia, to such an extent that it was almost certainly to Fursey's own brother, Ultan, that Gertrude of Nivelles appealed for reassurance as her own death drew near in 658.[56] Fursey's account of the other world can best be seen as a complement and a corrective to the penitential rigorism introduced into Gaul a generation earlier by his compatriot, Columbanus.[57] This penitential system dominated the life of many great convents and monasteries, among them Faremoutiers. Stringent penance formed the background to the dramatic deathbed scenes among the nuns of Faremoutiers that are described by Jonas of Bobbio in his *Life of Columbanus*. Indeed, death itself was dependent on penance. Only those whose sins had been stripped from them in a lifelong "ordeal of community,"[58] which included confession three times daily,[59] would be sure to pass gloriously to heaven. More than that: only those who had done sufficient penance would be allowed to set off on that journey. Jonas's account of the deathbeds of the nuns of Faremoutiers placed great emphasis on such delays. Sisetrudis was warned in a dream that she had only forty days in which to complete her penance. Her soul was taken from her and returned on the thirty-seventh day. Angels had held a *discussio*— a tax-audit—of her remaining sins. Three days later, exactly on the fortieth day, even these were paid off. Sisetrudis could die: "I will go now . . . for I am now better prepared for the road."[60]

Behind many scenes, one senses the absolute power of the abbess. As director of souls and regular confessor to her nuns, the abbess was a "silent well of secrets"[61] at the very heart of the convent.[62] She guarded the greatest secret of all—the appropriate moment of death. Only when a nun had totally forgiven her sisters, unburdening herself of all her hidden thoughts about them, would she be set free by the abbess to go.[63]

In such circles, we are dealing with a sense of the self drawn out by long delays. Whether in the space of one life alone (as was hoped to be the case among the nuns of Faremoutiers) or in the other world, the soul had to prepare itself fully before it came before the throne of Christ. It was not a self that waited, peaceably or with anxiety, to receive the magnificent, but essentially external, gesture of God's *indulgentia* for as yet unatoned sins. Every moment counted. All outstanding accounts must be paid off; every moment of the past mattered, lest any escape the memory of the penitent and so fail to be included in a conscious process of repentance and atonement. For persons considerably more frail than were the nuns of Faremoutiers, this was not a reassuring prospect. A long journey of the soul, similar to that endured by Fursey, awaited every one. And in that journey, what was at issue was the weight on the individual of the "unpurged" sins of a past life. In 678/9, Barontus, a late convert to the monastery of Saint Pierre de Longoret, near Bourges, underwent such a journey. He is an invaluable specimen for us, an average Merovingian: neither a thug nor a trickster, but a middle-aged former public servant with three marriages and far too many mistresses on his conscience.[64] He returned to earth badly shaken. Demons had clawed and kicked him as he made his way through the air above the countryside of Bourges. Barontus never reached the throne of God. Instead, he was brought before Saint Peter and was accused by demons who showed that they knew him better than he knew himself: "And they went over all the sins that I committed from infancy onwards, including those which I had totally forgotten."[65]

Barontus carried with him into the other world an entire life, in its full circumstantiality, made up of nothing other than the sum total of his specific sins and virtues. In that sense, the timorous Barontus was a sign of the future. In the concluding words of his monumental study, *Le voyage de l'âme dans l'au-delà*, Claude Carozzi pointed out that the penitent monk of this period "n'est qu'une première ébauche de la conscience de soi de l'individu en Occident" (a first sketch of the awareness of the self on the part of the individual in Western Europe).[66]

The text of the *Visio Baronti* ended with a citation from the *Homilies on the Gospels* of Gregory the Great: "Let us consider how severe a Judge is coming, Who will judge not only our evil deeds but even our every thought."[67]

Like the emergence of a new hybrid species, destined to dominate the ecology in which it is implanted, accounts such as the *Visio Baronti* represent the fusion of two traditions associated with the opposite ends of Christian Europe. On the one hand, Barontus belonged to a world already touched by penitential disciplines that had grown up in northern regions whose political and social structures were frankly postimperial. The notion of the *indulgentia* of God lacked day-to-day support in the practice of an absolute monarchy, whose power was shown by intermittent exercise of the sovereign prerogative of mercy. Despite the massive transfer to Ireland and northern Europe of the imaginative structures of the Bible and of late antique Christianity, the amnesty of God no longer stood alone and unchallenged in the minds of contemporaries, as it had once done in the late Roman Mediterranean. On the other hand, as the citations from the works of Gregory the Great make plain, texts such as the *Visio Baronti* drew heavily on the introspective, philosophical tradition of the purification of the self associated with the Greco-Roman world. Even in the presence of the overwhelming mercy of God, the Christian upholders of that tradition directed the attention of their charges, if only for a moment, away from false confidence in the *indulgentia* of God, as emperor, to insist on the authenticity of the conversion of the penitents and on their full responsibility for the working out of their own penance.

It is customary to keep these two worlds separate in our minds. The latter is associated with the prestige of a classical tradition of introspection and personal responsibility. The former is usually judged severely by historians of Dark Age Christianity. The penitential systems associated with the Celtic world are most usually treated as the products of a more "primitive" mentality: their widespread adoption in western Europe is seen as a symptom of the reemergence of "archaic" ways of thought in a barbarized society.[68] But the two systems were drawn together by a fundamental homology. Both were characterized by relative indifference to solutions based on a model of indulgence, which drew its cogency from the practice of amnesty in an absolute, late Roman state. Once the notion of the prerogative of mercy as an attribute of the "imperial" sovereignty of God weakened in the minds of Christians in such a way that appeals to God's power of *indulgentia* no longer provided a solution for the problem of the unatoned sins of the faithful, then the two traditions collapsed in on each other. What we often call the "highest" elements in classical and early Christian thought—the austere emphasis on slow, authentic change—joined what we are prone to call the "lowest" features of a barbarian Christian society—a penitential system in which satisfaction must be made for every sin. Both systems combined to create an imaginative struc-

ture that did justice to the silent weakening of the late Roman sense of the
untrammeled amnesty of God.

In this process, the image of Christ himself changed in a manner which
contemporaries barely noticed but which cannot but strike an observer who
passes from late antiquity to the northern world of the eighth and ninth centuries. Christ, of course, remained a great king. But He also took on the
features of a great abbot. The severity of his justice was no longer intelligible
solely in terms of absolute power, tempered by gestures of imperial amnesty.
What Christ judged, he judged now as an abbot. He searched the heart to
establish the sincerity of the penance of each person, deciding whether and
when this penance had taken its intended effect. What Christ delegated to
Saint Patrick was the right "to judge the penance" of his proteges.[69] Christ's
power was partly modeled on the powers of the abbot of a great monastery.
He became the *calvus*, the "tonsured" Christ of Anglo-Saxon Latin poetry.[70]
In the Old Icelandic *kenning*, Christ is the *meinalausan munka reyni*—"Lord
without stain, who tests the hearts of monks."[71]

This evolution did not occur in other parts of the world. In exactly the
same years as Fursey had experienced in one stateless society in Ireland his
visions of the other world, in another stateless zone at the other end of the
Roman world in the Hijaz, the visions of Muhammad had set in motion "one
of the most radical religious reforms that have ever appeared in the East."[72]
This reform went in the opposite direction to what was occurring in Western Europe. What emerged in the Qur'an and in the Islamic tradition, as it
crystallized in the seventh and eighth centuries, was a singularly consequen-
tial reassertion of the empire of God. In a scenario of the Last Judgment
more stunning and immediate even than that contemplated by Gregory of
Tours, God would make plain that not only amnesty but the power to obtain
amnesty through intercession depended unambiguously on God's sovereign
will. For even Muhammad's rights of intercession, of *shafa'a*, were defined as
absolutely dependent on God's prerogative of mercy: they existed only *bi-
fadhl rahmatihi*, out of the supreme bounty of his mercy.[73]

And this mercy remained consistently overwhelming. The most optimistic estimates of Augustine's interlocutors in the *City of God* as to what
the power of God's mercy might achieve for their fellow Christians became
a central feature of the imaginative world of early medieval Muslims. Whatever men or angels might think, God kept for himself "ninety-nine parts of
mercy."[74] At the very end of the Last Day, he would not be content until the
last Muslim crawled out of hellfire, blackened all over like a coal, except for
the unburned patches on his forehead and two knees—signs that even this

frailest of sinners had prayed the appropriate prayers of a Muslim. And God would joke with him, with the bonhomie of a great king, imperturbably certain of his power, and so in a mood, after a long day, to show mercy.[75]

It is helpful to take a step outside Western Europe for a moment, in this manner, lest we take its highly particular evolution for granted. In different regions, characterized by different social and political structures, a common Judaeo-Christian inheritance gave rise to very different imaginative structures. This is most apparent, of course, in the enduring contrast between Western Christianity and Islam. But, if we go back in time to the end of the sixth century, to the Italy of Gregory the Great, we can appreciate that within Christendom itself Byzantium and Western Europe had begun to go their separate ways.

In 594, as scholars of the period know, the *Dialogues* of Gregory the Great sketched out, almost for the first time, the "twilight" outlines of a world beyond the grave.[76] The fourth book of the *Dialogues*, in particular, is filled with vivid narratives of the experiences of individual souls in a highly circumstantial other world. In these narratives, the fortunes of individual souls depended on the extent to which they had succeeded or failed to make due amends through penance for their sins in this life. Yet only a decade previously, around 580, when Eustratius, a priest in Constantinople, wrote a treatise on the state of the souls of the departed, he approached the matter from an entirely different angle. What concerned Eustratius was to prove that all human souls, and most especially the vibrant souls of the saints, remained "alive" after death.[77] It appalled him to think, as his opponents suggested, that the saints died only "to rest and snore" until the Last Judgment. This was not so. Eustratius insisted that this world was flanked by a great city peopled by "citizens" who enjoyed a more vigorous existence than did the living on earth. Yet that was all that he was prepared to say. The basic category that concerned him in souls beyond the grave was their "life" and *energeia*, the effective activity of "living" persons. The "life" of the soul was what he defended against those who appeared to deny it. Eustratius barely thought of the life of the soul beyond the grave in connection with unatoned past "sin." Sin did not concern him greatly. He took for granted that all departed souls carried with them abiding "flecks" of human frailty. But these would be forgiven by God in a final, all-embracing, but profoundly unspecific, because "imperial," gesture of amnesty.[78]

Writing in Byzantium, Eustratius painted the other world with a broad, old-fashioned brush. In marked contrast to Eustratius, however, Gregory and his interlocutor, Petrus, set to work in the *Dialogues* with fine engravers' tools. They etched memorably individual portraits, using the acid of the unpurged

sins of a past life to catch a unique likeness of each person. They asked themselves, for instance, what complex calibration of God's justice could catch the
individuality of a man such as the deacon Paschasius. Paschasius had been a
learned clergyman, a lover of the poor, altogether a figure from a late antique
laudatory epitaph,[79] whose funeral had even been the occasion of a miracle
of healing. Yet he had been so pig-headed in his support of an antipope that
he made his last appearance as a phantom in the steam of a thermal spa to
ask an astonished bishop for his prayers.[80] A precise notion of temporary suffering after death, undergone for particular sins, offered a way of seeing the
respected, but problematic, Paschasius "in the round."

It was "sin" and "merit," acquired in this life and tested in the next with
meticulous precision, and not only the "life" of the soul, which mattered most
in Gregory's definition of the human person in this world and in the next.
In this shift of emphasis, we have come to touch upon a remarkable achievement of the early medieval Latin West. The period has usually been dismissed
as a Dark Age of Christian thought, an age of "theology in eclipse,"[81] characterized by "doctrinal stagnation and the riot of imagination."[82] But the
heated arguments in the other world reported by Fursey and the evidence of
lively conflicts of opinion in clerical circles all over northern Europe and the
British Isles that ranged over issues relating to sin, penance, and the notion
of impurity combine to give a somewhat different impression of the age.[83]
Its principal interests were not our own, and so it is easy to miss wherein
lay its principal achievements. What the spiritual leaders of the seventh century may have lacked in zest for those aspects of speculative theology that
we as modern persons tend to value, they more than made up for in a heroic
effort to cover all known life, in this world and the next, in the fine web of a
Christian notion of sin and forgiveness. Faced with this phenomenon, I am
tempted to coin a neologism. We are dealing here with the final stages of what
I would call the "peccatization" of the world: not with a "culpabilization" in
the sense of the fostering of a greater sense of guilt in Christian circles but
with something more precise and a good deal more significant—with the definitive reduction of all experience, of history, politics, and the social order
quite as much as the destiny of individual souls, to two universal explanatory
principles, sin and repentance.

When this happened, all that was not human grew pale. The *mundus*,
the physical universe, that "great city of gods and men," lost something of its
glory and of its reassuring immensity. In a vision told to Boniface in the late
730s in Frisia, a view from beyond the grave no longer included the *mundus* in its glory, as it had appeared to pagan mystics of an earlier age as they

ascended through its refulgent layers to the Milky Way and to the world beyond the stars.[84] What now mattered for the visionary was a view of the sum
total of human secrets. The basic model for such revelations was no longer
a longing to embrace the universe from a high point in the stars. It was a
longing to unveil the "hidden things" of the religious life, secret sins, secret
virtues, secret practices told in the confessional or whispered into the ears of
holy hermits—in sum, to penetrate the secrets of the individual. What the
monk reported by Boniface saw was not the *mundus*: it was "the individual
merits of almost all persons and the human race and all the world gathered
before his gaze as so many individual souls."[85]

And with that change—a change inevitably made to seem more abrupt,
more irreversible and unidirectional in the short space of one essay than it was
in reality, but a change all the same—we have reached the end of a very ancient world. It is an ancient world whose unmistakable profile we who study
late antiquity have learned to recognize. But the distinctiveness of that profile stands out also in contrast to other forms of Christianity in terms of those
imaginative structures that were central to its own life but which it did not
pass on to later ages. After the seventh century, a new style of Western Christianity emerged. It was greatly preoccupied with issues of merit, sin, and
identity and so found itself in need of a different imaginative world peopled
with more clearly focused faces not only of the saints but even of sinners—
the *non valde mali* of whom Augustine had written in his *Enchiridion*. The
new Christianity of early medieval Western Europe did not wish to appropriate the rich imaginative structures of its own, more ancient past. An ancient
sense of untrammeled power and mercy associated with the empire of God
was lost along the way.[86] As a result, late antique Christian views of the other
world have remained either opaque to us or can seem strangely out of focus.
The ancient other world, in its Christian form, is one of those many casual-
ties of time that we tend to sum up in the somewhat anodyne phrase, "The
Birth of Medieval Europe."

From Jericho to Jerusalem

The Violent Transformation of Archbishop Engelbert of Cologne

Jacqueline E. Jung

ON THE EVENING of Friday, November 7, 1225, the archbishop of Cologne was murdered. That surprise attack by a band of local noblemen left the city bereft of a charismatic, powerful, and decidedly controversial political and ecclesiastical leader. One year later the Cistercian monk Caesarius of Heisterbach, at the urging of the new archbishop Henry of Molenark, attempted to remedy the loss by composing a Vita of Engelbert, praising his deeds and ultimately proclaiming him a saint.[1] The text is an extraordinary document that contains lively narrative sequences, detailed accounts of political situations, and some remarkable theoretical wrestling with the notion of sanctity. For, as Caesarius was well aware, claims for the archbishop's holiness were not to go undisputed; many citizens appear simply not to have liked him much, and most were aware that his spiritual concerns were not abundant. Below the surface of Caesarius's candid biography lies a mass of questions that we can see him struggling to resolve, both for the sake of a consistent narrative and in order to persuade his skeptical audience. What is the nature of sanctity? How do miracles work? How do they relate to virtues in life? What is the relation between life and death and the afterlife? At the heart of these diverse questions lie distinct but often contradictory assumptions and expectations about Last Things. Caesarius knew he was treading on thin ice by proclaiming Engelbert a martyr who enjoyed company with God immediately following his unexpected violent death, for, as he and his readers were certainly well aware, an extended sojourn in purgatory would have been necessary for anyone else departing life with the spiritual failings of this archbishop. How were these conflicting assumptions about the "eschatology of immortality" to be reconciled?

As we shall see, Caesarius would return repeatedly to the fact of Engelbert's murder and to its gruesome relic, the corpse, in order to work out these issues. The shock and pain of death in this case provided the pivotal point. As the archbishop's blood flowed out, what had been spiritual deficiencies in life became wells of virtue, worldly activities were replaced by miraculous ones, and the man who in the end could not save himself in the flesh gained the power to save the souls of others. While my account of Caesarius's biography of Engelbert is a case study of one man's Last Things, it contains much that is relevant to a more general discussion of eschatology. Issues of life and death, body and soul, judgment and salvation form the crux of the narrative, and Caesarius's unconventional treatment of the eschatology of immortality makes the Vita an especially valuable document when we consider thirteenth-century views of the End.[2]

Our view of this text must be deepened and complicated on the other hand if we keep in mind that it was ultimately unsuccessful in its aims to provide Cologne with a new saint: Engelbert was never canonized (nor, it appears, was a formal canonization process even initiated), and the spate of miracles so dutifully recorded in the Vita seems to have died along with Caesarius in around 1240. The Vita did not attract interest until the sixteenth century, when it was reworked in 1575 by Laurentius Surius.[3] Eight years later Engelbert's name was entered for the first time into the Roman Martyrology, although his feast day was not celebrated publicly until 1617. Renewed interest in the archbishop's relics followed immediately; they were translated in 1622 and in 1633 received a glorious new shrine reliquary.[4] Tourists visiting the Cologne Cathedral Treasury today can marvel at the lavishness of the precious materials and the dramatic poses of the little bishop figurines that line the sides of the coffer, gazing attentively at the scenes from the life of Engelbert depicted on silver relief plaques just above their shoulders: Engelbert saying mass, Engelbert feeding the hungry, Engelbert stabbed amid a flurry of cloaks and horses' hooves. To be sure, there is a far greater emphasis on the archbishop's pastoral care and personal piety in these images then there is in Caesarius's Vita—a reflection of the very different concerns of the Church during the Counter-Reformation that were also manifested in the title of Engelbert's new Vita with its emphasis on his "defensione ecclesiasticae libertatis et Romanae Ecclesiae obedientia." The shrine, of course, is likewise couched in a drastically different visual idiom from that current at the time of his death—one need only compare the sprawling baroque effigy with the solemn wooden statue of Engelbert produced around 1240 (now in Münster).[5] Nonetheless, in the narrative panels that frame the archbishop's bones, the words of Caesarius continue to resonate.

During his nine-year reign, Caesarius tells us, Archbishop Engelbert II of Berg proved himself a fierce and enthusiastic civic protector.[6] His position established him as the most powerful official in the Holy Roman Empire after the emperor himself, and when after a tumultuous adolescence he grasped the reins of office, it was with evident glee. A member of one of Cologne's oldest and most formidable families,[7] he aimed to reestablish Cologne's preeminence after decades of political and economic turmoil, and he swiftly put to an end the war, famine, inflation, and interdicts that had characterized his predecessors' reigns.[8] He rebuilt crumbling defensive walls, resuscitated long-dead trade routes, and proudly assumed the role of a "new Solomon" as he stunned visiting kings and dignitaries with the splendor of his markedly improved city.[9] Along with his duties as chief imperial administrator and local prince, Archbishop Engelbert worked to renovate churches, welcomed members of the young mendicant orders (who were still treated with suspicion), and reestablished the by then hazy boundaries between secular and ecclesiastical privileges, successfully reclaiming for the church numerous properties long oppressed by local nobles.[10] At the same time, we are told, he exercised an ardent love for peace and zeal for justice, hearing and helping the local downtrodden in their plights against greedy lawyers, highwaymen, and even the ecclesiastical bureaucracy of which he himself was a part.[11] In this, Engelbert follows the model of lay male piety established in Odo of Cluny's tenth-century Life of Saint Gerald of Aurillac, but in contrast to Gerald, as we shall see, Engelbert displays no religious motivations or corresponding ascetic behavior.[12]

Like those of other charismatic power-holders (then as now), Engelbert's bold actions and forceful character caused sharp divisions in public opinion about him. Nevertheless, whether one loved and admired or feared and resented him, his far-reaching influence, diplomatic savvy, and administrative ingenuity were widely recognized and often appreciated by contemporaries. Nor did his lack of concern for pastoral duties or spiritual care seem to bother his contemporaries, who must have taken for granted the essentially secular, political nature of a powerful bishop-prince's duties. Although personal piety and an ascetic life did matter in questions of episcopal sanctity, as contemporary canonization documents make clear,[13] it is, as C. Stephen Jaeger has reminded us, abundantly evident from surviving bishops' biographies that "piety was not a requisite quality for the position [of bishop] in the same way that statesmanship and administrative skill were."[14] One can hardly obtain a clearer picture of the duties and qualities associated with the powerful bishop-princes of thirteenth-century Germany than from the verses written by the proimperial poet-propagandist Walther von der Vogelweide, praising Engelbert's achievements in the early 1220s:

Von Kölne werder bischof, sint von schulden frô.
ir hânt dem rîche wol gedienet und alsô,
daz iuwer lob da enzwischen stîget unde sweibet hô.
   sî iuwer werdekeit dekeinen boesen zagen swære,
   fürsten meister, dáz sî íu als ein unnütze drô.
getriuwer küniges pflégære, ír sît hôher mære,
keisers êren trôst baz dánne ie kanzelære,
drîer künige und éinlif tûsent megde kamerære.[15]

Noble bishop of Cologne, you have good cause to be happy. You have served the empire well—so well that your fame has grown in the meantime, and now hovers high. Should your esteem be offensive to any common cowards, you chief of princes, may that be to you an empty threat. Loyal guardian of the king, you are widely famous—better than any chancellor the guarantor of the emperor's honor, protector of Three Kings and Eleven Thousand Virgins.

Perhaps, joining in Walther's optimism, Engelbert took those words too much to heart and dismissed completely the threats that "common cowards" were indeed to pose. In any case, what began as a straightforward but irreconcilable dispute between the archbishop and his distant cousin Count Frederick of Isenberg over rights to a local nunnery ended in Engelbert's bloody death in 1225.[16] Modern scholarship, beginning with a 1917 article by Wolfgang Kleist, maintains that the original plan had been simply to kidnap not kill the archbishop.[17] Frederick, who under the mask of friendship was accompanying Engelbert on a journey to a church dedication ceremony in the outer reaches of the diocese, had treacherously arranged for some twenty-five of his men to wait in ambush along the sides of what Caesarius describes as a "concave road," a narrow path embedded between steep wooded hills near to the town of Gevelsberg. When the men, well concealed by the trees, leaped down to seize the vulnerable archbishop, the violence was evidently meant to stop there. But the plan backfired. For the archbishop, suddenly "made stronger," surprised the hitmen by struggling vigorously against them, and the attackers lost all control and drew their daggers. What followed, according to an eyewitness report, was a frenzied free-for-all, with the men brutally pounding, stabbing, and chopping away at the indignant, terrified, and ultimately helpless archbishop.[18] When Engelbert's companions, worried that he had been taken captive by his enemies, turned back to search for him, they nearly stumbled over his prone body lying in the dirt. One can only imagine their shock to find their proud and robust leader now a filthy, bloody corpse—"exceedingly horrible to see" and, to add insult to injury, even stripped of his characteristically sumptuous attire.

The scenes described here were to provide fodder for much imaginative speculation in later centuries—from the dramatic depiction on the side of Engelbert's baroque shrine, which represents the men in great swooping cloaks and mannered poses, to Annette von Droste-Hülshoff's Romantic ballad "Der Tod des Erzbischofs Engelbert von Köln" (1838), which calls to mind a dreamy, gentle Engelbert facing the band of villains amid a forest thick with crackling branches and dripping dew.[19] In contrast to those later, embellished versions of the story, Caesarius's account remains remarkably pragmatic. Just as in the miracle stories, he is careful to inform us which person performed what act at which point; and while the scene is a highly engaging read by virtue of its subject matter, Caesarius's primary concern seems to be to provide a full and accurate report of the struggle. Perhaps, paradoxically, it is the very matter-of-factness of this account, which does not appear to embellish anything and saves any moralizing until the end, that makes it so moving. Certainly it conforms to a tradition of history writing analyzed by Karl Morrison and exemplified by Caesarius's compatriot Otto of Freising, who "considered part of the historian's task to provide the reader with the illusion of being an eyewitness."[20]

But back to the narrative itself. Stunned, saddened, and most likely terrified for their own safety, the archbishop's companions next piled his corpse onto an offensive-smelling dung cart borrowed from a nearby farmer and trundled it along to the closest church. Engelbert's humiliation was deepened further when, upon arrival there, the pastor made clear his disgust for the gory heap. Claiming that the body would "contaminate" the church, he relegated it instead to a corner of his living quarters for the night, where it would do less harm. There a monk recently converted from the knightly class guarded it—his former profession, it was claimed, made him less likely to be disturbed by close contact with a murdered person. The body soon began to work miracles, healing those who dared touch it and provoking visions in those who sat mourning it.[21] These powers might help explain the fascination with which, soon afterward, the corpse was washed, eviscerated, inspected, and commented upon before being hauled back to Cologne, where the flesh was finally boiled away and buried in an "old tower."[22] The bones—clean, now, though thoroughly crushed in the onslaught—remained exposed as powerful and less revolting tokens of the offense. These and the blood-soaked cap and shirt were marched from town to town by Cologne officials to reinforce their complaints against the crime's perpetrators, and these articles acted as tangible stand-ins for the archbishop in passionate demands for justice and revenge. Within a year, the main instigators—most prominently, Count Frederick of Isenberg—were tracked down, tried, and publicly executed.[23] And it was one year after the murder, in November 1226, that the middle-aged Prior Caesarius from the monastery at Heisterbach presented to the new archbishop Henry of Molenark a Vita of Engelbert declaring him a saint.

Although the Vita was written at Henry's request—as the prefatory, conventional claims of modesty and unworthiness insist—there is good reason to believe that Caesarius was already deeply engaged in the tumultuous events surrounding the hero's life and death.[24] He included a passionate lament about the murder in a sermon composed immediately after the killing and probably, given the ambivalent attitude displayed toward the archbishop's life, even before the miracles began to occur. And in the prologue to a new collection of miracle stories known as the *Libri miraculorum* (1225–26), Caesarius announced his intention to include a Vita of Engelbert as Books IV and V. That plan was ultimately not borne out, probably because the subsequent official commission would have rendered it superfluous.[25]

Modern scholars, of course, are well familiar with Caesarius of Heisterbach as an enthusiastic observer, reporter, and interpreter of things miraculous, and his peers in thirteenth-century monastic communities also recognized him as such.[26] His *Dialogue on Miracles* was a best-seller, so to speak, even as he was writing it—much to his own annoyance, for in a letter to a Prior Peter of Marienstatt he complains of certain monks and nuns snatching up portions to copy before his careful revisions were complete.[27] Although representing a different genre, the Vita of Engelbert is no less characterized by vivid local color, narrative candor, and wide-eyed wit than those collections of exempla—the lively account of the archbishop's murder, supplemented by an eyewitness report, has been praised by modern commentators as "among the best [passages] that Caesarius ever wrote."[28]

As a historical document, however, the Vita remains as problematic and controversial as its very subject had been. By defying attempts to categorize it definitively as "true" historical biography or as a bit of myth-making hagiography, its structure has long frustrated modern scholars.[29] Its content presented no less a problem to Caesarius's own contemporaries (as he himself notes), many of whom were indeed skeptical that the worldly, wealthy man they knew could possibly be the healing, punishing, and vision-stimulating holy man whose pious activities were being recounted.[30] This, of course, is a dilemma that must have vexed many hagiographers of recognizable, recently dead persons: namely, how to reconcile a physical, time-bound life in the world with a spiritual, ahistorical holy existence. Saintly bishops—whose nonsaintly peers were frequently commemorated in laudatory episcopal biographies[31]—pro-

vided special problems for their biographers, who had to combine the traditions of hagiographical and biographical writing to produce a new picture of
a man who was both a secular administrative whiz and a pious ascetic. In fact,
in spite of the low expectations for piety in bishops as essentially political figures, all five bishops who both died and were canonized during the thirteenth
century—William of Bourges (d. 1209, can. 1218), Hugh of Lincoln (d. 1200,
can. 1220), Edmund of Canterbury (d. 1240, can. 1247), William Pinchon (d.
1234, can. 1247), and Richard of Chichester (d. 1253, can. 1262)[32]—displayed a
penchant for ascetic, distinctly mendicant-influenced ideals, acting as models
of humility, poverty, generosity, and so on. As in the case of Gerald of Aurillac, such behavior was closely tied to active thaumaturgical powers, so that
their sanctity was recognized and praised during their lifetimes.[33]

   This was distinctly not the case for Engelbert. In his sermon on the parable of the Good Samaritan (Luke 10: 30), preached immediately after the
murder, Caesarius openly laments the archbishop's journey in life from Jerusalem to Jericho—the route along which the man of the parable was attacked
by robbers and left for dead:[34]

And perhaps, as most people suppose, God wanted to erase his descent from Jerusalem to Jericho [through his death]. Through Jerusalem, in which the temple was and
therefore true religion, are indicated things spiritual; through Jericho, things worldly
and secular. While [Engelbert] had been bishop and duke, he directed his attention
less to those former things and went far down into the latter. This happened to such
an extent that one of our monks said to him, "Lord, you are a good duke, but not a
good bishop!"[35]

In the Vita, too, Caesarius does not hesitate to inform us of the future
archbishop's "complete and manifold" absorption as a youth in "the glories
of worldly things" (even while already holding several high ecclesiastical
offices);[36] he portrays him as completely entrapped by "nets of demons, tools
and snares of sinners."[37] How, then, was Caesarius to explain the postmortem
Engelbert, who appeared in visions performing mass—in one instance, his
own memorial mass—or clad all in white and riding a mule humbly into
church?[38] In seventy-nine recorded episodes over a period of ten years, this
new Engelbert healed the blind, deaf, crippled, and insane and punished dis-
believers, working miracles both through his relics at Cologne and through
his blood soaking the ground at Gevelsberg.[39] And his sanctity was recognized now not only by those men and women who experienced his powers
directly, but was also asserted by demons, who grudgingly praised the saint
and described his heavenly status through the mouths of possessed people.[40]

How could this be? The matter worried the knights and merchants who, Caesarius informs us, were apt to declare: "We cannot in any way believe that this proud, greedy man, entirely given over to the world, is able to work miracles"[41]—and the issue clearly bothered Caesarius as well.

And so, as a preface to his account of Engelbert's postmortem, holy activities, Caesarius offers a most unusual theory. The wonders that were occurring both at the archbishop's tomb in Cologne cathedral and at the site of his murder must not be regarded, he explains, as "the substance of sanctity, but are a certain signal of sanctity. Nor would it have been necessary," he continues, "that bishop Engelbert be distinguished by miracles after death if his life had been more perfect before death. The blessed Ebergisil and Saint Agilolf, both bishops of Cologne, both innocents murdered by guilty men, were crowned with martyrdom. They nonetheless were distinguished after death by rather few miracles, since it was not necessary that miracles recommend after death those whom a most holy life had recommended before death."[42] This argument represents a surprising departure from traditional theories of the miraculous—and it was deliberately so, as we can see from Caesarius's pointed distortion of the truth that many miracles had in fact long been attributed to the earlier bishops.[43]

As the compiler of a monumental collection of miracle stories, Caesarius was certainly aware of contemporary theoretical discussions of miracles and was one of the first to offer a definition of miracles as violating the ordinary course of nature.[44] But although the exact nature of miracles and their relation to individual sanctity was under debate at the time, most theologians agreed that true miracles were worked by God through a person distinguished by his or her individual merits.[45] Of course, it was difficult in the Middle Ages (as it remains today) for an individual to be acknowledged widely as a saint if he or she did not work miracles after death, regardless of his or her virtues during life. Nonetheless, miracles were tricky things; they could be performed fraudulently, for example by magicians or disguised demons, as well as legitimately by real saints, and medieval people were careful to distinguish between "true" and "false" displays.[46] One way of ascertaining that miracles were real and not delusions or falsely inspired was to examine the wonder-worker's life, whether it conformed in virtue to the astonishing deeds and whether this was a person through whom God would want to work.[47]

In the eyes of many of his contemporaries, Engelbert was clearly not such a person, and it was probably to counter popular skepticism that Caesarius contrived his unusual miracle theory. His claim here is that the miracles of Engelbert must be understood as signifying not a holy life—for as every-

one well knew, the archbishop was little concerned with either spiritual or
pastoral duties—but rather a holy *death*. In order for his miraculous capaci-
ties to be explained convincingly, Engelbert's murder had to be presented as
a type of radical conversion, a reversal and a negation of his former, worldly
life—the last-minute equivalent, one might say, to St. Francis's famous re-
nunciation of his father's goods while still a young man, and a satisfactory
substitute on earth for purgatorial penance. As Caesarius states in the first
chapter of the Vita, "The sanctity which he lacked in his life was replenished
in full by his death; and if he was less than perfect in his manner of living, he
was nonetheless made holy through his suffering."[48]

Although Caesarius insists throughout the Vita that Engelbert had died
"in defense of the Church," thus aligning him with traditional martyrs, he continually presents this especially gruesome manner of death as being of interest
in itself. It was the unwarranted outpouring of blood, the broken bones, the
grief and humiliation—for its own sake more than for its political significance
—that made Engelbert like Christ, Thomas Becket, and the other holy men
and women of the time who embraced physical pain as an exhilarating, expiatory state of being.[49] In one remarkable passage, Caesarius begins to justify
Engelbert's status as a martyr, citing various "causes" of martyrdom—inno-
cence as in Abel, love of law as in the Maccabees, and so on—and aligning his
hero, finally, with the internationally popular Thomas Becket.[50] (Engelbert
seems, in fact, to have provided Caesarius with a figure well suited for what
seems to be a particular sympathy of his for innocent victims of violent crime;
he proclaimed the martyrdom of Margaret of Louvain, a young girl who was
raped and murdered during a robbery of her family's home, in nearly identical terms.)[51] "In modern times," Caesarius argues, [Christ] "was murdered in
Saint Thomas, bishop of Canterbury, because of the need to maintain the liberty of the Church. The same cause of death existed in our leader Engelbert."[52]
Having found a suitable parallel, he proceeds to demonstrate the men's essential sameness on several points: "That man [Thomas] was murdered for the
freedom of the church of Canterbury; this one, truly, for the defense of the
church of Essen. That man freed the English church from the heavy yoke of
King Henry with his blood; this one, by a similar death, entrusted the church
to his protection from the unbearable demands of Count Frederick."[53]

However, Caesarius continues, Engelbert should be admired as an even
greater saint than his English counterpart because of the horrid particulars of
his death.

And although the blessed Thomas sustained many troubles, damages and exile before
his passion that Engelbert did not sustain, in [Engelbert's] passion it is certain that he

had, nonetheless, *more grief, anguish and distress* than Thomas had borne. That man indeed (as we read), struck in the head with a single blow, was left in the temple by sacrilegious men; this one, *his entire body bored through with many wounds by very many brigands*, was left naked on a dungheap. Saint Thomas was murdered by men who openly hated him; but Saint Engelbert [54] . . . by relatives and friends from whom he had anticipated nothing bad, and whom he himself had raised up. (emphasis added) [55]

"*This tends*," says Caesarius, "*to induce greater grief and to increase ill-feeling*" (emphasis added).[56] What Caesarius is arguing, in other words, is that for all the similarities in cause with St. Thomas, Engelbert surpasses that famous martyr in glory because he suffered more in his death. I have emphasized certain phrases within this passage in order to point out the importance Caesarius places on Engelbert's pain—both physical (the body "bored through with many wounds") and psychological ("greater grief" and "ill feeling"). Unlike early martyrs and those described in the slightly later *Golden Legend*, who likewise died under violent and painful conditions but remained joyous, Engelbert died *sad*.[57] In that respect he is assimilated to Christ, who was also abandoned by his friends and executed by people to whom he had done no wrong. Brutally mauled by "many brigands," including his own relatives and supposed allies, and abandoned as a bloody, naked, and vulnerable cadaver, Engelbert died not with a typical martyr's confidence and self-righteousness—enjoying the painless "anesthesia of glory" so characteristic of other martyrs [58]—but with a violent struggle, in confusion, pain, sadness, and humiliation. His emphatically undignified death contrasts with his orderly, controlled, dignified life. By genuinely *suffering*, both physically and psychologically, Engelbert inverted and negated his former secular life and was transformed—in the formulation of St. Paul borrowed repeatedly by Caesarius—from a "vessel of wrath" into a "vessel of glory."[59] That punishment on earth was enough to override any expiatory punishment after death that would otherwise have been necessary. For all his outrage and bitterness against them, Caesarius thus seems to have Count Frederick and his allies performing a service to the archbishop by shedding his blood.

The notion that suffering could function as a means of erasing sins or filling in moral deficiencies was not, of course, a new idea with Caesarius but had a long tradition in medieval thought. Writers such as St. Bonaventure applied it first of all to Christ himself—his suffering for the sins of humanity, it was held, overreached the bounds of ordinary human pain, to the extent that his body was more perfect than ordinary human bodies.[60] Engelbert's suffering, too, was greater than most people's—even than that of other martyrs such as Thomas—but this, it is argued, was because he was more in need of penance than they. Caesarius tells us that as the archbishop's companions washed and examined the corpse the day after the murder, they counted forty-seven wounds on it and bestowed on those wounds a profoundly personal meaning by associating them with certain holes in Engelbert's spiritual life.[61] As Caesarius recounts, "In every one of the members in which he had sinned, he was punished. He was punished many times in the head, namely on the crown, on the forehead, on the temples, lips and teeth—and so severely that rivulets of blood, flooding and flowing down, poured into and filled the hollows of his eyes, ears, nose and mouth to overflowing. He was also punished on the throat and neck, on the shoulders and back, on the chest and heart, on the stomach and hips, on the legs and feet."[62]

Through his very language, with its steady rhythm and repetition, Caesarius here directs us point by point through the saint's body, pressing us to envision and replay the torments it had experienced. Caesarius's insistence on the active role of his readers (or listeners) in that process is made explicit in the next clause; he has carefully enumerated the archbishop's wounds, he continues, "in order that you, reader, might recognize with what kind of baptism Christ deemed worthy to wash away whatever guilt his martyr had incurred through being proud, through seeing, hearing, smelling, tasting, thinking, being immoderate, working, touching, walking, and any other kind of frivolities, omissions and negligences of discipline whatsoever. . . . Surely, surely not without reason did he arrive at the glory of a martyr!"[63] It is important to recognize that there were liturgical precedents for Caesarius's graphic description of the dead man's body parts and the role they played in his spiritual state. The rites for the sick and dying in the late ninth-century Sacramentary of Sens, discussed by Frederick Paxton, provide a striking structural parallel in their call for the anointing of the sick person "on the neck, and throat, and chest, and between the shoulders, and on the five corporeal senses, on the eyebrows, on the ears inside and out, on the end of or within the nostrils, on the outside of the lips, and similarly on the outside of the hands, so that the stains that have in any way adhered through the five senses of the mind and body by the fragility of the flesh of the body, these may be cast out by the spiritual medicine and the mercy of the Lord."[64] Of course, Engelbert's death occurred too suddenly for the formal rites of the dying to have been performed. But both the language of the passage on the washing of the corpse and the ideas it contains on the linkages between body and virtue (or vice) make it clear that Caesarius understood the flooding of Engelbert's body with blood to substitute for its anointing with oil—a type of penance through blood such as has been studied in depth by Arnold Angenendt.[65] In this way, what had appeared in the Vita to be a chaotic and sloppily executed attack (see Appendix to this chapter) became an act highly charged with positive religious meaning.

The wounds on Engelbert's corpse were not to be perceived only as signs pointing to the martyr's past faults. Rather, they were also the tangible stage from which God performed an intensive series of supernatural spectacles. At first it was surprising for Caesarius that Henry, the cellarer of Hemmerode—who had tried to defend Engelbert from the attack—experienced "no horror" while guarding the body the night after the murder, "such as usually arises from [contact with] the cadavers of murdered people."[66] Caesarius attributes this unusual bravery to the "presence of holy angels, who were exercising a heavenly watch around the martyr's body." (But, he continues, "this Henry had been a knight prior to his conversion, and was therefore probably better equipped and more brave for this kind of work than most people."[67]) Such boldness in overcoming revulsion to handle the corpse was visibly and immediately rewarded in other cases. During the transport of the body back to Cologne, an older monk also named Henry was cured of a chronic limp when, "contemplating the blessed man murdered as an innocent by guilty men," he "touched the murdered man's bare arm with his own bare hand."[68] But the priest who had refused to let the corpse spend the previous night in his church—"claiming that the basilica would be contaminated, whereas it would in fact have been more greatly consecrated by the martyr's blood"—was "punished very severely, by divine will, on his body even today."[69] During its night at the monastery of Altenberg, the immanent power of the corpse and the intensity of the brothers' emotions were such as to induce in some of them "wonderful visions of the martyr's glory" while they slept.[70]

In an earlier paper in this volume, Peter Brown discusses the attitude toward the bodies and souls of the deceased manifested in the prayers of sixth-century religious men and women.[71] Those persons, he argues, were confronted with a "bruising paradox" as they washed and examined the lifeless flesh of their companions, for what they recognized in those moments was that "a human soul, released from the body and still 'soiled' with the dirt of life in a sinful world now drew close to the immense purity of God and His angels."[72] This attitude—and the sense of eschatology it entails—could hardly be more different from that manifested by Engelbert's friends as they cleaned his battered corpse and counted his wounds. Indeed, it appears that they perceived the experience in exactly the opposite terms: for them, the soul was made pure—and manifested its proximity to God—precisely through the messy materiality of the body. Bloody limbs that could heal or hurt a person on contact must have seen as virtually crackling with divine energy, so that along with grief, anger, and compassion, they also had the capacity to arouse feelings of awe and admiration. The friends of Engelbert did not need to pray that God have mercy on his "soiled soul," as Brown's sixth-century people might have. In contrast to those who understood divine mercy to come "as much from outside [the soul's] own power to cleanse itself as did the act of the washing of the soiled, helpless corpse,"[73] Engelbert's companions knew that the very fact of their having to clean the body of blood and dirt meant that the soul was *already* clean. The soul had been purified through the body's violation.

And so, just as baptism with water could send an initiate out into life with a "clean slate," Engelbert's bloody end acted as a purification ritual that negated his former life and readied him for immediate entrance into the heavenly ranks.[74] It thus constitutes the critical turning point in the archbishop's life, a parallel to the calls-to-holiness experienced by many male saints in middle age or female saints in youth.[75] Unlike his contemporaries Francis of Assisi and Elizabeth of Thuringia, whose holiness was visible to those who knew them,[76] however, Engelbert began to function as a saint only once his body had been hacked apart and his previous life forcefully inverted. Aligning him with the suffering Christ, Caesarius draws attention to the importance of the end in effecting that conversion. "The sun having hastened to its setting," he says,

the victim hastened to the altar with his sacrifice, so that an evening sacrifice (the most worthy under the Old Law) might be made to the Lord. Christ suffered on a Friday, at the sixth hour (that is, at midday), in order to display himself as a mediator between God and men. He wanted Engelbert, however, to suffer on the same day but at the end of the day, in order to show him crowned through a good end, and not through his preceding life. . . . Just as it was not proper under the Old Law to present a sacrificial animal without a tail, neither will a good life without a good end be pleasing to God.[77]

Caesarius's account of Archbishop Engelbert's death raises some provocative problems for current discussions of eschatology and the body. First, Caesarius is curiously, perhaps surprisingly silent when it comes to speaking explicitly of Last Things. He does not employ the traditional language of eschatology; no mention is made, for example, of the Second Coming, the Last Judgment, or the Resurrection of the Dead, and in several places Caesarius even explicitly refuses to speculate on the condition of the martyr's soul.[78] The question of what happened to Engelbert at the liminal stage of his death is, in fact, addressed directly only by two demons who happened to be at the scene and subsequently inhabited the bodies of a local man and a woman. One, possessing a man in Magdeburg, rejoiced at the murder of the archbishop even as he lamented his ignorance of the soul's whereabouts: Asked by a priest what had happened to Engelbert's soul, the demon responded sadly (*lugubri voce*), "Just as his eyes were covered with blood and darkened, his soul was torn away from us, and I don't know where it went."[79] The demon possessing a Cistercian nun outside of Cologne was rather more thorough in her account.[80] She, too, lost sight of the soul at the moment of Engelbert's death, a loss she attributed to his tearful confession the day before. "Alas!" she sighed when questioned about the soul, "it was snatched away from me and my companions who were all gathered around. [Engelbert] had prepared and washed himself so thoroughly before death . . . that we could have no claim on him."[81] The loquacious demon went on to volunteer the reason for Engelbert's current miracle-working prowess and to describe the power he exercised as an intercessor in heaven as well as on earth: "As he lay steeped in his blood, dying, he forgave his murderers with his whole heart, saying the words 'Father, forgive them' etc. On account of these words he has achieved such esteem from the Almighty that he is never refused what he requests of Him. And you should know this as a fact: no archbishop of Cologne has ever sat upon the episcopal throne who can accomplish so much with God, and whose rewards from God are so great."[82] Supernatural essence notwithstanding, it is difficult to hold this demon as a terribly reliable reporter, in light of the rest of the Vita. Caesarius certainly never mentions the archbishop reciting Christ's dying words in his last moments, and if we are to believe Engelbert himself, as he appeared in a vision shortly after the murder, his good-hearted forgiveness of his enemies did not endure beyond the grave. A canon of the Augustinian community of Klosterrath, while celebrating a memorial mass for Engelbert one week after his death, reported that the archbishop appeared to him during the service, dressed in pontifical robes and with a serene demeanor. After performing the ritual actions alongside the astonished canon, the apparition proclaimed: "Know for certain that all those who murdered me, or at whose instigation I was murdered, shall die miserably—and that more quickly than can be believed!"[83]

That assertion—rather hostile, it seems, for a saint, but typical of proclamations by ordinary ghosts[84]—did not completely come true; many more persons had been involved in the crime than were in the end capitally punished. Still, at least for Canon Ludwig, the martyr's words were not to be doubted. For immediately prior to his vengeful prediction, Engelbert had given what would be the most explicit statement in the Vita about the state of his soul after death. As Ludwig had reached the point in the commemorative mass where the names of the dead were recited, Engelbert had interrupted. "Brother," he said, "it is not necessary to name me among the dead, for I am with God and in the community of martyrs, enjoying indescribable joy."[85]

It is noteworthy that, throughout the Vita, Caesarius refuses to discuss Engelbert's glory in heaven himself because "we do not know what it is like nor how great it might be."[86] But he manages to make an aggressive argument for his sanctity nonetheless by placing testimonials in the mouths of both supernatural beings, who claim to have lost track of the soul, and of the archbishop himself, who claims already to be with God. Not only is Engelbert portrayed as attending God in the chorus of martyrs, but also, in the possessed nun's account, as enjoying particularly high regard from him. What this amounts to is a parallel to Engelbert's privileged status with the highest worldly authority, Emperor Frederick II (for whose son Engelbert acted as regent), during his lifetime. Indeed, the claim of the demon that Engelbert carried more weight with God than any previous archbishop of Cologne is not terribly different in essence from Walther von der Vogelweide's assertion that he had earned more esteem within the imperial administration than any other councilor. The emphasis, in this account, is on the earning of favors; it is not God's mercy that is at issue here, as it was in the early medieval cases elucidated by Peter Brown, but rather his justice, a justice that will repay a person's troubles during life with immediate entry into heaven after death while punishing wrongdoers with instant and painful retribution. It is perhaps revealing of the political climate of mid-thirteenth-century Cologne—and, most likely, of Caesarius's personal predilections as well—that the agency of God in effecting Engelbert's redemption seems to be secondary to Engelbert's own in suffering to achieve it. No thanks is given to God for his mercy, for example, nor do eschatological expectations about the Last Judgment and resurrection come into view directly. Engelbert's salvation occurs immediately, and he acts in the world as a punisher or healer with the same degree of freedom and vehemence as he had as a powerful bishop-prince. Indeed, God—like the emperor—seems to be out of town for much of this narrative.

Although his position vis-à-vis the status of the archbishop as a martyr-saint is obvious, Caesarius's reluctance to speak directly about the archbishop's soul probably stems from his own recognition of having created a new and not entirely unproblematic fusion of eschatological assumptions about personal redemption and immortality, a fusion that, like his unusual theory of miracles, may not have been wholeheartedly accepted by the public. And so his focus remains on the most striking and concrete evidence of the saint's downfall and exaltation, returning again and again to the broken body as the locus and vehicle of salvation—both Engelbert's own and that of the individuals who are cured by physical contact with it. The agony Engelbert experienced in his final moments thus replaced an extended stay in purgatory (which he clearly would have needed otherwise) and allowed him to gain full and immediate access to heaven.

That so much attention is lavished on Engelbert's suffering body as the site of salvation may also have important implications for the issue of gender and sanctity. As numerous scholars have pointed out recently, the body as presented in texts both by and about women was the special locus of female holiness.[87] Women's soft, penetrable bodies that wept, bled, and oozed or that were miraculously hardened and closed through prolonged fasting and virginity were seen as the primary instruments for identification and union with the Divine. By depicting Engelbert's body as open, permeable, and prematurely fragmented and by making precisely those physical qualities the catalyst for the archbishop's spiritual transformation, Caesarius has blurred the conventional boundaries between male and female sanctity.

Although throughout his life Engelbert conformed to the emphatically masculine model of sanctity established in Odo of Cluny's *Life of St. Gerald of Aurillac*,[88] his agonizing death and the subsequent critical role of his broken body transformed him into a different sort of man. At the end of his story, we behold the dreadful and touching metamorphosis of a formidable, aggressive, and distant public persona into a pathetic mass of bleeding, naked flesh, flesh that was later intimately handled in private spaces. This ultimately redemptive shift in identity contains implications that extend beyond this figure's personal history, however. For in Engelbert's painful passage from life to death (and from there, to glory), we witness that decisive change in models of sanctity so often associated with the decades around 1200, when—under the influence of the mendicant orders—friars, bourgeois laypeople, and women increasingly supplanted powerful clerics and rulers as the saintly objects of popular admiration.[89] The man who, like Gerald of Aurillac, had followed the old-fashioned paradigm of the just and mighty ruler, was forced in the end to take up the qualities of so many lowlier men and women of his day who strove fervently to imitate Christ in his suffering humanity.[90] Keeping in mind the Vita's deep concern with conversion and inversion, of sudden transformations and turnings-around, Engelbert's embodiment of two paradigms of sanctity is a judicious—if startling—solution. In order to become holy, clearly, Engelbert had to be in death everything that he was *not* in life. And when the archbishop encountered his radical turning point on that autumn night in 1225, he found that his body provided the fulcrum. For Caesarius and Engelbert's friends alike, that fear-inducing, wonder-working flesh was then embraced in awe as a tangible token of one personal and very painful redemption.

Engelbert's hard-won salvation, however, was not an end in itself. For

Caesarius, as for any pious devotee of saints, holiness resided not only in a person's acceptance into heaven but also—more immediately—in his or her propensity to communicate with the living and to aid in their salvation. And so while by relinquishing his elevated, worldly identity and adopting a more lowly, corporeal one, Engelbert redeemed himself and earned a place in the heavenly choirs of martyrs,[91] his story does not end there. It ends, significantly, with the intensive manhunt and execution of the villainous conspirators, most prominent among them Count Frederick of Isenberg.[92] Following Caesarius's example, I will conclude my discussion by examining the depiction of this other murder, a murder whose goal was essentially retributive yet became, in an unexpected twist, redemptive. Here, too, it is the body and the violence inflicted upon it that act as the pivot around which a profound moral and spiritual change takes place.[93] Moreover, the explicit connections and distinctions drawn in the narrative between Frederick's and Engelbert's deaths throw into higher relief the role of the murdered body in the archbishop's spiritual conversion.

Shortly after the death of Engelbert, Walther von der Vogelweide again gave voice to partisan sentiments surrounding the murder:

Swes lében ich lóbe, des tôt den wil ich iemer klagen.
sô wê im dér den werden fürsten habe erslagen
von Kölnè! owê daz in diu erde mac getragen!
    ín kan im nâch sîner schulde keine marter vinden:
    im wære álze senfte ein eichin wit umbe sînen kragen,
in wíl sín ouch niht brennen noch zerliden noch schinden
noch mít dem rade zerbrechen noch ouch darûf binden.
ich warte allez ob diu helle in lébende welle slinden.

He whose life I praise, his death I'll lament forever. And so I say—woe to him who has killed the noble prince of Cologne! Oh, that the earth can still bear him! I can find no torment bad enough to match his guilt: for him, an oaken stock around the neck would be far too mild. I don't want him to be burned, or chopped apart, or flayed, or broken on the wheel or even bound to it. I'm just waiting (to see) if hell will want to drag him, still living, down.[94]

Contrary to this passionate contention that no punishment save going to hell alive could possibly be horrific enough for the murderer of Engelbert, Frederick did suffer upon his capture in November 1226 an excruciating series of torments prior to his expiration.[95] The event comprises the final chapter of Book II, in which Caesarius presents it as the perfect retribution by casting it as a mirror image of Engelbert's murder. Whereas Engelbert's death had been spontaneous and chaotic, Frederick's was carefully orchestrated, involving a meticulous, piece-by-piece breaking down of his body by cool, indifferent, anonymous henchmen. Whereas Engelbert had been killed at night, Frederick's punishment takes up a full day, and he finally breathes his last at the break of dawn. Whereas the high-standing Engelbert had been laid low in a ditch, nearly invisible to his perplexed companions, the morally base and socially less lofty Frederick is elevated on a wheel set upon a tall pillar, his broken limbs all too visible to the onlookers below. Finally, whereas Engelbert had tried vigorously to defend himself, struggling against his attackers, Frederick accepts his punishment calmly and passively. Curiously, it is he, not Engelbert, who dies in the idiom of traditional martyrs: in prayer and without a struggle. Ever on the alert for things marvelous, Caesarius draws attention to the disparity between Frederick's arrogant, corrupt behavior in life and his humble and contrite attitude toward impending death, and he poignantly attributes it to a moral turnaround effected by Engelbert. The physical pain itself is what links them. While "it is fitting," he suggests,

that Frederick should perish in his body by a miserable and foul death, nonetheless we should hope that this same punishment was a medicine for his soul. For with contrition he shouted out both carefully and frequently, and both to himself and publicly, confessing himself a criminal, and patiently sustained the punishment carried out on himself, even offering his individual members to be broken to pieces, of his own accord. And when that merciless executioner wrought upon his back [Ps 128:3], inflicting sixteen blows with the hatchet, he did not utter a sound—so that everyone wondered.[96]

The thoughtful mirroring and inversion that Caesarius constructed in the death scene are most clearly manifested in the image of Frederick's *adventus* into the city as a prisoner. "But what's more," he relates, "God having arranged it, on almost the same day as when, one year before (*anno revoluto*), Engelbert was carried dead into the city [accompanied by] the grief of the masses, Frederick, with the desire of the masses, was brought as a prisoner through the opposite gate. And on the fourth day—when, that is, the first seven-day celebration was being performed with great attendance the previous year (*revoluto anno*)—this man was raised up on a wheel in an exceedingly unsightly manner and with many torments."[97]

The phrase Caesarius uses to convey the time lapse between the current action and the previous year, *anno revoluto*, captures beautifully the idea of turning around, of a movement from one point on a circle to the point directly opposite itself—in short, a conversion of the kind that, I have argued, forms the very backbone of Engelbert's own story.[98] As if to reinforce this idea, Caesarius even uses a reversal of words in the passage, moving from the construction *anno revoluto* when describing the double-entrance into the city walls, to *revoluto anno* when recounting Frederick's death. The torture wheel—*rota*—brings in a further, concrete image of that turning process so crucial to the narrative. It is only when he is placed upon that wheel, one year after the commemorative mass for Engelbert, that Frederick—astonishingly—is transformed from antitype, an inverted Engelbert, to type, that is, a parallel of Engelbert. For, like the archbishop for whose death he was responsible, it is through the absolute destruction of his body that the count is ultimately redeemed.

In Frederick's final moments, the points on the revolving circle converge at last; as the "merit of the martyr Engelbert who, dying, prayed for his enemies"[99] is passed on to his greatest enemy, the guilty one embraces that "grace" to pray for himself.[100] If bleeding, breaking, suffering, and praying during the process of death provided Engelbert with the ability to work wonders, then perhaps this extension of grace to an enemy likewise experiencing bodily fragmentation—allowing his own murderer to be saved in the end—can be counted as his greatest miracle of all.

Appendix

Caesarius of Heisterbach, *Vita et miracula Engelberti archiepiscopi Coloniensis*, ed. Fritz Zschaeck, vol. 3 of *Die Wundergeschichten des Caesarius von Heisterbach*, ed. Alfons Hilka, Publikationen der Gesellschaft für Rheinische Geschichtskunde 43 (Bonn: Peter Hansterns Verlag 1937), 234–328. My translation.

Book II, Chapter 7: *The Death of Engelbert and Its Aftermath*

They arrived at the place of ambush around dusk. And behold: Count Frederick, contemplating the enormity of his villainous plan and starting to abhor it, began to say to his men, "Woe to me, a wretched man! What kind of thing is this, that I wanted to do: to murder my lord and cousin?" But those others—the same men whom he himself had sparked earlier with the breath of Behemoth—soon rekindled him, inciting him to the evil deed with such force that, like an asp, he grasped again all the more ardently the very venom he had rejected not long ago.

Soon afterward, in a discussion with Herenbert, he revealed his will concerning the bishop's murder.[101] Then, in accordance with the instructions he had given his brother the steward, Frederick met up with Herenbert of Schwert and sped up ahead to where the lord archbishop was. When they reached the base of the mountain, the count declared: "Lord, this is our road." The bishop replied: "May the Lord protect us!" For, indeed, he was not without suspicion. Having lingered awhile, the count next positioned other attendants behind Engelbert, directing them to assist Herenbert in the act he had initiated. As the bishop entered onto the concave road flanked by two narrow footpaths, the count's servants who had been sent ahead made such a clatter as they awaited him that the lord archbishop himself wondered at the noise (so the cellarer of Hemmerode testifies today). Some of the attackers were approaching from the right side, others from the left, while still others followed behind with the count to observe the ambush. Then, as a signal to those who were hiding, Herenbert let loose a whistle so horribly loud that not only the men who were ignorant of the treachery were stunned, but so were the horses on which they were sitting. Soon those who had gone ahead drew their swords and turned back around. Seeing this, a certain soldier standing between the count's men and the bishop shouted in terror, "Lord, get on your horse right away, for death is at the door!" (A noble youth from Hemmersbach was leading the horse behind Engelbert's back.) Seeing that he had jumped onto the horse, the count's attendants threw themselves upon Engelbert, one of them severely wounding him on the leg. No one went to his defense except Conrad of Dortmund, who, with his sword drawn, threw himself upon Herenbert Rennekoie. But this Herenbert anticipated him, and struck him a heavy blow to the forehead. When Conrad turned away from him, Herenbert then wounded him between the shoulders [i.e., on his back]. Pay attention: This is the same Herenbert who shortly beforehand had forewarned the bishop of the plot, so that he would be able to extricate himself should the matter turn out differently than he hoped (*Vita* II:3). Seeing all this going on, "all" those who were with the bishop, "leaving him, fled" [Matt. 26:56], so that the words written about our Lord through the prophet were fulfilled in them: "I will strike the shepherd, and the sheep of the flock shall be dispersed [Matt. 26:31]."

After that, what happened to the bishop could not be fully ascertained, because of both the flight of his men and the imminent night. But the will of

God caused the following events to take place, in order that the chronology and the manner of the martyrdom could be made manifest. It so happened that Count Frederick was captured upon his return from Rome, and led as a prisoner to Cologne. Once there he openly confessed his own guilt and pointed out by name the other performers of the parricide, accusing even his own brothers (mentioned above) as likewise being guilty. Along with himself and another man, his scribe Tobias was captured. Placed in chains and in the hope of subsequent indulgence, he exposed in writing in what manner and by whom the blessed bishop was murdered, in agreement with the facts that the agonized confession in Rome of the count and the other abominable men had brought to light. This he did at the request of certain canons (those who had also strongly urged me to write), in order that the account could be written more accurately. This said about the matter, shall suffice.

And when the lord bishop had gone far enough along the concave road—so writes Tobias—the attendants who had been sent ahead, by seizing his horse's bridle, turned the horse around so violently that they wrenched the bridle from his hands. Unable to leave the road by either side (as it was concave and very narrow), the archbishop fled down the slope, in the middle of the road. But the men followed him, and Joachim wounded the horse on the thigh. Since they could not overtake him from either side of the road, Herenbert, on horseback, leaped off the road onto the steepest footpath and caught him (as he was to confess), seizing Engelbert violently by the collar of his cloak and dragging him down sideways as he bent forward, until they were both on the ground. But soon the bishop, who was stronger than the other man, rose up again vigorously and fled off the road into the bushes, with Herenbert still clinging, alone, to the edge of his cloak. When the count heard this clamor in the bushes, he rushed closer and is said to have shouted: "Grab him and don't let him go: For the man is being made stronger than we are!" Then the bishop uttered words of supplication, and said: "Saint Peter, with what [crime] do these men charge me?" Gnashing his teeth, Frederick replied: "Bring me the thief! Bring me the man who disinherits noblemen and spares no one!"[102] At this point Giselher, observing Herenbert clinging to the archbishop's cloak, rushed down and, chasing after them frantically, struck the first wound on Engelbert's head; and with the second blow, I believe, he cut off his hand; finally, that same Giselher ran his body through with his sword.—These words are Tobias's.

At the same time, Jordan, a man whom Engelbert had banished, rushed suddenly onto the scene to inflict the largest wound on his head (so he bragged in Isenberg), causing the bishop to cry a second time: "Oh woe!"

Then, turning to him again, Herenbert bored through him once more with his dagger, while Count Frederick wailed and shouted: "Woe to me, a wretched man! That's going too far!" When Giselher (whom I mentioned before) tried to chop off Engelbert's head, it was to Frederick that Godfrey, whom the Count had sent out to stop him, dragged Giselher by the hair. Still, barely ten paces separate the oak tree by which the men first attacked Engelbert to the place where he was finally dragged down, completely decimated (and where now, above the site of his martyrdom, a chapel has been constructed). It was at this spot that that herd, like rabid dogs and famished sons of perdition, bored into his whole body with the sharpest daggers prepared for the event, so that between the top of his head and the soles of his feet not a single part of his body remained free of wounds. This is just like what was said by the prophet regarding the figure of Christ, whose member Engelbert became by dying for the sake of justice: "Many dogs have encompassed me: the council of the malignant hath besieged me" and so on (Ps. 21:17).

Next it is said that one of the men sliced into the bottom of his foot, in order to appraise whether he was in fact dead. And then they all rushed back onto their horses, to reconvene at the place where the count was waiting, and left the body lying on the ground. Oh blind presumption! Oh madness not of men but of beasts, which did not shirk from so boldly, so cruelly, so odiously murdering the anointed one of the Lord, the priest of the Lord, a mighty pontiff, and not just any pontiff, but the father and prince of pontiffs—and, what should have been most terrifying of all, the most powerful duke and guardian of the Roman Empire. Having succeeded in the murder, the men, full of the devil, departed with their count—or rather that instigator of the entire malice—leaving the priest of the Lord to lie upon a dungheap as if he were not anointed with oil.

A certain knight named Leonius, who had remained with Engelbert when he was first attacked, chased after Henry the cellarer of Hemmerode, who had gone a little way ahead. "Oh lord cellarer," he said, "what should we do? Our lord the archbishop has been seriously wounded and taken captive by Count Frederick." By this he related simply that which he had seen, thinking that this is what had really happened. Unimaginably distressed, Henry replied: "Surely it would be proper to go back and see what is going on around him, or find out where he is being taken." They turned back immediately to the site of the murder, where they heard noises of the attendants wandering around in the woods. It was already night. And while they were walking about and looking around, they stumbled over the destroyed body of the martyr, which was full of holes and exceedingly horrible to see.

Greatly alarmed, the men left to retrieve from the nearest houses a stinking cart which had carried dung earlier that same day; this was by the cellarer's advice, so that the body would not perhaps be disgracefully treated by wild animals should it remain in the woods overnight. But behold: The body of that glorious prince, which when they left it was still partially clothed, they found almost completely naked when they returned. For aside from his leggings and overshirt, which hung about his neck, the attackers had left him with nothing; his undershirt and a little cap, though, were still to be found next to the body. All these things were so steeped in blood and so torn to pieces that the thieves had passed over them as if they were not of the barest use. But through them many healing cures have been effected, even today.

From Decay to Splendor

Body and Pain in Bonvesin da la Riva's
Book of the Three Scriptures

Manuele Gragnolati

BONVESIN DA LA RIVA'S *Book of the Three Scriptures* is an eschatological poem that describes hell in the *Black Scripture*, Christ's passion in the *Red Scripture*, and heaven in the *Golden Scripture*.[1] Enormous attention is given to the body within the whole text, which opens with contempt for the decay and rottenness of the earthly body and ends with triumphal praise of the splendor of the glorious body. In this essay I will analyze the meaning of the emphasis granted to the body in the poem and discuss the portrayal of Christ's passion as the midpoint in the transformation of the body from decay to splendor.

Bonvesin da la Riva was a tertiary of the Humiliati and arguably also of the Franciscans. He was born in Milan before 1250 and died between 1313 and 1315.[2] The *Book of the Three Scriptures* was written in the Milanese dialect in the last decades of the thirteenth century and was composed to be sung and recited orally to a wide and popular audience. It was a sort of oral preaching whose goal was more practical than explanatory or expositive.[3] The author announces his expectations at the beginning of the work, where he stresses that understanding is necessary but putting such understanding into action is absolutely essential:

Listening without understanding would have no effect, and the person who understood quite well would still accomplish nothing if he failed to put into action what he had understood. That to which man fails to commit his intellect and energy is of no avail. In this book of ours, there are three sorts of script. The first is black and full of fear; the second is red; the third is fair and pure, wrought in gold only, speaking of great sweetness. Thus, the time comes for speaking of the black script, of the birth of man, of life and death, of the twelve pains of hell, where there is great woe. May

God keep us from entering its doors! The red is concerned with the divine Passion, with the death of Jesus Christ, the queen's son. The Golden script speaks of the divine Court, namely, of the twelve glories of that excellent city. (*Black Sc.*, ll. 5–20)

These lines make it clear that the three sections of the book, represented by the three scriptures, are not independent but, on the contrary, strictly connected to each other: the opposition lies between the fear of black and the fair purity of gold, and the transition between the two is red. Expressions like "grand pagura" in line 10 or "gran dolzura" in line 12 foreshadow the emotional way in which the listeners should respond to the descriptions of the poem. This expected emotional response is exemplified in the following lines, which introduce the beginning of the black scripture and stress that "anyone who reads it with heart and mind should sigh and weep bitterly" (*Black Sc.*, ll. 23–24). Bonvesin's aim is the composition of a text that could provoke in his audience what Sixten Ringbom defines, when discussing different attitudes toward art images, as the "empathic approach" of the beholder that developed in the late Middle Ages: while listening to the poem, the public was expected to feel a deep and powerful emotional experience that would produce strong empathy involving both heart and intellect.[4]

In order to give rise to this response, Bonvesin uses various strategies throughout his work. The *Black Scripture* and the *Golden Scripture* are constructed both to mirror each other and to contrast with each other. The opposition between them is designed to provoke opposite emotions and is conducted according to what we could call, in Jean Delumeau's words, an "evangelism of fear" and an "evangelism of seduction": from the description of the misery of human life and of the torments of hell to the praise of the celestial glories.[5] In the *Red Scripture*, the empathic approach is encouraged by the identification of the red scripture with the actual passion of Christ, as though the very blood of Christ were the ink of the text. This image was expected to stimulate both the thoughts of the intellect and the emotions of the heart.[6] It also foreshadows the actual description in the central part of the poem that strongly emphasizes Christ's corporeal suffering and, in doing so, stresses his humanity and pushes the audience toward a feeling of proximity with him.[7]

The *Black Scripture* begins with a *De contemptu mundi*. This woeful vision of life originated in monasteries, was further developed in the convents of mendicant orders, and was finally transmitted to the whole of society as a "self-evident truth," which was expected to provoke in the public strong feelings of its own misery and pettiness.[8] The general deprecating tone of Bonvesin's description is fixed from the very first lines, which state that "the birth of man is of such kind that he is engendered in nasty entrails by blood that is commingled of vileness and filth" (*Black Sc.*, ll. 25–27). Bonvesin repeatedly stresses the miserable condition of the human body, which is weak, slack, and liable to continuous rottenness and decay (ll. 23–40). Even when men or women are beautiful externally, they are always ugly and filthy on the inside:

After he is grown up and fully formed, whether he be a male or a fine girl, he may be of a fair and excellent appearance outside, but no one, either knight or lady, is fair inside. There is no male or female of such beauty, whether small or great, queen or countess, that they are fair inside—this I boldly affirm. Instead, they are vessels of filth, vessels of great nastiness. No good thing issues from the body, only vileness. Out of the fair mouth come spittle and slime, through nose and ears and eyes pure nastiness. The vessel is fair outside, but inside there is a great rottenness. There is no food in the world, however precious it is, that does not rot inside as soon as it is hidden there. From the members of one's body, though they seem precious, issue no good fruit, only disgusting. (*Black Sc.*, ll. 41–56)

On earth everything changes, everything decays, everything is fragmented. Our wretched life is mutable, transient, precarious, and merciless:

Now rich, now poor, and now in misery, whether one is hungry or thirsty or in difficulties, the Wheel (of fortune) does not stop, it is always turning, out of control—now one smiles, now one weeps, and now one is ruined. . . . Or he will be sick, to his great discomfiture, with fever or gout or another affliction, so that there is no one so fair or so mighty that he may not become ugly and feeble in his great distress. One day, he will be singing, joyful and in good spirits; the next, he will be dejected and doleful. One day, he will be laughing, high-spirited and charming; the next, he will be mean and distasteful and hangdog. (*Black Sc.*, ll. 65–84)

The tone of the description becomes even darker when Bonvesin moves to the description of the decomposing dead body, which is described as becoming more and more rotten—just an ugly prey for worms:

The arms and legs, which were well-formed and fleshy, so fair and strong, nothing but skin and bones now. Truly, they will quickly rot underground in the ugly ditch. . . . O God, O wretched flesh, how slack and ugly you are, how disfigured you are, how vile you look. No champion or doctor or lawyer can be found to defend it from rotting. . . . The ditch is your lodging place, the worms your relatives. O flesh, why are you arrogant during our life? The worms await you the more eagerly the more you surrender yourself to rich food and excess. Your thoughts are few, for you do not think about the assault you are going to suffer. (*Black Sc.*, ll. 149–64)

As Philippe Ariès has pointed out, the connection between the moment of personal death, "one's own death," and the image of the rotting corpse, was common in the late Middle Ages. Decomposition and physical decay were not restricted to a "post mortem" condition but were "intra vitam": corruption was present in cadavers but also in the midst of life.[9] This is evident in Bonvesin's *De contemptu mundi*, where the putrefaction of the corpse is only one, even if perhaps the most striking, among the several imperfections of the earthly body. Immediately after the detailed description of the decomposing cadaver, Bonvesin attributes the cause of all this rot and suffering to original sin: "Pains and torments and death and thirst and hunger—all these things we endure through Adam's sin. Let us direct our lives along that narrow path that is pleasing to God who will raise us up without fail, and so we will certainly be counted as His 'leaven.'" (*Black Sc.*, ll. 165–68). Corruptibility, fragmentation, and decay, not the body itself, are negative and result from the Fall. Bonvesin holds out the promise, however, that if men behave properly, they will find the "salutary wealth" of heaven (l. 112) and, as we will see, eventually regain the very same body as on earth but redeemed from all its previous imperfections.[10] Only then will their glory be complete.

In the remaining lines of the *Black Scripture*, Bonvesin describes the moment of the sinner's death and his punishments in hell. According to this eschatological vision, the only thing the sinner can do when he dies is to regret his behavior and to express an impossible wish: "O poor miserable me, how unpleasant this is for me! If I must be punished with such a grievous torment, I would gladly return to the world with all my heart; I would do such penance that God would be satisfied with it" (*Black Sc.*, ll. 221–24). But it is too late, and as Bonvesin relates, it is impossible to attain salvation without the body: "O sweet Father most high, what great solace it would be if he could return to the world with his body! The soul issues forth, and thereupon he is dead. He came to his senses too late, nor did he see the light in time" (*Black Sc.*, ll. 225–28). Both body and soul are necessary and both are responsible for the destiny of each person. Hence damnation entails the eventual punishment of both: "Because both soul and body are guilty together, on the great Judgment Day . . . , body and soul will burn in this tormenting fire" (*Black Sc.*, ll. 242–44).

Bonvesin is perfectly aware of the theological doctrine that the body will return only after the last judgment and that until that moment the *anima exuta*, the separated soul, will be alone in the other-world. Nonetheless, his description of the twelve punishments of hell is mainly corporeal. A limitless physicality characterizes the twelve infernal torments of the *Black Scripture*, where the presence of the body is continuously implied and what is described is a fully somatomorphic soul.[11]

The first pain is the "dark fire that burns in that pit" (l. 298). The fact that the *anima exuta* could be tormented by corporeal fire was amply discussed by medieval theologians.[12] But here Bonvesin goes further: the senses and the faculties of the body are continuously implied in his description of the sufferings of hell.[13] For instance, in the tenth pain, diseases of every sort harrow the damned and disfigure their bodies:

The wretch is afflicted with every sort of disease; he is full of fistulas, morbid, delirious, feverish and paralytic, scabby from head to foot, malarial and gouty, bloated and pellagrous. Squinty and lame, his back crooked and verminous; his hideous and repulsive head hurts all over; the eyes are both rotten, the neck scrofulous; his teeth hurt him, he cries out, as if he were rabid. His arms are dislocated, his cheeks sunken, his tongue all swollen, his face emaciated, he is cancerous and half-blind, his shoulders slump, the stench of his ears stinks horribly. His limbs are swollen and gangrenous through and through; his inward parts are rotten and noisome, his chest is one (big) abscess, which keeps him in great pain. (*Black Sc.*, ll. 750–63)

Some other punishments deal with touch and with the pain that the body experiences when it is beaten and wounded. One of the most vivid examples is the seventh torment, where devils torture and slaughter the sinners' bodies with severe cruelty: "They tear them limb from limb with tooth and talon, they worry them and jab them and bruise them with sticks, with fork and knife they cut them up bite-sized, just as butchers do on earth with pigs and sheep" (*Black Sc.*, ll. 557–60).

The last affliction of the *Black Scripture* consists of the sinner's awareness that the Last Judgment will bring not the cessation but an increase of suffering because, Bonvesin tells us, all the punishments of hell that have been described will redouble with the resurrection of the body: "The unhappy man hopes for no improvement but always expects nothing but worse, namely, to be paid anguish twice over on the Day of Sentencing when the body (too) will have its torment" (*Black Sc.*, ll. 845–48). After all the corporeal description of the infernal pains, Bonvesin feels the need to restate the theological principle that the punishment of the body will occur only at the end of time and that only then will infernal suffering be complete and definitive. The damned soul makes it clear at the end of the *Black Scripture*: "How I am ruined and how I am destroyed! How I have despaired of all good hopes! Nevermore do I expect to be consoled; I await the Last Day, when the body will be paid. I await the Day of Sentencing with great trepidation, when the body will be punished, miserable accursed me. It will be no use then for me to beat my breast or to say *mea culpa*; I await it in great fear" (*Black Sc.*, ll. 869–76).

In the *Golden Scripture*, Bonvesin describes first the death of the just (ll. 25–80) and then the celestial condition of the separated soul before the resurrection.[14] But, as in the *Black Scripture*, the subsequent description implies the presence of the body. Here the twelve glories of heaven are presented as the opposite of the twelve punishments of hell, but the contrast between them is often mechanical and inconsistent.[15] In fact, the most striking feature of the twelve glories is that they describe a celestial realm that is presented as a place in which the imperfections and the limits of the earthly world are solved. This celestial reality has attained the purity that existed before the Fall, as though the world of Satan with its corruptibility, decay, sin, and pain had been completely overcome. The contrast stressed in the *Golden Scripture* does not really appear to be between hell and heaven but, rather, between the imperfect earthly condition described at the beginning of the poem and the regained perfection of the celestial one. The elements are exactly the same, but the essential transition is from decay to incorruptibility, from continuous change to stability. Even more striking is that this perfected physical reality of the celestial realm is described according to the contemporary theological discussion of the resurrection body.

Bonvesin was aware of the contemporary doctrine of the dowries with which the beatified soul endows the body that it gets back at the Last Judgment. In the twelfth century these *dotes* decrease from seven to four: *impassibilitas*, inability to suffer; *claritas*, beauty; *subtilitas*, a sort of incorporeality; and *agilitas*, a sort of weightlessness that enabled the body to move with the speed of light. After the mid-thirteenth century these dowries tend to drop out of theological discussion, but the cultural lag between theological speculation and more popular dissemination remained.[16] Lines 373–76 of Bonvesin's *De die iudicii* read: "The bodies will be glorified with four gifts: they will be formed harder than diamonds, more shining than the sun and thinner than any sound, and they will be faster and quicker than the eye."[17]

Bonvesin applies the doctrine of four dowries to the whole celestial realm, depicting it in the *Golden Scripture* as a sort of glorious reality, of resurrection reality.[18] The first glory gives a brief summary of the next glories and consists of "the great beauties of the land of the living, of the squares and the districts, which are shining and splendid beyond measure" (ll. 82–84). A long part of the description underlines the incorruptibility of the celestial world, which is presented as the explicit counterpart of the earthly condition that was described in the *Black Scripture*: "There nothing is lost, nothing grows old, nothing changes or spoils or decays; there is no subject of regret there, no one dies there, there is neither filth nor vermin nor scorpions nor snakes.

All things are safe there, fresh and youthful, always whole and lasting, enjoyable and neat" (*Golden Sc.*, ll. 125–30).

Apart from the fifth glory, which consists of the great joy that the blessed feel in the contemplation of the beautiful faces of the angels, Mary, and Christ, the remaining glories describe heavenly pleasures and delights that are similar to the earthly ones—such as perfumes, riches, servants, food, songs, or precious garments—but are finally redeemed of their mutability, temporariness, and decay.[19]

I will focus on the tenth glory, that is, "the great beauty, the fine appearance of the just man, his pure clarity" (ll. 601–2). Even though Bonvesin is still dealing with the separated soul, he seems to be describing the resurrection body. Bonvesin here resolves the limitations of the earthly body as expressed in the *De contemptu mundi* and finds a counterpart to its defects. The reference to the beginning of the poem is so explicit that the comparison is virtually required of the audience:

The resplendent face sheds such light that beside it the sun would be worthless. *The* tongue is of surpassingly sweet speech, *the* delightful eyes of surpassing splendor. *The* hair is of gold, shining and fair, *the* teeth of whitest white, *the* complexion brilliant, *the* hands very lovely, *the* feet very finely molded, every limb very fair and well formed. In that place, there is no man sick or ailing or in pain or too short or too tall or crippled or ruptured or old or misshapen or mute or leprous or lame or crooked or blind or freckled—Instead, each one there is healthy and lively, of middling size, whole and beautiful and fresh and well-formed, active and graceful, straight and clean and young, perfect and joyous. There no one is slothful or foolish or unseemly or thin or fat or smelly or feeble; no one is rotten inside or ugly or unseemly, nor does their breath smell bad nor are they repulsive in any way—Rather, everyone there is fine-looking, lively and quick, well-behaved and temperate and nimble and very seemly; everyone is fine inside and out, sweet-smelling and gleaming; their breath smells good, marvelously fragrant. In sum, what I am saying is nothing compared to the great beauty of the just man which never fails. (*Golden Sc.*, ll. 609–34)

The elements of the celestial person remain the same as on earth: face, tongue, eyes, hair, teeth, complexion, hands, and feet. But now the imperfections of the earthly body are cured, its lacks are filled, and its disproportionate parts are leveled. Moreover, this flourishing perfection will never fade. In heaven the transition of the body is from ugliness to beauty, from pain to impassibility, from partition to integrity, from decay to incorruptibility. In this euphoric praise of the splendor of the resurrection body, Bonvesin stresses both its integrity and lack of change. He wanted to involve the emotions of his listeners, and the idea of maintaining their own body, of continuing to be the same but in a new purified way, must have deeply seduced them.[20]

The poem places such importance on the body that body is everywhere, even when the author is aware of dealing with the separated soul. If it was possible to talk of the separated soul theoretically, it was very difficult to represent it without its body. Moreover, Bonvesin wanted to touch his audience, to make it feel the fear of hell and the seduction of heaven, to talk about something that would involve its deepest emotions. Only through such a corporeal reality, only through such emphasis on bodily pains and delights, could the listeners truly be involved and experience the description as real. Without such predominance of the body, they might have considered everything too abstract and too distant and would have not recognized the elements presented to them. Body was so important in the concept of the person as a union of soul and body that it was indispensable to both the idea of a frightening infernal punishment and the depiction of a seducing celestial glory. At the end of thirteenth century, Bonvesin is exploiting the potential of the somatomorphic soul that a long tradition of otherworldly journeys and visions had progressively developed, and he stresses that the separated soul experiences pain (in hell) and bliss (in heaven) immediately after death.

At the same time, Bonvesin highlights the importance of the Last Judgment as the moment in which the soul will be reunited with its body throughout the poem, and especially in the description of both the last pain of hell and the last glory of heaven. If, as we have seen, the twelfth torment of hell consisted of the soul's awareness that suffering will increase with the resurrection of the body, the twelfth joy of heaven is the knowledge that glory will endure or, rather, that it will be amplified after the Last Judgment. In spite of the splendor of the separated soul in heaven, complete bliss and "true sweetness" will be possible only with the resumption of the body:

The just man never fears he will suffer any torment—rather, he expects to see improvement on the Last Day, for his body will be a glory and great rejoicing. Then the just man will be doubly repaid. In his great love he expects to have true sweetness, for the body will rise in peace on the Last Day. . . . Soul and body will be in double glory then, in disport and in comfort. Dear God, how fine it would be to come to that bliss, to receive such glory, once one had seen the light in time! Therefore the just man overflows with joy and is all delight, because he expects that hour will come when his body will rise again to such glory. (*Golden Sc.*, ll. 689–707)[21]

Likewise just before concluding the poem, Bonvesin shows the blessed soul waiting for the resurrection and the subsequent increase of bliss: "I await the Last Day when my body will rise again and have pleasure and joy here and shine and delight in the purest splendor. The enjoyment I await cannot be told" (*Golden Sc.*, ll. 729–32). Body is fundamental and necessary for the fullness of glory, to the extent that Bonvesin's poem seems structured in order to underscore its importance. The *Book of the Three Scriptures* opens with the *De contemptu mundi*, which is characterized by a strong emphasis on the decay of the earthly body and ends with the seducing image of the resurrection body whose splendid beauty is described in the last part of the *Golden Scripture*. But what happens in between?

The *Red Scripture* describes Christ's passion and is part of a very well-developed genre of late medieval devotional literature both in Latin and in the vernacular. In the first lines of this section, Bonvesin indicates that the red scripture is Christ's passion, suggesting that it is red because the words are written with Christ's blood:[22] "Now I shall go on to speak of the red scripture, of the passion of Christ, to whoever would like to listen. It pleased him to bear it for us wicked men. These are wonderful words of weeping and fear. Now I shall tell you about the passion of the Son of the Queen—may she give me grace and excelling joy to speak properly of the divine passion, and save us thereafter from ruin in hell" (*Red Sc.*, ll. 1–8). The great emphasis given to Christ's physical sufferings represents the main characteristic of Bonvesin's depiction of his passion and is connected with the focus that contemporary spirituality put on Christ's humanity, stressing that it was the sacrifice of the cross that saved humankind and that the ransom for original sin was paid by Christ's suffering flesh.[23]

In Bonvesin's poem, attention to Christ's humanity is displayed with reference to his body. Two passages from other poems of Bonvesin show that Christ's body was conceived, through the figure of Mary, as flesh and blood. In the *De peccatore cum Virgine*, where Bonvesin takes explicit sides with those who defended Mary's bodily assumption to heaven, the sinner talks to Mary and says: "By birth we are together with you, made of the same blood and flesh. And you and your Son lived with human flesh, and with our flesh you are now in the supreme court. This is a great friendship, supreme queen, that you must have with all the people of the world" (ll. 111–16). Likewise, the poet says in the *Rationes quare Virgo tenetur diligere peccatores*: "Furthermore, the Queen has an excellent reason to help us sinners with great compassion: she is our kinswoman through her engendering, she dwells with our flesh in the eternal mansion. The glorious Virgin, and her Son as well, carried our flesh and blood hence. So she is our kin, nor can she say otherwise, nor can she wash it off herself whatever she does" (ll. 29–36).[24] Through Mary, Christ's body is made of the same flesh and blood as every other human being. They are the same blood and flesh that were despised in the *De contemptu mundi*.

But this decaying body, this flesh and blood, can suffer: they are, paradoxically, the instrument of salvation. On the cross, Jesus attempts to console his mother and says: "O sweet mother, who is groaning so, you know that I came into the world, as my father wished, to accept this Passion, dying on the wood of the cross. O sweet mother, you know that I came into the world, you know that I wished to take flesh from you so that the world which was lost might be saved through the cross on which I have now been set" (*Red Sc.*, ll. 346–52). As these words amply suggest, God took human flesh in order to gain the possibility of suffering, of feeling corporeal pain.[25]

In attempting to reach to the emotions of the listeners, the *Red Scripture* concentrates upon the moments in which Christ's body is most tormented. What most vividly expresses the incredible acuteness of the pain that his body experiences during the passion is blood. In contemporary spirituality, bleeding was associated with pain and was the most powerful symbol for cleansing and expiation:[26]

There was no spot two fingers broad on His entire body that was not broken and bruised to such a degree that the flesh looked almost as black as a kettle. They had no mercy on Him but laid it on with a will. The race of the Jews beat Him so violently that all His limbs were lacerated. His whole body seemed to be leprous, and His blood fell to the ground on every side. His flesh was everywhere battered and torn. The blood dripped down from His limbs to the ground. That renegade race had no pity but only kept laying it on and lacerating Him all over. (*Red Sc.*, ll. 53–64)

On the cross Christ's body becomes a piece of bleeding flesh and his four wounds are described as a "living fountain" that spills blood incessantly. Christ's blood flows like a river and is so prevalent that it is easy to visualize the script as red:

Both His feet and His hands were pierced with nails, from which He bore enormous suffering. So strong and sturdy, they were greatly tormented, the vigorous limbs nailed up there. Because His limbs were strong and vigorous, they bore all the more agonizing suffering. His hands hurt Him dreadfully, His feet were wracked, blood flowed out of the holes at four points. . . . Nails were driven into the limbs of the Lord, the feet, laid one atop the other, were pierced with a single nail. His sensitive limbs felt great anguish. From the living fountain, His precious blood flowed like a river from hands and feet; from the head to the feet, all the living flesh was seen to be torn and bloody. From His head to His feet, there wasn't a limb in His body from which blood did not drip and which was not twisted. (*Red Sc.*, ll. 153–70)

This representation of the wounded body of Christ on the cross inspired love and pity in the public, but also stressed the reality of Christ's flesh and suffering, thereby connecting the body of Christ with the rest of humankind. The extremity of Christ's suffering is explicitly connected with the vigor of his body. Lines 157–58 affirm that "Because His limbs were strong and vigorous, they bore all the more agonizing suffering."[27] This concept was a commonplace in thirteenth-century scholastic analysis.[28] Bonvesin is not as explicit as Bonaventure or Thomas Aquinas, but the idea is the same: the "role" or—we might say—the "mission" of the body is the experience of pain, and the more perfect the body, the better it can suffer.

As is made clear in the introductory lines to the *Red Scripture*, Christ's passion is not only incredible pain that must induce the listener to tears and fear, but it is also incredible love, the generous sacrifice that saves the world and that should induce humanity to consolation and hope.[29] In Bonvesin's poem Christ himself tries to console his sorrowing mother and underlines the contrast between unsurpassable suffering and the certainty of salvation:

Although I die under this torture, the third day will be my resurrection; you will see me then with great rejoicing; I will appear to you and to the disciples at that time. I will reveal myself before you then, O mother, you who are so prone to lament and grieve—dismiss your sorrow and your groaning; I will go and receive the high glory of the Father. You should rejoice, instead, O sweet mother mine, because I have found the sheep that was lost. Through this passion that I now bear the whole world will be saved, and so this must be. O sweet sweet mother, why are you upset if I die the death my Father wishes? Don't you want me to drink the cup that he has given me in peace, so that I may undo the work of Satan? (*Red Sc.*, ll. 357–72)

Through his passion, Christ rescues humankind from the "work of Satan." If we remember that in *Black Scripture*, lines 165–66, the "sin of Adam" was the cause of man's liability to pain, of the limitations and decay of his body, we understand that what Christ's passion attains is the possibility for humankind to eliminate all the imperfections and limitations of the earthly condition and to find again the lost purity of glory.

It is human suffering that induces redemption. And human suffering is possible through our body, which is—as we have seen—flesh and blood. Paradoxically, the same miserable and decaying body that was despised in the *De contemptu mundi* contains the means of redemption through the experience of pain. The "high glory" that Christ gains through his corporeal pain is the redemption from the imperfections that allowed his body to suffer and to be saved. Bonvesin explicitly shows this possibility with the figure of Christ: the beauty and the splendor of his resurrection face as described in the fifth glory (*Golden Sc.*, ll. 373–88) are an obvious counterpart of the humiliations and debasement that it had suffered during the passion (ll. 101–12).[30]

Bonvesin exemplifies what Bynum calls "the emphasis on the glory and salvific potential of suffering flesh" not only through Christ's passion but also through Mary's compassion, her "suffering with" Christ.[31] The great attention given to Mary's sufferings in the *Red Scripture* is common in contemporary accounts of the passion or of the deposition, both in literary works and iconographic representations.[32] In Bonvesin's poem, Mary's enormous suffering in seeing Christ's passion moves closer and closer to that of her son and ends in a sort of identification with it. Their sufferings are described in the same way: Mary's compassion blends with Christ's passion and she becomes him through her pain.

From Mary's first appearance on the Calvary hill, her sorrow is immediately physical: "When she had seen her Son in such a sorry plight, she felt overwhelming sorrow, so intense and so absolute that she was as if dead, her limbs so lifeless that no man alive could describe it. She bore tormenting anguish for her Son, agonized sorrow, sorrowful agony. She wept and groaned, she was so full of tears that her anguished heart swooned" (*Red Sc.*, ll. 137–48). When Christ's limbs are in agony on the cross, Mary's limbs express her pain: "Seeing her Son's limbs so torn, battered and bloody and so disfigured, bruised and wounded from head to foot, filthy and defiled with abuse and garbage, she was afflicted with immeasurable afflictions, with agonizing anguish, very harsh and profound. Her limbs were all weighed down with great sorrow, the sorrows she bore will never be counted" (*Red Sc.*, ll. 221–28). The idea of Mary suffering not only in her soul but also in her flesh was common in sermons and literature of the late Middle Ages.[33] This idea is connected with the identification of Mary's flesh with Christ's flesh: Christ's and Mary's bodies are a true unity, and what happens to his flesh also happens to hers. In this case, Mary's flesh feels the humiliations inflicted on her son's body and the nails driven into it.[34] At the same time, the human being was conceived of as a union of body and soul and pain was also understood as the experience of a psychosomatic unit. Mary's sorrow becomes therefore physical, expressed through her body.[35] She is not beaten directly and she does not bleed, but her emotional participation in her son's passion and her love for him transform psychic anguish into bodily pain.

Like Christ's, Mary's suffering is limitless. It is described as strikingly similar to her son's.[36] When the text was recited orally, it must have been difficult to distinguish Mary from Christ because they are described in the same way and they speak the same language. Thus Bonvesin expresses through words what in painting is expressed through the representation of Mary's body in the same attitude as Christ's.[37] Mary's love for Christ makes her suffering his. Through her empathic participation in Christ's agony, she unites with him. An earlier text makes the assumption behind such *imitatio*, or identification, clear. In explaining that Mary was "transformed into the likeness of Christ," Bonaventure quotes Hugh of St. Victor that "Vis amoris amantem in amati similitudinis transformat," the power of love transforms the lover into an image of the beloved.[38] In the *Red Scripture* Mary's love ("inama" in l. 283) for Christ moves her to ask not only for death but also for the opportunity to take part in the physical passion of her son. She begs the Jews to crucify her as well: "O God, precious son, whom my heart loves so, may you receive me into your Passion in my suffering and woe. O miserable Jews, you should kill me too, seeing that you nail my Son to the cross. Come and crucify the mother along with Him. Take vengeance on woeful me along with my Son by any death you wish" (*Red Sc.*, ll. 283–88). Although she is not physically on the cross, Mary suffers as though she were. Her pain is the same as her crucified son's. Indeed, through compassion, she suffers the crucifixion.[39] The boundaries between Mary and Christ are so confused that she can even ask for his compassion (l. 320). But during her immeasurable suffering, whose physicality is underlined by the summarizing expression "portar stradura disciplina" in line 252,[40] Bonvesin suggests her redemption:

His sweet mother, seeing these events, seeing her son lingering in great torments, and the dishonor, invective, and great abuse, and slander and mockery done to Him on the cross, writhed to and fro, so sorrowful was her heart, and wept with tears and great groaning, collapsing from anguish. Her lamentation was such that her grief cannot be described. . . . She could scarcely contain the suffering in her, so very harsh and great was her suffering. No greater woe could she have on earth than to see her Son's passion. She was groaning so, her limbs seemed to be dissolved in tears on tears, and she was stricken with much woe seeing her Son so torn and abused, dying little by little. She felt such anguish, she could not speak. But when her tongue tried to speak, her crushing suffering blocked her tongue, she writhed full of woe and sorrow. She could not speak, her voice failed her, she writhed and lamented and lamented and writhed, she sighed and wept, she wept and sighed—no one could have imagined the suffering she displayed. Such was her suffering that no man born ever felt equal anguish, felt equal pain. Through the mother's demeanor it was revealed that immeasurable suffering dwelt within. Oh the great compassion of our great Queen, of that sweet mother who is our remedy, who groaned and lamented so at such destruction, *taking for her Son very harsh discipline* (Portand per lo so fio stradura disciplina). (*Red Sc.*, ll. 213–53)

When Bonvesin utters "Oi grand compassion dra nostra grand regina," he highlights the connection between Mary's compassion and her status of queen, suggesting that what makes her a queen is her compassion. Through her "stradura disciplina," she attains the greatest glory. Not only do Christ's words to his mother in line 385—"you will come with me in time"—affirm that Mary will go to paradise after death, but, as we have seen, Bonvesin even believes in her bodily assumption to heaven.[41] "Regina"—queen—is the term that first defines Mary when her clarity is described in heaven (*Golden Sc.*, l. 327); it refers to her glory, which is complete because she is there with her body. We know what glory consists of: Mary's compassion, which is shown through her physical identification with the tormented body of her son, allows her to redeem the imperfection of the body through which she suffers and to attain the splendor of resurrection.[42]

If it is through his suffering that Christ attains glory for himself and the possibility of redemption for others, suffering is at least as central in the figure of Mary. But both Christ presented in his suffering humanity and Mary presented as the model of compassion are examples for the rest of humankind. With his writing and through the emotions it elicits, Bonvesin hopes to reform the behavior of his public. As he says in the opening of the poem, his aim is that the public respond to his poem with "heart and mind." At the end of the fifth glory, which consists in contemplation of the faces of Christ and Mary, merit is attributed to attendance at masses and help given to the poor, but also to love for Christ, which made the just man call up Christ's image in the heart and in the mind (*Golden Sc.*, ll. 401–2). The reference is to the contemporary well-developed cult of the Veronica: the material image of God was understood as a mediator between Creator and creature and the very act of viewing implied the desire of viewers to resemble the one they had in view.[43] Bonvesin's poem is a sort of "verbal Veronica." About the same time that the Veronica started to be conceived not as a portrait but as the imprint of the very suffering face of Christ on a piece of cloth, Bonvesin suggested that his account of the passion is written in the very blood of Christ. The poem aspires to the same goal as the Veronica: to mediate between Christ and man. The capacity to suffer bodily is what we have in common with Christ; suffering is what we can use in order to move toward him. Especially through the figure of Mary, suffering indicates a path to union with Christ:[44] Mary's compassion can be viewed as the exemplar of the empathic reactions that the poet is attempting to instigate in his public.

It is Christ and Mary's suffering flesh that gave them a site in which redemption can take place. But, as is made clear by Bonvesin in the passage from the *De peccatore cum Virgine* quoted above, their flesh is our flesh, and thus we too can suffer. After reminding his listeners at the beginning of the poem that their beloved bodies are decaying and rotting, Bonvesin indicates to them, through the example of Christ and especially of Mary, the way to redemption, whose sweetness he is about to describe in the *Golden Scripture*.

After the description of Christ's passion, Mary's compassion, and the anticipation of their glory attained through suffering, the final passage of the *Red Scripture* is a synthesis of the several practical suggestions scattered throughout the text, especially in the words of the blessed at the end of each glory.[45] Just before the description of the glories of the good man, which will entice the listeners, the central section of the *Book of the Three Scriptures* ends with an invitation to compassion:

> We have related the harsh Passion which Jesus bore unremittingly. There is no man of worth who could reflect on this without giving himself up to great *compassion*. There is no one on earth, once he has properly listened to the passion of that admirable Lord and how He was betrayed and tormented, no one so impudent or so hardened that he ought not to be filled with fear and affliction. There ought to be no one who would not bear in peace . . . when he heard the dreadful Passion which Jesus our true Lord bore for us. It should be no burden to him to bear deprivation, shame, and poverty through winter and summer, and hunger and thirst and cold, disgrace and sickness, affronts and wrongs of all sorts inflicted upon him. Tribulation should be no burden to him, nor forgiving those who affront him, nor living in penitence with great affliction, nor mourning for his sins with great contrition. Food and drink should give him no pleasure when he reflects that the King of Glory was slain thus for our sakes yet had never committed sin or culpable action. For the sake of us wretches, He was reduced to such degradation. (*Red Sc.*, ll. 425–48)

Con-passio, "suffering with," is the means by which we can assimilate to Christ and attain redemption: through patience, humility, penitence, and ascetic practices, our ability to experience suffering, body and soul, gives us access to salvation and to the wonderful fullness of glory. At the very end of the poem, after the explicit description of glory as integrity of the person, soul and body, without the fear of decay, Bonvesin stresses again that humankind gains glory through love: "We have told of the golden script, which is sweet to read, agreeable and refined. There is no person born who reads this script that should weary of winning such glory. If the script were only read with great love, there is no one in the world who would hesitate to live in penitence, so that he might gain such a life that he would never tire" (*Golden Sc.*, ll. 741–48). Through suffering with our miserable but so important body, Bonvesin tells us, we can win the sweetness of glory: we move from the corruption of the earthly body to the splendor of the resurrection body through suffering. Or, in the imagery of the threefold scripture, we move from the fear of black to the seduction of gold through the cleansing power of blood.

PART II

———

APOCALYPTIC
TIME

Time Is Short

The Eschatology of the
Early Gaelic Church

Benjamin Hudson

"GREAT FEAR FELL AMONG THE MEN of Ireland before the feast of John [the Baptist] of this year [1096], until God spared [them] through the fastings of the successor of Patrick and of the clergy of Ireland besides."[1] The panic of 1096 is a curious episode in Irish history, and this laconic statement in the contemporary chronicle known as the Annals of Ulster is one of its few records of society beyond the powerful princes and higher clergy. This cultural terror at the approach of a saintly festival that the Gaels believed to be a preview of the Day of Judgment leads to the question of why they were prepared to believe in the disasters associated with an event whose horrors were unknown elsewhere in Europe? Part of the answer is that the panic of 1096 reflects the interest in eschatology found among the Celtic peoples of Britain and Ireland. With the advantage of hindsight, that panic can be seen as the logical conclusion to ever greater speculations about final judgment that had become embedded in medieval Celtic intellectual and popular culture and reached a climax in Ireland in the eleventh century, as even sober historical texts concluded their factual narratives with accounts of the world's end.[2] This is most visible in works from the Gaelic-speaking lands where, in the rich harvest of literary and theological works, the theme of Last Things is found frequently and prominently, so much so that an excessive interest in eschatology and the supernatural has become an accusation hurled at medieval Irish theological works.[3]

The development of ideas about the final days that were important and, to the Gaels, believable found inspiration from a variety of sources, of which the Bible was the basis, especially the apocalyptic passages in the Gospels and the Book of Daniel.[4] In addition there were apocryphal texts such as the Apocalypse of Thomas, the Life of Adam and Eve, and the Vision of Paul that were circulating throughout Europe.[5] To these was added an original element from the heroic and adventure tales, with their rich store of pre-Christian belief, in which mortals and spirits together fought and loved in a landscape that was at the same time reassuringly familiar and hauntingly different. The resulting literary creations varied in content, from scholarly considerations of the Last Judgment (with descriptions of hell and its horrors as well as of heaven and its joys) to tales of fantastic voyages in which sailors met souls in the shape of birds waiting for the end of time or conversed with Judas, who was chained to a rock in the ocean. Two works—the Voyage of St. Brendan and the Vision of Tnúdgal—passed into the general canon of European literature. The Voyage of St. Brendan was circulating round Francia during the early eleventh century, when a monk of Cluny named Raoul Glaber incorporated several episodes in his *Five Books of Histories*.[6] By the following century, a Norman-French version of Brendan's voyage was composed for the court of the English king Henry I (1100–1135). The author, known only as Benedeit, had as a patroness Henry's queen, either his first wife Matilda or his second wife Adeliza.[7] The Vision of Tnúdgal became no less popular after its composition (in Latin) circa 1149, and its international popularity ensured that this vision would be translated into numerous vernaculars during the Middle Ages before it was finally written down in Irish, the language of its author, in the sixteenth century.

Early Views on Doomsday

The surviving writings from the primitive Celtic church give little indication of the rich harvest of eschatological thought that would later flourish. There is little involved speculation on the end of time, even though there was constant attention to the subject and a belief in its imminent appearance. The influence of the second-century bishop Irenaeus of Lyons is visible in the earliest writings, especially his treatise *Against Heresies*, which stresses the imminent coming of judgment.[8] In the fifth century, St. Patrick gave a simple statement of belief in his *Confession* with the notice that he was living in the last days, awaiting Our Redeemer who would return as judge of the living and the dead.[9] An only slightly more fulsome statement is made in the next century when, in the longest of the letters attributed to him, the British author Gildas described the depravity of humanity during the Last Days, which he identified as his own time, when the forms of Christianity were practised without any Christian spirit.[10] A generation later, Columbanus echoed his view on the imminent arrival of the Day of Judgment when he wrote that the world was in its last days.[11] As late as the eighth century, the same idea is repeated in the Old Irish gloss on 1 Corinthians 7: 29, in which a commentary on the passage *Tempus breve est* states "that is, this is the end of the world, it is not worthwhile to love it."[12] Even in poetry from the second half of the eighth century there was little elaboration, and the vernacular verses of Blathmac are sparing in their use of imagery to describe Doomsday.[13] Belief in the quickly approaching end of the world apparently inhibited any attempt to describe that conclusion.

Those unadorned recitations of faith did not exclude an interest in personal eschatology, as seen in a seventh-century after-death vision related by the eighth-century Anglo-Saxon historian Bede in his *Ecclesiastical History* concerning the vision of the Irishman Fursa [III. 19], which can be usefully compared with another vision story found in the same work, that of the Anglo-Saxon Drythelm [V. 12].[14] Both visions give an indication of eschatological thought, but with some significant differences. The vision of Drythelm is immediately concerned with Drythelm himself, but it also reveals a structured plan for souls after death in addition to a brief exposition on the fate of those souls at the Last Judgment and the state of the world. There is a fourfold division of souls—the good, the not entirely good, the not entirely bad, and the bad—which is later found in Irish works such as the first Vision of Adomnán. In contrast with Drythelm, Fursa's vision is personal and his soul is escorted by two angels through the otherworld, where he sees other angels reading from a book of life (*libellus vitae*) and learns that he is destined for Paradise. Waiting for the sinful, however, he sees four fires, which will purify the world. He is escorted untouched through a fire in which he sees burning the soul of a man whom he knew, but Fursa himself is burned by a demon for having accepted goods from that man and is warned by an angel of the dangers of accepting tithes acquired by sinful means. Fursa's vision shows the early Irish Church's preoccupation with private devotion and penance. There is no grand scheme; the individual's preparation is all that is important. The lack of interest concerning Doomsday in Fursa's account reinforces the attitude of immediate expectation found in the statements of Patrick, Gildas, and others. His vision does show the importance of the physical appearance of the body as a sign of divine judgment because the blow from a demon, according to Bede, had been seen by witnesses after Fursa's return/reawakening to this world. Physical pain or disfigurement from contact with otherworldly beings is occasionally found in other works. A contemporary of Bede named

Adomnán, abbot of the community on the island of Iona and upon whom was fathered the authorship of the two vision-tracts (which will be discussed later), claims that the monastery's founder Columba received a visible scar from an angel who was angry because of his refusal to carry out a divine order.[15] At this early date, there is a preoccupation with the form and nature of the body after death, a concern that would be amplified in later works.

By the eighth century, the plain statements of individuals who believed that they were witnessing the last days had given way to more elaborate literary expositions. The legends about Patrick that had developed in the centuries after his death, for example, illustrate this point. Part of the reason for the heightened interest in Patrick was the increasing power of the church of Armagh, whose head declared himself to be the saint's "heir" (comarbae) and for whom claims were being made, in virtue of that relationship, of primacy over all the churches in Ireland as well as Patrick's paruchia in Britain. Unadorned statements of faith made by the historical figure would be abandoned in favor of fictional incidents that demonstrated the power of the legend. The brief account of Patrick found in the early ninth-century *History of the Britons* attributed to the British historian Nennius ends with three petitions sought from God, the third of which was that the Irish would perish seven years before the Day of Judgment.[16] A century later, there was further elaboration on this theme in the hagiographical collection known as the Tripartite Life of Patrick, composed under the patronage of several of his "heirs," in the famous episode in which Patrick, now behaving like a hero from ancient sagas rather than a humble ecclesiastic, fasts against God in order to allow the Irish to escape the Last Days. The idea of ritual starvation is not unique to the Irish, and it was intended to force the opponent to grant a request or otherwise have his honor besmirched by the death of the one fasting. Patrick carried out his fast in order to receive a series of blessings from God that included his salvation of some of the damned, the assurance that he would be the advocate for the Irish, and the promise that Ireland would perish in a sea-flood seven years before the final Judgment, so that the Irish would not witness the terrors of the Last Days.[17] Similar claims would be put forward for other individuals, and for Finnian of Clonard it was asserted that he too would judge the Irish at Doomsday and anyone buried at his church would not be tormented in hell after Doomsday.[18] The desolation of Ireland prior to the end seems to have been a popular idea and is found in other works not associated with Patrick, such as the Colloquy of the Two Sages (*Immaccalam in dá Thuarad*), which claims that Ireland would be abandoned seven years before the Day of Judgment.[19] The approach of that day was considered so horrific and so painful that an early death was to be preferred to its terrors and suffering. The destruction of the Irish before Doomsday, then, was considered to be a divine mercy.

Voyages and the Otherworld

When Bede was writing his account of the vision of Fursa, considerations of the last times were finding their way into secular literature, as heroic elements would later be introduced into theological speculations. Examples of this are found in the so-called voyage literature, which provides evidence for popular beliefs about the Day of Judgment and the nature of souls. There might have been a tradition of voyaging in theological thought long before it appears in the surviving texts, and voyage imagery can be found in the writings of Columbanus.[20] One of the features that distinguished the stories of "voyages" (*immrama*) from the tales of mere "adventures" (*echtrai*) was that the former included journeying to islands that had connections with the otherworld, often as a way station for divine and human beings awaiting the Last Day.[21] At first the eschatological influence in secular literature is implied rather than explicit, which has led to some interesting speculations about the survival of pagan Celtic legends of the "Happy Otherworld."[22] One aspect of this otherworld was the land of eternal youth (*Tír na nÓg*), which in the popular mind could become confused with heaven.[23] Others have suggested to the contrary that remnants from a Celtic "Book of the Dead" have been added to Christian elements.[24] Still others have suggested that the otherworld elements are Christian in inspiration.[25] The surviving literature does show, however, how theological speculations were understood by the laity, and the way(s) in which those speculations were then incorporated into secular literature.

Connections of chronological freedom with the condition of the body are found in the voyage of Bran son of Febal (*Immram Brain meic Febail*), composed in the late seventh or the early eighth century. Bran and his company visit several islands of wonder, including an island of Joy and an island inhabited solely by women. An eschatological element is implied in the idea of perpetual youth while he is afloat, for when he leaves the island of women against the advice of the inhabitants and returns to Ireland, Bran discovers that centuries have passed and all that is remembered of him are merely some old tales.[26] Bran and his companions remain at the age they were at the time of their departure so long as they do not disembark on Irish soil, but when one of the crew leaps from the ship and touches the shore he immediately turns to dust. The idea of a chronological state-of-grace for humans who left their own land in order to travel on these journeys seems to have enjoyed some success with its audience and found its way into hagiography. A ninth-century litany of Irish pilgrim saints composed circa A.D. 800 states: "Twenty-four men of Munster who went with St. Ailbe on the ocean to visit the Land of Promise, who are there alive until Doom."[27] The famous Voyage of St. Brendan (*Navigatio Sancti Brendani*), now extant in an early tenth-century version, claims that the saint and his monks visited the community of St. Ailbe and his comrades during their voyage.[28] The origin for Brendan's association with Ailbe probably came from an earlier episode in the *vita* of Brendan, where he and his followers celebrate Christmas day on the island of the family of Ailbe.[29] More elaborate descriptions of Ailbe's community are given in the story of the Voyage of Uí Chorra (*Immram curaig húa Corra*). The Uí Chorra were three brothers who were consecrated to the devil and destroyed the churches of Connacht.[30] When they converted to Christianity and wished to make amends for their previous destruction, they rebuilt all they had destroyed and then, as a final act of contrition, sailed away on the sea. One of the islands they visited was the Land of Promise, where Ailbe and his monks awaited the Last Judgment. The brothers are forced to depart before sunrise because it would not be the place of their resurrection (i.e., the place of their burial); therefore they would be tormented if they saw the land and then had to depart from it. Before they leave, the Uí Chorra are told that the saint and his fellow travelers sing requiems for all who are dead in the sea.

The image of a community of mortals waiting for the end of time in a Land of Promise would enjoy a considerable longevity, and it is found in other materials that will be discussed later, such as the Vision of Adomnán, the Two Sorrows of Heaven, and the Voyage of Snedgus and Mac Riagla. The Land of Promise was an earthly version of Paradise, where rivers of milk and honey flow past a land filled with gold, silver, and gems.[31] Not surprisingly, the distinction between the Land of Promise and Paradise is not always obvious.[32] More startling, however, was the occasional effort to imply that Ireland was the earthly paradise by listing the similarities between the two.[33] This might explain why it was believed that a sea-flood would overwhelm the Land of Promise prior to the Last Days.[34] The divine mercy in destroying the body in order to spare the mind the terror of the Last Times that had, in the legends of St. Patrick, been granted to Ireland would be extended to an earthly paradise.

Those who waited for the Day of Judgment on islands in the sea were not always as saintly as Ailbe and his followers. In the Voyage of Uí Chorra the travelers journey to an island where they meet a disciple of Jesus who fled from Him until he came to the isle in the ocean where he remains until the end of time.[35] The figure of the penitent hermit awaiting judgment is found in two voyage tales, the Voyage of Máel Dúin (*Immram curaig Máildúin*) and the Voyage of St. Brendan. The story is essentially the same in both tales. A penitent, who is known as the hermit of Tory (an island off the coast of Donegal with a community dedicated to St. Columba) to Máel Dúin and Paul the hermit to Brendan, lives on a rock in the midst of the ocean with no visible supply of food.[36] In the story of Máel Dúin the hermit had been the community's cook, but later he became a thief and fled from the church with his stolen goods. He repented of his crimes, however, and went into exile. In Brendan's voyage there is no mention of any crime and the hermit simply leaves Ireland. A theme found in both episodes is that his spiritual progress is marked by changes in diet. The hermit of Tory initially is given seven cakes and a cup of whey water that sustain him for seven years. Then for another seven years he is given salmon. When Máel Dúin and his troop meet him, the hermit is living on a morsel of fish and a small loaf with a cup of good liquor, a ration also provided for the visitors. Paul the hermit is sustained by a slightly different diet for ninety years before he meets Brendan.

A penitential voyage and sojourn on an island in order to gain salvation was not limited to individuals but could be extended to entire groups of people, a prospect described in the Voyage of Snedgus and Mac Riagla, composed in the tenth century.[37] The story begins when a king named Fiachru son of Máel Coba is slain by the people of the kingdom of Ross, over whom he rules as a consequence of victory in battle. In order to prevent his kinsmen from avenging his death by a slaughter of those people, two clerics named Snedgus and Mac Riagla are sent from Iona by St. Columba to pass sentence. They judge that sixty couples are to be set adrift as punishment, and afterward the clerics decide to follow suit in order to be pilgrims for God. Their adventures are similar to those found in the voyages of Brendan, Uí Chorra, and Máel Dúin. At the conclusion of the tale, they visit an island that happens to be the one where the sixty couples from Ross are found, who tell the clerics that they will remain there until the Day of Judgment, living without sin and in the company of the prophets Elijah and Enoch. When Snedgus and Mac Riagla ask to see Enoch, they are told that he is in hiding until all go to the great battle on the Day of Judgment. There are parallels with secular tales that might contain survivals of the legend of the "Happy Otherworld," where beings live without blemish. For example, among the stories associated with an early Irish king named Connla the Fair, there is an adventure in which he is seduced by a fairy woman, who comes from a land where there is no sin, no mortality, and no hunger or thirst.[38]

Celtic literature frequently employs animals as substitute humans, and animals play an important rôle in voyage tales and other works with an eschatological interest. The purveyor of food to the hermit of Tory/Paul, for example, is an otter, a creature of mysterious powers in the Celtic literary canon. More frequently, however, the animal encountered in connection with eschatological themes is the bird. The image of the bird was used by Nennius, who claimed that when St. Patrick prayed, flocks of birds of all colors came to him in the same way that the Irish would come to him on the Day of Judgment, when he would lead them to the final reckoning.[39] The importance of birds in Irish eschatological works is emphasized in the Evernew Tongue (discussed below), in which the seventy-two flocks of birds created on the fifth day of Creation are described in elaborate detail. The Voyage of Snedgus and Mac Riagla describes a giant bird with a head of gold and wings of silver who recites human history from the beginning to Doomsday.[40] The story goes on to claim that a memento of this episode is a leaf from the tree that is preserved at Kells (then the head of the Columban *paruchia* in Ireland). In other tales, the bird is the form assumed by a soul after death as it awaits judgment. In the Voyage of Uí Chorra, the travelers sail to an island where they encounter birds that are the new bodily form for the souls of holy individuals. The bird-souls wait for the Day of Judgment in the company of a disciple of St. Andrew named Dega.[41] In the late tenth/eleventh-century tract known as the Vision of Adomnán (*Fís Adomnáin*), there is a description of three birds facing the Godhead, singing his praise.[42] Later in the same work, the prophet Eli preaches under the Tree of Life to souls in the shape of pure-white birds; among his topics are the perils of the Day of Doom, which leave his audience in fear.[43] Sometimes the form of the bird is a prison, as in the Voyage of St. Brendan, in which a flock of white birds announce that they are fallen angels who had approved Lucifer's rebellion without taking an active part in it. Their punishment is to wander the earth tormented by the absence of the divine presence, but on Sundays and holy days they are allowed to assume the form of birds and sing to the praise of God.[44] The place of birds within the eschatology of the Celtic world has some interesting parallels with the tradition of shape-shifting that is found in secular tales. In the Old Irish tale known as the Destruction of Da Derga's Hostel, the hero Conaire learns that his father is one such bird/man and therefore one of his taboos (*gessi*) is the hunting of birds.[45] In Welsh literature, the tale of Math son of Mathonwy, found in the *Mabinogion*, has an episode in which two men are transformed into different animals as punishment for a crime.[46] Confusion in the popular imagination between shape-shifting and resurrection could be the reason why the subject is addressed directly in an eleventh-century text called the "Tidings of the

Resurrection" (*Scéla na hEséirgi*).[47] The "Tidings" is concerned mainly with the question of the body after the resurrection, and it describes in detail the bodily appearance of the resurrected individuals, both normal and abnormal. The narrative takes great care to distinguish the resurrection at Doomsday from other forms of so-called bodily change, such as *metaformatio* (transfiguration into other forms such as werewolves).

At an early date the question of the soul was not confined to the bodily form taken after death or, in the case of the fallen angels, after disgrace. There was also the idea that souls rested and visited places on, or above, earth. A description of souls resting prior to the Last Judgment is found in the compilation that has been given the modern title *Catechesis Celtica*.[48] This is a collection of materials for sermons composed, if the extant manuscript is a guide, in the late ninth/early tenth century. In its present form the *Catechesis Celtica* is a product of a *scriptorium* in a Brythonic-speaking area (locations in Wales, Cornwall, and Brittany have all been suggested), but the text apparently is based on Irish materials.[49] Five places are enumerated where souls rest as they await the Day of Judgment: heaven for the saints and apostles; Paradise for patriarchs, prophets, and martyrs; Hades for the completely wicked; the light for the not entirely wicked; and a dark fog or mist for the more, but not totally, evil.[50] The *Catechesis Celtica* shows the connections among the Celtic intellectual centers through the avenue of the Latin language.

The kind of material found in the *Catechesis Celtica* seems to have had a wide circulation throughout the Celtic lands. The idea of the soul resting while awaiting judgment is found in later eschatological works, although there are different interpretations of it.[51] By the tenth century, rest was considered a divine gift for the damned, an example of Christ's infinite mercy. The Voyage of St. Brendan gives an example of rest for a damned soul in connection with Judas Iscariot.[52] When Judas is met by the saint, he is perched on a rock, lashed by sea and wind, but he says that his position is one of rest—provided through divine mercy—compared with the torments that await him in the evening. A different interpretation of rest is given in the Voyage of the Uí Chorra, where damned souls assume the shape of birds on Sunday and are allowed to leave hell.[53] The time of rest for the damned was reduced to three hours release on a Sunday in the Vision of Adomnán.[54]

Development of Eschatological Themes

The material from earlier tracts would be incorporated into later works, giving a continuity to eschatological speculations among the Irish. Beginning in the second half of the tenth century, texts appear that either are entirely devoted to the theme of the end of the world or consider the topic of the Day of Judgment at length. Not unexpectedly, much of the discussion revolves around the theme of the signs preceding Doomsday. There is, however, little indication of any special significance attached to the first millennium, in contrast with the general panic at the approach of the year 1096. Some of the texts from this period can be dated fairly closely, such as the Psalter of the Quatrains (*Saltair na Rann*) (composed in the fourth quarter of the tenth century), Vision of Tnúdgal (composed circa 1149) and the Fifteen Tokens of Doomsday (composed sometime after 1170). The date of composition for others is less obvious, although their word forms suggest a chronological range from the second half of the tenth century to the beginning of the twelfth century. These works include the Day of Judgment, Tidings of Doomsday, Evernew Tongue, Two Sorrows of the Kingdom of Heaven, Dispute of Body and Soul, and the first and second Visions of Adomnán. The latest date of composition for several of these texts—Two Sorrows of the Kingdom of Heaven, the first Vision of Adomnán, Tidings of Doomsday, and the Tidings of the Resurrection—is provided by the manuscript in which they appear, the Book of the Dun Cow (*Lebor na hUidre*), a Clonmacnoise manuscript compiled by Máel Muire mac Célechair (d. 1106), a scion of a family of hereditary clergy who had served that church for generations.[55] Also found in that manuscript are two of the early voyage tales, the Voyage of Máel Dúin and Voyage of Bran.

Consideration of Last Things within the context of a general overview of history is found in the Psalter of the Quatrains (*Saltair na Rann*).[56] This work was composed in the fourth quarter of the tenth century and is a vernacular summary of biblical history that concludes with an enumeration of the fifteen signs that will occur in the week preceding Doomsday.[57] In common with other Irish tracts, the Day of Judgment is placed on a Monday, so the poem begins with the previous Sunday and describes the events of the following week. On the Wednesday preceding the Last Day, all humanity is scourged by terrors, and on Friday all living creatures are slain. The earth is destroyed and reshaped on Saturday. The resurrection begins on Sunday with seven distinct risings, beginning with the apostles and ending with the seventh group, which includes everyone not included in an earlier group. Humanity will be separated into the saved and the damned, in accordance with Matthew 25: 32, although there is no indication of the nature of these groups as there is in Bede's description of the vision of Drythelm. The Psalter of the Quatrains uses ideas found in earlier works for its own narrative, such as the week of signs and terrors preceding the end of time that is noted in the *Catechesis Celtica*.[58] The fifteen signs of that week mentioned in the Psalter of the Quatrains are similar to the outline of signs that will be visible on the fifteen days leading to the final judgment presented in a work known as the *Collectaneum Bedae*.[59] Despite its attribution to Bede, the *Collectaneum* seems to be an Irish composition of the early Middle Ages; the study of it is hindered by the work's survival only in an early modern transcript.[60] The *Collectaneum Bedae* gives only the briefest notice of events, but it claims that all those still alive in the Last Days will die on the fourteenth of the fifteen days, so that they may arise with all the dead.[61]

The legend of the fifteen signs had a long currency in European literature. Remaining in an insular context, the narrative in the Psalter of the Quatrains seems to have been one of the sources for the late twelfth-century Irish tract known as the Fifteen Tokens of Doomsday (*Airdena inna Cóic Lá nDéc ria mBráth*).[62] That tract counts backward to the Last Day. Earlier Welsh works that are more closely allied with the poem in the Psalter of the Quatrains are two texts with titles both meaning Prophecy or Sorrow of Doomsday, *Yrymes Detbrawt* and, from it, the *Armes Dydd Brawd*.[63] The date of those pieces is uncertain; although they survive in a manuscript of the fourteenth century, they could be several centuries older. An interesting difference between the Irish and Welsh tracts is that in *Yrymes Detbrawt* the dead do not arise until the actual day of judging, rather than slightly before, as found in the Psalter of the Quatrains.

Other works were less interested in the signs preceding Doomsday than in the events of that day. As noted for the Psalter of the Quatrains, an enduring concern was the identification and the separation of those destined for salvation from those earning damnation. The issue of the division of the saved from the damned on the Last Day is considered in a work known as [The Day of] Judgment (*Bráth*), composed probably in the late tenth century.[64] The poem is concerned entirely with the fate of the damned, whose tortures are expressed in terms of pain inflicted on the body: bitter cold, great thirst, hunger, stifling smoke. The horror extends to the view presented to the lost soul, which sees terrible monsters, a burning sea, and devilish faces. The poem has some interest for cultural history with its list of those professions and classes especially vulnerable to damnation. The list begins with the legal profession, in the person of lying brehons (the interpreters of native law), before continuing with satirists, proud clergy and impious leaders. Such lists become less unusual and more precise in other texts, such as the first Vision of Adomnán, which gives two lists.[65] The first list includes such unpopular figures as the wicked manager of church lands (the *airchinnech*, an individual whose importance increases after the destruction of churches during the Viking Age), brehons, and unjust satirists before concluding with the heads of monastic schools (*fir léighinn*) who teach heresy. The second list is more secular and names dishonest artisans, cloth makers, traders, and wicked messengers who damage the reputations of others, as well as the expected impious kings or wicked *airchinnech*. Although some of the individuals such as the impious king or dishonest advocate figure in condemnation so frequently that they seem to be almost clichés, these lists do appear to reflect genuine concerns. For example, the maker of unjust satires (the *cáinte*) is condemned in the early Irish law tracts, and one code states that even if he is injured it is more proper to repudiate than to protect him.[66] Less obvious is the inclusion of other professions. Why were cloth makers especially vulnerable to condemnation or, for that matter, what manner of heresy was being taught in the monastic schools during the tenth and eleventh centuries?

Unusual among Celtic eschatological works is a tract that describes what happens after the Judgment. This is a work of the late tenth/early eleventh century called the Evernew Tongue (*Tenga Bith-núa*).[67] The story purports to describe an assembly at Mount Sion where the monarchs of the east were addressed by the spirit of the Apostle Philip, known as the "ever-new tongue" because his tongue was nine times removed by heathens and each time healed. The language used to address the group, it is claimed, will become the common speech of angels, animals, and humans after the Day of Judgment.[68] The Evernew Tongue also describes in grisly detail the great conflagration and destruction that accompany the Judgment, with the interesting information that the event will occur at midnight.[69] Great attention is given to the physical appearance of the day, as seven fiery winds come from heaven, the moon turns red, and the sun loses its light. The torments of the animals are described, with beasts crying in terror as the forests are laid low, the birds screaming at the rivers of fire, and the denizens of the sea suffering as the water heats.

A contemporary visionary tract is known as the [first] Vision of Adomnán (*Fís Adamnáin*), and it is one of the most important works of the period.[70] According to this tract, the famous Abbot Adomnán of Iona is said to have had a vision of the afterlife during the meeting called to endorse the "Law of Innocents" (*Cáin Adamnáin*). The Vision of Adomnán describes heaven and hell in addition to the end of time, and it has been described as the finest of all the medieval visions that exist prior to Dante.[71] As well as material from the Apocalypse of Thomas and the Vision of Paul, the Vision of Adomnán may incorporate material from a now lost work of Elijah preaching to bird-souls.[72] This complex tract raises a number of interesting questions, among which is its debt to Old English works, for parts of it resemble closely the vision of the Anglo-Saxon Drythelm as related by Bede. There is a fourfold division of humanity, and the division determines how close to the divine presence a particular individual will be. Unlike Drythelm, however, in the Vision of Adomnán the heavenly city is perceived as on a hill, with gates and gate-wardens protecting it from sinners. The particular penalty of the damned is to glimpse the heavenly city and then be forced away from it. Especially striking is the image of a bridge spanning the glen of hell; for the pious the bridge is narrow at the beginning but wide at the end, while for the sinful a broad beginning gives way to a narrow end from which the soul falls into the pit. The sinners are tormented by fire that is wrapped around them, piercing their flesh and pouring down in showers. Centuries before Dante's *Divine Comedy*, the author of the Vision of Adomnán saw specific punishments meted out to particular categories of sinners. Teachers who fail to fulfil their obligations, for example, wear cloaks of red fire with wheels of flame around their throats and are forced to eat raw, rotten dog flesh fed to them by little children, the ones who were cheated of their education.

Several texts that generally are dated to the eleventh century are more explicit concerning the state and division of bodies and souls during and after the Last Judgment. The Tidings of the Resurrection, which has been introduced above, is unique in the attention it gives to the question of the body in connection with the resurrection. The commentary concludes that everyone will have the age of thirty years, in conformity with the age of Jesus when he was crucified at the completion of thirty-three years, and their bodies will be formed perfectly, with full complements of hair.[73] An exception is the bodies of those who died as martyrs and who will bear their scars as marks of beauty. The resurrection at Doomsday is distinguished from other forms of bodily change resurrection such as *metaformatio* (transfiguration such as were-wolves). Could those erroneous forms of resurrection have been among the heresies taught by heads of monastic schools and condemned in the Vision of Adomnán?

The Tidings of the Resurrection not only indicates a more general concern for the role of the body as part of the resurrection but also shows an increased concern for children. On the question of the form that the resurrection will take for some babies, the Tidings of the Resurrection asserts that those who died in the womb or were aborted, as well as the malformed, will all be resurrected complete, while those of "two bodies in one union" (Siamese twins) will be separated and complete; all will have the proper form and full heads of hair.[74] The attention given to children might be a reflection of criticisms leveled at the Irish clergy; in the second half of the eleventh cen-

tury Archbishop Lanfranc of Canterbury would send a letter to Irish clergy
in which he felt it necessary to state the canonical position on the giving of
communion to infants at baptism, and into the twelfth century criticism continued to come from fellow clergy and the papacy.[75]

Mention should be made briefly of two other tracts. The first is known
as the Tidings of Doomsday (*Scéla Lái Brátha*), and it describes the division of the resurrected at the Last Judgment.[76] The author of this piece was
interested in chronology. Doomsday itself lasts a thousand years. The soul
condemned to the pit falls for thirty years before reaching the bottom. An
eastern orientation similar to that of the Evernew Tongue is found in the
work known as the Two Sorrows of the Kingdom of Heaven (*Dá Brón Flatha
Nime*).[77] The prophets Enoch and Elias are the two sorrows, waiting for the
end of time in order to die. This tract is important for its information about
the Antichrist, and among its sources are pseudo-Augustine's *De Antichristo*,
pseudo-Hippolyte's *De consummatione mundi*, and Adso of Montiér-en-Der's
De libellus de Antichristo.[78]

Even a cursory reading of the selected texts in this brief survey reveals
that there was no uniformity of interpretation on the subject of eschatology,
either personal or communal. To take one example, there was the issue of the
division of souls and the time of their separation, or, to state it somewhat differently, the nature of souls at Doomsday. Following the fascination of the
Irish literati with category, four interpretations are represented among these
texts. One group of texts has the souls divided into four states at the time
of death—the good, the not entirely good, the not entirely wicked, and the
wicked. To this group belong the first Vision of Adomnán and the Vision of
Tnúdgal. A second group follows the fourfold division but places the separation on the Day of Judgment; in this group are the Fifteen Tokens of Doomsday and the Tidings of Doomsday. The third category, found in an addition to
the Vision of Adomnán, sees a threefold division—the good, the indifferent,
and the wicked. A final category, found in the Two Sorrows of the Kingdom
of Heaven, endorses the same threefold parting, but the division is made on
the Day of Judgment. Those categories not only show the influence of earlier
works, but they also bring up the question of borrowing or loaning within an
insular context, for four similar categories are found in Anglo-Saxon materials.[79] Similarities between the first Vision of Adomnán and Bede's account of
the vision of Drythelm, for example, have been noted. This is not to discard
the very real possibility that the similarity might arise only from the use of the
same sources.[80] For example, the fourfold division at Doomsday is also found

in the writings of Haymo of Halberstadt (died 853), a writer well known at the Carolingian courts frequented by Irish scholars, while the threefold division at death is known from the writings of Pope Gregory the Great.

A second example of diversity of opinion seems to reflect development of an idea over the course of time. This is the purpose of the Fire of Doomsday, which was connected, in turn, with the problem of whether the body was cleansed or reformed at the Last Judgment, a topic mentioned in a number of texts. Early in the ninth century the purpose of the fire was seen as cleansing and the Old Irish Metrical Rule (circa 800), the Martyrology of Tallaght (circa 831–40), and the *Vita Brendani* preserved in the Book of Lismore suggest that all souls passed through the fire that would clean away sin.[81] After the mid-tenth century there appears to have been some change in that idea, and texts such as the Tidings of Doomsday, the Fifteen Tokens of Doomsday, and the Day of Judgment all declare that the fire will go beyond cleaning and that it will reform bodies in preparation either for admission into the elect or for casting into hell. There is little evidence of the belief that the saints would not suffer, although it was thought that the fire would feel like a soothing rain to the saints.

The interest in eschatology implied by the increased number of works that deal with some aspect of the subject had an influence on other types of writing. Historical works composed after the tenth century, for example, show an increasing popular preoccupation with matters concerning the Last Days. Two works that use the form of inspired prophecy to narrate a survey of history (*vaticinia ex eventu*) are now known as the Prophecy of Berchán and the Phantom's Frenzy. Both works, in their present form, are compositions of the eleventh century, and both are histories of powerful Gaelic princes— Berchán covers Ireland and Scotland while the Phantom's Frenzy is confined to Ireland. They conclude their accounts of Irish kings with lists of monarchs who, it was believed, would rule Ireland prior to Doomsday. Berchán notes that the final succession of kings will be one hundred and forty years after the death of the last Irish monarch in the historical survey, followed by the time of the Antichrist and concluding with the final conflagration, which will be an arrow of fire from the southeast.[82] The Phantom's Frenzy also gives a list of kings who will reign just before the Last Days, together with the events which will occur, such as the appearance of three suns in the sky and the movement of Lia Fáil, the ceremonial monolith at Tara.[83] The Phantom's Frenzy is particularly interesting because the author/compiler was Dub-dá-leithe of Armagh (died 1064), the "heir" of Patrick. The eschatological element in the Phantom's Frenzy appears to have been Dub-dá-leithe's contribution, for it is not found in an earlier work that it imitated, the eighth-century verse prophecy known as Conn's Frenzy (*Baile Chuind*).[84]

The Panic of 1096

How influential were these eschatological works beyond the walls of a church? Did they have a popular circulation or were they known only within a small circle of educated clergy? Even in more recent times there is great difficulty in assessing the influence of literature on society, but the comparatively greater survival of eschatological texts from the late tenth/eleventh century than from any other time might not be entirely a matter of chance, but rather a reflection of a popular interest in Last Things. Evidence for this is provided by the aforementioned panic at the approach of the feast of the Decollation of John the Baptist (August 29) in 1096.[85] Why did the Gaels believe that a particular feast day in the year 1096 would present a preview of the horrors of the Day of Judgment and might presage the immediate dawning of the dread day?

The reasons for apprehension can be set forth briefly. Even though the Gaels believed that they shared the general human guilt for the death of Christ, legend suggested that they were culpable to a slightly lesser degree because when an Irish king named Conchobar mac Nessa learned of Christ's arrest, he had gathered together a war-band to rescue Him but had died in an apoplectic fury upon learning of the crucifixion.[86] Concerning the death of John the Baptist, however, the same popular tradition believed that the Irish carried a particular guilt for his death because an Irish druid named Mog Roth supposedly carried out the murder, so greater atonement by the Gaels was in order.[87] Because of their sins, they would be punished in an especially deadly form. The belief in a significance to the feast of the Decollation of the Baptist is visible by the mid-tenth century, when the vernacular "life" of Adomnán, composed circa 956–64, warns of tribulation for the Gaels of Ireland and Britain around the feast of the Baptist.[88] By the end of the eleventh century, it was believed that if the feast day satisfied four conditions, this would presage disaster. First, the festival had to fall on a Friday; second, it had to fall in a bissextile (i.e., leap) year; third, it had to occur in a year with an embolism (an extra lunar month); finally, the year of the festival had to stand at the end of a chronological cycle. Three of the four chronological criteria were satisfied precisely by the year 1096: the twenty-ninth of August fell on a Friday, and the year was both bissextile and embolismal; it was not, however, at the end of a cycle recognized by the Irish.[89] This final point might not have been interpreted strictly.

The first type of terror (perhaps the only one, but this point is not obvious in the sources) would be a plague so savage that St. Patrick's gain of the immersion of Ireland prior to Doomsday would be as naught. The consequences were to be so fatal that three-quarters of Ireland's population would perish. What seemed to be physical confirmation of this scenario appeared late in the year 1095, when a plague began in August and continued for nine months to the beginning of May 1096. The mortality from the pestilence was severe, and it affected the aristocrat and the peasant indiscriminately. Among the dead were the bishops of Armagh and Dublin, the king of the Isles, and numerous lesser princes. Even the chronicles make note of the significance of the year: the Annals of Ulster, whose main comment has been quoted, have a marginal note that identifies 1096 as the "year of mortality" (*blíadhain na mortla*), while the Annals of Tigernach describe this as the "year of the festival of John" (*blíadan na féil Eoin*).[90] The Annals of the Four Masters, a seventeenth-century collection of earlier materials, notes that the Irish were saved through fasts, alms-giving, and donations of land to the churches, essentially a repetition of the remedy given in the vision.[91]

Literary expression of the horror that would be unleashed at the time of that feast is found in a work known as the "second" Vision of Adomnán.[92] The date when Adomnán became associated with this calamity is uncertain; it was certainly before the composition of his vernacular "life" in the mid-tenth century, and it was firmly established by the time of the composition of the "first" vision of Adomnán (*Fís Adomnáin*), which placed the saint's visit to the afterlife on the feast of the Baptist.[93] The "second" vision begins by listing the several chronological signs satisfied (at least in part) by the year 1096 that would foretell, it was believed, a tribulation upon the Irish known variously as "broom out of Fánad" (located on the north coast of Co. Donegal), a "fierce dragon which will search Ireland from the south-east," or the "rowing wheel."[94] Origins for these manifestations of vengeance have been sought in pre-Christian ceremonies. The "rowing wheel," for example, has been tentatively identified as a horn originally used in certain pagan rituals, the memory of which had been incorporated into Irish Christian apocalyptic thought by the eleventh century.[95] The answer need not have been so remote, however, and the "first" Vision of Adomnan mentions "wheels" (*rotha*) of fire round the throats of sinners in hell.

There are four sections to the "second" Vision of Adomnán: an introduction explaining the reason for the devastation, a description of the horrors, a plan to ward off the destruction, and examples of how successful such a course of action had been in the past. The treatise has an accumulation of ideas from earlier works. There is a list of the wicked individuals who are especially liable to suffer, among whom are ungodly teachers, impious kings, and those who are morally lax, a reworking of the categories of sinful persons also found in the first Vision of Adomnán and [The Day of] Judgment. Specific reference is made to the complaint of evils, some of which were usually found in these tracts (such as the destruction of holy places) and some that are not so usual (such as the practice of magic), with the additional accusation that the Irish were behaving as badly as pagans, except that they did not worship idols. In some ways this is not entirely different from contemporary interest throughout Europe in signs of the apocalypse as prophecies of current events.[96] There is a reference to Patrick's petition to save the Irish from the fire of Doom that follows Nennius's *History of Britain* and the Tripartite Life of Patrick. The idea of saintly intervention is repeatedly made in the second vision, which claims that injustices done to the churches have resulted in their patron saints refusing to revisit them or other places associated with their lives on earth: birthplace, place of baptism, place of death, and their burial plot. This is a refinement of the similar idea on the resting of souls found in the *Catechesis Celtica* and various voyage tales as well as the first vision attributed to Adomnán. Finally, there is color symbolism as the bodies of the damned will be made of black ashes, the color of their souls, which is found also in the Tidings of the Resurrection.

The Gaels survived the year 1096, but the hysteria that occurred and the sincerity of belief in its terrors may have helped hasten the progress of ecclesiastical reform among them. Within a generation a series of reforming synods had begun to change the administration, both physical and intellectual, of the Irish churches, while those in Scotland had reform helped along by royal support.[97] The reform of the churches among the Gaels followed the outline presented in the vision literature, as the claims of the hereditary clergy were set aside in favor of the reformed monastic orders. The heretical teachings were corrected, and liturgy and ritual were brought into conformity with the rest of Latin Christendom. The impious clergy were admonished in letters from popes and colleagues. The "heirs" of Patrick took holy orders and became bishops, an example followed by other members of the hereditary clergy.

The changes in the church were the beginning of the end for the Gaelic imaginative genius on the topic of Last Things. During the eleventh century, apocryphal literature from elsewhere in Europe was circulating round Ireland, and it began to influence insular works. But the final two productions to be discussed here—the Vision of Tnúdgal and the Fifteen Tokens of Doomsday—also had a popularity that overshadowed earlier works. A tale that would be one of the best known of the insular eschatological texts is the Vision of Tnúdgal (*Visio Tnugali*), which was composed circa 1149.[98] Probably written in the Irish monastery at Ratisbon, the vision was seen by a warrior from the south of Ireland named Tnúdgal. He travels through the otherworld, where he meets famous individuals from the past and from his own time, as in Dante's journey in the *Divine Comedy*. Even though this vision owes some debt to earlier Irish materials, in the main this treatise incorporates ideas and themes current throughout western Christendom. For example, the image of Satan chained in hell, graphically portrayed in a Leonese manuscript of circa 1047, is also found in the Vision of Tnúdgal.[99] A Cistercian influence also has been identified in this vision, especially in its celebration of St. Malachy, the friend of St. Bernard of Clairvaux.[100] Less well known, and possibly the latest of the distinctly Irish works, is the Fifteen Tokens of Doomsday, believed to have been composed sometime after 1170.[101] The Fifteen Tokens borrow heavily from earlier works, particularly the Psalter of the Quatrains, and would become a favorite source work throughout the Celtic lands, especially Wales. Those two works were almost a postscript to previous centuries of speculation on the end of time.

Contemplation of Last Things

Why were these speculations on Last Things so popular? Two suggestions can be offered. The first is that there were many similarities between eschatological and secular works. The presentation of theological ideas within the context of an adventure, such as the voyage tales, ensured an enthusiastic reception from a society with a taste for the heroic and fantastic. The idea of a chronological state-of-grace, visible as early as the eighth century in the Voyage of Bran, became intertwined with longevity as part of waiting for the end of the world found in the voyage of the Uí Chorra. The character of a penitent or saint waiting for Doomsday on an island in the ocean was as suitable for an adventure tale as it was for a hagiographical or theological work. Eschatological materials contained much that was exotic, such as descriptions of the fire of the great conflagration, the casting of the damned into hell, or the terrors of the final week. The apparently indiscriminate mingling of eschatological tracts with romance and adventure stories in the early twelfth-century Book of the Dun Cow shows how slight was the line between speculation on sacred themes and popular adventure or romance. A clear lack of distinction between theological speculation and popular entertainment is apparent among the works preserved in this volume because the eschatological tracts are preceded and followed by sagas and adventure tales. For example, the Two Sorrows of Heaven is followed by the tale of the Intoxication of the Ulstermen, while the Voyage of Bran is followed by the romantic adventure of the Wooing of Emer (the wife of the hero Cú Chulainn).

There was also the heroic aspect to form or shape, which reflects the Celtic fascination with the body as well as its importance in their culture. In Irish literature there are numerous examples of how the body was believed to reflect one's innermost thoughts and virtues. Dishonor might produce a blemish, usually on the face, while the color of the countenance could reflect righteous indignation, fear, or shame. The color symbolism employed in the second Vision of Adomnán or the details provided by the Tidings of the Resurrection concerning the appearance after resurrection illustrate a fascination with the human body. The idea of shape-shifting into a form other than human, especially the transformation of the soul into the shape of a bird, is found for certain saintly individuals in tales such as the Voyage of Uí Chorra.

The second suggestion is that these speculations on Last Things reflect popular concerns among the Gaels. Private devotion and prayer were a feature of the Irish church, and they are reflected in materials dealing with Last Things, as the earliest works were concerned with a personal eschatology. Pilgrimage or exile as a form of submission to divine will is also a recurring theme, and the religious houses founded on the Continent for the wandering Gaels testify to the popularity of forsaking one's homeland. Reverence towards saints was another popular aspect of Christianity in Ireland and Gaelic-speaking Scotland, especially the rôle played by saints either at the Last Judgment or in preventing terrors, actively or as interpreters. These reflections are not just limited to the eschatological elements in the voyage and vision literature but include the contemplation of the end of time as a theme for sermons.

The influence of specific groups on ideas about the end of time could have been more important than is now appreciated. Religious reform at the end of the eighth century could be part of the explanation for the theological influences on voyage tales. After the mid-eighth century, close association between the churches and the aristocracy led to accusations of worldliness in the church, and a reaction to it was the *Céli Dé* ("Clients of God") movement, which proposed to reintroduce a new rigor into ecclesiastical discipline and practice. As part of their program, it has been suggested that the *Céli Dé* themselves promoted the voyage tales.[102] Another group that appears to have had an influence was the Vikings. Various episodes in voyage tales are now considered to reflect information gained from sailing in the northern Atlantic. In the Voyage of Máel Dúin, there is a silver pillar, which could be a description of an iceberg, while a well of water that rises and falls as a rainbow could be an account of a geyser in Iceland.[103] More generally, the terror from Viking raids, in addition to their assaults with seeming impunity on churches, could be part of the reason for the apparent plethora of texts composed after the ninth century which discuss the end of time. Because their Christian victims saw them as the very creatures of evil, little additional imagination was required to consider the arrival of the Vikings as a warning of the approaching Doomsday. Works such as the Tripartite Life of Patrick or the second Vision of Adomnán connect the *geinti* (heathen) or *gall* (foreigner) with the approaching Day of Judgment. They would lead astray Christians, and the explanation of the *Gall-Gáidil* (Foreign Irish) offered in the eleventh-century Fragmentary Annals is that they had forsaken their baptism; even though the Vikings were wicked to the churches, those men were worse.[104] As the Viking settlements in Ireland became towns in the late tenth and eleventh centuries, the influence of the heathens among them on the local Christian community was a worry, and their influence is specifically cited as a reason for punishment in the second Vision of Adomnán. The Vikings also either caused or hastened various changes in the churches that were viewed with alarm in some quarters. Not only might Viking attacks on religious houses have led to a greater intellectual preoccupation with Last Things, but the very destruction they caused mandated the physical reorganization often resented by the clergy themselves, such as the rise of the *airchinnech* (the lay manager of church properties), who is frequently cited as a prime candidate for punishment at the Last Judgment.

The changes in eschatological ideas from the fifth to the twelfth century provide evidence of evolving intellectual concerns among the Gaels. The earliest Celtic writers such as Patrick, Gildas, or Columbanus content themselves with simple statements closely following biblical precedents. Their belief in the imminence of the end of time allowed little room for any elaboration on the theme. External events such as the collapse of imperial Roman administration in Britain slightly before Patrick's lifetime or the appearance of devastating plagues during Columbanus's career were as convincing proof of the approaching judgment as was the plague of 1095–96. After the seventh century there was an increased speculation on the nature of Last Things based on the Bible and apocryphal texts. While tales such as the Voyage of Bran imply rather than expound on those themes, later works such as the Voyage of Uí

Chorra make eschatological elaboration a fundamental part of the story. At the same time there becomes visible increased speculation about the pioneers of Christianity among the Celts. Thus Nennius includes a passage on the role to be played by Patrick on the Day of Judgment. In Ireland this reworking of hagiography included the production of vernacular versions of saintly *vitae* in the tenth century, such as that for Adomnán, but the most extensive production was the collection and amplification of the Patrician materials in the so-called Tripartite Life. The transformation of Patrick from the historic missionary to a figure more suited to the demands of a folk hero was completed when he bargains with God for the condition of the Irish at the end of time.

By the tenth century, less partisan minds had turned to the topic of the end of the world. Tracts such as the first Vision of Adomnán or [The Day of] Judgment note that the sinfulness of society as a whole announces the approaching finale. Specific classes or occupations are singled out for censure; by the twelfth century, the Vision of Tnúdgal identifies particular individuals. At the same time there was an increased interest in the chronological indicators of the approaching end. They were seen not in terms of a particular year but in the circumstances of a saint's feast or in the appearance of physical phenomena. While earlier works made passing reference to such concerns, by the tenth century much more attention was given to the theme of the fifteen signs of Doomsday or the horrors associated with the feast of John the Baptist. Changes within the Church itself could have had a part to play, and by the late eleventh century the Celtic churches were being criticized as antiquated by the proponents of ecclesiastical reform. A parallel concern was heresy or, to put it more mildly, beliefs not in line with current orthodox views; the first Vision of Adomnán speaks sharply of those whose teachings might lead others to doom. Stress from both intellectual and physical affairs could lead, not unnaturally, to contemplation of the Last Days and the rewards (or punishments) awaiting.

The crescendo to this eschatological interest appears to have been reached with the panic of 1096. The terrors of that year might have been one of the inspirations not only for the preservation of the earlier eschatological materials but also for the composition of the famous Vision of Tnúdgal, which dealt with Last Things on a personal level, almost a return to the theme of the Vision of Fursa related by Bede. A more physical influence might be the effort to locate the entrance to hell on an island in the midst of Lough Derg known as St. Patrick's Purgatory. Notice of it first appears in the written records in the twelfth century, when it was already famous as a pilgrim site.[105] After the mid-twelfth century, however, the topic of the end of time began to lose its originality. True, there were many texts—prose and verse—on the subject, but mainly they rework earlier materials. Partly this was the result of the changing nature of literary composition among the Gaels, a time of transition as the manuscript tradition began to pass from the religious houses to the laity.[106] Interest in topics associated with the Final Days continued, and works such as the Fifteen Tokens or the Evernew Tongue found admirers and imitators for generations. Their debt to earlier works is obvious, and those early texts allow for an understanding of the imagination and concerns of Gaelic society during a formative period.

Exodus and Exile

Joachim of Fiore's Apocalyptic Scenario

E. Randolph Daniel

When Israel was in Egypt's land: Let my people go:
Oppressed so hard they could not stand. Let my people go.
Go down, Moses, 'Way down in Egypt land.
Tell ole Pharaoh. Let my people go.

Your foes shall not before you stand: Let my people go.
And you'll possess fair Canaan's land: Let my people go.

Oh, let us all from bondage flee: Let my people go.
And let us all in Christ be free: Let my people go.

We need not always weep and moan: Let my people go.
And wear these slavery chains forlorn: Let my people go.[1]

When slaves sang this spiritual about Moses leading the people of Israel out of Egypt into the wilderness and Joshua leading them to the conquest of Canaan, they expressed their longing for freedom, for equality with their masters, and for a share in the prosperity of the United States. On January 1, 1863 Abraham Lincoln issued the Emancipation Proclamation freeing the slaves in those states that formed the Confederacy. On December 18, 1865, the thirteenth amendment abolished slavery. The fourteenth amendment with its "due process clause" was ratified on July 28, 1868. The slaves were liberated during and shortly after the Civil War. Nevertheless, some 130 years later, many African-Americans have still not arrived at the land of Canaan. Despite the success of a growing black middle class, many blacks are mired in urban ghettos, where a racially biased war on drugs, high unemployment, and police brutality persist. They have escaped Egypt, only to find themselves wandering in the wilderness for more than a century.

On November 7, 1917 the Bolsheviks successfully took over the revolutionary government of Russia. Eighty-one years later their dream of a stateless and classless worker's paradise has been totally shattered. The USSR has broken up into nationalist states, and Russia itself is groping its way toward capitalism.

So pharaonic oppression, deliverance, Sinai, and Canaan are still with us, powerful memories shaping our perceptions of the political world. The "door of hope" is still open; things are not what they might be. . . . This is a central theme in western thought. . . . We still believe . . . what the exodus first taught . . . first,—that wherever you live, it is probably Egypt;—second, that there is a better place, a world more attractive, a promised land;—and third, that "the way to the land is through the wilderness." There is no way to get from here to there except by joining together and marching.[2]

The original exodus had three components: the liberation from Egypt, the journey through the wilderness, and the conquest of the land of promise. Liberation has been the easiest step to achieve. The journey was longer and harsher than the Hebrews expected—Moses was dead before the people entered Canaan. The third and final step has proved truly elusive. Sometimes the liberated never reached it at all and remained in the wilderness. At other times Canaan proved disappointing, another Egypt. The exodus formed a paradigm that has shaped the hopes, dreams, and aspirations of reformers and revolutionaries, of the oppressed and those whose mission was to free the suffering, but Canaan has either eluded them or proved to be as oppressive as Egypt.

The Israelites conquered Canaan and established a monarchy, but it split into two kingdoms of which the northern fell to the Assyrians in the eighth century and the southern, Judea, to Nebuchadnezzar, whose exiling of the leading citizens became a symbol of disappointment with Canaan. This caused an anonymous prophet to envision another exodus:

Comfort, comfort my people . . . speak tenderly to Jerusalem and tell her this, that she has fulfilled her term of bondage, that her penalty is paid. . . . Prepare a road for the lord through the wilderness, clear a highway across the desert for our God. (Isa. 40: 1–3, New English Bible)[3]

Exodus led to captivity and captivity to a new exodus. The prophets had voiced God's discontent with Israel and Judea because they had failed to achieve the justice that the covenant demanded. When the dispersal of the northern people by the Assyrians was followed by the exile of the Judeans, the temptation grew to abandon Yahweh and to embrace the victorious deities of Babylon. The Judeans were dazzled by the opportunities in the metropolis, realizing how poor and off-the-beaten-track Jerusalem had been. Apocalypticism emerged in the prophets, Second Isaiah, Jeremiah, and Ezekiel, who created the notion of a renewed exodus and conquest to keep Judaism alive among the exiles. Cyrus, the Persian, permitted the return, but the second temple era had its own problems, culminating in the first Jewish War with the Romans in 70 A.D.[4]

Popes Leo IX (1049–54) and Gregory VII (1073–85) launched the papal reform movement confident that God would enable them to attain their goals despite opposition from churchmen and lay rulers. Gregory, who expressed his vision of a reformed church in apocalyptic terms, was one of the first reformist apocalyptics, the prophets who used language traditionally associated with the end of history to describe thoroughgoing clerical reform. Bernard of Clairvaux (1090–1153) was the preeminent reformist apocalyptic of the first half of the twelfth century, and his *De consideratione* (written 1145–53) became a manifesto for his disciples, who included Gerhoch of Reichersberg (1092/1093–1169), Hildegard of Bingen (1098–1179), and Joachim of Fiore (1130s–1202). Bernard urged Eugenius III to implement clerical reform, arguing that the pope had been given the position of vicar of Christ in order to purify Christendom spiritually. Bernard was upset that Eugenius, instead of working for reform, was preoccupied with judicial business, was surrounded by lawyers, and was taking the temporal sword. Bernard reminded Eugenius that the issue of Abelard and Gilbert of Poitiers was still hanging in the air.[5]

The trends that made Bernard uneasy intensified under the following pontiffs. The brief pontificate of Anastasius IV (1153–54) alarmed Hildegard, who addressed a scathing letter to him.[6] Gerhoch of Reichersberg sought to persuade Hadrian IV (1154–59) to implement the decrees of the synod of Rheims over which Eugenius had presided in 1148, to read *De consideratione*, and to address its concerns, but Hadrian instead became involved in an increasingly bitter dispute with Frederick I.[7]

The schism between Alexander III (1159–81) and Victor IV (1159–64) completed both Gerhoch's and Hildegard's disillusionment with the popes as the agents to achieve clerical reform. Gerhoch supported the legitimacy of Alexander III, but he came reluctantly to the conclusion that simony had been involved in the pope's election and that because Alexander refused to clear himself, he was quite probably a simoniac and certainly consumed by avarice. As such he was an "abomination of desolation" sitting on the papal throne. Alexander's usurpation of the rights of Frederick and Alexander's championing of papal justice and canon law were additional elements in Gerhoch's indictment.[8] Unable to believe that Alexander would struggle to realize reform, Gerhoch could only rely on his faith that somehow Jesus would reform the church just as he had come to his disciples on the stormy sea during the fourth watch of the night and reached out to Peter, whose lack of faith was causing him to sink beneath the waves (see Matthew 14: 25–33, Mark 6: 46–52, John 6: 15–21).[9]

Hildegard's *Sciuias* (written 1141–51) was Augustinian in its apocalypticism, giving a detailed portrait of the final Antichrist but also alluding to a period of improvement after his annihilation (see Robert Lerner's "Refreshment of the Saints"). Hildegard did, however, introduce the notion of a succession of periods before Antichrist characterized by five animals—a fiery dog, a yellow lion, a pale horse, a black pig, and a gray wolf.[10] Charles Czarski has shown that Hildegard completely altered her thinking when she wrote her *De operatione dei siue liber diuinorum operum simplicis hominis* (begun in 1163). Under the fiery dog, the princes of the empire will strip the clergy of their temporal wealth, and the era of the yellow lion will begin millennially with holiness, peace, and prosperity. The pacifism of the Christians will induce outsiders to attack, but reform will again triumph. Both kings and princes will cease to have any respect for the empire and the pope will rule only Rome and its immediate environs. The renewed holiness will finally be engulfed by heretics and other sinners until Antichrist comes. The *Liber diuinorum operum* is certainly reformist, and, as Czarski has cogently argued, the shift must have resulted from Hildegard's disillusionment with the papacy.[11]

Joachim of Fiore was born in the 1130s at Celico near Cosenza in Calabria. His father was a notary, and Joachim, the eldest son, was educated in his father's profession and then given a post at the Norman court at Palermo. Sometime in the late 1160s or early 1170s, Joachim left the court, went to Palestine as a pilgrim, and returned convinced that he ought to become a wandering preacher. He became a monk at Corazzo, a Benedictine house between Cosenza and Catanzaro, where he was elected abbot in the late 1170s. In 1184 Joachim was at the Cistercian house of Casamari, which is located up in the mountains east of Frosinone between Rome and Monte Cassino. Joachim was trying to persuade the Cistercians to take Corazzo into their order. Eventually this happened, but by that time (c. 1189) Joachim had left Corazzo, was leading an eremitical life, and was about to found San Giovanni in Fiore, the mother abbey of his Florensian Order. The new order was prospering before Joachim died in 1202.[12]

Three intuitions shaped Joachim's prophetic message. The first occurred when Joachim was in Palestine and involved concords between persecutions of Israel and persecutions of the church.[13] This intuition was the basis of book one of the *Liber de concordia*.[14]

The second intuition came to Joachim at Pentecost while the abbot was at Casamari (probably in 1184). Joachim thenceforward understood trinitarian relationships by analogy to the musical instrument called a psaltery that was shaped like an equilateral triangle but with a blunt top; it had ten horizontal strings and a hole in the middle. The hole represented the unity while the top represented God the Father by whom the Son was generated. The Spirit proceeded from both the Father and the Son. Visualize a triangle with the Father at the top, the Son at the lower left facing angle and the Spirit at the lower right facing angle. The line from the top to the left angle represents the generation of the Son, the line from the top to the right angle the procession of the Spirit from the Father and the bottom line the procession from the Son.[15]

The third intuition happened after Joachim had left Casamari (hence in 1185 or 1186). Joachim was working on his commentary on the Apocalypse and was wrestling with some difficulty when, on Easter eve, the solution came to him.[16] Joachim, I believe, realized that the Apocalypse was the inner wheel that corresponded to the outer wheel in Ezekiel's vision (Ez. 1: 4–21). The outer wheel was the history of the Hebrew people from Abraham to the return from Babylon, recorded in the scriptures from Genesis through Nehemiah. The Apocalypse or inner wheel thus "concorded" with the history of the Hebrews and contained the history of the church.[17]

Joachim began his *Liber de concordia* while he was at Casamari (c. 1183–85) and finished it no later than 1198. The first four books formed a prolegomenon in which Joachim worked out the concords between the history of the Hebrew people and the history of the Church. In this working out, Joachim defined the patterns of history to which I shall return shortly.[18] The *Psalterium decem chordarum* was begun at Casamari and finished about 1186. In it Joachim explored trinitarian relationships and began to formulate the pattern of three *status*. Book five of the *Liber de concordia* commented on the scriptures from creation week to the prophets, ending with a commentary on Daniel. The *Expositio in Apocalypsim* was begun at Casamari and was finished by 1200 when Joachim wrote his Testamentary Letter.[19] The *Tractatus super quatuor euangelia* commented on a harmony of the four gospels. Most scholars have considered it to be a late work because it is incomplete and is not listed in the Testamentary Letter. That omission, however, may have been because it was left unfinished.[20] Joachim intended to comment on all those books of the Bible that were considered suitable for spiritual or allegorical interpretation—the histories, the prophets, the gospels, and the Apocalypse. The wisdom books were excluded, as well as the letters of Paul and the other apostles, except for Job, which Joachim considered one of the four special books from the Hebrew scriptures (the others were Esther, Judith, and Tobit). Joachim commented on these four special books in book five of the *Liber de concordia*.[21] The four gospels corresponded to these four special books and to the four hubs and the living creatures on Ezekiel's wheels.

While he was a hermit at Petra Lata before he founded the abbey at S. Giovanni in Fiore, Joachim began but left unfinished a commentary on the life and rule of St. Benedict. Stephen Wessley dated it to 1186–88 and argued that in it Joachim was justifying himself by reference to the life of Benedict.[22]

Joachim thought visually and analogically. Trees, vines, and geometrical shapes underlay his thinking. He inserted *figure* into the *Liber de concordia*, *Psalterium decem chordarum*, and *Expositio in Apocalypsim*, and the *Liber figurarum* is a collection in which the figures are considered to be genuine works of Joachim, although the compiler was one of his disciples. Some of the figures in the *Liber figurarum* correspond to those in the other works, but even in these cases there are significant differences.[23] Like Bernard, Gerhoch, and Hildegard, Joachim was a monastic theologian. Theology was commentary on Scripture and primarily on the spiritual senses. Symbolism was intrinsic in Joachim's methodology.[24]

Joachim was widely respected as a prophet during his lifetime. In 1184 he went to Veroli to see Pope Lucius III. The abbot sought permission to write and confirmation that God had indeed revealed the *concordia* to him. While he was in the pope's presence, he commented on a sibylline text that had been discovered among the papers of Matthew of Angers, cardinal priest of San Marcello. This commentary is his earliest extant work, the *De prophetia ignota*.[25]

In 1186 Joachim went to Verona, where Pope Urban III (1185–87) renewed Joachim's permission to write. On June 8, 1188 Clement III wrote to Joachim from the Lateran Palace in Rome, mentioning Urban's permission and exhorting Joachim to finish his "Expositionem Apocalipsis and Opus concordie." Joachim came to Rome in this same year and received Clement's permission to leave his post at Corazzo, which became a daughter house of Fossanova.[26]

During the winter of 1190–91, Joachim was interviewed by Richard I the Lionhearted while the English king was wintering in Messina.[27] Joachim went to Rome again during the pontificate of Celestine III (1191–98), and on August 25, 1196, Celestine issued a bull formally approving the founda-

tion of S. Giovanni in Fiore and the constitutions of the Order of Fiore.[28]
Finally Adam of Persigny, a Cistercian, interviewed Joachim while he was in
Rome. The extant account dates the interview to 1196, but Marjorie Reeves
has argued that it must have been in 1198 after Innocent III had become pope
because it refers to him.[29] In addition to his contacts with the popes and with
Richard I, Joachim maintained active ties with the rulers of Sicily and Calabria, William II (died 1189), Tancred of Lecce, and Henry VI.[30]

Bernard of Clairvaux in his *De consideratione* wrote: "Quaternity sets
limits to the earth; it is not a characteristic of the deity. God is trinity, God is
each of three persons. If it pleases you to add a fourth divinity, I am already
convinced that what is not God should not be worshipped."[31]

Bernard was attacking Gilbert of Poitiers.[32] Bernard's attack on Gilbert
probably caused Joachim to write a treatise in which the Calabrian abbot accused Peter Lombard of teaching that the godhead was a *quaternitas* rather
than a trinity. Lateran IV took Lombard's side and condemned Joachim's
attack. This condemnation provoked a furious reaction among Joachim's
Cistercian and Florensian disciples.[33] This reaction is reflected in Pseudo-
Joachim, *Super Hieremiam prophetam*, completed by 1248 at the latest.[34]

In 1248 Friar Gerard of Borgo San Donnino was in Provins, where he
cited the *Super Hieremiam* to Friar Salimbene.[35] In 1254 Gerard published
a *Liber introductorius in euangelium eternum* at Paris, which probably consisted of an introduction and all or parts of the *Liber de concordia*, *Expositio in
Apocalypsim*, and *Psalterium decem chordarum* with glosses by Gerard in which
Gerard interpreted the third *status* radically. Gerard was a Franciscan, and the
order was currently involved in a bitter dispute with the secular masters at
the University of Paris. They seized on the *Liber introductorius*, arguing that
it reflected the antichristian heresies that the mendicants were propagating.
The condemnation of Gerard's *Liber* and the subsequent condemnation of
extracts from Joachim's works by the Commission of Anagni raised questions
about Joachim's orthodoxy that are still argued.[36]

Hence modern scholarship has focused on two issues—Joachim's doctrine of the trinity and his division of history in three *status*. Interpreters
who have favored a radical understanding—making Joachim the progenitor
of Hegel—have argued that Joachim was a tritheist who gave more weight to
the three persons than to the unity and gave the Holy Spirit a mission equal
to and separate from that of Jesus Christ. The third *status* of the Holy Spirit
would involve as complete a break from the present *status* of the Son as that
status had made from the first *status* of the Father. In particular, the clerical

church and the sacraments would cease to function when the *ecclesia spiritualis* arrived, just as the synagogue had earlier been replaced by the church.

Defenders of Joachim's orthodoxy argued that his trinitarian theology was completely orthodox and even tried to prove that the treatise condemned at Lateran IV was a forgery. Despite whatever changes the third *status* might involve, the clergy and sacraments would persist unchanged to the end of history. Scholars quoted random passages from Joachim's works in defense of their views. Many of these passages had been cited by the Commission of Anagni.[37]

Marjorie Reeves has compiled a major revision of all prior interpretations. Methodologically, she has argued that the figures are the keys to understanding Joachim's thought. McGinn, West, and Zimdars-Swartz have all followed Reeves's lead in this respect. Reeves has also compelled scholars to recognize that Joachim used several patterns of history and that the three *status* had to be understood in parallel with the two *tempora* and the patterns of fives and sevens.[38]

Augustine of Hippo tried to discourage speculation about the end and was pessimistic about the future. Reform for him was strictly personal. Joachim has been contrasted with the Augustinian tradition because Joachim expected the apocalyptic crisis in the imminent future and because he expected the third *status* of the Holy Spirit to be significantly holier and more spiritual than the second *status* of the church.[39]

Joachim, however, was fundamentally Augustinian. His understanding of the trinity relied on Augustine's analogy to the faculties of the human mind, memory, reason, and love.[40] Moreover, Augustine's eight *etates* are the foundation of Joachim's understanding of history. Augustine relied on the genealogy of Jesus in Matthew 1: 2–17, which supplied forty-two ancestors from Abraham to Joseph divided into three groups of fourteen each (Abraham to David, David to the exile, the exile to Jesus). This was supplemented by the twenty generations that Luke gave from Adam to Abraham (Luke 3: 23–38). Augustine sought to undermine the *anno mundi* dating that fed constant expectation of a millennial seventh worldweek by using the generations rather than numbers of years to define the *etates* before Jesus because generations, especially those before Abraham, involved extremely varied lengths of time. Augustine therefore divided the time before Jesus into five *etates*, the first two of ten generations each, the last three of fourteen each. Augustine's sixth *etas* began from the Incarnation and lasted until the end of the world. Its length was indeterminate so that its end could only be surmised by the onset of various signs. The seventh ran parallel to the sixth, but the sixth was terrestrial, an age of suffering and trouble, while the seventh was heavenly—the rest of the souls who had died in Jesus and were awaiting the final resurrection. Augustine equated the millennium of Apocalypse 20: 1–6 with the entire history of the church, in order to blunt the thinking that it would be the seventh worldweek of earthly bliss. The eighth *etas* of eternity was beyond history.[41]

Properly we call the *concordia* a similitude of equal proportion of the New to the Old Testament, equal I say as to number but not as to dignity, when namely person and person, order and order, war and war by means of a certain parity gaze as it were into each other's faces.[42]

Moreover that understanding which is called concords resembles a continuous highway that goes from the desert to the city. Along the route there are low spots where the traveler is uncertain about the right direction to pursue and there are also mountain peaks from which the pilgrim can look both backward and forward and measure the right way by contemplating the path he has come.[43]

Concordia was not typology or allegory. Events, persons, places, institutions, and orders in a particular generation have similarities or parallels in the same generation in the succeeding *status* or *tempora*. Josiah was the twenty-eighth from Jacob in the line of Jesus' ancestors and the thirty-sixth from Jacob counting by the judges of Israel. Josiah, king of Judah from 640 to 609 B.C., carried out a major reform inspired by "some form of the book of Deuteronomy."[44] Josiah, however, tried to stop pharoah Necho II of Egypt from marching to the Euphrates but was defeated at Megiddo and killed.[45] Pope Leo IX (1049–54), who lived in the thirty-sixth generation of the church, initiated the papal reform movement, but his expedition against the Normans resulted in a bitter defeat.[46] Josiah and Leo "concord" with each other.

By means of the *concordia*, the *uiator* could look back from a "mountain peak" and by seeing the road that had been traveled, discern the main shape of the road that still lay ahead. To reveal the concords and interpret them was the task that God had given Joachim.[47]

The first intuition gave Joachim the notion that the persecutions that the Hebrew people had suffered paralleled those suffered by the Christians. This is the subject of book one of the *Liber de concordia*, written at Casamari and left untouched thereafter.[48]

Joachim began anew with the first twelve chapters of book two, part one. Joachim contrasted Jewish insistence on a literal, earthly fulfillment of the promises to Abraham with spiritual, heavenly Christian expectation and then defined the *concordia* (chapter two) and allegory (chapter three). Chapter four introduced the *prima diffinitio*—the pattern of the three *status* and their parallel, the evolution of the three orders of the married, the clergy, and the monks (chapter five). Chapter eight introduced the *secunda diffinitio*—that of the two *tempora* to which correspond the Jewish and gentile peoples and the two testaments or covenants.[49]

Both *diffinitiones* were patterns extrapolated from series of generations. The first series consisted of the ancestors of Jesus according to Matthew's and Luke's genealogies. The second and third series begin with someone in the first series but continue beyond it to the generations of the common era, each of which is computed at thirty years, although Joachim refused to commit himself on the length of the generations after the fortieth (1170–1200 A.D.), in which he was living when he wrote. The first series included sixty-three generations, divided into three groups of twenty-one each.[50] Joachim likened this series to a tree of which the first twenty-one generations are the root projecting upward (the *initiatio*), the second twenty-one the trunk sending forth limbs and leaves (*fructificatio*), and the final twenty-one the full blossoming and the gradual decay (*consummatio*).[51]

Joachim conceived the *prima diffinitio* as A or as the ten-stringed psaltery, shaped like an equilateral triangle with a blunted top. The psaltery, as we have seen, described the generation and procession of two persons from one, of the Son and the Holy Spirit from the Father.[52]

The first *status*, representing the Father and the married, had its root in Adam, its fruition in Jacob, and its consummation in Uzziah (Ozias) (king of Judah, 783–42 B.C.). The second *status*, which began with Uzziah, who was the twenty-first generation before Jesus, flowered in Jesus, and began its final stage in the twenty-second generation after the Incarnation, belonged to both the Son and to the Holy Spirit, primarily to the Son who was generated from the Father and secondarily to the Holy Spirit who proceeded from the Father. Like the Son from the Father, the clergy proceeded from the married and the monks like the Holy Spirit came from both the married and the clergy. Hence the third *status* began twice, the first time in the reign of Asa (Judah, 913–873 B.C.) with the appearance of Elijah and Elisha and the second time with Benedict of Nursia. Joachim tried to draw these three trees in the *Liber de concordia* but never succeeded. The closest representation is Table Seven, in which the first column represents the generations of the first *status* from Adam to Joseph, the third column represents the generations of the second *status* from Uzziah to generation forty-two after Jesus, the second column represents the first beginning of the third *status* with the generations from Asa to the forty-second generation after Jesus, and the fourth column represents the second beginning of the third *status* from generation sixteen of the church to the forty-second generation after the end of the second *status* or the eighty-fourth of the church. The three *status* are organic, living entities sprouting from each other, overlapping and progressively moving step by step from the world of the married and from the promise that the Hebrews would conquer the land of Palestine to the ultimate virginal monastic contemplatives whose "conquest" would be complete peace and silence in which to contemplate God.[53]

Joachim described the lower case Greek omega, ω, which symbolized the *secunda diffinitio*, as one rod that proceeded from two. The first *tempus*, identical to the first *status*, consisted of the generations from Adam to Joseph, husband of Mary, and corresponded to the procession of the Holy Spirit from the Father, to the letter of the Hebrew scriptures, and to the *populus iudaicus*. The second *tempus*, which was the same as the generations of the second *status* from Uzziah to the forty-second generation of the church, corresponded to the procession of the Holy Spirit from the Son to the letter of the Christian testament and to the *populus christianus*. From the letter of the two scriptures proceeded the spiritual understanding (*spiritualis intelligentia*), and from the two peoples came the *uiri spirituales*, or monks.[54] Thus the two *diffinitiones* describe the same historical pattern, the progression from the original exodus to the still future monastic "land of promise."[55]

Joachim began to explicate these two *diffinitiones* in book two, part one, chapter twelve. The development of the *prima diffinitio* ended with book two, part two, chapter nine. From chapter ten to the end of the first part of book four, Joachim devoted himself to the *secunda diffinitio*.[56]

In book three, part one Joachim interpreted the seven seals of the first *tempus*, and in part two the corresponding seven openings of the second *tempus*. Using the image of the wheels of Ezekiel Joachim devised another pattern of generations in which the first four *tempora signaculorum* represent four animals, each with six wings, and four *ordines*, those of the apostles, martyrs, confessors, and virgins to which were alloted six generations each for a total of twenty-four. The fourth opening ended in 720 A.D. The fifth opening, the *sedes*, would have sixteen generations and would last from 721 to 1200 A.D.[57]

Moreover the forty-first generation alone is to be accepted as double, so that it could rightly be called twice the sixth, for the chief reason that there is to be a double tribulation under the sixth opening in likeness of the passion, in which, the shadows being doubled, Christ has suffered. Indeed in the forty-second generation, which will be like a sabbath, the seventh seal will be opened, about which the Apocalypse has spoken: "And when he had opened the seventh seal, there was silence in heaven for about half an hour." (Apoc. 8: 1)[58]

In the second *tempus* when the seals were to be opened, ten generations were to be subtracted from the sixth and seventh seals and added to the opening of the fifth seal. The opening of the fifth seal would extend therefore from 720 to 1200. The sixth seal would follow and last only one generation. During it, two persecutions would occur. Then the seventh seal would ensue, an era of sabbath.

The seals embraced forty generations, from Abraham to Jehoiachin, to which were added the forty-first designated by Shealtiel and the forty-second that belonged to Zerubbabel. Hence forty generations were counted down to the beginning of the Babylonian Exile. Shealtiel, the forty-first, reigned during the Exile. Zerubbabel led the return to Palestine in the forty-second generation.[59]

Joachim's objective was to equate the history of the Hebrews from Jacob to the Exile with the history of the church from Jesus to Joachim's own fortieth generation (1170–1200). Specifically Joachim equated the generations from Josiah to Shealtiel with the period from Pope Leo IX (1049–54) to 1200. Thus Joachim made the history of the church from the beginning of the papal reform movement correspond to the events that began with Josiah's reform in Judah and ended less than a century later with the deportation of the Jews to Babylon. The parallel between Josiah and Leo IX has already been pointed out.[60] Ioachaz's removal from Jerusalem to Egypt by pharoah Necho "concorded" with Gregory VII's flight to Salerno and Henry IV's elevation of Clement III as antipope. Joachim's forcible submission to the Babylonians paralleled Henry V's effort during his coronation "to extort a privilege of investiture" from Paschal II.[61] After Joachim died, Jechonias, his son, reigned until Nebuchadnezzar removed him and put on the throne Zedekiah, the paternal uncle of Jehoiachin and son of Josiah, a king whom Joachim called "homo pessimus et iniquus." Joachim described the years after the death of Josiah as a "time of confusion" and noted:

Thus also in the church a certain confusion has been created by the intervention of worldly princes on whose strengths schismatic men relied, so that sometimes both indecently and illegally two and two at the same time seemed to go up together to the papacy, about whom the stupefied people doubted a long time and opposed parties of men had opposed sentiments. And even if one of the two was catholic, the other schismatic, this did not upset the concords.[62]

Joachim was referring to the Alexandrian schism, which finally ended when Alexander and Frederick agreed to the Peace of Venice in 1177. That peace, Joachim said, was broken "in the days of pope Lucius and especially of

Urban, in whose pontificate the church suffered almost beyond endurance."
Then Joachim added: "Whether moreover on this occasion the church will
have lost something of its liberty to these sons of the new Babylon, may she
see who better knows that which [the church] has suffered."[63] Then Joachim
summed up his point:

The summit of the concordia of these [five] generations is this that there we have read
that the king of Babylon fought against Jerusalem, and here Roman emperors against
the liberty of the church. And some of the kings of Judah obeyed the king, but repented and tried to stand in their liberty by relying on the strength of the Egyptians;
another [king] went over to the [Babylonians] without war and was led to Babylon. Here some of the Roman pontiffs inclined toward and agreed with the emperors
on some occasions, but at other times tried to resist them with the help of various
princes; some [pontiffs] decided entirely to humble [themselves] under the [imperial]
hands and to live pacifically.[64]

The struggle between the reforming pontiffs and the emperors had cul-
minated in a Babylonian exile of the church, according to Joachim. The emperors from Henry IV through Henry VI persecuted the popes and deprived
the church of its liberty. The popes themselves were partly to blame, especially
Alexander III and his successors, because of their vacillating policies. Joachim,
however, counseled the popes to submit because the exile was God's will. Although there were some "spiritual Christians" who tried to live holy lives,
the overwhelming majority of the Latin Christians were driven solely by carnal desires and by worldly ambitions. Using Lamentations as a text, Joachim
included a scorching indictment of the simoniac clergy and the monks who
were cenobites only on the outside.[65] "Until this present place we have rowed
securely navigating past landmarks that we knew well. Henceforth, we must
voyage cautiously, keeping careful lookout from side to side during the rest of
our journey. We are like seamen who sail unfamiliar coasts, even if we are close
inshore, because to steer by what we have heard is one thing, but by what we
have seen is very different, although both are equally possible from God."[66]

The concords permitted Joachim to interpret God's plan securely down
into the 1190s. The abbot was confident that he correctly understood the
events that had ensued since 1049. Beyond 1200, however, only the scriptural concords could be discerned clearly. Their imminent parallels remained
dim. Joachim dated Holophernes's assault, recorded in the book of Judith,
during the exile. He also tried to date Haman's plan against the Jews,
which is recorded in Esther, to this same period. Joachim therefore expected
two antichristian persecutions of Latin Christendom while it was in "Baby-

lon." Joachim, however, could only speculate on the identity of the future persecutors.[67]

Josiah's successors had been literally conquered and exiled. The exile of the papacy and of Latin Christendom was figurative. Simony and the pursuit of worldly goals had become so pervasive that the church had become Babylon rather than Jerusalem. Even the popes had been lured into pursuing temporal power, especially by embarking on military adventures. The combined effect of the antichristian persecutions would shatter Babylon as John of Patmos had predicted in Apocalypse 18; in other words these assaults would purify Latin Christendom of the simoniac clergy and of monks who were only outwardly followers of Benedict.[68]

The exilic prophets had interpreted the return to Jerusalem from Babylon as another exodus and journey in the wilderness.[69] Joachim used the same imagery when he wrote that:

> The forty-second generation will begin in the church in the year or hour that God knows better [than we do]. In that generation, indeed, after the general tribulation has purged the weeds from the grain thoroughly, a new *dux* [i.e., a new Zerubbabel] will ascend from Babylon, a universal pontiff of the new Jerusalem, that is of holy mother church; in whose type it is written in the Apocalypse [7: 2]: "I have seen an angel ascending from the direction where the sun rises, having the sign of the living god." And the remainder of those who have been released from exile [will journey] with him. He will ascend, moreover, not by actual walking or by a journey from one place to another, but because complete liberty will be given to him to reform the Christian religion and to preach the word of God, because the lord of hosts has begun to reign over the entire earth.[70]

After the "antichrists" have purged the clergy, then a reform pope will lead a figurative return to Jerusalem. This pope will realize the Gregorian dream of a holy and purified Latin Christendom that then will dominate the entire world.

In book two of the *Liber de concordia*, Joachim had drawn a figure of three circles, resembling the circle figures in the *Liber figurarum*.[71] In the *Liber de concordia* version, each large circle contained three smaller circles that enclosed texts. In the first circle (that of the *primus status duodecim patriarche*), the texts referred to the sons of Israel entering Egypt, leaving Egypt, and entering the promised land. The second circle, labeled *secundus status duodecim apostoli*, cited the apostles preaching in the synagogue, then going to the gentiles, and receiving their hereditary, gentile Christianity. The third circle, inscribed *tertius status duodecim spirituales uiri*, referred to the *uiri spirituales* who would preach in the world to gain others, who would cross over to a harsher monastic life, and to those who would have faith in the *uiri spirituales* and thus enter the rest the prophets foresaw. In this version of the circle figure, each *status* is an exodus involving precisely the three elements of liberation, journey, and conquest. The first was a literal journey; the other two were figurative, the last more spiritual than the second.

Joachim was very much a disciple of Bernard, whom he called an "*alter Leui et alter Moyses*"[72]: "But nevertheless [Bernard has been made] like a leader and teacher of all by the prerogative of grace. Because he was taught by the spirit and the hand of God was with him, he has been made like another Moses, who led his brothers and their sons, not his sons, from Egypt. . . . He did not lack an ally like another Aaron, who was the high priest Eugenius, Roman pope."[73]

Joachim compared the Second Crusade to the journey of the Israelites in the wilderness. Both the Israelites and the crusaders "perished in the desert" and turned against their leaders, but Bernard, Joachim added, defended himself in his *De consideratione* by comparing the crusade to the Sinai journey.[74] Joachim equated Cîteaux, La Ferté, Pontigny, Clairvaux, and Morimund with the five tribes that received their inheritance first in the promised land in the first *status* and the five patriarchates in the second.[75] Joachim refused to identify any candidates for the concords to the seven tribes that received their inheritance later and to the seven churches to which John of Patmos had written in the Apocalypse, but the author of the anonymous *Vita* certainly thought that Joachim intended them to come from his own foundation, the Order of Fiore, and this same thinking may well have motivated the monks of this order.[76]

The third *status* was already becoming fruitful when Joachim was writing in the 1180s and 1190s. The founding of Cîteaux and its daughter houses was a step toward its realization. Bernard of Clairvaux was its Moses. Joachim understood the *status* of the Holy Spirit as a third exodus, one that had begun already at the end of the eleventh century and was going to come to complete fruition when the church was completely reformed after 1200.

Two paradigms shaped Joachim's thinking, the exodus and the exile. The former included three components—liberation, journey, and conquest. The Israelites had been freed from Egypt, had journeyed in the wilderness, and had conquered Canaan, but eventually they were conquered and the people of Judah were deported to Babylon. Jesus and his apostles had been a second "exodus," but simony and worldliness had transformed Latin Christendom into another "Babylon." A third exodus, however, had already begun and under papal and monastic leadership would culminate in the coming, contemplative land of promise.

Like the American slaves and the Communists in Russia, Joachim would have been deeply disappointed had he lived to see the actual future he imagined. Scholastic theology triumphed over monastic theology, and clerical reform never occurred. The early promise of the Florensian Order was not fulfilled. The advent of the friars excited Joachimists but proved finally unavailing as a means of thoroughgoing clerical reform. For Joachim even the envisioned exodus proved elusive.

Arnau de Vilanova and the
Body at the End of the World

Clifford R. Backman

THE PROSPECT OF CHRIST'S second coming can be terrifying. Even if the scenes described by John in Revelation do not represent the actual events of that day to come, there is little about the end that is not unsettling to contemplate. The terror results primarily, of course, from concern about our own fates or those of our loved ones. St. Augustine taught medieval Christians that no one—not even the most devout and blameless—can afford to be without fear when Judgment Day arrives: our fates have long been sealed, he proclaimed, and all we can do is to live piously and hope that we number among those whom God has chosen to admit into his heavenly kingdom. But one can never be sure. No one, he emphasized, *deserves* salvation—that is, no one can claim to be worthy of spending eternity in God's presence— and only those whom God has inscrutably selected will receive that greatest of gifts. Augustine's interpretation of predestination was not universally accepted, but the influence of his uncertainty principle was widespread and long felt. Most early medieval artists represented Christ as a stern judge, a king with a bad temper, rather than as a loving and gentle savior. His power received more attention than his love, and power inspires awe. Besides, the popular assumption of the early medieval period was that in all probability only professed monks and nuns would be saved on Judgment Day, if anyone would be at all; knowing how slim one's chances were only enhanced the trepidation people felt when contemplating the end. Christian faith, in other words, provided early medieval people with many convictions, but a conviction of certain salvation was not one of them. Mark Twain's wry summation of one of his fictional characters, that "he possessed all the calm confidence of a Christian with four aces," is a description that would not have, nor could ever have, fit most early medieval faithful—with or without the cards.

But a second cause of the terror is the sheer dreadfulness of the event itself, even for those who are saved. Christian history ends with a bang, not a whimper; and the prospect of immense multitudes of sinful souls condemned to eternal torment evokes pity, even in someone like Augustine (although admittedly not in harder hearts like Jerome, Peter Damian, or Dante). Heavenly judgment is too severe a matter to feel complacent about. But a consistent note to be found among medieval theorists about the end is that whatever happens will be just. God will do the right thing, and we can take some comfort, however small, in that knowledge. Nevertheless, the unimaginable nature of that day means that a sense of uneasiness towards it is never far off.

Numerous medieval writers, however, argued that whereas the end is unimaginable, strictly speaking, it is still knowable. They believed that the works of the Hebrew prophets—particularly Isaiah, Ezekiel, and most of all Daniel—positively bristled with clues about what to expect and, more especially, when to expect it. The Revelation of St. John, moreover, provided a coherent blueprint of what to expect because it was, of course, the only work of authentic Christian prophecy. All that was necessary was to decode this extraordinary text. Interpretations changed over the centuries, with some writers favoring allegorical readings, others a variety of symbolic approaches, still others (though less frequently) a literal assessment. Whatever the approach, however, certain passages and images from the text soon came to dominate and center apocalyptic exegesis: the repetition of the sevenfold division of things (the seven churches of Asia, the seven angels with seven trumpets, the seven seals, etc.), the Whore of Babylon, the saintly reign of a thousand years. And even though most churchmen, beginning with Augustine, sternly condemned the practice, these images and motifs became increasingly used as tools for calculating the arrival of the end. By assigning numerical values to the letters of the Greek alphabet, Jerome identified the Beast whose number is 666 (mentioned in the thirteenth chapter) with the then-contemporary Vandal king Genseric, thereby intimating that the end was close at hand. In the eighth century, Bede laid the foundation for Joachim of Fiore's popular heretical interpretation in the twelfth century by arguing for a seven-stage division of universal history, from Creation to Judgment Day, on the basis of the "seven churches" theme. Although Bede carefully avoided assigning specific dates to each period to remain orthodox, the clear implication of his book was that he and his contemporaries were living in the seventh age. Adso of Montier-en-Der, writing for his queen in the tenth century, drew heavily on both Jerome and Bede in positing his own apocalyptic millennialism.[1]

The legitimation of this sort of exegesis, this fascination with identifying repeated motifs, figures, and numbers in Scripture in order to unlock hidden secrets that would guide one to the Last Day, had many elements in it, varying from author to author, but at least one definite characteristic was shared by them all: namely, the belief that, however awful and inscrutable God's power may be, his love for us is at least great enough that he would sprinkle a few clues around for us. The observable structural order of creation—the regular cycle of the seasons, the constancy of the fixed stars for navigation, the predictable reaction of the body to various elements (foods, herbs, sensations, or whatever)—carried and encouraged the implicit hope that God's creation was capable of being understood and that if God's creation could be understood, so too might his will, thereby improving one's chances of salvation. More than that, they hoped, God's love led him to scatter clues to his divine plan within the Scriptures themselves, the part of creation to which medieval Christians were enjoined to pay the closest attention. At the literal level, in other words, the Scriptures informed the faithful of how to live their lives, but at the hidden level they also gave away the due date—the specific point in time by which the faithful had to get their lives in order to improve their chances of salvation. Writers and enthusiasts of this sort of scriptural exegesis, so intent on discerning the "pattern in the rug," so to speak, would have well understood and endorsed Samuel Johnson's famous dictum about gallows and fortnights.

Among late medieval writers to tackle the subject, one of the most interesting is the Catalan physician-turned-mystic Arnau de Vilanova (ca. 1240–1310). Long known to historians of science for his twenty-odd volumes of writings on topics ranging from epilepsy to pharmacology, his late career as a religious reformer and apocalyptic alarmist has until recently been overlooked. Indeed, he is still virtually unknown to most medievalists, which is ironic because in his day he was one of the best-known figures in Europe.[2] As professor of medicine at the University of Montpellier, he held the most prestigious position in the medical establishment; as an occasional diplomat for the Barcelona-based Crown of Aragon confederation, he was a prominent figure in French and Italian courts; and as personal physician to over a half-dozen kings, princes, and popes, he enjoyed extraordinary access to the centers of power. If that weren't enough, widespread rumors that he had poisoned at least two of the popes he treated, Boniface VIII and Benedict XI, made him notorious, and the nature of his treatments of those pontiffs added to his reputation as something of a magus. A linguistic polymath, he translated his own scientific writings and those of others back and forth between Latin, Greek, Arabic, and Catalan. (While he seems to have had only a smattering of Hebrew, he was familiar with much of the Jewish tradition of medicine as well.) Much of the high regard historians of science have had for his work arises from his early championing of experimentation in the pursuit of scientific truth. Like only a few others before him, Arnau bridged the gap that often existed between medical theory and medical practice, and in the process he made significant contributions to the development of modern science.[3]

But Arnau was no proto-Enlightenment rationalist. A powerful emotionalism pervades all his writings, both scientific and religious, and in his treatment of the ill—most famously in his care of Boniface VIII—he frequently took recourse to magic amulets, incense, mysterious rites and chants, astrological portents, and numerological symbolisms. His treatise on lovesickness (*De amore heroico*) especially emphasizes the point that human passions, sensations, and intuitions often provide a more reliable insight to human actions than cool, theoretical thought. In Arnau's mind, whatever worked was right, and he remained open at all times to considering instinct and revelatory emotion as equal to the powers of reason and controlled experiment. Indeed, he believed that medical knowledge itself could be the result and consequence of divine revelation.

Despite his high connections and busy pen, Arnau may have remained unknown to most Europeans until 1299. But in that year he took the extraordinary risk of reading to the Dominican scholars at the University of Paris the newest redaction of a work that he had originally written in 1288 and had kept hidden ever since, a work called *De tempore adventus Antichristi*.[4] He was in Paris on a diplomatic mission for James II of the Crown of Aragon at the time, and he apparently could not resist the temptation of trying out his ideas. The timing was not accidental. Fluent in Arabic and familiar with Islamic beliefs and culture, Arnau was aware that the year 1288—the year in which he had his revelation about the approach of Antichrist—was, according to the Islamic calendar, the year 666, a reckoning rich with apocalyptic meaning. Moreover, by the time of his diplomatic errand to Paris in 1299, Pope Boniface VIII had already announced the Jubilee celebration for the following year. Religious excitement filled the air, and Arnau felt certain that the time was ripe for his announcement of the arrival of the end, which, on the basis of the ninth and twelfth chapters of Daniel and several passages in Revelation, he had determined would occur sometime between 1366 and 1376—a time close enough to inspire urgency, yet far enough away to keep alive hopes for the spiritual and social reforms needed to prepare the world for that day.

Arnau's hopes for a prophet's welcome collapsed, however, when the Paris theologians condemned his book and chastised him, a layman, for daring to venture into matters beyond his concern or ability. He appealed his case and kept appealing it until it came before the papal consistory in 1301. By this time his case had become a cause célèbre. Fortunately for Arnau, his trial for heresy coincided with a painful attack of gallstones in Pope Boniface VIII, and Arnau's successful treatment of the malady put the usually irritable pontiff in a conciliatory mood. While vigorously rejecting the ideas put forth in the *De tempore adventus Antichristi*, Boniface demurred from anathematizing either the book or its author and in the end rebuked Arnau only for having presented his ideas in public as a layman without prior permission from the Holy See.[5] Arnau characteristically interpreted Boniface's action as a tacit approval of his ideas and launched energetically into a string of new treatises and screeds that elaborated both his hypothesis about the end and the reforms required to prepare mankind for it. His success was notable. According to one papal courtier, Arnau's predictions of the end gained support "even among the leaders [of the Church, i.e., the cardinals] . . . they say that his predictions have already begun to come true, and they fear that all his warnings will come to pass."[6]

After still more works emerged from Arnau's pen, most notably a series of tracts attacking the intelligence and legitimacy of the "pseudo-religious pseudo-theologians" of the Dominican order, a spectacular trial at Perugia ensued in early 1304 and made him a kind of media star. (Decades later he was still mentioned, with a glint of admiration, by Chaucer at the end of the Canon Yeoman's Tale.) A number of grim Dominicans, who regarded his claim to have unlocked, finally, the knotty mystery of the prophets and Revelation as an unendurable layman's presumption, wanted to see his works condemned and their author imprisoned. There is some evidence that their concerns were not entirely theological. The same courtier who noted Arnau's success at winning converts to his apocalypticism also claimed to have overheard one cardinal lamenting to another Arnau's cure of Boniface's illness: "If only that Arnau hadn't come! For the simple truth of the matter is that [Boniface] would be dead and buried by now, if not for him."[7]

The next pope, Benedict XI, was himself a Dominican and had little patience with lay prophets of Arnau's sort, especially with ones who could claim a certain degree of intellectual bona fides. Making matters worse, Arnau had since turned his energies away from Joachimite apocalyptic prophecy (on the assumption that he had already done all that he could to prove his case about the approaching end) and towards the social and ecclesiastical reforms that he thought must happen in order to prepare the world for Antichrist's, and thence Christ's, approach. While no formal link appears to have occurred, Arnau allied himself sympathetically with the heterodox splinter group of the Franciscan Spirituals, the radical branch of the Franciscan order that was the most zealously devoted to the idea of evangelical poverty and Church reform. The Spirituals, in short, believed that the *imitatio Christi* incumbent upon all clergy carried with it an absolute obligation to renounce all wealth and property and that the Church as it then existed, with its vast estates, magnificent palaces, and concern for collecting ecclesiastical taxes, had either lost or was in danger of losing all spiritual authority—precisely at the point in time when Antichrist's approach seemed imminent and therefore the need of the faithful for a purified Church was at its highest. This was the spirit behind Arnau's declarations of his "evangelical detestation of the corrupt practices within the Catholic orders" and especially among the "dragons and serpents" of the Dominicans, who reviewed Arnau's every utterance with a suspicious eye from their comfortable—and in Arnau's opinion, wholly undeserved— university posts.[8]

As previously mentioned, tensions came to a head in early 1304 when Arnau, with a characteristic lack of realism, approached Benedict at a church council in Perugia in order to gain papal approval for his latest eschatological theories. To say that he failed is an enormous understatement. Benedict showed not even the slightest interest in or sympathy with Arnau's imaginings, but he also happened to fall extremely ill during the council and agreed to put himself under Arnau's medical care. Once again the physician took precedence over the prophet, and Arnau did his best. Benedict died, however, and suspicions arose anew about Arnau's complicity. (We do not know enough about Benedict's symptoms to guess what actually killed him.) Arnau landed in prison, without a papal or royal patron to protect him, and with inquisitors lining up for the opportunity to put him through the interrogational wringer. Petitions poured in from sympathizers across Europe asking for mercy on his behalf, but there seemed to be little hope. Arnau had always relied, whether he admitted it to himself or not, on the hope of a papal benefactor who might be willing to countenance his religious fantasies in return for his medical knowledge. With no pope on the scene, however, and indeed with rumors running rampant that Arnau had contrived to poison Benedict because of that pope's insensitivity to his spiritual pleadings, matters looked grim.

But then something very strange happened: the cardinals, immersed in
the task of choosing a new pope, decided to free Arnau. No one knows precisely why, but several explanations seem possible. First, a number of the
cardinals may simply have wanted Arnau out of their hair as they worked on
the delicate negotiations of selecting a new pontiff. The presence of a popular, reform-minded rabble-rouser like Arnau certainly would not have made
the scene of backroom bargaining any easier, given all the attention being
accorded to his imprisonment. Releasing him would seem a much better
option than leaving him, and supposedly his supporters, on the site of such
important negotiations. Another possible explanation is that those cardinals
who were reportedly avid supporters of Arnau's prophecies managed to persuade the others that his ideas, while strange enough, were not intrinsically
heretical—for how could one prove him wrong without waiting to see what
happened in 1376 (the terminus of the ten-year span in which he predicted the
end-times would begin)? This is perhaps unlikely, for there is evidence that
to many observers it was Arnau's lay status, not his ideas themselves, that was
the issue.[9] A greater possibility exists that Arnau's age (he was then approximately sixty-five) and the shock of his imprisonment and rumored complicity
in two papal murders convinced many at court that he had been left a broken
man who would soon enough disappear from the scene.

If such was the case, those hopes did not last long. Freed from prison,
Arnau, whose health remained vigorous, went into a self-imposed exile at
Messina, the site of the royal court of the Catalan Sicilian monarch Frederick III. He remained at court for about a year, during which time he penned
a treatise for the king's benefit called the *Allocutio christiani de hiis que conve-
niunt homini secundum suam propriam dignitatem creature rationalis* (The Address of a Christian Regarding Those Things That Pertain to Man by Virtue
of His Dignity as a Rational Creature).[10] In this work Arnau argued energetically for a rationalist view of the world and of mankind's unique place in it.
God gave man the ability to reason, and, Arnau stressed, there has to be a reason for that: "God and Nature do nothing purposelessly," he had written as
early as 1288. The created world operates according to endlessly complex but
inherently rational principles (although, as in many aspects of Arnau's own
medical work, his interpretation of the rational seems excessively broad by
modern standards), and God has given Man the power of reason in order that
he might understand those principles. This is proof-positive, in Arnau's mind,
that God wants mankind to figure out the order and meaning of life. God's
truth lies imbedded in the physical world just as it suffuses and defines Holy
Scripture; all that is required is to read correctly the evidence of his Truth

that God has planted all around us. And since reason is the key to that ability, and since all mankind, by definition, possesses that trait, then unlocking the heavenly mysteries is not and cannot be the exclusive domain of the clergy.

This was startling and dangerous stuff. Perhaps still shaken by his close escape at Perugia, Arnau did not circulate the *Allocutio* and left much of its religious argument implicit and hinted at, rather than explicitly asserted. Indeed, after making his initial argument, he quickly turned most of his attention in the *Allocutio* to advising Frederick of Sicily to adopt a number of specific social and institutional, as well as spiritual, reforms. The *Allocutio* is Arnau's first work that bears unmistakable evidence of his allegiance to the heterodox splinter group, the Franciscan Spirituals (or Spiritual Franciscans), although some traces of his leaning towards them came earlier.[11] This would seem to have invited an ecclesiastical backlash, but none came—presumably because the cardinals were still engrossed in the difficult search for a new pontiff, one that would ultimately result in the election of Clement V and the papal exile to Avignon.

Arnau took advantage of the relative calm and the amenities of Frederick's court to produce his major religious work, the *Expositio in Apocalypsi* (Commentary on Revelation).[12] We do not know for certain whether he finished the book during his Sicilian tenure, but he almost certainly wrote most of it while there. He mentions Clement V, who became pope well into 1305, at a point over three-fourths of the way through the long book, and we know that Arnau only ended his island idyll in order to present his *Expositio* to the new pope, hoping once again to win a papal protector and legitimator. The *Expositio* both fascinates and infuriates; more than any other of his religious books it shows all of its author's strengths and weaknesses. Passages of considerable insight, of venomous spite, and of gargantuan hubris all jostle with one another for position on the page. We do not know Clement's specific reaction to the book, but he clearly dismissed it and this must have disappointed Arnau considerably because only a few years earlier Clement (then Bertrand de Got, archbishop of Bordeaux) had expressed sympathy for Arnau's plight in the contest between Boniface VIII and the Dominicans over Arnau's theories about the Antichrist. Still Arnau did not give up hope. As late as 1309, when he was near seventy, he continued to send his new writings to Clement; and on at least one occasion, he traveled to Avignon in order personally to read a new work to him.[13]

The *Expositio* begins cagily. Arnau distinguishes carefully between *visio* and *intellectus*, "vision" and "understanding." Only true prophets, those uniquely blessed by God and the precursors of the Christian clergy, possess the power of *visio*; but *intellectus*, while a God-given gift in the way that any remarkable human talent is, is something that is at once both lesser and greater than *visio*. It is lesser because its possessor cannot claim the same sort of mystical union with God that a true prophet enjoys and that enables him to speak as a mouthpiece for the Lord himself, but greater because those with *intellectus* may yet legitimately claim to understand the truth of someone else's vision, provided that God grants such a person the power to understand, and even to understand that vision better than the prophet himself who experienced it. Arnau's point is not that God favors an Adam Smithian sort of specialization of labor but rather that God suits both his revelations and the understandings of them to the points in history when they are needed. Citing the case of Daniel—the figure on whom Arnau's calculations of the end most depend—Arnau asserts that Daniel's prophecies, for example, as understood by the Jews of the second century B.C.E. sufficed for the needs of that time. But as centuries passed and Christ's appearance on earth ushered in a new revelation of God's design for man, such prophecies take on different meaning and require different interpretation, for "the messages contained in visions lie buried deep within them" and "God, who is the author of all visions, grants the proper understanding of them . . . whenever He wishes and to whatever extent He wishes." [14]

The various explications of Daniel's prophecies by Christian writers, whether mystical, moral, symbolic, allegorical, or literal, have once again been geared, according to Arnau, to the specific needs of the times they were written, so that those later expositors' understanding of the vision is "even greater than" that of the original prophet. The time has now come, Arnau concludes, to move beyond these sequential and one-dimensional interpretations, to synthesize their wisdom, and to offer a full and final reading of the Scriptures. By pairing the works of the prophets with the apocalyptic text of Revelation, Arnau argues, the certain truth of what we can expect at the end, what it will mean, and when we may expect it, can at last be revealed. What makes this possible is the very bounty of God's goodness: since he has always given as much revelation of his Truth as was needed throughout history, now that history is soon to end, the time has come for God to make his final revelation via the person or persons who possess both the spiritual health and the reason-based *intellectus* that will allow them to see the Truth and to see it whole. [15]

In this way Arnau cleverly avoids claiming prophetic gifts for himself—which would have guaranteed the reopening of charges of heresy against him—while nevertheless establishing himself as a legitimate prophetic voice.

And what does that voice say about the end (apart, that is, from the timing of its arrival, which he had already dealt with in earlier works)? His *Expositio* offers, for all its claims to completing and perfecting the explication of the Revelation, a thoroughly, if not quite conventionally, Joachite eschatology, although he does refine Joachim's system somewhat by emphasizing throughout the heightened importance to be played by the "proclaimers of evangelical truth" who made up Arnau's most ardent followers—both among the Franciscan Spirituals and among evangelical laypersons. He follows the standard format of verse-by-verse glosses. The angel of 1:8, who announces the revelation to John, is likened to the "angelic pope" predicted by Joachim but also represents the *universi praecones incorrupti evangelicae veritatis*. In fact, Arnau suggests, the latter group is likely to be more important than the "angelic pope" and his clergy because the trumpet blast that began John's vision came from behind him (1:11): God, Arnau hints, always speaks directly to his established clergy, and this sort of indirect communication can only signify that it is the nonclerical faithful who will receive, and who in fact already have received, the full *intellectus* of the end.

Most of the rest of the *Expositio* repeats, with some slight modifications, the traditional Joachite interpretation. Thus the three persons of the Trinity correspond to the three ages (*status*) of history, to be calibrated against the seven periods (*tempora*) of history as represented by the seven gifts of the Holy Spirit and the seven churches of Asia to whom John speaks. Since the seven churches symbolize the Church as a whole, all of the spiritual and social reforms that must be accomplished before the end must be spearheaded by the angelic pope, but Arnau introduces an evangelical *correptor* (from *corrigere*, "to correct" or "to improve," rather than from *corripere*, "to snatch" or "to steal") who will serve as the pope's spiritual adviser and guide.

But what, specifically, will happen to the faithful once the *correptor* and the "angelic pope" have fulfilled their missions and have purified as much of the expectant world as possible? What will our bodies physically experience? Bodily resurrection of the dead and the physical assumption of the living have stood at the center of Christian eschatology at least since Paul wrote his epistles.[16] But will the faithful enter paradise in their healthy twenty-year-old bodies or in the weakened persons of their dotage? Will physical imperfections, even relatively harmless ones like nearsightedness, persist? Does it matter? Here the *Expositio in Apocalypsi* remains maddeningly silent—but then, so does Revelation itself. The fact that Arnau, following John, never attempts to describe God's appearance in anthropomorphic terms but only refers to it as "an impression of light" tells us little. John mentions crowds and voices, multitudes and choirs, but angels, not humans, dominate his vision, and consequently Arnau's exposition.

The fact that Arnau's medical writings and medical activities continued throughout the last two decades of his life, after his evangelical conversion, suggests that he saw his medical and religious callings as compatible. "All the sciences share in a common usefulness, namely the acquisition of perfection in the human soul, preparing it, in effect, for all future happiness," he wrote in his *Commentum super canonem "Vita brevis."* Moreover, he repeatedly referred to medicine as "the most noble of sciences" and "the summit of nobility." He singled out St. Luke, a physician, as uniquely important among the four Gospel writers; in his *Address at Bordeaux*, for example, he boldly chastises his critics: "I tell you, that if anyone rejects my religious writings simply because they were written by a physician, then he does not walk in the path of Christ, since Christ himself did not exclude physicians from understanding the sacred teachings." And in what might have appeared in another writer as a mere rhetorical flourish but in his case clearly flirted with danger, he often described Christ himself as the *medicus supremus* and *medicus summus* of all Creation, whose Truth was literally the best medicine for mankind.[17]

Correlating physical health with spiritual health was a common conceit in the Middle Ages, but Arnau took the idea to new heights. Two basic paradigms existed for understanding human nature, and each had an influence on Arnau's medical and religious thinking; the first, associated chiefly with the Jewish tradition, defined man as enlivened flesh, an essentially corporeal being temporarily brought to life by God's infusion of spirit; the second, more explicitly Christian in nature, viewed man as embodied soul, an essentially spiritual (and thereby timeless) being momentarily given a physical aspect. Both paradigms posited a correlation between physical and spiritual well-being, but the connection was considerably stronger and more explicit in the latter—and it was this fact that lay behind the large dose of what we today would call magic in medieval Christian medicine.[18] Arnau's use of amulets, incense, and astrology in treating Boniface VIII's gallstones in 1301 reflected this connection because the "magical" aspects of the treatment aimed, in theory, at curing the spiritual component of Boniface's ailment while the "nonmagical" treatments (warm baths, soft foods, weak broths, and some herbal medicines) addressed the physical component. Boniface himself indirectly endorsed the soul-related nature of medicine and the body when, joyfully recovering from his complaint, he announced to the papal court "I did not realize it until now, but now I proclaim it aloud—this man [Arnau] is the greatest cleric in the world!" To describe Arnau as a *clericus* clearly implied a recognition in him of some sort of spiritual power. Boniface's words no doubt also bolstered Arnau's hopes of papal support for his apocalyptic prophesying.[19]

Those hopes were dashed, however, when Boniface refused to endorse Arnau's eschatology (although Arnau made it a point, in subsequent years, to point out that Boniface had never formally condemned his ideas either). When Boniface died two years later, after being assaulted by Philip IV's henchmen at Anagni, Arnau penned a blistering essay, *De morte Bonifacii VIII*, in which he attributed the pontiff's death to the sickness of his soul rather than to the violent humiliations inflicted on his aged body. What was that soul-sickness, according to the physician? Boniface's refusal to recognize the truth of Arnau's religious message.[20] An assertion this audacious might well have led to arrest, were it not for the fact that Boniface had left so many enemies behind him. One can easily imagine some figures at court furtively enjoying Arnau's declaration that Boniface had died of his own spiritual wickedness. Whatever the case, no trouble arose from the essay and its extraordinary claims. It is worth noting, however, that Arnau did not dare to offer a similar spiritual autopsy of Benedict XI.

Shortly after completing his Revelation commentary, Arnau tried during the papal interregnum to gather support from other branches of the Church. He appealed to a handful of bishops, mostly Catalans and Provençaux, whose sympathy he thought would be helpful; but he also turned, somewhat unexpectedly, to the Carthusian monastic order, which was then embroiled in a debate with its critics over the propriety of giving severely ill brethren meat to eat to improve their strength as opposed to the ideal of complete meat avoidance. While often overlooked by historians, the questions of whether to eat meat was briefly as significant an issue to the Carthusians as the definition of poverty was for the Franciscans in the years around 1300. The relative smallness of the order and its austere isolation probably account for the neglect and also raise the issue of how Arnau got involved with the Carthusians. It seems highly unlikely that the order sought out Arnau's help in resolving its dietary dispute; he was far too suspect a character. Instead, Arnau probably saw his entering the fray as a way to regain some of his lost respectability after the debacle at Perugia and his Sicilian exile. However it came about, Arnau quickly produced a treatise *De esu carnium* (On the Eating of Meat) that defended the practice of meat abstinence in both medical and spiritual terms. Though still unpublished, it offers a useful window into Arnau's thinking on human nature and may suggest what, if anything, he expected to happen on the Last Day.[21]

Every aspect of human life, Arnau argues, is suffused with moral meaning. The decisions of everyday life—whether to drink a cup of wine, to work at one's trade, to bathe, to make love with one's spouse, or to read a book—are both the products of and influences upon our moral and spiritual well-being. (In the health regimen that he composed for King James II of the Crown of Aragon, Arnau even attributed a moral element to the act of breathing: not only did the king's body require fresh air for health, but so too did his mental capabilities and powers of judgment, and therefore the earthly well-being, and ultimately the spiritual fate, of James's subjects depended on the king's proper breathing.) As God's supreme creations, our souls and bodies are, in their natural state, wholly healthy and perfect. True, the temporal encapsulating of our souls in human flesh carries with it the unavoidable stain of original sin, but the waters of baptism restore us to pristine perfection. From that point on, life is a continuous moral combat in which nothing is without spiritual meaning.

Arnau's case for Carthusian meat abstinence rests on five main arguments: the logic of love, the necessity of tradition as the best defense against heresy, the evidence of medical science, the authority of Scripture, and the evidence of direct observation. It is an interesting combination, one that reflects Arnau's privileging of the traditionally Christian definition of human nature as soul-within-a-body as opposed to the traditionally Jewish notion of body-given-life. Three of the arguments deal with the soul, while only two deal with the body, and yet in this text Arnau is writing specifically as a physician rather than as an apocalyptic prophet. The arguments run roughly as follows.

1. The logic of love. Critics accuse the Carthusians of failing to love their ill brethren by withholding from them a form of nutrition that would alleviate their bodily suffering, yet the Carthusians' vow of meat abstinence results from, and serves as an expression of, their absolute love of God. It is demonstrably illogical, Arnau argues, to insist that a practice that emerges from the greatest of all possible loves can ever devolve into, or be interpreted as, an absence of love. To love God with such totality is to love all those who offer God the same love, the same vow, the same totality.

2. Tradition as bulwark against heresy. Given his own notoriety as a heterodox thinker, Arnau here flirts openly, if characteristically, with danger. He identifies two types of heresy: overt opposition to the Church's teachings and authority and the assertion of novel ideas about the universal human condition—in essence, the redefinition of human nature. The Church's own long history, he points out, validates the practice of abstinence, whether from meat or any other substance, and therefore to assert the illegitimacy of meat avoidance in principle is in effect to reject the Church's historical authority and is therefore tantamount to heresy. On the second point, he argues that to insist that human bodily survival is impossible without meat consumption is essentially to redefine the very nature of the human body—a universalizing activity if ever there was one—that runs contrary to medical knowledge, the teachings of Scripture (where does the Bible say that Jesus ever ate meat?), and the observable longevity of vegetarians. Arnau concludes by pointing out that Jesus himself, according to both Matthew and Luke, urged his disciples: "Do not worry about your life and what you are to eat, nor about your body and how you are to clothe it. For life means more than food, and the body more than clothing" (Matt. 6: 25, Luke 12: 20).

3. *Medical evidence.* This point receives the most amplification and specificity; indeed, it accounts for over half of Arnau's text (disregarding the introductory and concluding passages). It shows Arnau at his most Galenic, emphasizing the proper balance of "vital forces" and "humors." Setting aside violent causes for the time being, he says that death results either from disease or from malnutrition. If a condition arises from disease, the proper course of treatment is medicinal—in which case the introduction of meat into what has previously been a meatless diet will either prove to be futile and irrelevant at best or will prove harmful at worst by disrupting the natural balance of forces and humors. If the problem is indeed nutritional, however, then substitutes for meat (such as egg yolks and diluted wine) represent more medically sound choices because meat itself is most appropriate for individuals regularly engaged in vigorous physical activity, which is hardly an accurate depiction of Carthusian life.

4. *Scriptural authority.* This brief section of the treatise comprises a highly selective dietary summary of biblical history. No fatted calves here: Arnau mentions only those examples that meet his purposes. David gave bread, figs, and raisins to the servant of the Amalechites; Jesus distributed bread and fish to his famished followers; while Paul instructed the Romans that "People range from those who believe they may eat any sort of meat to those whose faith is so weak they dare not eat anything except vegetables. Meat-eaters must not despise the scrupulous" (Rom. 14: 2–3).

5. *The evidence of our eyes.* Arnau notes with a certain malicious glee—the same sort of emotion that lay behind his delighted singling out of incompetent Dominican physicians at Paris—that Carthusian monks are indeed famous for their longevity, with many reaching the age of eighty and a few particularly blessed individuals reaching ninety, one hundred, and beyond. A diet lacking meat, he concludes, shows no deleterious effect on the monks in general and therefore cannot in any way be considered a fault or shortcoming

in their life regimen. Those who cannot recognize this obvious fact are fundamentally unqualified to judge Carthusian practice. The net result of these arguments, whether explicit or implicit, is that what is good for the soul is good for the body, though not necessarily vice versa, and herein lies the essential difference between the Christian and Jewish traditions with which Arnau was so familiar. A healthy soul provides proof-positive of a healthy body, barring exceptional circumstances, while an unhealthy body offers only an indirect and imperfect index of spiritual health. Death is not necessarily a failure, regardless of the age at which it strikes. But spiritual death or spiritual illness (as in the case of Boniface VIII) directly influences, and may even determine, physical well-being. This sounds confusing: if the soul is healthy and pure, why should that not guarantee physical soundness? And doesn't the fact of final illness and death therefore imply something about one's failed spiritual state?

What makes Arnau's thought interesting is his insistence, here and elsewhere, that death itself is a natural phenomenon when it comes as the denouement of a lived-out existence and is in such a case morally neutral. Spiritual health, in other words, makes physical health essentially irrelevant; illness—unless it be the natural decline of bodily vigor at the close of a long life—may serve as a warning sign for individuals to engage in necessary spiritual regeneration. Christ, as the *medicus supremus* of all Creation, presents sickness to mankind as nothing so much as an opportunity for reform. But for those whose souls already exist in vigorous purity—like the Carthusians (and, by clear implication, Arnau's much-favored Spiritual Franciscans, who also practiced austere physical self-denial)—bodily malaise, while a genuine suffering that deserves attention and treatment, cannot be simplistically equated with spiritual disease.

So what does this imply for the end of time? It's hard to say, and Arnau himself never dared venture a guess. It seems likely, however, that he expected the end to make physical soundness itself irrelevant even though the faithful may be assured of the resurrection of their bodies. Arnau seems far too implicated in a materialist understanding of human nature to posit anything like a literal rejuvenation of the dead—a miraculous return of the youthful, vigorous, and hale bodies of our early adulthood instead of the decrepit, worn-out things we leave on our deathbeds—which leaves us with the assumption, given all that went before, that Arnau presupposes that the physical state of the resurrected faithful is an irrelevance. He makes no claim to know the physical condition of the saved, although his understanding of the body as organic material suggests that he would dismiss the notion of youthful bodies being restored to those who died at great age. Bodies on that day may or may not be cleansed of illness or decay; the essential point is that the spiritual joy of the faithful will make such a question inconsequential. The joy of reunion with God will, if anything, make us unaware of our bodies— for who could turn their eyes away from the Lord in order to inspect their limbs? We cannot and will not know exactly what is going to happen on that day. But what a blessing God has given us, he concludes, in at least letting us know, via the encrypted messages in Scripture and Creation, *when* to expect that of which we cannot know *what* to expect.

Of Earthquakes, Hail, Frogs, and Geography

Plague and the Investigation of the Apocalypse in the Later Middle Ages

Laura A. Smoller

For nation shall rise against nation, and kingdom against kingdom: and there shall be famines, and pestilences, and earthquakes in divers places. (Matt. 24: 7)

Then the angel took the censer, filled it with fire from the altar, and threw it to the earth. And there were noises, thunderings, lightnings, and an earthquake. So the seven angels who had the seven trumpets prepared themselves to sound. The first angel sounded: and hail and fire followed, mingled with blood, and they were thrown to earth. (Revelation 8: 5–7)

Before the outbreak of the universal pestilence later known as the Black Death, according to a letter seen by the fourteenth-century chronicler Heinrich of Herford, a tremendous earthquake struck the Austrian region of Carinthia. In the same year, "fire falling from Heaven consumed the land of the Turks for sixteen days"; "it rained toads and snakes for several days," by which many men perished; and "pestilence gathered strength" in many parts of the world.[1] Similarly, the chronicle of the Austrian monastery of Neuberg recorded both the Carinthia earthquake and disturbing phenomena associated with the initial outbreak of the plague "in eastern parts." First, through the corruption of the air, men and beasts were changed into stone.[2] Second, a "lethal rain" mixed with pestiferous snakes and worms fell "in the regions where ginger comes from," which instantly killed all it touched. And, third, not far away, "a terrible fire burned from the sky" and consumed all it fell on, so that the very stones "burned as if they had been naturally changed into dry wood." The smoke from that fire was extremely contagious and killed many merchants a long way away. Even those who escaped carried its deadly contagion with them and so brought the plague to Greece, Italy, Rome, and neighboring regions.[3]

A similar confluence of signs appears in a letter written in Avignon by Louis Heyligen and quoted in the chronicle of an anonymous Flemish cleric. According to this letter, a province in the eastern regions of India had suffered terrible and unheard-of storms for three days. On the first day "it rained frogs, snakes, lizards, scorpions, and other poisonous animals." On the second day, there was thunder and lightning, and "hailstones of an incredible size fell," killing nearly every person. On the third day, "fire with a fetid smoke descended from heaven" and killed the remaining people and animals in the area and destroyed all the cities and towns there. According to Heyligen's letter, it was assumed that these storms had caused the great plague that then spread with south winds blowing from India to Christendom.[4]

Earthquakes at home. Rains of fire, hail, snakes, and toads in the east. These contemporary authors described the onset of the great pestilence not just with terrifying omens, but specifically with language drawn from Christian apocalyptic. Plagues, after all, feature both in Revelation (16: 8–11, 18: 8) and in the apocalyptic portions of the gospels (Matt. 24: 7, Luke 21: 11).[5] Chroniclers who described such portents at home and abroad mapped God's apocalyptic torments onto an orb whose image already was pregnant with the religious meanings apparent in the great *mappaemundi*. In these chronicles, snakes, toads, hail, and fire all rained down in the east: the land of marvels and monsters, of Prester John and Gog and Magog, of the enemies of the faith and of potential Christians. Plague moved from east to west, from pagans to Christians. Mapping its progress represented an attempt to understand, and thereby control, the disease.[6] But it also helped situate plague within an apocalyptic frame of reference. At the same time, these signs and prodigies were not without meaning in scientific efforts to explain plague. Earthquakes, snakes, toads, and stinking smoke also formed part of medical descriptions of the plague's etiology. The plague treatises, I will argue, form a critical moment in a longer trend of attempts to naturalize the apocalypse. This trend in turn was one aspect of the larger late-medieval project to naturalize marvels by extending the explanatory scope of natural philosophy. At a time when scientific speculations about the apocalypse had become problematic, plague writings reopened the door to such an analysis. They did so by their reliance on phenomena that defied strict categorization either as purely natural causes or as wholly supernatural apocalyptic signs.

In summary, plague in many ways both invited and defied the attempt at naturalizing. By mapping plague onto a geography with eschatological import and by locating its causes in apocalyptic-sounding signs, I will argue, fourteenth-century authors entered into a tangled web of symbols. Each aspect of their treatment of the plague set off a whole host of free-associations in the realms of natural philosophy and of apocalyptic. Fourteenth-century writers appeared to be unwilling to say that plague was either entirely natural or entirely apocalyptic. Their writings, by their very ambiguity, opened up the possibility that plague might be simultaneously natural and apocalyptic. By implication, these treatises raised the possibility that the apocalypse might indeed be explained by natural causes. Thus, the speculations plague engendered helped set the stage for a thoroughgoing scientific investigation of the apocalypse in the following century.

Mapping the Plague and the Geography of the Apocalypse

In the fourteenth-century writings about the plague mentioned above, the authors locate the most bizarre phenomena associated with the outbreak of pestilence in the distant east. Likewise, according to physicians at the University of Paris, the effects of the triple conjunction of 1345 that caused the plague would be felt more in "southern and eastern regions," areas in which their text strongly implies a number of portents such as falling stars have been seen.[7] These phenomena, which, as we shall see, had meaning in both apocalyptic and scientific interpretations of the plague, explained the observed fact that the disease traveled from east to west. Mapping has been called a form of conquest and control of territory,[8] and mapping plague's progress was perhaps an attempt at mastering and possessing the feared disease, just as the naturalizing of its causes, as we shall see, marked an effort to bring inexplicable tragedies under the control of human understanding. But in plotting plague's progress on a map of the world, fourteenth-century authors found themselves mapping plague on an earth that already had religious meaning, and, specifically, eschatological import.

Home to the plague's origin and the most striking phenomena associated therewith, the east had, in fact, long been associated with both marvels and with apocalyptic traditions. From classical times, the east was the land of monstrous races, unusual animals, untold-of wealth, and incredible diversity. It was the site of both the earthly paradise and of flesh-eating scarcely human monsters.[9] If fire and worms were going to rain down anywhere, why not in the east? But if plague was mapped onto a world that put the disease's mysterious origin in the already marvelous east, that same *mappamundi* provided localization for aspects of the drama of end times, whose nearness the plague and its harbingers seemed to indicate. It was clear, for example, that the last act of that drama would be played out in and around Jerusalem (Rev. 20: 9), the world's center in the *mappaemundi* and the setting of history's central moment: the crucifixion.[10] In *The Travels of Sir John Mandeville* (probably written in the first decade after the appearance of the Black Death), the author asserts that the Last Judgment will take place at the foot of Mount Tabor in the Vale of Jehosaphat.[11] One strand of the considerable body of Antichrist lore put that fiend's birth or at least his youth in the cities of Capernaum, Chorozin, and Bethsaida in Galilee.[12] But, just as the *mappaemundi* visually depicted the history of salvation moving in time and space from Eden, at the map's top, to Jerusalem, at its center, a fuller chronology of end times would also have to show a movement from the periphery in towards that center.

One aspect of an apocalyptic movement from periphery inwards appears in the Cedar of Lebanon vision that circulated from the early thirteenth century and found a new life in the hands of a number of chroniclers in the wake of the outbreak of the Black Death. That prophecy, like other late medieval visions of the apocalypse, looked to a period of peace and calm before the final confrontation that would usher in the world's end. Among the features of that time of peace would be a universal conversion to the Christian faith or, as the Cedar of Lebanon vision expressed it, "Within fifteen years there will be one God and one faith. . . . And the lands of the barbarians will be converted."[13] This prediction rested ultimately upon the passage in the gospel of Matthew in which Jesus tells his disciples, "And this gospel of the kingdom will be preached in all the world as a witness to all the nations, and then the end will come" (Matt. 24: 14).[14] After the conversion of the barbarians, according to the same vision, there was to be "a universal passage of all the faithful" to the Holy Land prior to the appearance of Antichrist. Mapping this scenario in space and time would produce a movement from the periphery—locus of conversion—to Jerusalem, the center and goal of pilgrimage.[15] And since Christendom had already reached the western limits of the world, as Hugh of St. Victor had pointed out in the twelfth century, by the fourteenth century everybody knew that the lands to be converted lay to the east (beginning, lamentably, with the Holy Land itself).[16] This final conversion was one of the goals of the thirteenth-century Franciscan missionaries to Asia like William of Rubruck and was the hope implicit in both *Mandeville's Travels* and the belief in Prester John, a Christian king somewhere off in the mysterious east.[17] The eastern locus of this end-time missionizing thus meant that the movement of the unfolding apocalypse—at least insofar as conversion was concerned—would be a movement from east to west, just as plague itself moved from east to west, from the lands of infidels to the lands of Christians.

In fact, several fourteenth-century chronicles dealing with plague adduce an anecdote that reflects at least the hope that these eastern lands would be converted to the faith in plague's train. The English chronicles of Henry Knighton and the monastery of Meaux, for example, relate how an eastern ruler or people decided that the plague raging in their lands was the result of their lack of Christian faith. Sending representatives to Christendom in order to begin the process of conversion, they discover that plague is present among Christians as well and return home with the conclusion that their planned conversion would in fact be futile.[18] This tale may be read as anti-apocalyptic; after all, plague does not initiate a final universal conversion in the story. Nonetheless, it demonstrates that the plague's appearance at least engendered the hope that the anticipated universal conversion was at hand.

Another type of motion embodied within apocalyptic beliefs has to do with the movement of enemies. Again, here, plague writings appear to parallel this eschatological geography. As described in Revelation, when Satan is released after being bound for a thousand years, "he will go out to deceive the nations which are in the four corners of the earth, Gog and Magog, to gather them together to battle" (Rev. 20: 8). These forces will advance upon Jerusalem ("the camp of the saints and the beloved city"), where they at last will be consumed by a fire from heaven (Rev. 20: 9). In this movement of apocalyptic enemies, there is also a motion from periphery to center, from the four corners of the earth to Jerusalem. Unlike the movement of universal conversion, however, this amassing of enemies was understood in the fourteenth century to be not simply a movement from east to west, but also a movement from west to east. In the final days, there would be enemies without and enemies within Christendom, all of whom would converge upon Jerusalem. As Roger Bacon wrote, "For [Gog and Magog] must obey [Antichrist]: therefore, if they break out from one part of the world, he will come forth from the opposite direction."[19] But who precisely was meant by the phrase "Gog and Magog," and whence would they come?

One tradition increasingly elaborated in the Middle Ages equated Gog and Magog with enemies from without, specifically with the barbarian, indeed almost antihuman, tribes long since enclosed behind an iron gate by Alexander the Great. By the fourteenth century, these enclosed peoples had also been firmly identified with the ten lost tribes of Israel and were associated with the Amazons (who were said to be either their guards, their wives, or their overlords). Near the end, according to this series of traditions, Alexander's gates would be opened, and Gog and Magog would rush out to join the forces of Antichrist and to terrorize Christians.[20] Where exactly one might find Alexander's gates and the enclosed nations was less clear, however. By most accounts Gog and Magog were to be found somewhere in Asia. But some authors placed them in the Caspian Mountains; some, in the northern extremes of Asia; others, in islands of the northern sea; and yet others, in the extreme northeast corner of the orb.[21] Even with these discrepancies, it is apparent that the release of Gog and Magog from the iron gates would result in a roughly east to west movement as the forces of Antichrist moved on from Asia towards Jerusalem.[22] Could this east-to-west movement of enemies have been linked to the westward progress of plague?

There may indeed have been some interconnections, as fourteenth-century chroniclers mapped the plague's progress onto an east-west trajectory already understood to have eschatological significance. Here again the bizarre signs that accompany the plague's eastern outbreak in the fourteenth-century chronicles come into play. Interestingly, textual descriptions of the enclosed tribes of Gog and Magog not infrequently are accompanied by references to snakes, worms, and reptiles—the very portents fourteenth-century authors localized to the initial focus of the plague in the east. The widely read *Revelationes* of pseudo-Methodius, for example, describes the enclosed tribes as living filth, who on their release not only will feed upon human flesh and blood, but also "will eat unclean serpents, scorpions, and all of the most filthy and abominable kinds of beasts and reptiles which crawl upon the earth."[23] In *Mandeville's Travels*, the ten lost tribes (Gog and Magog) are enclosed within a range of mountains surrounded by a great intraversible desert that is so "fulle of dragounes, of serpentes, and of other venymous bestes that no man dar not passe."[24] And Roger Bacon in the *Opus maius* reported the very words by which Alexander the Great supposedly described these horrid tribes as poisonous reptiles: "O Earth, mother of dragons, nurse of scorpions, guardian of serpents, and sinkhole of demons, it would have been easier for you for this hell to be enclosed within you than to give birth to such races! Woe to the earth, producer of fruit and honey, when so many serpents and beasts assail her!"[25] Snakes, scorpions, vermin, and reptiles textually accompany the outbreak of the plague in the east as well as the release of Gog and Magog and the peoples enclosed by Alexander.

A second tradition about Gog and Magog, stemming from an Augustinian reading of Revelation, interpreted the names allegorically as referring simply to the enemies of God in general and not to any literal race of peoples in any specific geographical location. This interpretation encouraged Christians to see Gog and Magog as the enemy within, reinforcing the equation of Gog and Magog with Jews, not so much the ten lost tribes, but those Jews still living among medieval Christians.[26] These two interpretive traditions could come together, as in the treatment of Gog and Magog in *Mandeville's Travels*. There the author avers that when the enclosed Gog and Magog (ten lost tribes) break out in the final days, they will join forces with Jews living among Christians, who will lead them into Christendom "for to destroye the Cristene peple"[27] and then, presumably, to march on Jerusalem. Gog and Magog in *Mandeville*, although localized and identified specifically as Jews, combine the notions of internal and external enemies of Christendom.

This eschatological movement of enemies coming from within may also have been in the minds of fourteenth-century chroniclers writing about the plague. The massive burnings of Jews in the plague years, after all, rested upon the belief in an international conspiracy of Jews to poison the water supplies of Christendom, a conspiracy seen as an alliance of enemies without and enemies within.[28] The interpretation of Gog and Magog as enemies within finds expression also in the fourteenth-century chronicle of the cathedral priory of Rochester. The chronicle's author, probably William Dene, asserts that the recalcitrance of now-scarce laborers after the plague must arise from the influence of Gog and Magog. "It is therefore much to be feared," he writes, "that Gog and Magog have returned from hell to encourage such things and to cherish those who have been corrupted."[29] William Dene seems to lean towards the Augustinian exegesis by saying that "Gog and Magog have returned from hell," for he neither identifies Gog and Magog with any known enemy, such as the Muslims or the Jews, nor gives them a specific earthly home base. Rather, they are belched forth from hell—literally the bowels of the earth—not unlike the earthquakes described by other fourteenth-century authors. In contrast to the eastern rains of snakes, worms, frogs, and fire, earthquakes in fourteenth-century plague writings take place close to home: in Carinthia for Heinrich of Herford, in England itself for the chronicler of the Yorkshire abbey of Meaux.[30] Spewing out noxious fumes from the belly of the earth, earthquakes bespoke internal corruption hiding under the surface and waiting to break out, just like the enemy within, be it the Jews or the lax Christians who would be Antichrist's prey.[31] The earthquakes close to home in plague chronicles resounded with reminders of the enemy within, just as snakes and poisonous reptiles raining in the east pointed to the enemy without.

The geography of the apocalypse thus could impose itself upon and provide one set of meanings to the geography of plague. Its progress mapped, charted, and analyzed by fourteenth-century authors, plague nonetheless defied the possession and control that geographical knowledge represented. Even as authors attempted to "tame" plague by mapping its progress, the multiple meanings in the places associated with plague could lead readers and authors into an endless web of free associations in which earthquakes, snakes, and toads served simultaneously as metaphors for corruption, apocalyptic signs, and natural causes of disease. The same pattern is apparent in fourteenth-century authors' attempts to give plague a natural explanation. Although they appear to believe that explaining plague by natural causes will lay their apocalyptic fears to rest and bring the disease within the control of human understanding—if not prevention and cure—their explanations lead them into the same web of eschatological signs, portents, and free associations. It is almost an unspoken hope in these writings that if plague can be explained in natural terms, then it cannot betoken the nearness of the end. But it proved impossible to read the plague as entirely natural and not at all apocalyptic. Fourteenth-century chronicles can jarringly announce the apocalypse and naturalize the very signs that indicate its nearness without comment or coming down on one side or the other.

Apocalyptic Signs and Natural Causality
Before the Black Death

Many fourteenth-century authors described plague in overtly or implicitly apocalyptic terms by relating the epidemic to other physical signs associated with the end in scripture and prophecies. The understanding of such signs had gone through a number of changes in the centuries leading up to the Black Death, however. Whereas previously medieval Christians had assumed that such apocalyptic portents would be sent directly by God, in the thirteenth century some natural philosophers were assigning natural causes, such as astrological configurations, to apocalyptic portents.[32] By century's end, however, there had been a backlash against a scientific study of the apocalypse.

According to Scripture, key signs and portents would herald the nearness of the apocalypse. Many of these signs figure in the fourteenth-century plague writings. Earthquakes, for example, had particular religious meaning. Earthquakes appear frequently in Scripture, not simply as manifestations of divine anger and mechanisms for the deliverance of the just, but also specifically as apocalyptic signs. For example, in Isaiah 29: 6–7, God's promised deliverance of Jerusalem from her enemies is effected by thunder, earthquake, storm, and devouring fire. An earthquake accompanies Christ's death on the cross and rolls back the stone covering his tomb in Matthew. Yet another earthquake frees the apostles Paul and Silas from prison in Acts 16: 26. Most importantly, earthquakes feature among the signs of the end enumerated in the synoptic gospels (Matt. 24: 7, Mark 13: 8, Luke 21: 11). And the largest constellation of earthquakes occurs in Revelation itself, in which there are no fewer than five earthquakes accompanying the torments unleashed therein against the enemies of God (Rev. 6: 12, 8: 5, 11: 13, 11: 19, 16: 18).[33] Earthquakes in Scripture thus can be direct manifestations of God's anger, including the fury reserved for the enemies at end times.

Many medieval chroniclers interpreted earthquakes along similar lines, as the result of God's wrath or as warnings thereof. These earthquakes have—it is implied—supernatural causes. For example, in Gregory of Tours's *History of the Franks*, earthquakes appear among a number of other portents (visions in the skies, comets, unusual weather, and rains of snakes and blood) announcing disasters, including epidemics of plague and dysentery and the appearance of false prophets. Gregory implies that these are signs of the end by quoting apocalyptic texts from Matthew and Mark alongside his enumeration of such portents. He also describes these portents as "the kind which usually announce the death of a king or the destruction of entire regions," again likely envisioned as the result of God's direct action and not the workings of secondary causes.[34]

The thirteenth-century chronicler Matthew Paris, too, made much of earthquakes and other *supernatural* portents as apocalyptic signs. His writings demonstrate the way in which, under the influence of Aristotelian natural philosophy, authors were carefully separating out natural and supernatural events. In Matthew Paris's conception, such phenomena point to the apocalypse precisely because they can have no natural causes. As he wound up his *Chronica majora* in the year 1250, for example, Matthew noted the singular number of "prodigies and amazing novelties" in this twenty-fifth half-century "since the time of grace," a half-century he fully anticipated would be the world's last. Among these prodigies were eclipses, floods, unexplainably large numbers of falling stars, and earthquakes.[35] Not simply the number of portents, but specifically their inability to be explained by natural causes pointed towards the looming apocalypse. For example, Matthew Paris had described an earthquake that happened in England in 1247, thought to be particularly significant of "the end of the aging world" in that England lacked the "underground caverns and deep cavities in which, according to philosophers, [earthquakes] are usually generated."[36] A large number of falling stars was particularly troubling again because it defied natural explanation. Since "no apparent reason for this can be found in the *Book of Meteors* [Aristotle's *Meteorology*]," Matthew concluded that "Christ's menace was threatening mankind."[37] Matthew thus implied that earthquakes and other phenomena arising from natural causes were noteworthy but not apocalyptic. But those for which no natural cause could be found pointed menacingly toward the end.

Matthew Paris's analysis of earthquakes and falling stars reflects the thirteenth-century scholastics' ongoing project of explaining more and more events—and particularly *mirabilia*—through natural causes.[38] Phenomena that appear as wonder-inducing signs in early medieval chronicles—like rains of fire—meet with scientific explanations, often highly dependent on astrological theories, in thirteenth-century authors such as Albertus Magnus, Thomas Aquinas, and Roger Bacon. One might conceivably use natural philosophy to investigate and explain most marvels and prodigies. The logical extension of this movement would be that even those phenomena associated with the Last Days in prophecies and Scripture could be explained scientifically, with the assumption that God regularly can and does act through secondary causes.

In fact, the bleeding edge (to borrow a computer term)[39] of this project of naturalizing marvels was the attempt to apply scientific reasoning to the study of religion and, in particular, the apocalypse. The preferred mode of analysis for such an investigation was astrology. The thirteenth-century Franciscan Roger Bacon was the most outspoken advocate for the application of mathematics to eschatology. According to Bacon, astrology was particularly useful in looking to general changes on earth, such as changes in laws and sects, meaning that one could use the stars to predict such changes in religion as the arrival of Antichrist.[40] Bacon used astrological theories to conclude that only one more major religious sect was to appear on earth in the future. That final sect had to be the lying, magical sect of Antichrist. Bacon was confident that further study of the stars would tell him when that sect would arrive, and in the *Opus maius* he offered this advice to Pope Clement IV: "I know that if the Church should be willing to consider the sacred text and prophecies . . . and should order a study of the paths of astronomy, it would gain some idea of greater certainty regarding the time of Antichrist."[41]

After the Parisian condemnations of 1277, however, in which a number of astrological propositions were condemned, few were willing to take up Bacon's charge. Bishop Stephen Tempier's list of condemned propositions contained several dealing with astrology. His caricature of the science of the stars associated it with the worst sort of condemned fatalism: an affront on human free will and God's omnipotence.[42] Probably as a result, several authors in Paris around the year 1300 in fact expressed skepticism about the ways in which astrology might be used to predict the time of Antichrist's advent. Arnau de Vilanova, for example, was quite happy to use scriptural figures to set an exact date for Antichrist's arrival: 1378. Nonetheless, he completely dismissed astrologers' claims to be able to predict the time of the end, asserting, "Just as [God] acted supernaturally in the work of the world's creation, so, too, he will accomplish the world's consummation supernaturally."[43]

John of Paris, writing in response to Arnau's treatise, flatly denied that humans could have certain knowledge of the time of Antichrist's advent, whether using Scripture, prophecy, or astrology to calculate that time. John was willing, however, to use the movements of the stars to offer a conjecture of the world's age. That figure, in turn, he fitted to prophecies about how long the world would endure in order to conjecture that the world would end in some two hundred years.[44] All the same, John rejected the notion that astrology could generate a certain prediction of the time of Antichrist's advent.

Henry of Harclay, responding to both John's and Arnau's treatises, even more sharply attacked the claims that astrology—or any method of calculating—could predict the time of Antichrist's arrival. Ridiculing a number of apocalyptic prognostications, Henry thundered that the predictions of astrologers and other calculators were "*vanissimi.*"[45] And, concluding, he specifically stated that the apocalyptic signs of Mark 13: 24 (a darkening of the sun and moon) would be miraculous, and not natural eclipses.[46]

The message of all three authors was that end times were not susceptible to any kind of natural explanations or predictions based thereon, precisely what Matthew Paris had argued in 1250. In the mid-fourteenth century, one of England's most prominent astrologers would rush to proclaim that he had predicted the outbreak of plague and would spend pages using astrology to investigate the date of Creation, but he would shy away from any attempt to use astrology to predict the time of the end.[47] But by the fifteenth and sixteenth centuries, astrological predictions of the world's end were increasingly common. The plague writings of the mid-fourteenth century helped effect that change. They did so by presenting the plague ambiguously as both an apocalyptic sign and a natural event.

Plague as Apocalyptic Sign in Fourteenth-Century Texts

Indeed, earthquakes and other prodigies supported a sometimes open and sometimes implicit apocalyptic discourse in several fourteenth-century chronicles about the plague. By linking the plague and the portents surrounding it with other apocalyptic signs drawn from Revelation or the Gospels, or by quoting key prophecies and passages from Scripture, these chroniclers—usually writing in the immediate wake of the initial outbreak of plague—interpret the appearance of pestilence as one of several signs of the end.

A number of authors associated the plague with known apocalyptic prophecies. For example, the Irish chronicler John Clynn, who apparently perished in the plague himself, inserted in his chronicle the widely circulated Cedar of Lebanon prophecy, now said to have been revealed in a vision to a Cistercian monk in Tripoli in 1347.[48] Along with the now long-past falls of Tripoli and Acre, the prophecy foretold famines, great mortality, and other torments prior to a fifteen-year period of peace and then the final onslaught of Antichrist. Clynn followed up his quotation of the prophecy with the remark, "It is unheard of since the beginning of the world that so many men would have died in such a [short] time on earth, from pestilence, famine, or some other infirmity." And he made specific reference to an earthquake "which extended for thousands of miles, [and] toppled, absorbed, and overthrew cities, villages, and towns" and to the [subsequent?] pestilence that deprived these settlements of any inhabitants.[49] Thus, for Clynn, the earthquake was directly linked to the plague, and both numbered among the apocalyptic torments described in the Cedar of Lebanon prophecy.

Within this context, perhaps, are to be understood other signs and portents Clynn listed in the years prior to 1348. For the year 1337, for example, he described flooding, freezing weather, a sheep and cattle murrain, and the unexpected appearance of roses on willow trees in England during Lent (which were taken to various locations and displayed as a spectacle).[50] And for the year 1335, Clynn related that a large cross was erected in the square in Kilkenny, and many people had themselves branded with the sign of the cross (with a burning iron) as a sign of their pledge to go to the Holy Land. The Cedar of Lebanon prophecy Clynn would quote for 1348 predicted a "general passage by all the faithful" to the Holy Land following the times of tribulation. Looking back in 1348, those pledges too might be seen as a fulfillment of prophecy. The Cedar of Lebanon vision seems to have offered Clynn an overarching explanation for all the various signs he described. In pointing to a period of peace after torments, the prophecy could offer hope and comfort as well as provide meaning to the calamitous events.[51]

Scripture itself provided a key for understanding plague's apocalyptic meaning for other fourteenth-century authors. For example, John of Winterthur, a Swiss Franciscan, remarked upon an earthquake in the Austrian region of Carinthia that preceded the outbreak of the plague, as he traced the disease's progress from "lands overseas" to Christendom (although without describing any marvelous portents such as a rain of fire in the east). "The aforesaid earthquake and pestilence," he wrote, "are the evil harbingers of the final abyss and the tempest, according to the words of the Savior in the gospel: 'There will be earthquakes in various places, and pestilence, and famines, etc.'" (Matt. 24: 7; Luke 21: 11).[52] Another chronicler, William Dene, writing in the chronicle of the cathedral priory of Rochester, did not dwell on apocalyptic signs or portents before the plague. Nonetheless, as noted above, he specifically drew a line linking the demands imposed by now-scarce laborers after the plague to the work of Gog and Magog, God's enemies in the Last Days (Rev. 20: 8).[53] Chroniclers like John of Winterthur and William Dene described the events of the mid-fourteenth century as fulfilling the predictions of Scripture.

Heinrich of Herford, one of the authors quoted at the outset of this essay, brought both Scripture and prophecy to bear upon his analysis of plague's role as harbinger of apocalypse. In his chronicle, tracing the world's history up to 1355, he, too, left several pointed indications that the plague and other current happenings were to be understood in apocalyptic terms. First, like John of Winterthur and William Dene, he cited scriptural passages that pointed to the Last Days. Immediately before he described the earthquake and rain of fire, serpents, toads that preceded the plague (in his entry for 1345), Heinrich lamented the sorry state of the world around him, a world full of "dissensions, rebellions, conspiracies, plots, and intrigues . . . among both secular and regular clergy"; "disturbances of young against old, ignoble against noble in many cities, monasteries, and congregations"; simony, to the extent that clerics traded appointments "for money, women, and sometimes for concubines" or gambled for them over dice; and many "disturbances and contests over kingdoms, principalities, archbishoprics, bishoprics, prebends, and other things of that kind." To Heinrich, it looked as if things were turning out "just as the apostle foretold in 2 Timothy 3[: 1–7] and 2 Corinthians 12[: 20]."[54] The references were apocalyptic. In 2 Corinthians 12: 20, Paul had written, "For I fear, lest, when I come, I shall not find you such as I would." Promising that "in the last days perilous times shall come," Paul had detailed in the overtly apocalyptic 2 Timothy 3 the selfishness, disobedience, dissensions, and lawlessness that would reign near the end. Even before he began to discuss the plague and the prodigies surrounding its appearance, Heinrich implied that current events pointed to just those "perilous times" of which the apostle had warned.

Second, Heinrich made oblique reference to other apocalyptic prophecies, namely to the same Cedar of Lebanon prophecy that John Clynn inserted into his chronicle when he described the plague's progress in Ireland. The reference came in Heinrich's one hundredth, and final, chapter, under his entry for the year 1349, in which he described a number of disturbing events: the appearance of a ghost or phantasm, the killing of the Jews for the charge of well-poisoning (a claim Heinrich strongly disputed), the progress of plague, and the appearance of the flagellants. Heinrich condemned the flagellants for their contumacy and disrespect for the clergy, even describing how they had killed two Dominican friars. He opened his discussion of the obstreperous flagellants by saying, "In this year, a race [*gens*] without a head suddenly arose in all parts of Germany, causing universal admiration for the suddenness of their appearance and for their huge numbers."[55] He added that they were called without a head "as if prophetically," both because they literally had no head or leader and because they figuratively had no head or prudence guiding them. The phrase "race without a head" comes from the Cedar of Lebanon prophecy. This prophecy, as mentioned above, described a period of torment, then a fifteen-year period of peace, and finally its end when "there will be heard news of Antichrist."[56] Thus in dubbing the flagellants the "race without a head," Heinrich was inviting his readers to see their appearance as part of the apocalyptic scenario laid out in the Cedar of Lebanon vision. In fact, Heinrich had already specifically connected the flagellants with the "race without a head" and the appearance of Antichrist in the introductory matter to his hundredth chapter. There, in a summary list of the notable events that had occurred around the year 1348, he simply stated, "A race of flagellants, without a head, foretold the advent of Antichrist."[57]

In addition to quoting Scripture and prophecy to link up his own times to end times, Heinrich further implicitly sounded an apocalyptic alarm simply by the sheer number of signs, portents, torments, and *mirabilia* that he described in the final two decades of his chronicle (ca. 1337–55). Beginning in 1337, Heinrich told of a rain of blood, the births of several monsters, a plague of locusts (echoes of Revelation 9: 3?), visions, phantasms, conspiracies, and rebellions, as well as the earthquake, fire from heaven, and rain of toads surrounding the outbreak of plague. In fact, in the introduction to the final chapter of his chronicle, Heinrich pointedly observed that "the beginning of the reign of this Charles [IV of Bohemia, r. 1346–78] seems to be memorable on account of the number of monsters, portents, and other singular happenings that then appeared."[58] He then strung together a list of all the various portents and *mirabilia* that he had already mentioned or would describe in the pages to come. Heinrich did not here specify what we are to make of this clustering of signs, but, given his quotations of Scripture and prophecy, we are perhaps to conclude that, like Matthew Paris in 1250, Heinrich saw the increased number of marvelous phenomena as an indication that the world was nearing its end.

In the final pages of Heinrich's chronicle, however, he interjected that note of caution sounded so frequently in medieval discussions of the end's timing.[59] "And note," he wrote, "that this eighth year of Charles's reign was the 5317th from the beginning of the world, the 3661st from Noah's exit from the ark," and so on, listing counts of years for various other chronological schemes.[60] As Richard Landes has pointed out for the early Middle Ages, such countdowns were inherently eschatological, by either explicitly or implicitly allowing readers to calculate the number of years left until the world's fated 6000th year.[61] Heinrich here followed Bede's calculation of the age of the world, a figure much smaller than other estimates of its age and one that put the end of the sixth (and presumably final) millennium several centuries distant even from Heinrich's time. Further—and here Heinrich showed his realization that this type of countdown could be apocalyptic—Heinrich felt compelled to continue with a discussion of the unknowability of the time of the end. "The time remaining in this sixth age," he reminded his readers, "is known only to God. It is not for men to know the times or moments that the father has reserved to his power" (Acts 1: 7).[62] Indeed, in Augustinian fashion, he stated that the seventh age of repose for the blessed, "its door quietly opened," had begun with the sixth age and ran along concurrently with it.[63] While Heinrich was quite willing to string together contemporary apocalyptic signs and quotations from Scripture, he showed understandable and customary caution in definitely announcing the immediacy of the end.

Although this sort of caution frequently accompanied apocalyptic predictions, the explicit pointers to eschatological texts and prophecies in the chronicles of Heinrich of Herford, John Clynn, John of Winterthur, and William Dene strongly suggest that the constellation of bizarre *mirabilia* described by other chroniclers, such as the earthquakes, hail, and rains of toads and snakes with which I began this essay, were also meant to have apocalyptic echoes. Thunder, hail, and fire falling from heaven figure not simply among the plagues of Egypt (Ex. 9: 23–26), but also in Revelation, in which the first trumpet blast of the seven angels with seven trumpets results in hail and fire mingled with blood (Rev. 8: 7), and the pouring out of the seventh of the vials of God's wrath brings about earthquakes, thunderings, and a plague of enormous hailstones that destroy the city of Babylon (Rev. 16: 21). Indeed, in the letter of Louis Heyligen quoted by the anonymous Flemish chronicler, the reference to "thunder, lightning, and hail of marvelous size," may well be a nod to Revelation 16, in which "every [hail]stone [was] about the weight of a talent" (Rev. 16: 21).[64] The same anonymous chronicler even more ominously described a hailstorm in 1349 in which the egg-sized hailstones had faces, eyes, and tails.[65]

Fire and smoke were other apocalyptic signs featured in fourteenth-century texts about the plague. Stinking smoke attendant on heavenly fire appears in both the Neuberg monastery chronicle and Heyligen's letter among the causes of the outbreak of the plague in the east. The image of fire raining down from the heavens as described in words in these fourteenth-century chronicles could have triggered visual memories of illustrations connected with Revelation.[66] God sends fire from heaven to destroy Satan's army after his final unloosing in Revelation 20: 9. And fetid smoke emerges from the bottomless pit, along with locusts, in Revelation 9: 2–3.

Frogs, too, have scriptural resonances. They number among the plagues of Egypt (the second plague, Exodus 8: 1–15; also Psalms 78 and 105), along with a plague of festering boils (Exodus 9: 8–12). The rain of toads and frogs in fourteenth-century writings about the Black Death also would remind readers of the unclean spirits of Revelation 16: 13, spirits in the form of frogs (*in modo ranarum*) that issue from the mouths of the dragon, the beast, and the false prophet. These frogs, too, are depicted in illustrations of Revelation, and commentators equated the frogs' croaking voices with the blasphemous words issuing from the mouths of the preachers of Antichrist.[67]

Thus, the unusual precipitation of fire, hail, snakes, and toads reported in the chronicles of Heinrich of Herford and the Neuberg monastery and in the letter of Louis Heyligen had an implicitly apocalyptic meaning.[68] The message did not need to be spelled out. With or without quotations from Scripture and prophecy, such chroniclers presented the plague in a decidedly apocalyptic fashion.

Earthquakes, Frogs, Snakes, and Storms as Part
of a Natural Explanation of Plague

If the frogs, hail, earthquakes, and other unusual weather surrounding the outbreak of the plague in the east could be read as apocalyptic portents, they nonetheless figure as well in fourteenth-century scientific explanations of the plague. In fact, the whole cluster of bizarre signs associated with the initial outbreak of plague in the chronicles of Heinrich of Herford and others finds its way into medical and scientific treatises as well. These phenomena form part of the natural causes of plague detailed in fourteenth-century scientific writings about the disease. Further, the very chroniclers who insert apocalyptic portents into their treatment of plague sometimes explain these signs using natural philosophy. In scientific writings as well as in monastic chronicles, fourteenth-century authors presented the plague as simultaneously a sign of God's final wrath and a phenomenon capable of receiving a natural explanation.

The best-known scientific discussion of plague from the mid-fourteenth century is the treatise composed by the medical faculty of the University of Paris. As historians frequently note, the Paris physicians blamed the plague on the famous "triple conjunction" of Saturn, Jupiter, and Mars on March 20, 1345.[69] But this conjunction forms only a part of the faculty's analysis of the causes of the plague, which they argue had both a remote cause (the heavens) and a proximal cause (the earth). The conjunction of March 1345 was the remote and universal cause of the plague, and it had the effect, argued the Paris physicians, of drawing up warm, moist vapors from the earth, which were corrupted by Mars (which ignited them and particularly caused corruption because it was retrograde) and Jupiter (whose quartile aspect with Mars [?] caused a bad disposition in the air inimical to human nature). The configuration of the heavens also had the effect of generating many winds, particularly warm, moist southern winds. Thus the triple conjunction served as a universal remote cause of plague.[70]

The Paris doctors also described a more proximal cause of plague, namely air corrupted by bad vapors (also a result of the triple conjunction) and spread about by the south wind. Corrupt air was even more harmful to the body than corrupt food or water, asserted the doctors, because it could more rapidly penetrate to the lungs and heart. Such pestiferous vapors could arise from stagnant water or unburied bodies or could even escape directly from the earth during an earthquake. When they rose and mixed with the air, the whole air would be corrupted, and an epidemic would result.[71] In other words, earthquakes functioned not simply as signs of divine wrath, but in a medical understanding of plague they also were the source of noxious vapors that corrupted the air, causing disease in humans.

Another proximal cause of plague in the Paris medical faculty's opinion was a change in weather. Here, the physicians were following good Hippocratic teaching, which looked to changes in weather as a cause of epidemics. In particular, unusual weather throughout the four seasons could produce a pestilential year, the Paris doctors argued, and they noted that the preceding winter had been warmer and rainier than usual. Further, they feared that the next spring might bring yet another round of pestilence should the winter again prove abnormally warm and wet.[72] While the Paris physicians do not directly mention hail as a feature of plague-generating weather, they nonetheless finger an excess of warm rains (presumably some of which would be accompanied by thunder, lightning, and hail) as culprits in a pestilential year.

Furthermore, the Paris doctors, like the chroniclers with whom I began, added a geographical component to their description of plague's origins. The Paris physicians pointed to the south and east as the ultimate source of plague and the location of the most noteworthy phenomena associated with the corruption of air and outbreak of pestilence. The physicians had stated that the upcoming year might well be another plague year should the winter again be warm and wet. Nonetheless, they asserted that any such plague would be less dangerous in France than in "southern or eastern regions" because the conjunctions and other causes detailed in their treatise would have more effect in those regions. And, they noted, there had been "numerous exhalations and inflammations, such as a *draco* and falling stars."[73] The sky had in fact taken on a distinct yellow and red tone from the scorched vapors, the doctors declared, and there had been frequent lightning, thunderings, and intense winds from the south, carrying great amounts of dust with them. These winds, said the doctors, "are worse than all others, [in] quickly and more completely spreading bodies of putrefaction, especially strong earthquakes, [and] a multitude of fish and dead animals at the seashores, and in many regions trees [have been] covered by dust." Further, the doctors noted that "some say they have seen a multitude of frogs and reptiles which are generated from putrefaction." All of these, the faculty of medicine wrote, "appear to precede great putrefaction in the air and the earth."[74] "No wonder if we fear that there is a future epidemic coming!"[75] Because the work of the south wind was so crucial in spreading corruption in their explanation, the doctors implied that corruption would arise in the south and east and be dispersed by the winds.

Certainly the faculty of medicine in Paris were no scientific revolutionaries. Their explanation of epidemics arising from corrupted air was completely standard according to Galenic medical theory. And their list of signs and causes of corruption, from unusual weather to earthquakes to frogs and dead fish, again was completely standard. Scholastic science held that frogs, toads, snakes, and worms could be generated from corrupt matter and that such animals were inherently poisonous.[76] In early modern Europe, there would be a strong association between toads and the plague, and persons of all social strata would wear amulets containing various preparations made from toads and arsenic to guard against pestilence.[77]

Nonetheless, the way in which these phenomena cluster together in the Paris medical faculty's treatise is striking. In fifteen lines (of printed text), we move from a reference to southern and eastern regions, to falling stars, to a reddened sky, to thunder and lightning, to dust storms, to earthquakes, to dead fish, trees overcome by dust, and at last to frogs and other reptiles.[78] One could just as easily be reading the work of Heinrich of Herford as that of the Paris medical faculty. A reader might indeed think these were the "signs in the sun, and in the moon, and in the stars" of Luke 21: 25. And yet they fit entirely within the medical explanation of the plague arising from corruption in the air.

Earthquakes occupy the central position in another fourteenth-century scientific explanation of the plague, a *quaestio* entitled "Whether the mortality of these years is due to divine command or from some natural cause?"[79] The author of this treatise dismissed the astrological explanation of the plague that featured so prominently in the Paris physicians' treatise (and in other treatises) with the remark that the plague had lasted much longer than the conjunction (some five or six years, whereas Saturn spends at most two and a half years in any one sign of the zodiac).[80] Rather, the author of the *quaestio*, following "Ypocrates," concluded that the most probable natural cause of the current mortality was a "corrupt and venomous exhalation from the earth, which infected the air in various parts of the world and which, when breathed in by humans, immediately suffocated them with a manner of extinction."[81] He noted that air that is shut up in the earth in caverns or in the bowels of the earth is corrupted by earthly fumes and becomes poisonous to humans, as happens in the case of wells that have long been sealed up. When they are opened, the first people who go down into them frequently suffocate, causing ignorant *vulgares* to assume that there is a basilisk down in the well.[82] The author also explained that earthquakes were caused by "the exhalation of fumes closed up in the bowels of the earth, which, when they beat against the sides of the earth and cannot get out, shake and move the earth, as is apparent from natural philosophy."[83] In regards to the current epidemic, he specifically cited the Carinthia earthquake on the feast of St. Paul in 1347 (the same earth-quake mentioned by Heinrich of Herford and others), noting that the plague had begun its journey through German-speaking lands in Carinthia after the earthquake there.[84] He blamed the actions of the winds for spreading the cor-rupt air about haphazardly, explaining the desultory pattern of the plague's spread.

The *quaestio*'s author continues with a rather curious observation. In further proof that the fumes inside the earth were noxious to humans, the author noted that "according to Avicenna and Albertus [Magnus], in some earthquakes men are changed (*transsubstanciati*) into rocks, and chiefly into salt rocks on account of the strong mineral virtue in terrestrial vapors."[85] If the vapors released by earthquakes could effect such a dramatic transub-stantiation, surely they also could initiate a pestilential corruption of the air. What is most remarkable in this statement is not so much the logic, but the assertion that earthquakes can change men into rocks. While the author al-most certainly had in mind the biblical story of Lot's wife being changed into a pillar of salt, Sodom and Gomorrah in Genesis 19 were destroyed in a rain of fire and brimstone from heaven, not an earthquake. The whole dis-cussion is, however, vaguely reminiscent of the chronicle of the monastery of Neuberg, which described both an earthquake and the subsequent poisonous vapors that changed men into stone in the east, followed by rains of fire, poi-sonous snakes, and worms, and finally the outbreak of the plague.[86] Perhaps the author of this treatise was aware of the same traditions that informed the Neuberg chronicler's description of men being transformed into stones. He presumably was writing in some southern German or Austrian region because he mentions specifically only the Carinthia earthquake (and indeed makes ref-erence to the destruction of Villach, as does the Neuberg chronicle). But the author of this *quaestio* offers an explanation of the phenomenon drawn from natural philosophy, probably from commentaries on Aristotle's *Meteorology*.

The medieval scholastic understanding of earthquakes in fact depended upon the explanation put forth in the second book of Aristotle's *Meteorology*. Aristotle had explained that earthquakes arise when the sun warms an earth made moist by rains, giving rise to winds (evaporation) inside the earth, which causes the earthquake. The most violent earthquakes result in those places where the sea flows into subterranean caverns, thereby impeding the outward flow of wind. As a result, a great amount of wind is compressed into a small space, from which it eventually breaks forth with great violence.[87] Be-cause earthquakes are generated by moisture, evaporation, and wind in this theory, they are a species of weather.

Medieval commentators elaborated upon Aristotle's theories. Albertus

Magnus discussed earthquakes in book 3 of his *De meteoris*, under the general rubric of impressions caused by cool, dry vapors. According to Albert, earthquakes happened when dry vapors trapped within the earth were too heavy to escape easily. He noted that the vapors that were emitted from the earth during an earthquake were frequently laden with dust, causing the sun, moon, and stars to appear bloody or blackened. Furthermore, Albert stated that the vapors enclosed within the earth, deprived of light and air, possessed the nature of poison. In the days before an earthquake, such vapors would seep out through the "pores" of the earth and kill animals that kept their mouths to the ground, such as sheep. Then, after a large eruption of such vapors in an earthquake, a pestilence would almost invariably follow. As if to confirm this line of reasoning, Albert added that he himself had witnessed an incident in Padua in which a long-closed well was opened up. The first and second persons to enter the well to clean it out died instantly "from the vapor of that cavern," while a third, who merely leaned into the well, was indisposed for the next two days.[88]

In Pierre d'Ailly's late fourteenth-century treatise on weather (*De impressionibus aeris*), the discussion of earthquakes immediately follows a treatment of winds. D'Ailly attributed earthquakes to the actions of warm, dry vapors enclosed within the earth (*spiritus*), which, on account of their subtle nature, seek to escape from the earth. When their free escape is impeded, an earthquake results.[89] He explained a number of phenomena associated with earthquakes based upon the actions of these vapors, including the strange noises that frequently accompany earthquakes (rumblings and the fact that in Aristotle's phrase, "the earth seems to moo") and the sun's darkened appearance during earthquakes.[90] At times, an earthquake could cause both vapors and stones to be thrown from the earth, in a boiling fashion, as vapors brought small stones up with them, and those stones falling caused other stones to dislodge.[91] Thunderous rumblings, darkening of the sun, and a rain of stones—many of the signs associated with plague by chroniclers—all could result from the actions of earthquake-causing vapors, according to d'Ailly.

Further, d'Ailly compared earthquakes to sicknesses in the human body, associating earthquakes with disease metaphorically, just as the chroniclers, Paris doctors, and anonymous *quaestio* had associated earthquakes literally with the plague. First, following Aristotle, d'Ailly noted an earthquake's similitude to bodily paralysis or tremors in animals.[92] In such cases, d'Ailly said, a superheated vapor within the body (the animal's or the earth's) causes a trembling motion. Second, d'Ailly adds that a similar effect is sometimes seen in humans after they produce urine, when subtle vapors sneak into the body through the natural paths of the urine (*per vias naturales urinales*), disperse throughout the other inner parts of the body, and cause a tremor of the whole body as they exit through the pores.[93] D'Ailly also explained the pattern of aftershocks following an earthquake by comparison to disease, in this case tertian or quartan fever, in which the entire amount of the febrile vapor seeking expulsion was not released in the original fever (or earthquake).[94] Earthquakes thus behaved much as sicknesses in the body of the earth in which excessively warm vapors were expelled from the earth's body. By equation of macrocosm and microcosm, earthquakes pointed to sicknesses in the human body and in fact were noted to be a cause of epidemics.[95]

Earthquakes, bizarre weather, toads, worms, and serpents all featured in medical analyses of plague because they caused or resulted from the corruption that was the epidemic's cause. Yet these phenomena were also the very signs that gave plague its apocalyptic punch. Indeed, the earthquakes, thunder and lightning, rains of blood, worms, and snakes, and the other marvelous phenomena that show up in fourteenth-century writings about the plague had multiple significances. There was an overlap between their apocalyptic and scientific connotations even within the same treatise. Such language set up a chain of associations in readers' minds, so that an earthquake could at the same time serve to release corrupt air and to point to Matthew 24 or other apocalyptic passages in Scripture. By and large the authors of such treatises left these overlaps unexplained without comment. These phenomena neither served as natural causes of the apocalypse, as they might have for Roger Bacon, nor appeared specifically as supernatural, and therefore apocalyptic, signs, as they might have for Matthew Paris or the Parisian authors around 1300. The very ambiguity of these portents, as I will argue, was profoundly important. Perhaps nowhere is this overlap and ambiguity between the natural and the supernatural more apparent than in the chronicle of Heinrich of Herford.

Heinrich of Herford's Chronicle

Heinrich of Herford's *Liber de rebus memorabilioribus* is particularly noteworthy for the number of signs and portents the author describes in the final decades of his chronicle, which ends in 1355. As noted above, Heinrich makes specific mention of a cluster of portents at the start of the reign of the emperor Charles of Bohemia in 1348.[96] Given his citation of apocalyptic texts from 2 Timothy and 2 Corinthians, his use of other apocalyptic language,[97] and his deliberate pointing to the cluster of portents around the time of the plague, it is apparent that Heinrich meant to give his text an apocalyptic slant. And yet, Heinrich also frequently appended to his descriptions of just such marvels explanations drawn from natural philosophy. No longer are these portents seen through the lens of an either/or dichotomy either as natural events or as supernatural apocalyptic signs. In Heinrich's chronicle, the same events are often uncomfortably and unexplainedly both.

For example, for the year 1337, Heinrich described in immediate succession the following prodigies: a rain of blood in Erfurt, a nine-year-old girl bearing a child by her father, and the birth of a baby girl with breasts, pubic hair, and menstrual periods. Then he immediately quoted a passage from Albertus Magnus's *Physica* in which Albert explained just such a monstrous birth. Such monsters, according to Albert, result from an abundance of the material of the first seed and the strength of the heat and virtue forming the infant. "And in my own times," Albert wrote—and Heinrich quoted him—"there was displayed a girl who had been born with breasts and with hair under her arms and in her groin, and her mother asserted that she also suffered from a monthly flow, which without doubt happened on account of the heat that formed and matured [the fetus]."[98] This same principle is at work in the births of children who already have teeth, according to Albert. The sexually precocious girls of 1337 thus could be explained by natural causes. Heinrich did not offer here an explanation—marvelous or scientific—for the rain of blood in Erfurt, although he was careful to note that he himself had seen "its drops captured in a white linen cloth."[99] (The same sort of attention to first-person observation marks the pages of Albert's treatises also.) Several pages later, however, the reader is again inundated with a wave of portents and with a scientific explanation of them.

Under the year 1345, Heinrich opened his discussion of the Black Death, with his quotation of a letter describing the earthquake in Carinthia on the feast of the conversion of St. Paul, a rain of fire in the land of the Turks, and a rain of toads and snakes. Under the same year, he recounted the stories of a number of battles, the appearance of a devil (*dyabolus*) who killed or harassed several men in the household of one Thyderic Sobben, and ghosts (*fantasmata*) who were carousing in a church in Mendene.[100] In the following brief entry for the year 1346, Heinrich noted some important political events: the election of Charles of Bohemia as king of the Romans and the death of King Philip of France. The bulk of his remarks for the year 1346, however, concerned yet another marvelous phenomenon, this time the birth in Westphalia of a lamb with two heads, the lower one a lamb's head and the upper one a bird's head. The monster seemed "both to have been a portent and to be attributed to the virtue of the stars." [101] Heinrich again appended quotations from Albertus Magnus's *Physica* and *De meteoris* offering explications of the birth of monsters. These quotations, however, can apply not simply to the two-headed lamb that Heinrich has just described, but also to the portents in the east in the letter he had quoted with respect to the outbreak of plague.

Following the description of the two-headed lamb, Heinrich quoted three passages from Albertus Magnus. In the first, from the *Physica*, Albert explained monstrous births similar to the two-headed lamb Heinrich described, using as an example the birth of piglets with human faces. In such a case where the offspring had the characteristics of two very different beings, the operation of the heavenly bodies had to be at work, for the seeds of humans and pigs (or, mutatis mutandis, sheep and birds) were too different for any progeny to be engendered. Rather, the seeds would mutually corrupt one another. But the planets could induce the pig's seed to take on a form outside of its ordinary capacity, as, for example, when the sun, moon, and some other planets were all in a certain region of Aries and no human could be generated. [102] Presumably, the lamb's bird head was formed in this manner. Next, and with no explanation of why, Heinrich quoted two passages from Albertus Magnus's *De meteoris*. Both dealt with the generation of animals in an unusual manner, but not this time with two-headed sheep, human-headed pigs, or even pig-headed humans. Rather, the two passages Heinrich lined up here describe the generation of animals in the clouds, with resulting rains of small frogs, fish, worms, and, even once, a calf. Heinrich seems to be thinking back to his entry for the previous year about the rain of toads and snakes in the east that preceded the outbreak of plague.

According to the passages Heinrich quoted from Albert, these phenomena, too, were susceptible of natural explanations. As heat causes rainwater to evaporate, Albert had argued, it can draw up a little earthly matter mixed in with the moisture. That mixture, once taken up into the air, begins to harden and to become skin. The continual exposure to heat produces a spirit within that skin, to which the virtue of the stars adds a sensitive soul, so that an animal results. The beings so generated are usually aquatic animals like frogs, fish, and worms because in such rains the watery element prevails over the earthy element. [103] As in the case of the calf that fell from the sky, however, the body of a perfect animal could be formed in the clouds, a fact to be explained by the virtue of the stars. [104] The joint actions of evaporation and the stars, thus—although Heinrich does not explicitly draw this connection—could be responsible for the marvelous rain of toads and serpents that preceded the plague as well.

The same conflation of the natural and the apocalyptic comes in Heinrich's treatment of the flagellants. On the one hand, his most overtly apocalyptic language comes in his description of the flagellants, of whom he wrote, "[the appearance of] a race of flagellants without a head foretold the advent of Antichrist."[105] At the same time, here, too, comes his most blatant scientific explanation of a presumed apocalyptic sign. Heinrich dwelt at length on the flagellants (for more than four pages in the modern edition), whom he condemned as imprudent, defiant, and a corrupting influence. He apparently was drawing on firsthand experience of their rituals, saying that he himself had seen the sharp points at the ends of their whips embedded in their flesh so that they could not easily be pulled out and noting with the empathy of one who had been there that "it would take a heart of stone to watch such behavior without shedding tears."[106] He also quoted at length (perhaps in its entirety) a treatise on the flagellants composed by one Gerhardus de Cosvelde, "rector of the scholars in the city of Münster in Westphalia."[107] This remarkable treatise offered an explanation of the flagellant movement based entirely on astrology.

Gerhardus's analysis of the flagellants rested upon the horoscope he erected for the moment of the sun's entry into Aries on March 12, 1349, the beginning of the astrological year. (The horoscope is also reproduced in Heinrich's chronicle.) For Gerhardus, the key component of this horoscope was the third mundane house, beginning with Aries and containing the planets of the sun, Saturn, Mars, and Mercury.[108] According to Gerhardus, the third mundane house presided over faith, religion, and mutations of religion. The sun was in a position of particular strength in this horoscope (Gerhardus indeed dubs the sun the "lord of the year"), and its position in the mundane house signifying religion meant that it would "multiply a religion and sect."[109] Further, Gerhardus declared that the new sect foretold by the horoscope would have its origins "in the east," since Aries was an eastern sign having significance mainly over Germany, according to Alchabitius, author of a widely used medieval textbook of astrology. Thus the new sect would thrive chiefly in Germany.[110] The fact that Mars and Mercury were in conjunction in the horoscope signified beatings with whips and the effusion of blood.[111] Because the two planets were in Jupiter's *domus*, their influence would lead men to join this sect—and not without hypocrisy (all attributed to Alchabitius).[112]

Every detail of the flagellants' activities finds an astrological explanation in the treatise Heinrich quotes. The flagellants wear a grey hood before their eyes, and thus a saturnine aspect, because in the horoscope Saturn is in the sign of Aries, which has significance for the head.[113] In their rituals, they "fall down to the ground horribly" because the planets signifying the flagellants are in one of the "falling" (*cadens*) mundane houses.[114] The cause of their (partial) nudity is found in the fact that Saturn is both combust (i.e., within a given number of degrees of the sun) and in Aries, the sign of its dejection. Their strange garments arise from the influence of Venus, which is in Saturn's *domus* in the horoscope and is a signifier of women's clothing.[115] The flagellants claim to be inspired by a stone tablet brought down from heaven by an angel. This "fiction" is caused by the falling Saturn (i.e., the planet is in its dejection and in a cadent mundane house), which signifies about heavy things like stones, as well as about oracles and the apparition of secret things.[116] The lying nature of the sect, as well as its instability, result from the baleful appearance of the sign of Scorpio in the midheaven (the tenth mundane house in a horoscope), for Scorpio signifies sorrow, lying, and instability. The fact that Scorpio appears in the tenth mundane house, the *domus* of Jupiter, results in people believing the flagellants' lies and calling them miracles, "on account of Jupiter's faith."[117] In short, Gerhardus concludes, "I say that in my estimation *this sect is purely natural*, and that they are acting under a species of fury called mania. . . . And the sect will not last long, but will end quickly and with confusion and infamy."[118] The apocalyptic "race without a head" is now explained entirely by the stars. If this is not Heinrich's conclusion also, he gives us no sign here, for he moves immediately to a discussion of political events and leaves the flagellants behind.[119]

Even the succeeding passages in Heinrich's text, however, leave the reader poised between marvelous and scientific explanations of events. Under the year 1351, Heinrich described an unusual plague in the town of Hameln. A pit was being dug and cleared out in grounds belonging to one of the town's citizens when one of the workers suddenly fell down and at once expired. A second worker went into the pit to retrieve the body and suffered the same fate. The word quickly spread, but no one knew the cause of the plague. A third worker was sent into the pit, but this time with a rope tied around his waist, so that he could quickly be hauled out. Again, the pit proved poisonous, but the worker was able to give a sign as he was becoming stiff and stupefied and was pulled out half-dead. A fourth worker entered the pit and died as the first two had. Opinion was divided, according to Heinrich, on the cause of this singular plague. Some leaned towards a marvelous explanation. They maintained that there must be a basilisk in the pit, able to kill instantly by its breath or even its very glance. Others tended towards a scientific analysis. They held that the earth in the pit had been poisoned by the fact that in the past there had been many latrines in the same place. At length, the pit was filled with a brothlike mixture of boiling water and flour, and the plague was ended, either by the death of the basilisk or by the purging of the poisons from the pit.[120]

This story very closely parallels passages from scientific treatises on earthquakes. In the *De meteoris*, for example, Albertus Magnus claims to have witnessed just such an incident when a long-closed well in Padua was opened up, a happening he attributed not to a basilisk, but to the venomous nature of vapors remaining enclosed within the earth for a long time.[121] There is also a like passage in the anonymous *quaestio* attributing the Black Death to earthquakes. The author of that *quaestio*, like Albert, adduced such a scenario to prove how poisonous were the fumes released by earthquakes. He further remarked that ignorant people attributed deaths just like those Heinrich here described to the existence of a basilisk in the pit, whereas the explanation was properly to be found in the poisonous vapors enclosed within the earth.[122] Heinrich is clearly aware of both sorts of explanations as he describes the venomous pit of Hameln. Just as he does with the monstrous births and rain of worms and snakes in his chronicle, however, he refuses here to give the nod to either a purely marvelous or a purely scientific explanation. This little "plague" in Hameln, like the universal bubonic plague, is ambiguous in Heinrich's chronicle, capable of multiple interpretations. In the case of the little Hameln plague, Heinrich offers us two competing, and by implication mutually exclusive, explanations. Either there is a basilisk in the pit or the latrines once on that site poisoned the soil. In the case of the universal pestilence, however, the interpretation is not posed in either/or terms. We may understand the earthquakes, fire from heaven, rain of toads, and pestilence *at the same time* as proceeding from God's wrath, as being signs of the approaching end, and as resulting from natural causes.

Multiple Meanings and the Trend to Naturalize the Apocalypse

Why might plague in the minds of fourteenth-century authors bear such a multivalent analysis? Why might one aspect of a description of the plague—frogs, say—carry us effortlessly from biblical imagery (Exodus and Revelation) to natural philosophy? Why does the same cluster of phenomena (earthquakes, frogs, worms, rains of fire) pop up as readily in a natural philosopher's analysis of the disease as in an apocalyptic letter about marvelous prodigies in distant and nearby lands? How is it that an author like Heinrich of Herford came to move effortlessly from apocalyptic texts to Albertus Magnus's *De meteoris?*

First, nature was not a category separable from theology. "Caeli ennarrant gloriam dei" (The heavens proclaim the glory of God; Ps. 18: 2). For medieval Christians, the world was God's handiwork, and any effort to understand the world—such as natural philosophy—came square up against the fact that nature was the fabric of God's plan. That meant that the earth was never just the earth, but that even for a naturalizing author such as Roger Bacon the world was also the orb of the *mappaemundi*, the area in which God's plan of salvation unfolded, sometimes literally—as in the Ebstorff map—the body of Christ. Any time one mapped events on the earth, one was fitting them into a geography and a chronology put in place by the Creator. Place, time, and event all had eschatological meaning. The sorts of slippages in meaning and free associations I have been detailing here were the logical outgrowth of this cosmology. Once an author began to map a phenomenon like the plague onto that orb, he was entangled in an endless string of associations and cross-references. If plague began in the east and moved toward the west, one could not help but think of both Prester John and Gog and Magog, of the potential Christians and the feared enemies of end times. If the plague was accompanied by earthquakes, one's mind was drawn to both Matthew 24 and Galenic medicine. One could follow a trail of snakes and worms that led from apocalyptic portents to meteorology to medicine and finally to the geography of Gog and Magog.

It is not surprising that the same cluster of phenomena appear in monastic chronicles and medical discussions of the plague. An event like plague could not be understood entirely apart from God. Once an author began to describe plague with the language of natural philosophy, miasma-generating earthquakes inevitably shaded into apocalyptic earthquakes, and corrupt vapors inside the earth began to look like corrupt enemies within Christendom. Existing eschatology shaped and informed the map on which fourteenth-century Christians plotted the epidemic's course. While mapping can indeed represent the act of possession, of physically and intellectually grasping space, mapping the fourteenth-century Black Death rather inserted it into an orb already freighted with meaning, where earthquakes, plague, frogs, and hail hovered in a polysemic limbo between physical undoing and apocalyptic unveiling.

Second, the ambiguity of the portents in the fourteenth-century plague treatises must be seen additionally as a species of caution in predicting the time of the end, whether reading portents or using astrology or some other branch of natural philosophy to do so. By leaving open the question of whether this plague and these earthquakes were a sign of end times or simply a manifestation of a bad run of weather, fourteenth-century authors could hedge their bets. Heinrich of Herford softens his quotations from 2 Timothy, 2 Corinthians, and the Cedar of Lebanon vision by offering a horoscope explaining how the action of the heavens could engender the appearance of "the race without a head." Flagellants now appear as sufferers of a form of mania and perhaps not as the harbingers of Antichrist. John Clynn reproduces the apocalyptic Cedar of Lebanon vision, yet leaves blank pages at the end of his chronicle "for the continuation of this work, if perhaps in the future any human witness should remain, or any member of the human race."[123] The Paris doctors mention falling stars, thunder, lightning, earthquakes, and frogs, yet set these apocalyptic emblems within a clearly scientific context. These multivalent signs allowed fourteenth-century authors safely to predict and not predict the end at the same time.

This reluctance to come down firmly on one side or the other is apparent in the plague writings discussed above, texts that hover between natural and apocalyptic explanations of the plague. The Paris physicians, for example, end their discussion of the plague's astrological and earthly causes with the remark that epidemics sometimes proceed from God's will.[124] The author of the *quaestio* on earthquakes suggests in his introductory question that there is an either/or opposition between a divine cause of the plague and a natural one. At the end of the *quaestio*, however, he collapses that distinction, noting that God can as easily lift a naturally caused plague as he can one proceeding from supernatural causes.[125] The portents mentioned by chroniclers like Heinrich of Herford meet in the same chronicle sometimes with an apocalyptic interpretation and sometimes with one drawn from natural philosophy. And in the chronicle of Neuberg monastery, apocalyptic-sounding fire falling from heaven, a rain of snakes and worms, and the changing of men into stones are all explained as resulting from "a malign impression of the superior bodies acting as efficient cause."[126]

In their very caution, however, the authors of these plague treatises played a pivotal role in allowing a rehabilitation of the thirteenth-century attempts to naturalize the apocalypse. Unwilling to call the plague definitely either an apocalyptic sign or a natural event, mid-fourteenth-century authors simply had it both ways. In so doing, they collapsed the post-1277 distinction that insisted—as had John of Paris, Arnau de Vilanova, and Henry of Harclay—that the apocalypse would be a supernatural event and therefore could not be predicted by natural philosophy or astrology. The unspoken implication in plague writings is that there are scientific explanations behind the portents associated with the apocalypse and that, insofar as it is possible, God will work through natural causes in the destruction of the world. Thus one might indeed use natural philosophy to investigate the apocalypse. The very hesitancy of fourteenth-century plague authors to announce the end thus opened the door to renewed speculation about the apocalypse using natural philosophy.

By the early fifteenth century, the latest apocalyptic-seeming disaster, the Great Schism, had engendered just such an analysis. Spurred on by a reading of Roger Bacon, the French cardinal Pierre d'Ailly began cautiously using astrology to investigate the time of the end. Before he made his predictions, d'Ailly offered a careful defense of astrology and its ability to predict religious change. His defense hit at the very issues raised by Parisian authors around 1300 like John of Paris, namely, the extent to which the appearance of Antichrist would arise from natural or supernatural causes. D'Ailly's conclusion, following Bacon, was that all religions save Christianity and Judaism were under the control of the stars. Even those two faiths, inasmuch as they had natural components, were subject to astrological control (the stars, for example, could explain Jesus' excellent physical *complexio*). D'Ailly's subtle distinction of the realms of natural and supernatural causality meant that the other religions, such as the anticipated sect of Antichrist, would fall under the heavens' sway. Using that justification and cautiously hedging his calculations by nodding to the will of God, d'Ailly offered an astrological prediction of Antichrist's advent for the year 1789.[127]

A generation later, in 1444, an astrologer named Jean de Bruges was even more confidently applying astrological reasoning to the study of the apocalypse.[128] Relying heavily on the example set by Pierre d'Ailly, Jean based his prediction of the end on the pattern of conjunctions made by the planets Saturn and Jupiter. He paid particular attention to the triplicity, or group of zodiacal signs, in which each conjunction occurred. (Astrologers divided the zodiac into four triplicities, each of which was held to share the characteristics of one of the four elements: earth, water, air, and fire. Successive conjunctions of the two planets tend to stay within the same triplicity for around 240 years.)[129] According to Jean, the world's end would have to take place when Saturn-Jupiter conjunctions entered the fiery triplicity around the year 1765. Just as a conjunction in one of the watery signs had signaled the Flood, the future return to the fiery triplicity would have to bring about the world's end in a deluge of fire. In his prognostication, then, Jean did not simply use the stars to predict the time of the world's end. He also specifically provided an astrological explanation of the phenomena that would bring about that consummation, namely the rain of fire of Revelation 20: 9.[130] More sure in his predictions than Pierre d'Ailly, Jean unabashedly described the apocalypse in natural terms. He was no outlier. By the early sixteenth century, such predictions were abundant.[131]

In this context of renewed natural speculation about the apocalypse, we can perhaps begin to understand the zeal that drove Christopher Columbus on his famous voyages across the Atlantic. As Pauline Moffit Watts has demonstrated, Columbus acted under a clear sense that the world's end was at hand and that his own travels marked the beginning of the universal missionizing and conversion of the final days. Heir to speculations reopened in the wake of the plague, he derived his date for the apocalypse from a reading of Pierre d'Ailly's writings on astrology. But, again like the authors of the fourteenth-century plague treatises, Columbus also was aware of the geography of the apocalypse and its motion from periphery to center. His ultimate goal thus was not simply to reach the east by sailing west, or even to bring about the conversion of the Indies, but rather to see a crusade to Jerusalem, where history would reach its culmination. In a letter urging Ferdinand and Isabella to undertake just such a crusade, Columbus cited d'Ailly as his source for the prediction that the world would not endure beyond one hundred and fifty-five more years—and divine inspiration for his confidence that the crusade would succeed.[132]

In the decades following the Parisian condemnations of 1277, it was not at all clear that such astrological prediction of the apocalypse would survive. Authors like Arnau de Vilanova, John of Paris, and Henry of Harclay around 1300 had asserted—as Matthew Paris had implied in 1250—that the world's end would not be accomplished through natural causes and therefore could not be forecast using natural philosophy. Roger Bacon's confident prediction that mathematical sciences would help the church foreknow the time of Antichrist lay unfulfilled. But by the fifteenth century, scholars again began to use the science of the stars to examine the world's end, cautiously at first, then with more alacrity. In between those two moments, the plague writings of the mid-fourteenth century played a pivotal role. On the one hand, fourteenth-century authors clearly set the outbreak of pestilence in an apocalyptic frame of interpretation, mapping plague's progress in a course that paralleled the eschatological geography of the *mappaemundi* and highlighting the disease's outbreak with apocalyptic signs like earthquakes, hail, frogs, and rains of fire. On the other hand, the same authors offered an interpretation of plague— and the marvelous phenomena surrounding its appearance—as a completely natural phenomenon.

Unwilling definitively to announce that the world was about to end, fourteenth-century authors allowed their presentations to hover between dubbing the disease purely apocalyptic or purely natural. In their indecisive ambiguity, they refused to set the problem in the terms defined at century's beginning, in which the apocalypse was to have nothing whatsoever to do with natural causes. In so doing, they left open the possibility that events might in fact be seen simultaneously as apocalyptic and resulting from natural causes, precisely the situation Roger Bacon had so confidently envisioned in the *Opus maius*. Doubtless these authors were terrified and sought to understand the overwhelming disaster around them in any and every way possible, even in ways deemed to be incompatible. In their very human reactions to plague, these writers reopened the door to naturalizing the apocalypse.

PART III

THE ESCHATOLOGICAL IMAGINATION

Community Among
the Saintly Dead

Bernard of Clairvaux's *Sermons for the Feast of All Saints*

Anna Harrison

BERNARD IS FAMED for the friendships he enjoyed. He pours out, in his sermons on saints as in his sermons on the Song of Songs, ardent expressions of longing and love for his brother and for other friends, living and dead, and one can find such expressions in his letters as well. A hunger to be remembered by his now dead brother infuses his lamentation on Gerard: "How I long to know what you think about me, once so uniquely yours," Bernard writes. "Perhaps you still give thought to our miseries, now that you have plunged into the abyss of light, become engulfed in that sea of endless happiness."[1] For these reasons alone—that is, because of the tight hold that friendship exerts on him and because of his longing to be remembered by his brother—one might expect to discover in Bernard's writings signs of *this-life-like* relationships among the saintly dead. Moreover, Bernard's various works are shot through with references to the common life and to relationship with others more generally. In this essay, I consider Bernard's sense of the relationship among heaven's inhabitants. I focus on his five Sermons for the Feast of All Saints,[2] and I look closely at the two images that are central to his discussion of the experience of saintly souls in heaven: the image of the bed and the image of the feast. My analysis of these images within the larger context of Bernard's work indicates that despite his charged preoccupation with his brother's love for him, despite his broader interest in friends and friendship, despite his attention to the common life and to the relationship between self and other, Bernard thinks little about interaction when he thinks about the dead.

Although the love that was alive on earth continues to move in heaven, it does change. Addressing his dead brother, Bernard exclaims:

God is love [1 John 4: 8], and the deeper one's union with God, the more full one is of love. . . . Therefore. . . . Your love has not been diminished but only changed. . . . All that smacks of weakness you have cast away.[3]

The image of the heavenly feast is evocative of such change. More specifically, Bernard uses that image to talk about the dissolution of the will of each soul into the will of God; and through this image he conveys, too, a sense—however tentative and ambiguous—of the union of all souls in heaven. Bernard uses the image of souls resting on separate beds to talk about the maintenance, in heaven, of the self each soul was on earth, as well as the soul's passionate, gratifying encounter with God.[4] Neither of these images nor any other, however, communicates a sense of relationship among the saintly dead that resembles relationships forged in this life.

Community Among the Saintly Dead

Bernard tells us something about the earthly life of saints in his Second Sermon for the Feast of All Saints. Paul is the only saint Bernard mentions by name in this sermon. A "zealous and most fearless warrior," Paul has heeded the "blast of the war trumpet"; Paul's words are those of "a vigorous leader striving boldly."[5] The life of a soldier-saint is, "from the womb to the tomb,"[6] a series of menacing skirmishes. It is characterized by the laborious business of striving toward salvation and by perpetual insecurity, as the saints are tossed between the hope that they will triumph in their battle and secure a place in heaven, on the one hand, and on the other, the fear that they will not stay the course but will succumb to temptation and tumble back into sin. The Sermon on the Mount is the saint's battle plan, and victory consists in fulfilling the "law of the combat,"[7] which is enjoined by the Beatitudes.[8]

Because of the arduousness of the combat and the terrible and continual uncertainty of the outcome of the conflicts, the soldier-saint can never relax his vigilance. The anxious motion of a successful battle is rewarded in heaven by rest (and appears all the more frenzied in comparison with that rest). In Bernard's description of heaven, images of rest predominate. Bernard's preferred expression in describing the further reaches of contemplation enjoyed in this life is *quies*,[9] and *requies* and *somnus* are the words that he uses to describe the state of saved souls, who are "delivered at last and for ever from all that could trouble their peace."[10] The saints now enjoy the rest that they sought while on earth, when they were caught between their longing for rest and the demands of charitable obedience (to their superior, to their Rule, to their God).[11] Slumbering on their beds, the saints are no longer torn between tranquility and labor; they are no longer buffeted between hope and fear:

> For this most sweet bed-covering of the soul, she now washes or moistens with no tears, since God has wiped every tear from her eyes. . . . This is, I say, a most sweet and most health-giving rest for the soul, a clean, secure, undisturbed conscience. Therefore, let the purity of her conscience be the soul's pillow, tranquility its headrest, serenity its cover, so that she may sleep in the meantime [until the resurrection] deliciously in the bedcover and rest [there] happily.[12]

Bernard paints a deliciously languid picture of souls, who, finally free from the burden of self and others, sleep a wakeful sleep, flooded with untroubled memories; taking great delight in their storehouse of memories, that which was a source of anguish in life is now a source of joy:

> [The souls of saints] are inwardly free from all trouble, in the sweetness of their soul, they recollect their years, they rejoice for the days in which they were humbled, with delighted admiration they consider the dangers that they have evaded, the labors that they have carried out, the battles that they have won.[13]

In that "city of rest,"[14] the souls of the saints possess in their hearts great joy indeed. And yet, souls do not experience full joy: they are waiting for all who will be saved to fill up heaven, and they are waiting and longing for their glorified bodies so that they may consummate their bliss. What Bernard emphasizes is their longing for their bodies. For the souls' desire for their bodies is such that their love for God "suffers a kind of contortion and makes a 'wrinkle' [Eph. 5: 27]."[15] Only after the resurrection will this distracting desire for the body cease.[16] Luxuriating on the bed of their conscience, mulling over their memories, and awaiting expectantly the return of their bodies, the souls of the saints appear *self*-preoccupied. But if we look at some of Bernard's other writings, it becomes clear that the bed on which each soul rests is also the site of the soul's passionate desire for God and intimate, pleasure-filled, encounter with God.[17] The bed *is* the soul, and the soul is the bedroom of the King.[18] The image of souls sleeping, remembering, and waiting, the stark separateness of each of the beds in which each soul enjoys God and desires God[19] does not suggest interaction among the saints. There is scant indication that heaven's inhabitants are even aware of one another.[20]

The feasting of the holy souls at heaven's banquet table is among the few images in all five sermons that depict the saints as gathered together. Joined in a common meal, the hungry souls of saints feed with unending desire on the words and the works of Christ.[21] This image of saints feasting evokes commensality and commonality more than it does "soul-to-soul" intercourse. Nonetheless, Bernard does not elaborate on the communal setting of the heavenly feast, on the social aspects of eating.[22] Furthermore, when he is discussing the feast, he seems much more interested in the food than in the company.[23] But to say this is once again to bring attention to community, but community in a very particular sense.

The image of the saints collected around a table, triumphantly feasting on Christ, calls to mind the eucharistic meal; it suggests the incorporation of all souls into Christ.[24] In order to understand what associations the image of feasting on Christ may have had for Bernard, it is helpful to turn to other instances in which he talks about eating Christ. In a passage from his Sermon Seventy-One on the Song of Songs, Bernard writes about the spiritual food that Christ offered to Martha and to Mary. Explaining that for Christ to nourish is to be nourished, Bernard describes the person who eats spiritual food as being simultaneously eaten by Christ:

So it is that while he feeds others he is himself fed, and while he refreshes us with spiritual joy he himself joys in our spiritual progress. My penitence, my salvation are his food. I myself am his food. . . . I am chewed as I am reproved by him; I am swallowed as I am taught; I am digested as I am changed; I am assimilated as I am transformed; I am made one as I am conformed. Do not wonder at this [John 5: 28], for he feeds upon us and is fed by us that we may be the more closely bound to him. Otherwise we are not perfectly united to him. But if I eat and am not eaten, then he is in me but I am not yet in him [John 6: 57]. But if I am eaten but do not eat, then he has me in him, but it would appear he is not yet in me; and in neither case will there be perfect union between us. But he eats me that he may have me in himself, and he himself is eaten by me that he may be in me, and the bond between us will be strong and the union complete, for I shall be in him and he will likewise be in me.[25]

If heaven involves complete and perfect union with Christ, then union with Christ in heaven means something like being digested and transformed into Christ and digesting and transforming Christ into oneself. Bernard follows this graphic description of incorporation with a passage in which he considers in more technical terms the soul's union with God. Between God and man there exists "a communion of wills and an agreement in charity" (*communio vuluntatum et consensus in caritate*).[26] In another sermon, he writes:

Man and God, because they are not of one substance or of one nature, cannot, indeed, be said to be one; nevertheless, they are with sure and complete truth said [to be] one spirit [1 Cor. 6: 17], if they adhere to each other with the glue (*glutino*) of love. Certainly, it makes a unity not so much by a coherence (*cohaerentia*) of essence as by a sharing of wills (*conviventia voluntatum*).[27]

The transformation that the saved soul undergoes is a transformation of will. It is the will of the saint that in heaven is incorporated into the will of Christ; fleshly love (*amor carnis*) will be absorbed (*absorbendus*) into the will of God.[28] In *On Loving God*, Bernard talks about the soul being "poured into the will of God" and compares this pouring into with a little drop of water that seems to forsake itself (*deficere a se tota videtur*) as it takes on the flavor and color of the wine into which it is infused.[29] He speaks also about the "fired-iron" being made like (*simillimum*) the fire, "the previous form having been cast off."[30] He wonders and he rejoices:

When will it experience this kind of state, so that the spirit, drunk with divine love, forgetful of itself, and its very self made as if a broken vessel [Ps. 30: 13] in God, and wholly advanced in God and adhering to God [1 Cor. 6: 17], [is] made in one spirit with him and says, "Do my flesh and my heart fail, God of my heart and my part, God, in eternity [Ps. 72:26]?" . . . Indeed, to lose yourself in a certain manner, just as if you were not you . . . , and to empty your very self, and to be almost annihilated (*paene annullari*), is of heavenly life not of a human state. . . . O pure and stainless intention of the will, surely the more stainless and purer because now in this [will] there is left behind nothing of the self admixed, by which the will is the more pleasant and sweeter, because it is wholly God that is felt! To be moved in this way is to be deified.[31]

As Etienne Gilson has pointed out, such images of fire, water, and wine highlight the *likeness* of the soul to God (but not the sameness), the *seeming to be* the same as God (but not being the same).[32] When Bernard speaks about the soul without using images, he talks sometimes about the soul's transformation in God, sometimes about the soul being almost annihilated, and sometimes about the preservation of the substance of the human being in God. While it is true that Bernard explicitly and repeatedly insists that the substance of God and the substance of the saved do not become one, it is important not to minimize the extent to which he insists on the identification of God and the soul, the extent to which the saved in heaven are transformed in becoming more God-like. The passage quoted from above continues: "Otherwise, how will God be all in all [1 Cor. 15: 28], if anything of humanity survives in humanity?"[33]

Bernard's images of the soul pouring into God and disappearing like water poured into wine, even his more formal explication of the will of the soul conforming completely to the will of God, might strike some of his modern readers as threatening something one might call "self." For Bernard, however, the soul is not really *its* self *until* its will is lost in God's will. The soul becomes "like God" and fully itself by becoming—at least in some respects—other than it was in life.[34] From a certain perspective, annihilation (of the will) *is* restoration: "the soul that is unlike God is unlike itself."[35] In some sense, it is by moving away from that which we were in life that we become who we are and were meant to be.

Read in the light of these several quotations from Sermon Seventy-One on the Song of Songs and this passage from *On Loving God*, the image of the saints feasting on Christ is one of transformation, a transformation that is really a self-realization, in which the soul is shorn of the skin of self-will.[36] And, shorn of self-will, the soul's will becomes one with the will of God. Furthermore, these passages may suggest that the saints are assimilated to, dissolved in, and lose themselves not only in Christ but also in one another. For if each saint is united "by the concurrence of wills to God," the implication may be that the soul of each saint is united to the soul of every other saint. But Bernard does not quite make this assertion. Bernard hints at this kind of unity among all of heaven's inhabitants—saved souls and holy angels—in his First Sermon for the Dedication of a Church, when he says (using 1 John 4: 16) that souls are joined with one another in love and knowledge through love of God.[37] When we put this in context, we see even more clearly the intimate union of each "living stone" of the heavenly church with every other:

The stones cohere to one another by that double glue (*glutino*) of full knowledge and of perfect love. [They cohere to one another] so greatly, since they are joined reciprocally by greater love the closer they stand to that love that is God. But there is no mistrust that can separate them from the reciprocity, where there is nothing in the one that the other does not suffer happily; the beam of truth penetrates everything. For because "the one who adheres to God, is one spirit" with him, indeed, there is no doubt that the blessed who adhere perfectly to Spirit with him and in him penetrate the whole.[38]

By considering the image of feasting on Christ in the context of some of Bernard's other writings, we have seen that the image suggests that the saved in heaven are united through the common experience of feasting. But if we think of experience insofar as it is located in the will, the other images we have considered, in combination with Bernard's more formal discussions, suggest that Bernard may have also considered this experience a *shared* one, in which boundaries between the wills of saints are dissolved into one another through and in Christ. The souls of the blessed "penetrate the whole." And yet, Bernard does not talk about the souls of saints pouring into one another as he does about each soul pouring into God. Bernard does insist, however, that the personal memories of each soul are retained in heaven. And this certainly suggests that very real boundaries between individual souls abide eternally.[39]

Such perduring of boundaries is very important to Bernard. In his sermon on the death of his brother, Gerard,[40] we learn that Bernard was laden down with sorrow and anger at the "bitter separation" wrought by death. The loss of Gerard is one that daily recalls itself to him. He catalogues lovingly the numerous pleasures (and the utility) of his brother's companionship and declares his continuing need for him. Vivid hurt and fierce love rage: "Gerard was mine, so utterly mine."[41] Although in heaven Gerard rejoices in "a sea of endless happiness," the language of brutal physical rending characterizes Bernard's experience of his brother's death: Gerard was "snatched from" Bernard's embraces, "torn from" Bernard,[42] life without Gerard is a galling wound.[43] Death accomplished what was unthinkable while Gerard lived: "While you lived when did you ever abandon me?"[44] His brother's was not the only death that left Bernard heavy with dejection and neediness: the author of Bernard's first *Life* speaks of Bernard's desire to buried next to his "special friend"[45] Malachy (archbishop of Armagh and papal legate, who wished to be a disciple of Bernard), and in his own *Life of Malachy*, Bernard articulates his hope for reunion with the friend whom death has taken from him.[46] In his Sermon on Blessed Humbert (a monk who left the Benedictines to become a follower of Bernard), Bernard laments that death has deprived him of "a dear friend, prudent counsellor, a strong supporter."[47] In the same sermon Bernard bemoans the death of his brother and his companions (probably referring to Gerard, who died in 1138, and perhaps to Malachy, who died in 1148, the year in which Humbert also died).[48] Addressing himself to God, he enumerates the cruel gifts that these several deaths have delivered:

"Friend and neighbor Thou hast put far from me, and my acquaintance because of my misery" [Ps. 87: 7]. Thou hast drawn them from their misery leaving me alone in mine. Thou hast taken from my side those who were related to me according to the flesh and related to me more closely according to the spirit. . . . Would to God thou wert willing to slay once and for all him whom Thou scourgest, instead of keeping me thus alone, miserable man that I am, in order to make me endure repeated deaths, many and cruel![49]

In spite of Bernard's intense grieving for the intimacies of lost friendship, he does not describe heaven in his Sermons for the Feast of All Saints as being peopled by intimates or as a place in which wished-for reunions and renewed companionship with particular friends take place. Heaven is not compensation for this loss.[50] The presence of a particular loved one that Bernard longs for in his writings on Gerard and Malachy, especially, seems very different from that kind of "togetherness" evoked by the language of incorporation into Christ, in which, as we have seen, all souls' wills conform to Christ (and, seemingly, to one another) in union with him.

The differing emphases that I have found, on the one hand, in the Sermons for All Saints and, on the other, in some of Bernard's other writings may in part reflect the different purposes for which the several texts were written. But Bernard himself was sufficiently preoccupied by the difficulty of reconciling the soul's assimilation into God with the maintenance, in heaven, of the affections built up in this life to address this concern in his sermon on Gerard. There he writes:

How I long to know what you think about me, once so uniquely yours. . . . Perhaps you still give thought to our miseries, now that you have plunged into the abyss of light, become engulfed in that sea of endless happiness. It is possible that though you once knew us according to the flesh, you now no longer know us and because you have entered into the power of the Lord you will be mindful of his righteousness alone, forgetful of ours. Furthermore, "he who is united to the Lord becomes one spirit with him" [1 Cor. 6: 17], his whole being somehow changed into a movement of divine love. He no longer has the power to experience or relish anything but God, and what God himself experiences and relishes, because he is filled with God.[51]

Gerard continues to be enormously important to his brother; alone and lonely, Bernard wonders with terrible uneasiness whether he may no longer be of significance to Gerard. Bernard's apprehension is more poignant when we take into account his cry: "Who ever loved me as he [did]?"[52] Yearning to be loved and to be remembered by him who loved him so vehemently, Bernard asserts that in heaven Gerard's being joins with God in such a way as to satisfy Bernard's own desire. The passage from Bernard's Sermon Twenty-Six that I quoted from above continues:

But God is love [1 John 4: 8], and the deeper one's union with God, the more full one is of love. . . . Therefore . . . Your love has not been diminished but only changed; when you were clothed with God you did not divest yourself of concern for us, for God is certainly concerned with us. All that smacks of weakness you have cast away. And since love never comes to an end [1 Cor. 13: 8], you will not forget me forever.[53]

This passage seems to affirm that the particular affections we establish on earth do continue in eternity. Such an insistence is echoed in a sermon Bernard wrote for the Feast of St. Victor:

It is not a land of oblivion [Ps. 87: 13] that the soul of Victor inhabits; . . . Does the heavenly habitation harden the souls that it admits, or deprive [them] of memory, or strip away kindness? Brothers, the breadth of heaven dilates, not contracts, the heart; it delights, not estranges (*alienat*) the mind; it enlarges, not tightens (*contrahit*) the affections (*affectiones*). In the light of God, memory is made clear not obscured; in the light of God, that which is unknown is learned, that which is known is not un-learned.[54]

Memory is vitally important to Bernard. As he elsewhere insists, "it is agreed that the soul is immortal, and it will not live hereafter except with its memory, or else it would come to pass [that it would] not be the soul hereafter."[55]

Greedy for the pleasures and for the efficacy of friendship, Bernard be-lieves that "social intercourse, especially between friends," cannot be purpose-less and that feelings of friendship are part of what it means to be a human being.[56] Bernard asserts that the memory of those whom we value in life and our affections for them do not dissipate in heaven but are preserved. But as the passage from the Sermon for Gerard quoted from above also makes clear, souls in heaven love in a manner distinct from the manner in which they loved on earth. This is because in heaven "all that smacks of weakness" is cast away. His *Steps of Humility* helps us to make sense of just what this weakness may mean to Bernard.

In Chapter Four, which concerns self-knowledge, Bernard explains that "neither love nor hatred can give a judgment of truth." After alerting his reader to the unjust judgment that hatred gives rise to, Bernard warns that unjust judgment can also be born of love. He remarks: "I know that it is decreed in human law, and in both secular and ecclesiastical causes, that special friends of the litigants may not try their cases, in case they are misled or mislead others by their love. . . . love can make you diminish, or even hide, your friend's fault."[57] Read in the light of his sermon on Gerard, Sermon Seventy-One on the Song of Songs, and Bernard's five Sermons for the Feast of All Saints, this passage would suggest that incorporation into Christ reforms earthly love into a love that is stripped of the prejudice and partiality that colored that love in life. All of this raises important questions about how much of who we are, as well as who and how we love, *is* the dross ("weakness") that adheres to us in consequence of sin.[58] It therefore raises questions about what aspects of relationships we may have cherished in this life will be transposed into heaven and what aspects jettisoned—that is, it provokes questions about the foun-dation for and preservation of a personal, *this-life-like* relationship among the saints. In his Fifth Sermon for All Saints, Bernard writes:

See, for there is nothing of security in this our fellowship (*communione*), nothing of perfection, nothing of rest (*quietis*); and nevertheless, this also: how good and how jocund it is to live together with brothers [Ps. 132: 1]! For everything offensive that occurs, whether interiorly or whether exteriorly—when in these things our heart and soul is one in God—is certainly found so much more tolerable by that very sharing of brothers (*consortio fratrum*). How much sweeter will that be when there is no occasion of dissension, where perfect charity connects all in indissoluble agreement so that as the Father and Son are one, so we shall be one in them [John 17: 21]![59]

This is the fullest statement in these sermons on the nature of the earthly community. The passage indicates that barriers to love are struck down in heaven—where all souls love one another in the love of Christ—precisely because the constraints of sin are no more. But the passage just quoted raises an important question. For if each soul's love washes over all members of the heavenly community—the soul's affections having been liquefied and poured into the will of God[60]—what becomes of the privileged status of some relationships in life over others?[61]

In Bernard's writings, we can trace a tension between "special friendships" in the eternity of heaven and the dissolution of the will into the comprehensive love of Christ. At least when he is considering his brother's death, the absorption of the will into Christ seems to be a source both of joy and of anxiety for Bernard. Bernard seems to want to retain certain aspects of the self that will render individuals familiar to one another in heaven (memory) but to exclude that dross of the self that adheres to us in consequence of sin (including partial, prejudicial love and those aspects of the soul that keep us from loving others well). Bernard also seems to yearn for love that is not empty even in heaven of the special tenderness and partiality with which it was stamped on earth. In his sermon on Gerard, Bernard writes: "It seems to me that I can almost hear my brother saying, 'can a woman forget the son of her womb. And if she should forget, yet, I shall not forget you.'"[62] This tension is part of a larger, more complicated tension between, on the one hand, remaining who we were in this life and, on the other hand, peeling away those aspects of the self that are the accretions of sin[63] and being incorporated into God in heaven. This tension makes it difficult to understand what the relationship *among* the saints might look like.

Bernard focuses in these sermons on two kinds of experiences of the saints. The first is the experience—represented by rest or sleep—that is common to the saints but not shared by them. The second is the experience—represented by feasting—that is common to and, in a sense, shared by the saints. It is important to point out, however, that *requies* and *somnus*—as well as feasting—seem to represent not a single activity but the *total* experience of the saints in heaven. At the end of his Second Sermon, Bernard writes: "These are, I say to you, brothers, these are the whole affairs of the saints: this food, this sleep of theirs."[64] Rest—and feast—seem to mean taking delight in everything.[65] There is, then, a sense in which *each* of these experiences (rest and feast) *is* the total experience of the saints in heaven; they are not, therefore, separate and distinct from each other. Nevertheless, one image, rest, emphasizes a sense of the individual soul (separate from other souls), the other, feasting, a sense of the union of all souls with one another—although there is no real sense of souls fusing with one another or of one soul substituting for or becoming another soul. We do not, however, find in these sermons an image that conveys the transport into heaven of that which was so important to Bernard: the special, particular friendships that he valued in this life. The focus throughout Bernard's five Sermons for the Feast of All Saints is squarely on the self and on the self's relationship to God—not on the self's relationship to other selves. The question of relationship with other selves does not seem to have been foremost on Bernard's mind. And the questions that he does not ask tell us a great deal about what his concerns were.

Community of the Resurrection

In his Third Sermon, Bernard describes three stages of the soul's existence: in the corruptible body, without the body, and with the glorified body. The threefold stages of the soul's existence might lead one to ask whether Bernard envisions three distinct forms of community, corresponding to each stage of the soul's existence.[66] Does Bernard have a vision of the resurrection community that is distinct from the community of souls in heaven before the resurrection?

In the passage that closes the Life of St. Malachy, Bernard indirectly refers to reunion with Malachy, as he refers to Malachy's burial. He talks about this reunion not in the context of a soul-to-soul meeting in heaven before the resurrection but as a coming together that takes place after the resurrection:

Good Jesus! yours is the deposit which was entrusted to us. Yours is the treasure which is buried with us. We are keeping it to be transferred to you at that time when you propose to demand it. Only grant that he may not go forth without his comrades, but may we have him as our leader whom we had as our guest and grant that we may reign with you and with him too, for ever and ever [Rev. 22: 5].[67]

But the import of this passage is not that Bernard looks forward to meeting with Malachy at the resurrection *instead* of immediately upon entering heaven. Furthermore, in other writings concerning the dead whom he had known personally, Bernard does not talk about reunion at the resurrection. In his sermon on his brother, Gerard, and in his sermon on Humbert, he mentions the resurrection, but in neither case is it a scene of reunion.[68]

It is true, nevertheless, that in a certain sense there is a new form of community at the resurrection. Although each individual's battles are over the moment she or he enters heaven, the war is really not over until all who will be saved are there. In the following passage Bernard makes one of his strongest statements in these sermons on the importance of the resurrection community:

For into that most blessed house they shall enter neither without us nor without their bodies, that is, neither the saints without the common people, nor the spirit without the flesh. Nor is it proper that complete blessedness be present until the person to whom it is given is whole nor that perfection be given to an imperfect church.[69]

Certainly, then, the presence of the whole church makes the celestial city whole. But there is no indication in these sermons—and this is what is important for my concern—of any change in the relationship among the saints, of the flowering of a new form of community corresponding to the much-discussed resurrection.[70] What then are we to make of Bernard's avowal that saints yearn for us?

That Church of the first-born await, and we are neglecting them; the saints desire us and we loiter; "the just await us" [Ps. 141: 8], and we pretend not to notice (*dissimulas*). Let us rouse [ourselves], brothers: let us rise with Christ, let us "seek those things that are above" [Col. 3: 1–2]. Let us desire those who are desiring us, let us hasten to those who are expecting us. With the desires of our souls, let us seize upon before hand those who are awaiting us.[71]

Although Bernard asserts that the saints are waiting for the whole community of the saved and for the restoration of their whole selves, he spends more words and writes with far greater urgency about the resurrection body than about the resurrection community. The souls of the saints "want their bodies back."[72] They "solicit" their bodies, they "supplicate" God for their bodies, they "pray and cry out to the Lord for the consummation which is still withheld from their desires."[73] They do *not* cry out for the friends they had while on earth; they do not cry out for community. While it is clear that the souls of the saints await their bodies in order to experience fully the joy of heaven, it is not clear that they, for the same reason (if for any!), await their friends. The absence of body prevents soul from fully tending to God. Bernard makes no such claim about friendship or about community.

The weighty consideration Bernard gives to the resurrection in these sermons indicates that he is finally more concerned with the whole self than with the whole church. Or, rather, when Bernard thinks of the community after the resurrection, he thinks about it as the context within which souls get their "bodies back." That Bernard should focus on the resurrection community with the resurrection body in mind makes sense. The very purpose of establishing community between the holy souls in heaven and the monks at Clairvaux is primarily to rouse desire for heaven and to spur the *individual monk* on in his individual battle for heaven.[74] The perfecting of the relationship between inner and outer person that is begun within the monastic community is not achieved until after the resurrection, when the soul receives its glorified body. It is true that Bernard insists that the happiness of the saved will increase at the resurrection. But this seems to be because on that "last grand festival day" the happiness of the saints will increase because distracting desire for their bodies is stilled—a desire that now keeps their souls from fully tending to God. Furthermore, their happiness will increase on the "dawn of that new day," when the saved will for the first time see "God as He is."[75] But, it remains unclear what kind of causal relationship—if any—exists between experiencing the beatific vision and the gathering of the entire community of the saints.[76]

Conclusion

None of Bernard's Sermons for All Saints contains a treatise on community among the saintly dead, and he has not produced such a treatise anywhere in his writing. Bernard does, however, refer to community again and again throughout his writings, and the topic would appear to be an important one for any study of his spirituality. Scholars have long noted a burgeoning in the twelfth century of new groups and structures that multiplied the ways one could "live religiously."[77] Caroline Walker Bynum has called attention to the studied equilibrium between self and community fostered in this period. She has argued that this century is characterized in part by a concern to think about self in relation to groups and vice versa—a concern, she contends, that is without parallel in the earlier Middle Ages. Bernard holds a position of pivotal importance in the twelfth century; his influence on his contemporaries was enormous. My research into Bernard's sermons reveals, however, the surprising conclusion that—for all his emphasis on self, desire, friendship, and the common life—Bernard does not elaborate a theory of the heavenly community.

Bernard's conception of community among the saints in heaven is limited: although he does talk about common experience among the saints and about reciprocity, or sharing of experience, interaction among the saints simply does not figure prominently in his thought. It appears that Bernard has not fully worked out the relationship between self, God, and the other who is a friend. Longing for the ecstatic loss of self in God in heaven, he nevertheless betrays some trepidation about what that loss of self seems to imply for the precious relationships we have established on earth. Known for the fervent friendships he carefully cultivated in life, Bernard's heaven is not, as I noted above, restitution for the toll on friendship that death takes. Although memory guarantees the continuation of self, the way we love in heaven seems to move us away from the self we were on earth as our wills dissolve into the will of God. Nor does Bernard have a conception of community after the resurrection that is distinct from the community among all souls before the Final Judgment. Indeed, Bernard has a far greater interest in the resurrected person than in the resurrection community. In his vision of the glory of eternity, it is this self—whole at last and tending to God with a desire that will never diminish and that will be bathed in utter satisfaction always—that enthralls Bernard.

Heaven in View

The Place of the Elect in an Illuminated Book of Hours

Harvey Stahl

For the faithful in the later Middle Ages, the afterworld was not the place it used to be. It was larger and in many ways nearer. Although the bliss of heaven, which the righteous hoped to enjoy after the Last Judgment, was still the distant ideal, the living were increasingly occupied with the fate of the human soul on the long road between death and the general resurrection, with an intermediate stage in which purged souls could benefit from prayers recited in this world and in which the righteous already enjoyed the company of saints. This shift in interest, which is evidenced in theological and visionary texts as well as in penitential and funerary practices, is also registered in the visual arts. From the late thirteenth century, it not only appears in scenes of purgatory but is elaborated in a large and varied group of images showing Christ and Mary enthroned with multitudes of saints and the blessed faithful. Where is this place in the afterworld? What is experienced there? How does it differ from the Jerusalemic ideal? This essay responds to these questions as they are raised in the illuminated frontispieces to a Book of Hours made in France about 1315–20. The illumination suggests that unlike the imagery of purgatory, which developed primarily within Last Judgment iconography, these scenes of the heavenly court arose largely from the imagery of the Triumph of the Virgin, a subject that also had eschatological implications. And because these frontispieces employ the imagery of reliquaries and utilize their characteristic strategies of presence and revelation, they raise issues of bodily continuity and perception at a time when both were central to debates about the soul's knowledge of God before the general resurrection.

The two frontispieces that are our subject are found in a richly illumi-

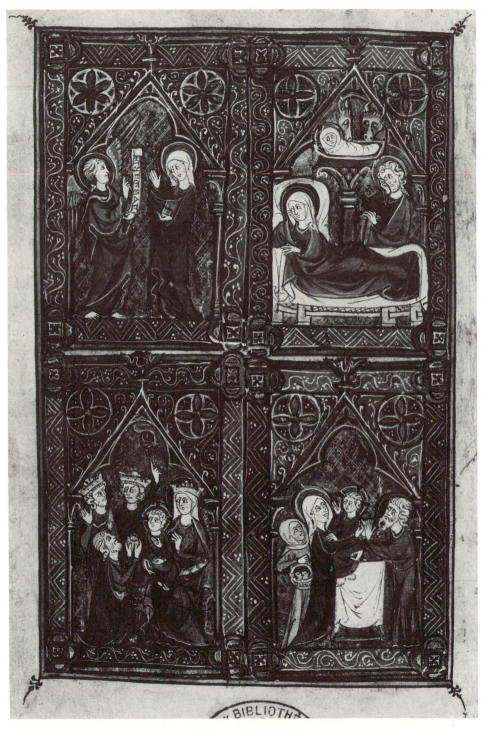

Figure 1. Infancy scenes. Book of Hours, Cambrai, Bibl. Mun. ms 87, fol. 16v. Photo: author.

nated Book of Hours preserved in the Bibliothèque Municipale at Cambrai.[1] The illuminations are preceded by the usual liturgical calendar and followed by the Hours of the Virgin and other prayers in Latin and in French.[2] Several initials in the text show the patrons—a lord and lady—and their arms. They are usually identified as Isabeau de Rumigny and Gaucher de Châtillon d'Autresche, châtelain de Bar, who were married in 1312, a date that accords with the style of the initials.[3] That style is also found in manuscripts created in Cambrai, Thérouanne, and Amiens.[4] Although the two full-page miniatures are contemporary with the rest of the book, they are on heavier parchment and were each painted by artists who did not work in the rest of the book. Thus there is no way to know if the two full-page miniatures were planned from the outset or added soon afterwards, possibly in response to the unusual program of text illuminations, as has recently been suggested.[5]

Both frontispiece miniatures are illuminated on the verso. The first is divided into four separately framed compartments illustrating the Annunciation, Nativity, Adoration of the Magi, and Presentation in the Temple (Figure 1). Each of these scenes is painted on a separate piece of parchment that has been pasted onto the page and then surrounded by a common frame. I shall return to this unusual composite page shortly.

The page facing the Infancy cycle is blank, but on its verso is an illumination showing an elaborate building with contemporary Gothic details, seen in a kind of transverse cross-section (Figure 2). Its interior is divided into three stories with central, intermediate, and lateral spaces, all filled with figures. These figures and their arrangement warrant careful inspection. In the top central compartment are Christ and Mary, both nimbed, crowned, and wearing golden robes.[6] Mary holds a book and gestures with an open hand to Christ, who sits to her right and blesses her. In each of the adjacent spaces stands an angel, one bowing a vielle and the other playing a portable organ. Beyond them to the left is a large group of nimbed male saints and, to the right, crowned female saints, all gesturing toward the center. Below Mary and Christ, in the second level, is a large central figure who wears a papal tiara and faces outward, his hands together in prayer. The surrounding figures, largely ecclesiastics, all turn toward him.[7] In the adjoining spaces are angels, one plucking a guitern and the other a psaltery, and, beyond them, male saints at the left and female saints at the right.[8] At the lowest level, the central compartment is divided into two, again by gender, this time with unclothed men and women, all with tiny red and blue flowers penned over their bodies. Next to them angels play a harp and a bagpipe. At the extreme sides are saints on horseback, each riding toward the center. The left one is dressed

Figure 2. Mary, Christ, and the faithful elect. Book of Hours, Cambrai, Bibl. Mun. ms 87, fol. 17v. Photo: Médiathèque Municipale, Cambrai.

in full ceremonial armor and is probably St. George; at the right St. Martin cuts his cloak for the beggar.[9] Other figures are outside this structure. Just above the roof line are two censing angels. Four corner medallions overlap the frame: in the two upper ones are seraphim; in each of the two lower ones an angel stands between small trees and lifts a bird up toward the main compartment. In the lateral medallions, which the frame overlaps, are Ecclesia with her chalice and banner and, at the right, the blindfolded Synagogue.

The subject of the painting has been variously interpreted. It has been identified as a Coronation of the Virgin, but Mary is not being crowned—she already is—nor is she offered a scepter or other regalia. Moreover, she is at Christ's left, whereas in Coronation scenes at this time she is usually at his right. Nor is this a traditional All Saints picture, for then we would expect to see a hierarchy of saints beginning with the apostles, not one with such prominent churchmen and with the anonymous resurrected. Nor can this be an image of the Second Coming or Last Judgment, for the twenty-four elders and the resurrected Christ are absent, and neither theme would account for the range of musical instruments the angels play, which do not include the traditional trumpets signaling the general resurrection. And if these are the resurrected already enjoying paradise, then one would expect traditional attributes, such as the Fountain of Life, or to see the landscape elements within the architectural structure rather than outside of it. The *Catalogue général* refers to the subject as the City of God and in many ways Augustine's text does form the basis for this painting which represents, I believe, the union in time of Christ and the earthly Church, as represented by Mary and the congregation of the faithful elect.

A *City of God* manuscript created about 1120 at Canterbury will serve to introduce several of the most important themes at play.[10] This manuscript also has two consecutive frontispieces (Figures 3, 4). The first is divided into three registers and shows, from below, men peacefully at work in the fields, or good regimen, then violent death, or bad regimen, and finally angels and devils competing for the souls of the deceased. One angel already lifts up a soul. Its presumed destination, seen in the second miniature, is a multilevel structure enclosed by towers and a roof. At the top is Christ enthroned and blessing, with music-making angels in a landscape to either side; just below, at a second level, are the twelve apostles holding palms and seated between cities with open gates. The lower two levels form a distinct structure within the larger one, a building shown in cross-section, with niches defined by wide arches carried on heavy columns with detailed bases and capitals. This part is dominated by an enthroned and crowned female figure, presumably Eccle-

Figure 3. Righteous and evil deeds. Augustine, *City of God*, Florence, Bibl. Laurenziana ms. Plut. XII.17, fol. ɪv. Photo: Bibl. Laurenziana, Florence.

Figure 4. Heavenly and earthly cities. Augustine, *City of God*, Florence, Bibl. Lauren-ziana ms. Plut. XII.17, fol. IV. Photo: Bibl. Laurenziana, Florence.

sia, holding a scepter and open book.[11] Alongside her are two women who gesture toward holy figures with scrolls. Beneath are prelates and kings, also with palm branches, who face a central seraph before the open gates of paradise, with its four rivers extending into the margin below. I take the image to represent the Heavenly City to which the blessed enter to reign with Christ and the saints. It is not a straightforward illustration of the New Jerusalem for, in spite of the scales and the references to paradise, nothing in this two-page sequence suggests that the general resurrection and Last Judgment have taken place. Rather, following Augustine, it is the joyous place where the blessed reside in the spirit until the general resurrection, when they will be united with their bodies. But what then is this lower structure? It would have to be the Church that sojourns on earth but "even now is the kingdom of Christ and the kingdom of heaven."[12]

In many ways the Cambrai miniature takes this lower structure as its subject and setting. It repeats several elements from the earlier depiction, such as the music-making angels and Christ and the apostles, but it omits the traditional attributes of paradise—the landscape, miniature cities, rivers, and guarded gate—and adds figures who are unnimbed and even unclothed. There is a more differentiated hierarchy, with multitudes in each category, and with pride of place given to officials of the church. And it is preceded not by a contrast of good and evil, as in the Canterbury *City of God*, but by Infancy scenes, so that the context is the history of the Incarnation rather than judgment. Finally, Christ exceptionally appears to the left of the Virgin and is the less active figure. The narrative focus changes: the emphasis is not on Christ and a heavenly city that includes the Church but on Mary, who symbolizes the Church, defined here by the faithful who constitute it, by the hierarchy that structures it, and by the role it has in the history of redemption. Whether we understand her as interceding for the faithful or as entrusting them to Christ, they are in her Church and Christ seems to be, for the moment, *chez Elle*.

An analogous representation of Ecclesia with a hierarchy of the faithful appears in a drawing after the destroyed Strassburg manuscript of Herrad of Hohenburg's *Hortus Deliciarum* (Figure 5).[13] The accompanying text identified the upper figures as diverse ranks of apostles, popes, prelates, abbots, and abbesses, and the lower ones as adolescents with, alongside, clerics, monks, hermits, knights, and male and female laity.[14] The battle between Good and Evil that we saw in the first illustration of the Canterbury *City of God* now occurs outside this structure, while inside, as the text explains, are those who, above, regenerate the Church through their teaching and those who, below, by their obedience, each in their class, work each day and faithfully prepare

Figure 5. Ecclesia and the faithful. Drawing from Herrad of Landsberg, *Hortus deliciarum*, ed. and trans. Aristide D. Caratzas (New Rochelle, N.Y.: Caratzas Bros., 1977).

Figure 6. Sponsus and sponsa and elect. Psalter, Munich, Bay. Staatsbibliothek, clm. 835 fol. 29v. Photo courtesy Bay. Staatsbibliothek, Munich.

their affairs for the coming of the Spouse.[15] But he has not yet come, and there is no music or rejoicing.

The reference to Christ as "the spouse" points to a critical aspect of our subject, one also seen in an early thirteenth-century English Psalter, now in Munich (Figure 6).[16] This full-page illumination is also divided into registers with holy figures arranged in distinctive groups of saints, some distinguished by gender. Angels play musical instruments in both parts.[17] On the central axis is Christ seated on a rainbow arc and blessing within a mandorla flanked by seraphim; below is the crowned Ecclesia dressed in fine robes and enthroned in a mandorla with apostles to either side. Here she appears as the *sponsa*, for she is youthful and wears her hair long and her mandorla, held by angels, is an extension of Christ's. More important, in the middle of the five lower medallions is the *Agnus Dei*, an allusion to the Marriage of the Lamb in Revelation 19: 7. Its presence among the surrounding saints is consistent with medieval commentaries on this passage. Haimo of Auxerre and Richard of St. Victor explain that all the elect are present and exult at the marriage, which is that of Christ and the Church, and that they are brought into the company of angels and saints.[18] This is also the interpretation we find in Joinville's *Credo*, a work composed and originally illustrated about 1250–60. A late thirteenth century exemplar shows Ecclesia embracing the lamb at the wedding table, where she is joined by crowned saints, as angels nearby cense and play musical instruments (Figure 7).[19] Although the composition depends upon the tradition of Marriage of the Lamb illustration found in contemporary Apocalypse manuscripts, the accompanying text makes clear that it shows how the righteous come into the presence of Christ: "We firmly believe that saintly men and women who have passed away, and the prudent men and women who are now living, will have eternal life and bliss in heaven, and they will be at the table of the Lord."[20] In the *Credo* and also in the Psalter, the next subject is the Last Judgment, but heaven is an independent image.[21] Whether the setting is the wedding table or a hieratic vision of the assembled faithful, Christ receives the Church and the Elect. In both the *Credo* and the Psalter, the Last Judgment is the next subject illustrated, but heaven is an independent image, it is a joyous place of the union of Christ and the Church.

Marie-Louise Thérel's magisterial study, *Le triomphe de la Vierge-Église*, traces how this imagery of the Church as a queen or as the *sponsa* or as the embodiment of the faithful was continually in tension with that of Mary in the same guises.[22] But with the acceptance of the bodily assumption of Mary, these meanings converged and her coronation clearly marked the glorification of all humanity within the history of salvation. Although these meanings

Figure 7. Marriage of the Lamb and Last Judgment. Joinville, *Credo*, St. Petersburg, National Library of Russia ms. Lat. Q.v.I, 78. Photo: I. P. Mokretsova and V. L. Romanova, *Les manuscrits enluminés français du XIIIe siècle dans les collections soviétiques, 1200–1270*.

Figure 8. Coronation of the Virgin and Last Judgment. Ivory diptych, Metropolitan Museum of Art. acq. 1970.324.7a–b. Photo: Metropolitan Museum of Art.

were implicit in representations of the Coronation of the Virgin from its beginnings in the twelfth century, it is only in the mid-thirteenth that the elect begin to appear alongside the crowned and enthroned Mary. One early example is an ivory diptych made in Paris about 1260–70 (Figure 8).[23] The cuttings for the hinges make it certain that the panels were always connected as they are now, with the Coronation of the Virgin at the left, preceding the Last Judgment, as we saw in the analogous subjects in the Psalter and *Credo*. The details of the Last Judgment are traditional for this time, except that the carver is particularly innovative in the use of arches within arches to suggest three levels, one below the other, corresponding to the Christ in judgment, the resurrection, and hell. In addition, the scene of heaven, which would normally balance the hell scene at the lower right, is represented on the left leaf where, beneath the Coronation, is a procession of figures—a mendicant, a king, a pope, and possibly a deacon—whom one angel descends to greet as a second leads them toward a ladder ascending to heaven. This group almost certainly derives from a composition for the Last Judgment, for related diptychs made by the same Parisian atelier either show the resurrected rising in their tombs, already dressed like those approaching the ladder in the left leaf, or else all three parts—resurrection, heaven, and hell—immediately below the figure of Christ in judgment.[24] However, no diptych at this time shows a subject beginning on one leaf and continuing onto the next, and the very high quality of the ivory makes it unlikely that its carver was simply filling the available space beneath the Coronation. Rather, I believe the unusual placement of this group under the Coronation ivory is purposeful: it is an early example of a narrative structure found in some of the finest Parisian diptychs, a structure in which complementary themes, gestures, and patterns of reading are deliberately played off one another, often to dramatic effect, and in ways that deepen the devotional import of the ivories.[25] In this case the rising forms of the left panel, with its ladder, its stair-step sequence of levels, and the highly placed figures of Mary and Christ, complement the low figure of Christ and the obliquely descending diagonals of the right panel; similarly, the angel pointing up to the Coronation at the lower left contrasts with the devil pointing down to the hell mouth at the lower right. This is not just a Coronation scene with a bit of the Last Judgment beneath; it is a thematically integral diptych that defines heaven largely in Marian terms. In the circular reading that is typical of many of these diptychs, Mary seems to receive the elect both before and after the Last Judgment, and humanity continually triumphs in her Coronation. The ivory accurately indicates how the elect are increasingly destined to Mary's protection, whether the context is linked to the Last Judgment or not.

In his book on purgatory, Jacques Le Goff comments that "Purgatory, in its upper reaches, may be nothing less than evidence of the reality of a beatific vision prior to the Last Judgment."[26] Although those "upper reaches" are never named as clearly as purgatory is, there can be no doubt of the currency, after about 1240, of the belief in the souls of the elect being gathered together and having access to a vision of the divine before the Last Judgment. The nature of this vision was under intense scrutiny at that time, especially in the quodlibetal discussions of William of Auxerre, Bonaventura, Albertus Magnus, and Thomas Aquinas.[27] Discussions of this in-between place, frequently referred to as the *patria*, employ such metaphors as the bosom of Abraham or the place "across the Jordan."[28] Key to these texts is the essential desire of the soul for unity with the Deity, a fulfillment expressed in terms of proximity and vision, of seeing God "face to face." In this desire, Mary often plays a figurative role both in terms of access, as the *porta coeli* or *scala coeli*, as the ivory suggests, and as the *Sponsa*, as a sign of the union of soul and body in the marriage of Christ and his Church.[29] That relation is important because, as Caroline Bynum has shown, the very definition of self in this context depends upon notions of the glorified soul's continuity with body; indeed, the qualities or *dotes* the beatified soul bestows on the glorified body are one element in its restoration of identity.[30] The *patria* and Mary's role become vivid in a different way in sermon and visionary literature. Helinand of Froidmont (c. 1160) tells of the miracle of the man who died, was shown purgatory, and was then led by an angel to the east, where a wall set apart a beautiful, sunny, flower-filled field for the souls of saints before the "regnum dei."[31] In a contemporary example, a pleasant place presided over by Mary precedes a vision of the lower world, and in numerous mid-thirteenth century exempla Mary herself is the guide and the place is one distinguished not by flora but by the company of saints over which she herself presides.[32] By the time of the ivory diptych, Mary is not an unfamiliar figure in these "upper reaches."

Although this imagery was slow to appear in the visual arts, by the second decade of the fourteenth century many works had begun to elaborate the themes and motifs we have seen in the Cambrai miniature. What Panofsky referred as the "new style" *Allerheiligenbilder* made their appearance.[33] In these All Saints images Christ and Mary are above a large and sometimes diverse group of saints and musical angels, the setting may be sky or clouds, and heretofore traditional elements, such as the *Agnus Dei*, are not always present. In some, the souls of the faithful are lifted by angels into orders of the elect; in others, Mary and Christ are enthroned with Christ at Mary's right, as though to suggest that the multitudes of surrounding saints are in her protection or that she is their representative.[34] This is also the suggestion in Cimabue's influential fresco of c. 1280 in the upper chapel at Assisi, where Christ and Mary share an impressive throne and Mary, to Christ's right, gestures to the surrounding company of the elect as if to present them to the blessing Christ (Figure 9).[35] The emphasis of the image, which follows scenes of Mary's death and ascension, is clearly that of the Triumph of the Virgin, and the same is true of a number of independent panels that show Mary and Christ enthroned, alone or with a multitude of saints, but with Christ at her right even as she is crowned.[36] It is also the case in Nardo di Cione's fresco of Heaven in the Strozzi Chapel at Santa Maria Novella in Florence, a work of c. 1350 in which Christ and Mary are crowned and enthroned together above a large assembly of the elect and angels (Figure 10). With the resurrection of the dead and Christ in judgment on the adjacent wall and with hell on the opposite one, the arrangement would seem to be that of a traditional Last

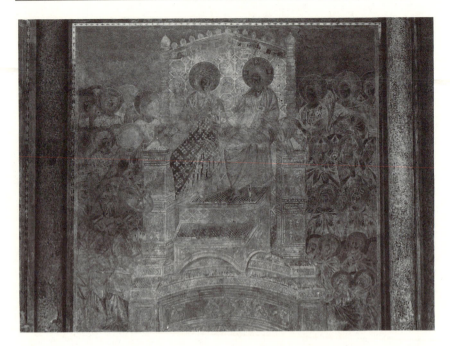

Figure 9. Cimabue, *The Heavenly Throne*. S. Francesco, Assisi. Photo: Sacro Convento, Assisi.

Judgment, except that here, as in the Munich and Cambrai pages, the angels and elect are in distinct ranks and references to the Church figure prominently.[37] Here again the Marian imagery is central. In this case it probably reflects Dominican hymns sung at the church, hymns which address Mary as Queen and ask to be gathered up into the company of heaven.[38] The painting is particularly interesting in our context because unlike the Hell fresco, which is indebted in many details to Dante's poem, the Heaven fresco seems to depend directly on Aquinas's theology of a century earlier; if it parallels the *Paradisio*, it is in the way they both describe Mary's role in providing access to the beatific vision.[39] Indeed, the very proximity of the Heaven and Last Judgment frescos underscores Mary's distinctive role in the former: how she gives the painting a devotional focus and enables it to take on institutional implications and to figure the soul's embodiment and protection in the timeless period of the afterworld.[40]

So far our discussion has dealt with the Cambrai painting as though it merely extended the forms we found in earlier manuscripts, albeit substituting

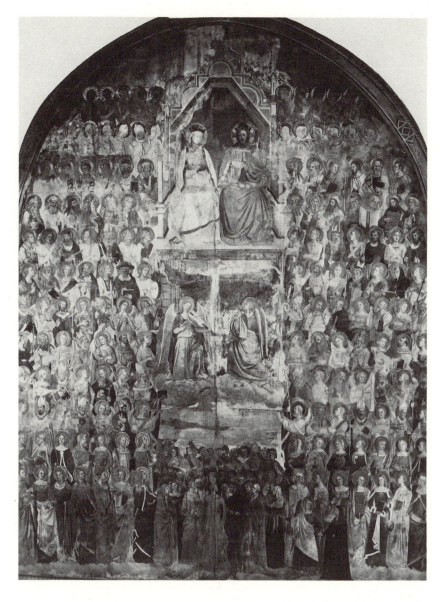

Figure 10. Nardo di Cione, *Heaven*. Fresco, Strozzi Chapel, Santa Maria Novella, Florence. Photo: Alinari/Art Resource, NY.

Figure 11. Floreffe reliquary of the True Cross (open). Louvre, Paris. Photo: Réunion des Musées Nationaux, Paris.

a Gothic structure for the Romanesque forms of the Canterbury miniature or for the geometrically partitioned one of the Munich page. But this would not explain the most striking features of the Cambrai miniature: its gilt forms, the miniaturization of a three-story structure, or the narrow decorative strips that frame each compartment. Although the forms may be architectural, they refer not to the built forms of Gothic churches but to those of metalwork reliquaries. An apt analogy is the Louvre reliquary of the True Cross from Floreffe, a work of about 1255–60 (Figure 11).[41] All those details in the miniature that make no sense as an architectural cross-section fall into place when they are seen in terms of metalwork: the miniature's narrow lateral compartments with musical angels correspond to the inner part of the reliquary's wings, the part that covers the side of the object when it is closed; each of the broader lateral compartments, which are exactly half the width of the central compartment, correspond to the parts of a reliquary wing that close over the front of the object; and the small pinnacles above the roof of the lateral compartments, which are normally alongside the central tower, are now at the far sides, a position they would have only when the reliquary is open. Moreover, there are similar decorative details, such as leaf work along the edges and borders and, most telling of all, supportive footings for the base of the object. This is not a picture of a reliquary, but it reproduces certain reliquary forms in unusually explicit detail.

It is well known that reliquaries from at least the eleventh century began to take on the general form of churches and that by the mid-thirteenth century, they evolved into modern buildings with contemporary-looking details, as in the case of the shrine of St. Taurin at Evreux of about 1245, with its gables and aediculae, or the shrine of St. Gertrude at Nivelles, with its elaborate roses and side aisles. The essay by Bruno Boerner in the catalogue of the recent exhibition devoted to the Nivelles shrine makes a compelling case that these architectural reliquaries derive from earlier shrine reliquaries and never lost the associations they had with sarcophagi and with the idea of Holy Jerusalem.[42] But these later reliquaries, with their Gothic details, also have institutional associations: it is now the modern Church that superintends the way to Jerusalem for the relics of the saints within. Ecclesiology intersects with eschatology.[43]

Although illuminations have always used architectural forms as framing devices, those made at this time in the region of Cambrai often make specific reference to metalwork shrines. A telling example is the Crucifixion page before the Canon of the Mass from an early fourteenth-century Missal made for the cathedral of Cambrai (Figure 12).[44] The architectural forms enclose the body of Christ much as a monstrance encloses the host. By depicting the figure of Christ as if enshrined rather than merely enframed, the illumination underscores both the corporal presence of what it describes pictorially and what the priest is about to offer liturgically. The implications of this multivalent image are far-reaching and would require a separate essay to develop. Suffice it to say that looking into the space of a reliquary shrine is not the same as looking into that of an ordinary picture: the space in a shrine is uniquely reserved, sacrosanct, and empowered, a place where matter is especially durable and potentially affective, a place not of narrative performance but of symbolic exchange between this world and the next. From the spectator's point of view, a picture with such an interior space offers a different structure of representation, one that authenticates visual experience no less than perspective will in the centuries which follow.

The Cambrai page is a variation of this type of pictorial construction, a variation similar to those we encounter in a series of triptychs, compartment

Figure 12. Crucifixion. Missal, Cambrai, Bibl. Mun. ms 154, fol. 98v. Photo: author.

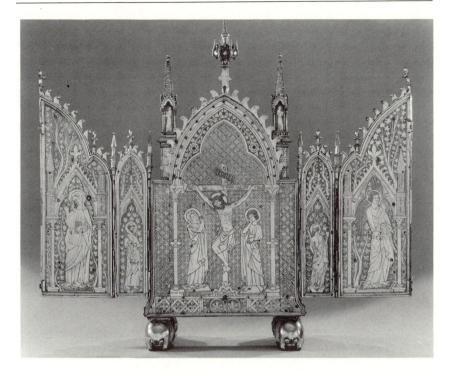

Figure 13. Floreffe reliquary of the True Cross (rear view). Louvre, Paris. Photo: Réunion des Musées Nationaux, Paris.

reliquaries, and box reliquaries of the True Cross made in the Rhine-Meuse region in the twelfth and thirteenth centuries.[45] The Floreffe reliquary may again serve as our example. A rear view with the wings open shows the angel on one wing and Mary on the other (Figure 13), enabling us to envision that when the reliquary is closed, the Annunciation is seen on the front. When it is opened, there are scenes from the Passion on the wings while, on the platform in the center, two angels stride outward and hold up the relic of the True Cross (Figure 11). What this and the earlier Cross reliquaries develop is a program keyed to the viewer's unfolding encounter with what is normally invisible. The setting is the history of salvation. Opening is synonymous with revelation. And inside is the sacred residue that links past to future and that is proffered for view.

This arrangement causes us to look again at one of the most unusual aspects of the Cambrai manuscript: the pasted-down scenes of the Infancy

of Christ on the preceding folio (see Figure 1). The page is altogether unexpected and seems at first glance to be a nineteenth-century pastiche created
by cutting out miniatures from a contemporary manuscript, probably a small
psalter, painted by a different artist who worked in a more purple palette and
used a different set of decorative motifs. The page is indeed a pastiche, but
there are several reasons why it is probably not a nineteenth-century one.
It conforms to no neo-gothic conception I am aware of for a manuscript
frontispiece. Moreover, the manuscript was never on the market, and it is inherently unlikely that someone after the fourteenth century would have been
so successful in choosing a pictorial source from a date and region consistent
with that of the rest of the book.[46] In fact, pastedowns are found in medieval
manuscripts from at least the twelfth century and are commonplace in Books
of Hours by the fifteenth.[47] Most important, there is much to suggest the
page is a creation of the early fourteenth century made as a companion to
the following miniature, which was itself probably a contemporary addition.
The green color used for its surrounding frame matches that of the following page and the dimensions of the two frames are almost identical.[48] They
also occupy approximately the same position on the verso of their respective
pages, so that one is literally in front of the other, the upper half of the first
miniature, with the Annunciation and Nativity, corresponding approximately
to the upper level of the second, with Christ and the Virgin enthroned. Moreover, a detailed examination of the four pasted-down pieces of parchment
shows that they have been carefully trimmed so that their inner edges slightly
overlap along the vertical median, the lateral edges fit snugly against the surrounding border, and there is space between the upper and lower edges and
the border. The careful treatment of these edges may well be a way of suggesting that the pastedowns are analogous to the hinged, moveable wings of
a temporarily closed reliquary. If this is the case, the Cambrai artist also took
inspiration from reliquaries in order to recreate, in a codex, a similar revelatory structure of viewing. While this would be an altogether exceptional
situation in manuscript painting, it is consistent with the references to metalwork on the following page and with the high level of invention seen in the
rest of the manuscript.

Whether this first miniature refers to a closed reliquary or simply functions to introduce the next one, and whether its viewer was the original patron
or a later reader who turned these pages as she prepared to recite the Hours
of the Virgin, these two illuminations function together as reminders of the
Incarnation and Mary's place in the history of redemption. They underscore
the custodial role of the Church, the congregation of the saints who reside

within it, and the future that awaits all of the blessed in the fullness of time. In this the two pages form a powerful introduction to the cycle of illumination that follows, especially to those initials that pit the female reader against the devil's temptations and invoke Mary's aid.[49] They present the viewer with the reassuring image of the destiny she is about to seek in her prayer. Indeed, one of the prayers in her manuscript is a French poem that concludes by asking that when she dies and her soul is separated from her body, angels take her soul to the place of joy where she will "see God face to face."[50] This phrase, which customarily refers to the beatific vision, is a clear statement of her expectations immediately following death. Such longings are common in devotional books at this time and often result in innovative depictions of the deity and the "place of joy."[51] But the image she saw in her Hours was neither a literal nor a mystical depiction of the deity; rather, it was an image that holds another field of representation, that opens to a higher level of the sacred where communion with the saints and a vision of God become possible.

This intersection of painting, reliquary forms, and eschatology is not unique to the Cambrai miniatures but is found in many later, often well-known works of art. Of these one of the most interesting is Hubert and Jan van Eyck's Ghent Altarpiece of 1432 (Figures 14–15). We know that some kind of framework surrounded the panels of the altarpiece and enabled it to be opened and closed. In her 1971 study, the late Lotte Brand Philip reconstructed the lost framework for the nine extant panels as a gigantic wall tabernacle combining the traditional functions of an altar reliquary with that of a rood screen (Figures 16–17).[52] Although details of Philip's reconstruction are controversial, her drawings underscore the parallels in both content and structure to the Cambrai miniatures, especially between the way the Annunciation on the exterior, painted in darker or gray tones, opens to a far larger and brilliantly colored spectacle of Christ and Mary enthroned above an all-inclusive hierarchy of saints. Reconstructions by other authors show a less elaborate structure but one still related to reliquaries.[53]

The Ghent Altarpiece is a theologically complex work that cannot be fully discussed in this brief essay. Its emphasis on Christ, on sacrifice, and on the liturgical and paradisial have no direct counterpart in the Cambrai miniature. But there are some striking similarities, such as the presence of mounted saints and the emphasis on the ecclesiastical as well as general features that relate to the tradition of the works discussed above, such as the groups of male and female saints or the prominence of musical angels. The Ghent panels of Adam and Eve, so different in scale and mood from the other panels, are no more extraneous than the Cambrai roundels with Ecclesia and Synagogue;

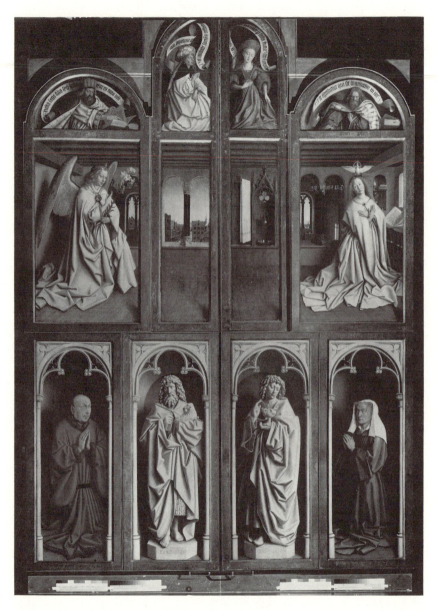

Figure 14. Jan van Eyck, Ghent Altarpiece, 1432 (closed). Cathedral of Saint Bavo, Ghent. Photo: Giraudou/Art Resource, NY.

Figure 15. Jan van Eyck, Ghent Altarpiece, 1432 (open). Cathedral of Saint Bavo, Ghent. Photo: Giraudou/Art Resource, NY.

both are reminders of those rejected in the old order that this new one supplants. This new order, with its two levels, is still the essentially Augustinian one of a new heaven and a new earth enjoyed by the community of saints in the Canterbury manuscript.[54] Moreover, the youthful Mary is still the *sponsa*: her crown is decorated with bridal flowers and the text behind her head comes from the office of the Assumption. Indeed, visitors in the first centuries after its completion understood the altarpiece in terms of the mystery of the Coronation.[55]

What is interesting in this is not the possible influence of the Cambrai Book of Hours on the van Eycks, which is unlikely,[56] but that while neither the Cambrai miniatures nor the Ghent Altarpiece are connected with bodily relics, both cite reliquary forms and use the reliquary as their operative metaphor. This is not surprising because reliquaries had long been a medium for developing new visual strategies of disclosure, presence, and authority. Although these ideas may have crystallized around relics, once in place they

Figure 16. Lotte Brand Philip's reconstruction of the frame for the Ghent Altarpiece (closed). Photo: Lotte Brand Philip, *The Ghent Altarpiece and the Art of Jan van Eyck* (Princeton, N.J.: Princeton University Press, 1980).

Figure 17. Lotte Brand Philip's reconstruction of the frame for the Ghent Altarpiece (open). Photo: Lotte Brand Philip, *The Ghent Altarpiece and the Art of Jan van Eyck* (Princeton, N.J.: Princeton University Press, 1980).

were easily transferred to painting and to subjects in which it was particularly desirable to stress the revelatory function of the image and the temporal continuity and material authenticity of what was pictured within.

In the works we have seen, the afterworld—at least that place celebrating the company of saints and proximity to the deity—was not shown consistently but it did move closer to earth. After all, in principle it was accessible right after death and, in both text and pictures, it was increasingly formulated as a projection of somatic and affective qualities a person possessed in this world. By the early fourteenth century, even optics and perception had a place in the afterworld, as writers tried to describe the differences between ocular and imaginative vision in order to define the *lumen gloriae*.[57] This situation must have provided a special kind of challenge for painters, for it had the double effect of promoting a naturalization of the afterworld while eliminating distinctions between experience before and after the general resurrection. We see this especially in the Ghent Altarpiece, where Eyckian realism draws so fine a line between heaven and earth and between Jerusalem and the place the saints wait. Yet for the viewer of the Cambrai Hours and for those in Vijd chapel in Ghent, reliquary imagery was still critical, for it provided both a metaphor for understanding how souls are preserved in transit to the end of time and a threshold to signal the visionary. With the work of Jan and others, these thresholds depended less and less upon an external apparatus; they could be folded into the works themselves, both into the technique of painting, with its vast potential for distinguishing levels of reality, and into their settings, which continue to refer to church interiors and exteriors. But for the Cambrai artist that apparatus was essential, for it enabled the painter to create a different kind of painting, not by painting differently but by inserting one structure of representation into another.

The Limits of Apocalypse

Eschatology, Epistemology, and Textuality in the *Commedia* and *Piers Plowman*

Claudia Rattazzi Papka

THAT BOTH DANTE'S *Commedia* and Langland's *Piers Plowman* are in some sense apocalyptic poems has been noted throughout their critical traditions, because both appropriate elements from the biblical Apocalypse, the Revelation to John, and include scathing critiques of secular and ecclesiastic powers, coupled with cryptic prophecies of millennial regeneration. While much work has carefully traced these allusions and attempted to decipher their historical and spiritual significance, less attention has been paid to the formal and narrative consequences of the use of apocalypse in these two poems.[1] In order to consider these literary or "authorial" aspects of apocalypse, it is useful to understand the apocalyptic text as a "fiction of judgment": a work that claims access to divine revelation while acknowledging its status as a human artifact, and in which visions of order and meaning are presented by the author as if from a divine perspective.[2] Comparing the *Commedia* and *Piers Plowman* in light of this more specifically textual definition of apocalypse makes it clear that many of the poems' most fascinating elements stem from the poets' engagement with the problems engendered, at the narrative level, by the exigencies of apocalyptic textuality.

Apocalypse claims to reveal that which only God can know, and thus constitutes, both eschatologically and epistemologically, a kind of oxymoron. The fiction of judgment furthermore claims to represent in human language what should, since it transcends the human order, be ineffable in its terms. As the apocalyptic author confronts the ends of human experience and the limits of human knowledge concerning those ends, she or he must therefore also face, at a very practical level, the limitations of linguistic representation. For the medieval Christian culture to which both Dante and Langland belong, the relationship of truth to textuality is particularly vexed: the status of the word is simultaneously highly suspect and absolutely enshrined. The serpent deceived humanity through language in the beginning, as the Antichrist will at the end; but the text in which these truths are inscribed comprises and constitutes "untouchable" language, guaranteed by the Incarnation of the Word in Christ and the fulfillment of the Old Testament in the New. While the Incarnation restores the possibility of human salvation and makes glimpses of it possible, it is only the return of Christ that will restore a prelapsarian epistemology. The promise of the Apocalypse is thus in part hermeneutic, and the unveiling of the meaning of that notoriously enigmatic text itself is only to be fulfilled in conjunction with the parousia. Textuality that makes claims to revelation is thus particularly problematic, and the authorizing strategies necessitated by the apocalyptic stance are typified by the frequently occurring divine command to write what has been seen—the moment in which the visionary is sanctioned and endowed with the prophetic mission. This mission is by definition a rather dangerous one, as the apocalyptic author must transmit a transcendent vision of what ought to be to a world that decidedly falls far short of that ideal.

Dante and Langland, in their respective visionary poems, demonstrate a profound awareness of these semiotic, rhetorical, and historical limits of apocalyptic textuality. They confront their readers with that awareness in self-reflexive moments in which they seem to grapple with the status of their own "makynges" (as Langland calls them) and with their roles as the makers of judging fictions. Both poets address the rhetorical question first, as they begin their journeys, and I discuss the profound differences in their styles of narrative authority in the first two sections of this essay. This analysis suggests the basic framework within which comparisons of Dante and Langland are generally placed: Dante's arrogance is epic and his formal precision and schematic exactitude could not be more different from Langland's associative, wandering modus operandi, which is coupled with a self-deprecatory narrative persona to produce the effect of a near-total lack of authorial control.[3] But to consider these stylistic differences rhetorical is to suggest a profound reevaluation of the usual perception of Langland's poetic talents as somehow inadequate by inserting the notion of an more intentional "inadequacy"—of poetic "failure" as rhetorical choice. It also implies, for Dante, the consideration of the context in which he wrote as crucially constraining his stylistic choices and visionary claims in their very rhetoric of unconstrained transgression.

In order to address these questions, the third, fourth, and fifth sections of the essay consider the apocalyptic culminations of the *Commedia* (in the Earthly Paradise cantos with which the *Purgatorio* concludes) and of *Piers Plowman* (in the last four passūs of the Vita). Here both poets engage the three-pronged issue of fallen language, biblical textuality, and incarnate Word, and thus provide the basis for a semiotic comparison that demonstrates a rather different relationship between the poets than their narrative rhetoric suggests. Here I argue that Langland's audacity actually in many ways outstrips Dante's, for while Dante's apocalypse, with all its build-up, finally reveals only allegories, Langland actually shows us Christ and lets him speak—in Midlands Middle English, no less—providing a moment of "unmediated" perception of the divinity, not only for the visionary, but also for his audience. In the final section of the essay, I continue my consideration of Langland's apocalypse into the final passus of *Piers Plowman*, where revelation gets clouded over again as history reasserts itself in all its unglory. Here I trace the imagery of plague in the poem in order to suggest what may be one of the differences in context that leads to the difference in apocalyptic style between Dante and Langland, at the two ends of the fourteenth century. I conclude that the repercussions of the eschatological trauma of the plague can be seen in *Piers Plowman* to include an epistemological aftershock that shakes the foundations of apocalyptic textuality represented by Dante's generic apotheosis. Finally, I suggest that Dante's text is itself conditioned by a rather different historical nexus of death and apocalypse, the pressure of which is marked, however, by its absence in the *Commedia*.

"A te convien tenere altro viaggio . . ." (Inf. 1: 91)

"It behooves you to go by another way if you would escape from this wild place,"[4] the shade of Virgil tells Dante, coming to his spiritual and poetic rescue in the "selva oscura" where the action of the *Commedia* begins. In that dark wood, Dante has strayed from the true path—"la verace via" (*Inf.* 1: 12)—and found himself confronted by three feral and allegorical beasts, the last of which, a hungry wolf, has blocked his progress completely. Virgil proposes a radical, eschatological detour whose first turn is into prophecy, as he predicts the arrival of a "veltro," a greyhound that will save Italy from

the avaricious clutches of the wolf. Virgil guides the poem across an epistemological threshold with the cryptic language of that-which-shall-be-fulfilled
and then links the path to that fulfillment with the "viaggio" on which he
proposes to take Dante:

Ond 'io per lo tuo me' penso e discerno
    che tu mi segui, e io sarò tua guida,
    e trarrotti di qui per loco etterno . . . (*Inf.* 1: 112–14)

Therefore I think and deem it best that you should follow me, and I will be your guide
and lead you hence through an eternal place . . .

Dante will be led on a tour of the eternal fires of hell and the temporary ones
of purgatory, and then, with another guide, he will ascend among the blessed
in heaven. In the one hundred cantos that follow this introductory précis,
Dante sustains a supreme fiction, "recording" the disposition of the damned
and the saved with a precision of biographical and taxonomical detail that allowed the identification of the souls of and by Dante's contemporaries, and
the legacy of which was a late medieval otherworld that often looked remarkably like the poet's own.[5]

    The authority claimed by and granted to Dante is extraordinary, as is his
audacity, for the poet repeatedly transgresses the limits inscribed by the biblical apocalypse tradition. In this tradition, Paul "knows not" the details of
his revelatory *raptus* and cannot repeat in human speech the *arcana verba* he
has heard (2 Cor. 12: 1–4). John witnesses the parousia and the raising of the
dead, but when the books of judgment are opened he does not tell us what
was written therein (Apoc. 20: 11–15). Dante, however, describes precisely
the mechanisms of his bodily passage through the realms of the still disem-
bodied souls, as well as the divine initiation and justification of his journey.
And if, for example, when Beatrice tells him that he must write exactly what
he has seen and heard for the sake of the world that lives badly (*Purg.* 32: 103:
"in pro del mondo che mal vive"), part of what he records is a dark narration (*Purg.* 33:46: "narrazion buia") he claims not to understand, nevertheless
these *arcana verba* are (at least putatively) inscribed verbatim in his poem.
And while John cannot tell us the judgments recorded in the apocalyptic
books, Dante actually claims that divine judgment is inscribed in *his* book.[6]

    Dante's is the paradigmatic fiction of judgment, in which divine and
authorial perspectives (judgment and fiction) are almost seamlessly inter-

woven.[7] The eschatological vision Dante presents is embodied in a text the structural perfection of which further undergirds the poet's assertion of the literal, revealed truth of his *sacrato poema*, whose inexorable teleology culminates with the beatific vision he claims to have been granted.[8] Dante, in other words, goes all the way, and the egregiousness of his experience—as well as the absolute novelty of his poetic recording of it—is emphasized throughout the poem. Dante writes that, when Virgil proposed this "altro viaggio," he balked, comparing his imminent journey to those of Aeneas and Paul and protesting his unworthiness; but the comparison and Virgil's response serve in fact to emphasize Dante's chosenness and to suggest (as the "veltro" prophecy does) that Dante's journey has a purpose of profound significance, not only for himself. Dante is aware of the transgressions in which he is involved and incorporates that awareness in a rhetoric of humility that narratively serves to elicit responses that further authorize his undertaking.

> Ma io, perché venirvi? o chi 'l concede?
>   Io non Enea, io non Paulo sono;
>   me degno a ciò né io né altri 'l crede.
> Per che, se del venire io m'abbandono,
>   temo che la venuta non sia folle. (*Inf.* 2: 31–35)

But I, why do I come there? And who allows it? I am not Aeneas, I am not Paul; of this neither I nor others think me worthy. Wherefore, if I yield and come, I fear that the coming may be folly.

"*And merueylousliche me mette . . .*" (*C. Prol.* 9)

"And I dreamt a marvelous dream," the voice of Langland's narrative alter ego, Will, reports, framing his vision across the limits of consciousness, but not necessarily of truth, in the oneiric realm.[9] In the B version of the poem, the dream places Will "in a wilderness, I could not tell where"—an allusion to the same allegorical space Dante describes as a "selva oscura," that is, a place in which one becomes lost. Will is not directly confronted by threatening beasts, however; instead, he sees a broad landscape. On a hill to the east is a tower, and in "a deep dale bynethe, a dongeon" yawns darkly. In the C-text, the wilderness is gone and the authorial voice immediately glosses the allegorical landmarks: the tower is Truth, while the dungeon contains Death.
    In different ways, then, both the B and C versions suggest that what Will

is seeing is a realm not unlike Dante's, where salvation and damnation define both space and time. But what Will then sees, on which the rest of the Prologue is focused, is what lies between the eschatological and epistemological poles of the Dungeon of Death and the Tower of Truth. It is a "fair feeld ful of folk," containing "alle manere of men . . . / Werchynge and wandrynge as the world asketh" (Prol. 17–19).[10] Langland shows us not the otherworld but this world, vividly, in all its chaos and corruption, as Dante does only indirectly, through his dialogues with those for whom this life is already over and whose choice of truth or death has already been made. Langland's field full of folk—his subject and his audience—is as yet unjudged; it still lives what Beatrice, Dante's second guide, calls "[il] viver ch'è un correre a la morte": the life that is a running toward death (Purg. 33:54). Langland's first guide, a linen-clad lady who descends from the tower and later identifies herself as Holy Church, similarly points out to Will:

The mooste partie of this peple that passeth on this erthe
Have thei worship in this world, thei wilne no bettre;
Of oother hevene than here hold thei no tale. (B. 1: 7–9)

Most people who pass through this world wish for nothing better than worldly success: the only heaven they think about is on earth.

Will, as he tends to do throughout the poem, asks for an explanation: "Mercy, madame, what may this be to mene?" (1: 11). And, characteristically, the explanation he gets, lengthy and theologically sound as it is, does not exactly answer his question. Holy Church tells him unequivocally that "Treuthe is the beste" (1: 85, 135), but when Will says she must teach him more specifically how he can know truth, she calls him a fool, says his wits are dull, and gives him still more examples and explanations of truth and the "trewe," the very proliferation of which seems to undercut the clear, unified monolith Will seems to think truth should be. He then tries a different tack, asking Holy Church to tell him how he can know the false. And thus begins Will's epistemological pilgrimage, in the course of which he will seek truth—the three-part path to salvation also known in the poem as "do-well," "do-bet," and "do-best"—and will hear "of other heaven than here" many different tales.[11]

A fundamental difference thus emerges between the two poems: Dante presents himself as a chosen visionary to whom is revealed—and explained—the disposition of the souls after death, and to whom the dos and don'ts of salvation are thus rather specifically shown, without his really asking (indeed, he protests his unworthiness). Will, on the other hand, is constantly demanding examples and explanations, actively seeking answers from an ever-proliferating network of "authorities," who certainly do not give one the sense of doctrinal reliability that Dante's interlocutors exude, if only because their versions never quite match up.[12] And the eschatological closure that is the precondition (or pretext) of Dante's vision is wholly absent from Langland's, in which everything still seems to be in process—including the poem itself, with its multiple versions, meandering, associative style, and repeated resistance to closure.[13] Will is shown actively in search of meaning, which proves always multiple and elusive, while Dante has meaning thrust upon him in its most absolute, ultimate form. For Dante the doors of apocalyptic understanding are flung open, while Will beats against them with his head and with his pen. And while Dante is, throughout the *Commedia*, sanctioned and encouraged in his pilgrimage and his poetic project, Will is repeatedly challenged and discouraged; Dante is given divine commands to write, while Will is told that he is wasting his time.

In the B-text, for example, Ymaginatif—the personification of one of the mind's creative faculties—menacingly (and rather paradoxically) counsels Will to abandon his creative efforts:

Amende thee while thow myght; thow hast ben warned ofte
With poustees of pestilences, with poverte and with angres
. . .
And thow medlest thee with makynges—and myghtest go seye thi Sauter,
And bidde for hem that yyveth thee breed; for ther are bokes ynowe
To telle men what Dowel is . . . (B.12: 10–18)

So mend your ways now, while you are still able. Often enough you have been warned by outbreaks of Plague, by poverty, and by many afflictions. . . . Yet for all this, you do nothing, but play about with poetry when you might be saying your Psalter and praying for those who give you your daily bread! Are there not enough books already, to expound Do-well . . . ?

Apocalypse in the Garden

In both the *Commedia* and *Piers Plowman*, a complex constellation of concerns is introduced by an allegorical recapitulation of biblical history from Genesis to Apocalypse. In the *Commedia*, this takes place explicitly in the Terrestrial Paradise, where the human root was innocent (*Purg.* 28: 142). In *Piers Plowman*, too, there is God's garden, where a magnificent tree grows bearing a fruit called Charity. When Dante wakes in his Eden, after passing through the final fire of purgatory, Virgil promises him that here he shall eat of a marvelous fruit:

> Quel dolce pome che per tanti rami
>   cercando va la cura de' mortali,
>   oggi porrà in pace le tue fami. (*Purg.* 27: 115–17)

That sweet fruit which the care of mortals goes seeking on so many branches, this day shall give your hungerings peace.

When Will sees the Tree of Charity, he asks his guide (who in the B-text is Piers himself and in C is Liberum Arbitrium) to shake down some of the fruit, wanting to "assaien what savour it hadde" (B. 16: 74). It was of course precisely this action—characterized by Dante as Eve's refusal to remain under any veil (*Purg.* 29: 27)—that caused the biblical banishment from Eden, with which the problems of eschatology, epistemology, and textuality all (from a medieval Christian perspective) began. Accordingly, death, history, and language are central themes in the final cantos of the *Purgatorio*, and in the allegorically parallel last four passūs of *Piers Plowman*,[14] in both of which schemes of salvation history frame a revelation that undoes the Fall and apocalyptically links alpha and omega, the beginning and the end, while at the same time crucially involving the poet pilgrims themselves and the status of their texts.

    Langland focuses first on the eschatological implications of the Fall, for when the ripe fruit falls for Will, the Devil snatches it away, "And made of holy men his hoord *in Limbo Inferni*" (B.16: 84); the fruit includes "Adam and Abraham and Ysaye the prophete, / Sampson and Samuel and Seint Johan the Baptist" (16: 81–82), who, despite their holiness, must dwell in hell because they lived before Christ. The historical aspect is developed, with all its typological force, as the kidnapping of the prophets and patriarchs begets the Incarnation. Old Law and New Law overlap when Abraham and Moses appear as Faith and Charity with their own two versions of "do-well" that gloss the retelling of the life of Christ from the Annunciation to the betrayal by Judas. Abraham expounds the mystery of the Trinity to the dreamer while also recapitulating the highlights of his role in Genesis and asserting his eschatological task as the keeper of the souls "Lollynge in my lappe, til swich a lord us fecche" (16: 269). It is typical of *Piers Plowman* that allegory proliferates in this nonlinear way, and it is no wonder Will gets confused when Moses appears, as *Spes*, in search of Christ, who must seal the text of the commandments Moses carries, which are not the ten we expect but the simple twofold mandate: "*Dilige deum et proximum tuum*" (from, e.g., Matt. 22). Will thus reaches another epistemological impasse, for Abraham's version of the path to salvation was to believe firmly in the triune deity:

"Youre wordes arn wonderfulle," quod I tho. "Which of yow is trewest,
And lelest to leve on for lif and for soule?" (B.17: 25–26)

"Your words astound me" I said. "How can I tell which of you to believe—which of you to trust to save one's soul?"

The problem of apparently competing doctrinal authorities is resolved, at least rhetorically, by the Samaritan whom the dreamer next encounters, who tells Will that both Abraham and Moses are correct, although they have both failed to help the stricken man the Samaritan has succored on the side of the road. The Samaritan explains:

May no medicyne under molde the man to heele brynge—
Neither Feith ne fyn Hope, so festered be hise woundes,
Withouten the blood of a barn born of a mayde. (B.17: 93–95)

No medicine on earth, not even Faith and Hope, can heal that man; his wounds are so festered. The only cure is the blood of a child born of a virgin.

The inexorable logic of redemption demands the sacrifice of the incarnate God, which Will indeed witnesses in his next dream. It begins with the singing of the "Hosanna" that accompanied Christ's entry into Jerusalem (Matt. 21: 9), which Dante also hears in his Eden.

In the *Commedia*'s Earthly Paradise, the "osanna" accompanies a phantasmagoric procession replete with apocalyptic allusions, and its Christological associations are amplified by the cry of one hundred angels who emerge from the chariot at the center of the procession:

Quali i beati al novissimo bando
surgeran presti ognun di sua caverna,
la revestita voce alleluiando,

cotali in su la divina basterna
si levar cento, *ad vocem tanti senis,*
ministri e messagier di vita etterna.
Tutti dicean: *"Benedictus qui venis"* . . . (*Purg.* 30: 13–19)

As the blessed at the last Trump will rise ready each from his tomb, singing Hallelujah with reclad voice, so upon the divine chariot, *ad vocem tanti senis,* rose up a hundred ministers and messengers of life eternal, who all cried *"Benedictus qui venis"* . . .

Dante cites this last phrase from the same triumphal moment in the Gospel of Matthew (21: 9), where it typologically heralds the eschatological event to which the resurrected "ministers and messengers of eternal life" also allude—for Christ's entry into Jerusalem preceding his Passion is analagous to his Second Coming, as bridegroom of the heavenly Jerusalem (Apoc. 21: 9). This eschatological dimension is less explicitly present in Langland's use of the allusions because he is indeed retelling the story of the life of Christ and has now come to the episode of his Passion—his death. But for both Dante and Langland, the transcendence of death is at the heart of these sections of their poems. And it is also linked, in the Edenic contexts, to the transcendence of language and of history, whose postlapsarian inadequacies parallel those of the rendered-mortal body. Apocalypse undoes Genesis in that humanity regains its immortality, language becomes immediate, literal, and transparent, and history becomes, as it were, immaterial. Langland figures the first transformation in its most literal—that is, historical—sense, precisely by retelling the story of Christ's death and resurrection. For Dante, however, all this apocalyptic expectation leads not to the revelation of Christ—a Christ who actually speaks, and whose words are recorded, in *Piers Plowman*—but to the revelation of Beatrice, Dante's most allegorical figure. Dante transforms history into allegory, as textual apocalypse inevitably does, moving into a prophetic mode that exploits the seemingly immediate language of images while acknowledging the "narrazion buia" their representation actually represents.

Dante's Eden, "la divina foresta spessa e viva" (*Purg.* 28: 2), serves as the stage on which an allegorical pageant appears, led by what at first appear to Dante as seven golden trees. These in fact turn out to be seven gold candelabra, which are followed by a retinue of twenty-four "elders" and four winged beasts, images that draw upon the iconographic literacy of medieval readers for a portentous, prophetic effect. But the images Dante inscribes, like the credos espoused by Abraham and Moses in Langland's garden, call into question the epistemological relationship between Old and New Testaments, as well as the epistemological status of Dante's own vision. In an address to the reader on the subject of the four winged beasts, Dante recalls the biblical intertexts of his vision and their discrepancies, while simultaneously authorizing his own text:

A descriver lor forme più non spargo
    rime, lettor; ch'altra spesa mi stringe,
    tanto che a questa non posso esser largo;
ma leggi Ezechiel, che li dipinge
    come li vide da la fredda parte
    venir con vento e con nube e con igne;
e quali troverai ne le sue carte
    tali eran quivi, salvo ch'a le penne
    Giovanni è meco e da lui si diparte. (*Purg.* 29: 97–105)

To describe their forms, reader, I do not lay out more rhymes, for other spending constrains me so that I cannot be lavish in this; but read Ezekiel who depicts them as he saw them come from the cold parts, with wind and cloud and fire; and such as you shall find them on his pages, such were they here, except that, as to the wings, John is with me, and differs from him.

The truth of Ezekiel's and John's visions of the four beasts is not undermined by the differences between them—they are, in a sense, synoptic. And while Dante's assertion of his agreement with John on the fact that the beasts each have six wings suggests the stronger truth-value of the New Testament version, it more importantly serves to vouch for the authenticity of Dante's own vision, which is thus understood to be another version of this same truth.

Langland seems to promise a similarly transcendent epistemology in the passus that constitutes the poem's most literal apocalypse, in which Christ himself appears and Will witnesses his Passion—the death of the Word made Flesh, with which Death is conquered and the Devil is made to relinquish the stolen fruit of (pre-Christian) Charity. Langland retells the story of the Passion primarily as told in the gospel according to Matthew, but drawing also on the other synoptic gospels and on the apocryphal gospel of Nicodemus, the primary medieval source for the legend of the Harrowing of Hell. For once, Langland is engaged in a synthetic, rather than a dispersive, narrative project, bringing together these different (but equally true) versions of the Truth and giving them one voice in his text—or rather, uncharacteristically silencing the voices whose versions of reality compete everywhere else in the poem—for Will actually *sees* Jesus being tried and condemned and nailed on the cross, and he describes it literally. It is as if he were describing the images along the stages of the cross painted around the apses and naves of some medieval churches, just as Dante describes the apocalyptic images familiar from the mosaics of early Christian ecclesiastical decoration. Both Dante and Langland thus draw upon visual imagery and its description to compensate for the overload of signification these moments represent. But while for Dante these images, for all their biblical pedigree, remain veiled in allegorical configurations that demand exegesis (a demand the critical tradition from its earliest representatives eagerly obliged),[15] for Langland they constitute the literal truth of the Word and do not require explanation but rather only typological fulfillment.

From "*narrazion buia*" to "*parole nude*"

After Dante has witnessed the apocalyptically charged pageant and the resurrection of his "Word" (Beatrice, whose Christological significance is elaborated in the *Vita Nuova*), the central element in the procession, the chariot that bore her to him, now becomes the focus of attention as it undergoes a series of allegorically allusive metamorphoses.[16] The *carro* is invaded by a fox, assaulted by an eagle, and then becomes the seven-headed dragon of Apocalypse, ridden by the equally familiar *meretrix*, who is, however, accompanied, kissed, and beaten by a novel giant who then drags the dragon and its rider into another *selva*. When this apocalyptic pastiche has finally come to an end, Beatrice suggests that in witnessing it Dante has reached a new moral and poetic level at which he can cast off fear and shame "sì che non parli più com' om che sogna" (*Purg.* 33: 33: "so that you may no more speak like one who is dreaming"). An epistemological hierarchy is implied by Beatrice's words, telling him he can transcend even the visionary mode of John, another dreamer of some of Dante's images, who was seen "dormendo, con la faccia arguta" (29: 144: "asleep, with keen visage") at the end of the parade of biblical books in the first, more allegorically obvious, part of the Earthly Paradise procession. Beatrice seems to acknowledge that the meaning of the latter part of the spectacle is somewhat less self-evident, for she provides an explanation, in language, of the images. But this exegesis, rather than enlightening, actually culminates with the infamous "enigma forte" (33:50) of the *Commedia*'s second major prophecy:

... io veggio certamente, e però il narro
    ... un cinquecento dieci e cinque,
messo di Dio ... (*Purg.* 33: 40, 43–44)

... for I see surely, and therefore I tell of it ... a Five Hundred, Ten, and Five, sent by
God ...

One can imagine the blank look with which these words leave Dante,
for Beatrice must assure him that events will soon make clear the meaning of
her "narrazion buia," whose darkness is perhaps also a function of its being,
precisely, the narration of what she *sees*—it is an image, translated into words;
a number that is somehow an object, a thing, and does not quite make sense
linguistically. She nevertheless tells Dante that he must report what she has
said: "Tu nota; e sì come da me son porte / così queste parole segna a' vivi"
(33: 52–53: "[Note this], and even as these words are uttered by me, so teach
them [mark them] to those who live"). And when you write them, she adds,
don't hide what you saw happen to the plant. What he sees and what Beatrice
says, the visual and the verbal signs to which Dante is being exposed and
which he must somehow translate for earthly consumption, are thus confused
or conflated, their epistemological relationship unclear. Indeed, as Beatrice
goes on about that plant—recalling both its Edenic and its Christological
significance—she sees that Dante is still quite dumbfounded, and with some
annoyance she says:

Ma perch'io veggio te ne lo 'ntelletto
    fatto di pietra e, impetrato, tinto,
    sì che t'abbaglia il lume del mio detto,
voglio anco, e se non scritto, almen dipinto,
    che 'l te ne porti dentro a te per quello
    che si reca il bordon di palma cinto. (*Purg.* 33: 73–78)

But since I see you turned to stone in your mind, and stonelike, such in hue that the
light of my word dazes you, I would also have you bear it away with you—and if not
written, at least depicted [painted]—for the reason that the pilgrim's staff is brought
back wreathed with palm.

Dante's incomprehension is described by Beatrice in another paradoxical
conflation of visual and verbal modes of understanding—her words blind him
and turn his mind stony and opaque—but her solution to his bafflement in the

face of her "dark narration" is the instruction that he store her words in images "painted" in his memory as the sign of his pilgrimage. The prophetic mode of representation Dante adopts in this eschatologically charged section of his poem engages the hermeneutic of "the revelation that conceals" and demonstrates that, despite having regained Eden, he has not fully transcended the limits of his genre, in which images must stand as shorthand for the proliferating polysemy of apocalypse that appears to the human mind as a "narrazion buia." But then, in the final moments before Dante will experience the vision of heaven, the description of which occupies the thirty-three cantos of the *Paradiso*, but which itself lasts only an instant, Beatrice makes him a promise:

Veramente oramai saranno nude
    le mie parole, quanto converrassi
    quelle scovrire a la tua vista rude. (*Purg.* 33: 100–102)

But [truly,] henceforth my words shall be as simple [naked] as may be needful to make them plain [reveal them] to your rude sight.

The promise of "naked words" represents the epistemological plenitude of unmediated understanding that eschatological apocalypse promises to fulfill, and in which Dante will participate by partaking of the beatific vision. The Edenic interlude, replete with the prophetic imagery of Ezekiel, John, and more contemporary apocalypticists, is thus for Dante but a step along the way to the revelation that constitutes the *Paradiso*. Before that revelation he must yet pass through the river Eunoe, Dante's invented counterpart to the classical Lethe (which also flows through his Terrestrial Paradise), the waters of which, Beatrice says, will revive his stunned faculties ("la tramortita sua virtù ravviva": *Purg.* 33: 129) and prepare him for the "trasumanar" (*Par.* 1: 70) that makes his *raptus* to the empyrean possible. But in an address to the reader in the final lines of the *Purgatorio*, Dante suggests that despite the eschatological and epistemological revelation he is about to experience, and despite Beatrice's promise of "parole nude," his own words continue to be bound by textual limits he describes in their most literal, physical sense:

S'io avessi, lettor, più lungo spazio
    da scrivere, i' pur cantere' in parte
    lo dolce ber che mai non m'avria sazio;

ma perché piene son tutte le carte
    ordite a questa cantica seconda,
    non mi lascia più ir lo fren de l'arte. (*Purg.* 33: 136–41)

If, reader, I had greater space for writing, I would yet partly sing the sweet draught which never would have sated me; but since all the pages ordained for this second canticle are filled, the [brake] of art lets me go no further.

Beatrice promises "parole nude" and in many ways delivers them in the *Paradiso*, explaining the heavenly hierarchies and the physics of immortality as unallegorically as possible; but the paradox of apocalyptic textuality is by no means resolved in the *Commedia*'s final cantica. It is, however, ultimately "deified" when Dante, in his concluding vision of the Trinity, sees the image of a book, the single volume in which all the universe is bound. This is the book of divine order, the book that guarantees meaning in all "ciò che per l'universo si squaderna" (*Par.* 33: 87: "that which is dispersed in leaves [un-bound] throughout the universe"), a book whose eschatological and episte-mological equivalent the *Commedia* itself attempts to be.[17] The book is both the object and the site of beatific plenitude, but it is also, as an image of the physical book from which Dante's *lettor* reads, a reminder of the distance be-tween our words and God's words of creation, incarnation, and judgment.

When the personification Book appears in Langland's vision, between Christ's death and his triumph over it, he is described as "a bolde man of speche . . . wihte two brode yes" (C.20: 240, 239: "a man with two broad, open eyes . . . who was very outspoken").[18] Like the two wheels of the chariot in Dante's Earthly Paradise vision, these two eyes denote the Old and New Testaments—two ways of seeing what is from the Christian perspective one truth, that of the Old Law fulfilled in the New—as well as suggesting the es-chatological fulfillment to which they ultimately "look." This temporal and typological ambiguity (or polysemy) is present as Book authoritatively as-serts both the promise and the threat of Christ's resurrection, in the speech that serves as the prelude to Will's witnessing the Harrowing of Hell.

And yut y, Boek, wol be brente bote he aryse to lyue
And comforte alle his kyn and out of care brynge
And alle the Iewene ioye vnioynen and vnlouken,
And bote they reuerense this resurexioun and the rode honoure
And bileue on a newe lawe, be ylost lyf and soule. (C.20: 264–68)

And yet I, Book, will be burnt but he rise to live and comfort all his kin and bring them out of their cares and unjoin and unlock all the joy of the Jews; And all but those who adore this resurrection and honor the cross, and believe in a new law, will lose life and soul.[19]

The ambiguity of Book's words permit several readings. The conventional one has Book staking himself on the assertion that Christ will live again, and is generally linked to an anti-Semitic interpretation of the effects of Christ's rising on the "Iewene ioye." However, the grammatical parallelism of Book's promises—linking the verbs arise, comfort, bring, unjoin, and unlock—may in fact undergird a reading in which the "unlocking" of the millennial promise of the Hebrew Scriptures ("the Iewene ioye") is predicated upon "this" resurrection—a reading which could be described as "two-eyed" in its conflation of the literal with the typological. This double vision is appropriate in the context Book is introducing, for the Harrowing of Hell will show that the death of the Jewish patriarchs is not final, despite the Old Law, because of its fulfillment by the New. But as Langland transcribes the Harrowing from the gospel book into his own, these ambiguities reach a level of both epistemological and eschatological transgression, as the words of the Incarnate Word are inscribed by the poet into his text and in his own vernacular, and his book becomes a Book of apocalyptic pretensions.[20]

An angel threatens *"Princepes* of this place, prest vndo this gates" (C.20: 272) for the king of glory is on his way, while Lucifer, Satan, and Hell itself debate the eschatological question of the Devil's right to sinners after the Fall. Christ will deny this right in his upcoming speech with an argument previewed by Satan himself in his accusation that Lucifer lied to Eve when he promised her the knowledge of good and evil:

And byhihtest here and hym aftur to knowe
As two godes, with god, bothe goed and ille.
Thus with treson and tricherie thow troyledest hem bothe
And dust hem breke here buxumnesse thorw fals bihestes . . . (C.20: 317–20)

And you promised that after they would know, as two gods, with God, both good and ill. Thus with treason and treachery you deceived them both and made them break their obedience through false promises.[21]

Gobelyne concurs, "We haen no trewe title to hem" (20: 324), and as the light he recognizes as God appears, Satan concludes that they have now "ylost oure lordschipe a londe and in helle" (20: 349) because of that lie. It is a lie that proves the limits of human epistemological possibility, which Christ "quytes" by stretching the previous limits of human eschatological possibility, so that, as Christ says, punning and suggesting the way his own mercy cheats death, "gyle be bigyled thorw grace at the laste" (20: 392).

Christ announces his presence in hell, body and soul, to retrieve the prophets and patriarchs who proclaimed the law he himself fulfills, an action whose justice he asserts through a series of juxtapositions that turn on the notion of Old Testament retribution—"*Dentem pro dente, et oculum pro oculo*" (Ex. 21: 24, C.20: 385a)—and prove that "*Non veni solvere legem, sed adimplere*" (Matt. 5: 17, C.20: 395a). Christ makes clear that this harrowing is the type of the resurrection of the dead, for "thenne shal y come as kynge, with croune and with angeles, / And haue out of helle alle mennes soules" (412–13), and he suggests that then, too, he will be stretching the limits of justice with his grace. Langland's Christ thus reveals his triple typological identity, as the fulfillment of the Old Law in the New, and as promise of a final law, when he will reign on earth.[22] At the same time, the legalistic maneuvers of Christ's speech, its slippery punnings and pairings, are at once paralleled and opposed to the lies of Satan to Eve, so that Christ's language undoes the semiotic rupture of the Fall just as Christ's mercy undoes Satan's treachery: "Y may do mercy of my rihtwysnesse and alle myn wordes trewe" (431).

Christ tells Satan he has no right to the just souls of the prophets and patriarchs because he got Adam and Eve not by right but by guile, the antidote to which (its complement) is the grace by which his death redeems the Fall. But Langland's Christ goes on to suggest that his compassion for humanity, because of his own human nature, may go even further than this already generous deal:

Ac to be merciable to man thenne my kynde asketh,
For we beth brethrene of o bloed, ac nat in baptisme alle. . . .
For bloed may se bloed bothe afurst and acale
Ac bloed may nat se bloed blede, bote hym rewe.
     Audivi archana verba, que non licet homini loqui.
Ac my rihtwysnesse and rihte shal regnen in helle,
And mercy al mankynde bifore me in heuene. (C.20: 417–18, 437–440)

And how can I, with my human nature, refuse men mercy on that day? For we are brothers of one blood, though we are not all of one baptism. . . . For a man may suffer his kind to go cold and hungry, but he cannot see them bleed without pitying them. *And I heard secret words which it is not granted to man to utter.* My righteousness and my justice shall rule over hell, and my mercy over all mankind before me in heaven.

The day of wrath might in the end be a day of mercy, Christ suggests, for all those who share the "blood" of human nature, which Christ, himself a creature of blood whose blood has been shed, cannot bear to see bleed. At this point, at the height of Langland's revelation of the apocalyptically speaking Christ, at the point where a heterodox universalism is almost being espoused, Langland inserts the Pauline paradigm of visionary restraint and epistemological aporia. The appropriation of Paul's words constitutes a kind of apocalyptic ellipsis, despite the fact that in some sense the transgressive words (the promise of universal salvation) have already been uttered.

This moment represents the epistemological apotheosis of the poem, when Christ speaks the "parole nude" that mark the limits of Langland's apocalypse, which appropriately ends with the chaining of Satan—the action, in John's Apocalypse, that signals the start of the millennium. In Langland's text, however, it initiates the descent back into allegory after revelation, a return to the personifications framing the dramatic reenactment of the life of Christ that at first continues the sense of triumphant resolution found in the finale of the Harrowing episode, imparting a sense of closure and culmination alien to the rest of Langland's poem. Peace and Righteousness are finally reconciled, and Truth and Love sing and play music until "the day dawned . . . That men rang to the resurreccioun" (C.20: 470–71). The eschatological context is quickly recast in its temporal form—it is the celebration of Christ's resurrection, Easter, not the Last Judgment—"a return to time which confirms in reality the truth of his vision."[23] At the end of this passus, all the levels of Langland's allegory are marvelously in synch, and the opening of the following passus adds a final element to the apocalyptic concordia as Langland inscribes for the first time the moment at which he not only "waked" but also "wrot what y hadde ydremed" (C.21:1).

From Comedy to Tragedy

Almost immediately, however, confusion returns, first epistemologically, with Will's inability to understand what he sees at the opening of his next dream, then eschatologically—after the allegorical narrative of the founding of Holy Church (to which Augustinian interpretation equated the millennial binding of Satan)—in the appearance of Antichrist and the descent into chaos with which *Piers Plowman* concludes.[24] While in Passus 20 Truth can emphatically exclaim, "Trewes . . . thow tellest vs soeth, by Iesus!" (462), in Passus 21 truth has once again become fragmented and elusive, and Will's vision is clouded and confused as he sees the figure of Piers-as-Christ:

And thenne calde y Conscience to kenne me the sothe:
"Is this Iesus the ioustare . . .
Or hit is Peres the plouhman? who paynted hym so rede?" (C.21: 9–11)

So I called to Conscience to tell me the truth about it—"Is this Jesus, the knight . . .
or is it Piers the Ploughman? And who stained him so red?"

Conscience replies that they are Piers's arms, but that it is Christ who bears
them. And Will, ever the quibbler, asks why Conscience uses the name Christ
when the Jews called the son of God Jesus. The discussion is markedly anticli-
mactic after the previous passus's rendering of the Passion and Harrowing of
Hell, in which Christ is unambiguously Christ, the text is unimpeachably true,
and paradox and polysemy enable understanding rather than impede it.

The defeat of truth culminates with the arrival on the scene of Antichrist,
instantly undoing the work of Piers Plowman, who had gone off, in Passus
21, to till truth throughout the world:

Auntecrist cam thenne, and al the crop of treuthe
Turned hit vp-so-down and ouertulde the rote,
And made fals sprynge and sprede and spede menne nedes;
In uch a contrey ther he cam, kutte awey treuthe
And garte gyle growe there as he a god were. (C.22: 53–57)

Antichrist . . . came . . . and overturned all the crop of Truth, tearing it up by the roots,
and causing Falsehood to spring up and spread and supply all men's needs. In every dis-
trict where he came he cut down Truth, and grew Guile instead, disguised as goodness.

In the face of this epistemological debacle, Conscience calls on Kynde (Nature) for help and calls on all the people to take refuge in Unity/Holy Church,
attempting, it seems, to regain the harmony signaled by Christ's "kynde"—
his assuming of human nature—and realized socially in the ecclesiastical allegory that dominates Passus 21, in which Piers heads the building of the
fortress Holy Church, whose Unity must stand against the assaults of Antichrist. The people seem largely to ignore Conscience, but Kynde hears his
plea. Rather than the deification of human nature exemplified and promised
by Christ, however, Kynde now sends the agents of its destruction:

Kynde cam aftur with many kyne sores,
As pokkes and pestilences, and moche peple shente;
So Kynde thorw corupcions kulde fol mony.

Deth cam dryuyng aftur and al to duste paschte
Kynges and knyhtes, caysers and popes.
Lered ne lewed he left no man stande
That he hitte euene, that euere stured aftur. (C.22: 97–103)

Nature followed with a host of cruel diseases, slaughtering thousands with foul con-
tagions, and sweeping all before him with his plagues and poxes. Then Death came
dashing after, crushing to powder both kings and knights, emperors and pontiffs. He
left none standing, priest or layman, but hit so squarely that they never stirred again.

This Langlandian danse macabre inscribes the indiscriminateness of
death. It is a social equalizer, but from a moral perspective Kynde's assaults
are essentially ineffectual, for when, at Conscience's pleading, Kynde ceases
from his attacks, "to se the peple amende," Fortune, Lechery, and Covetyse
immediately take hold among "tho fewe that were alyue" (C.22: 109–10) and
they gather a new army to continue Antichrist's assault. If one assumes these
references to large-scale death and disease refer to the events of the Black
Death (as most readers of the poem do), then the paradox of the plague seems,
in Langland's eyes, to be that while it is indeed meaningful—an event of
divine retribution (as Reason had asserted at C.5: 115, when he "preuede that
this pestelences was for puyre synne")—it is not seen as meaningful by most of
those who survive it, or rather its meaning is perverted so that they interpret
it as a judgment that has spared them and so licensed their licentiousness.[25]
Langland's epistemological and eschatological position seems to stem
from the historical circumstance of a society that has been given a sign, the
fulminating judgment of the plague, but has failed utterly to glean its significance. Indeed, that the entire apparatus of salvation represented by Holy
Church has been undermined in the wake of the plague has been asserted
throughout the poem, from the Prologue's recounting of the parsons and
priests who complain to their bishops "That hire parisshes weren povere sith
the pestilence tyme" (B. Prol: 84) and abandon them to live in more profitable
London, to Dame Study's long diatribe against those friars who speculate
and preach in ignorance, with cataclysmic results:

Freres and faytours haen founde vp suche questions
To plese with proude men senes this pestelences,
And prechyng at seynt Poules for puyr enuye of clerkes,
That folk is not ferme in the faith ne fre of here godes
Ne sory for here synnes; so ys pruyde enhanced
In religion and in al the reume amonges riche and pore

That preyeres haen no power this pestilences to lette.
For god is deef nowadayes and deyneth vs nat to here
And gode men for oure gultes he al togrynt to deth. (C.11: 54–62)

Since the Plague, Friars and other impostors have thought up theological questions just to please the proud. And they preach at St. Paul's out of sheer envy of the clergy, so that folk are no longer confirmed in the faith, or taught to be charitable with their goods and sorry for their sins. Not only in the Religious Orders, but among rich and poor throughout the whole realm, pride has spread so much that all our prayers are powerless to stop the pestilence. [For God is deaf nowadays and does not deign to hear us, and for our guilt he grinds good men to death].

The disastrous repercussions of the friar's pride and greed become the focus of the final passus of *Piers Plowman*, as one such friar talks his way into Unity, promising he can heal Contrition, who has been wounded by Hypocrisy in the psychomachic battle that conflates the imagery of plague with that of war. Conscience explains that the parson has given Contrition plasters for his sores that are too slow and painful, and the friar instead sells him a plaster and some prayers "for a litel suluer" (C.22: 367). The result of the friar's commodification of salvation is that Contrition forgets to cry for his sins and, comforted by the friar's flattery, he leaves Unity, making true penance, and therefore salvation, impossible. The sins attack Unity once more, but the friar has so "enchaunted" its inhabitants with his "dwale" (opiate) that there is no one left to help Conscience defend it, and so he declares he will set out on a pilgrimage to find Piers Plowman, who will destroy pride and give the friars a "fyndynge"—a provision for their livelihood—so they will no longer destroy salvation by claiming to sell it independently of true penance. In his last words, Conscience calls again on Kynde to avenge him and help him until Piers can be found. The implication is that the cycles of plague that rent the social and moral fabric of late fourteenth-century England will continue to "grind good men to death" until Conscience and Piers together can recall to the inhabitants of Unity how they may be heard by a God who is for the time being deaf to their imprecations.

This is, of course, what Langland tries to do in and through his poem, just as Dante must write "in pro del mondo che mal vive." It is also the message of Langland's prophecies; ambiguous as they may be in their specifics, they all foretell a period of disaster. Dante's prophecies rather suggest an imminent redemption in which he and his poem play an important part. Langland makes no such presumption at the apocalyptic level Dante reaches, but rather seems to intend his text as an edifying guide to the perplexed that acknowledges its inability to rise above that perplexity. The book of divine order from which Dante claims to copy is closed to Langland, who can only show its perverted paraphrasing by the multitude of voices he dreams, and for whom the only unequivocal truth is in the transcendence of the Word made Flesh. While Dante's revelation in the Earthly Paradise takes him beyond apocalypse to the promise of the beatific vision, Langland's revelation of Christ leads only to the disintegration that goes on and on in the anticipation of apocalypse.

As Robert Lerner has pointed out, the Black Death did not generate any real novelty in the nature (or even the amount) of apocalyptic expectation in Western Europe.[26] Indeed, the chiliastic currents evident in both Dante and Langland are part of a long and steadily flowing river of millenarian tradition in early and medieval Christianity. The similarity of the poets' diagnoses of what ails their respective societies is profound, as is their shared millennial "hope for supernaturally inspired, imminent, and sweeping this-worldly change,"[27] and both poets express their apocalyptic mentalities in the prophetic moments that punctuate the *Commedia* and *Piers Plowman*. Both poets furthermore demonstrate a certain influence of Joachite ideas and the often connected concern with poverty and the mendicant orders, as well as the more specific conviction that the root of their society's corruption lies in greed. With these elements, the apocalypses of Dante and Langland are "updated" with the concerns that mark fourteenth-century apocalypticism, much of which was generated around the internecine conflicts of the Franciscan order.[28] And again, in large part, Dante and Langland share these "modernizations" of their apocalyptic material. The picture, then, in terms of ideological content, seems much as Lerner paints it—a picture of continuity between the early and late years of the fourteenth century.

Dante and Langland, however, differ crucially from most of their apocalyptic predecessors and contemporaries in that their fictions of judgment are explicitly presented as fictions, in the etymological sense of the *fictio*, the "made thing." These are literary productions, rather than treatises, letters, confessions, or manifestos; they are poems, and vernacular poems at that, but it is precisely in their status as vernacular poems that the differences in their apocalypses lie. These differences, as we have seen, are manifested both rhetorically and semiotically, but their origins are fundamentally historical.

The paradox of apocalyptic textuality, of the fiction of judgment, is powerfully inscribed in Dante's *Commedia*, where moments of apocalyptic rhetoric are almost invariably coupled with moments of textual self-referentiality. Dante repeatedly asserts the truth of his vision and his message and enlists the denizens of his otherworld to reinforce the heavenly authorization for his mission as both pilgrim and poet, and the "divine" status of his *sacrato poema* is further authorized by its remarkable formal harmony and complexity. But the metatextual moments, such as those in the Earthly Paradise cantos discussed above, periodically remind us of the inescapable gap between the apocalyptic vision and the apocalyptic text, between revelation and representation.

For Langland, however, the crucial gap seems to lie elsewhere: it is not so much representation that undermines revelation, but rather history itself, and the gap is not so much between the fiction and the judgment as between the judgment and the world. The nature of this gap is suggested by David Herlihy's positing of an epistemological rupture consequent to the years of plague that separate Langland's apocalypse from Dante's. Herlihy argues that the result of this catastrophe was the sense that "the human intellect had not the power to penetrate the metaphysical structures of the universe": while earlier philosophers like Aquinas (and Dante) believed a divine order both existed and could be understood by the human intellect, their late-medieval counterparts had no such confidence.[29] In *Piers Plowman*, the plague has destroyed not only the social order but also man's ability to understand the significance of that destruction, and that inability is reflected in—and in a sense allegorized by—the poet's resistance to the proclamations of the fiction of judgment. When Christ appears in Passus 20, his revelation is more truly apocalyptic than anything in the *Commedia*, but while Dante's poem moves teleologically to its culmination with the beatific vision, Langland's falls back from its apocalypse to the chaos of the field full of folk, where history is still in progress and the attack of Antichrist is not the End, but just the beginning of yet another pilgrimage in search of a truth that can no longer, or not yet, be found on this earth.

A final, critical paradox suggests that just as there are specific textual repercussions of death (in the form of the plague) for Langland's apocalypse that have generally been ignored, so too the critical tradition has generally eschewed exploring the impact of a specific historical nexus of death and apocalypse on Dante's text. While *Piers Plowman* is now frequently considered in the context of the later Lollard controversies, when forms of vernacular religiosity were branded heretical around the turn of the century and well into the fifteenth, Dante's connection to the persecution of the Spiritual Franciscans and their lay followers, which is historically so much stronger (the heresy trials were actually occurring as Dante wrote the *Commedia*), is only beginning to be sketched.[30] Rather than undermining the view of the *Commedia*, of which Dantisti seem perhaps overly fond, as a poetically transcendent fiction of judgment—a view Dante himself promotes in his "sacred poem"—this context in fact suggests the historical incentive for Dante's narrative stance as *scriba dei*. Because death was a real consequence of apocalyptic claims for some of Dante's like-minded contemporaries, he had to adopt a dual rhetoric of ultimate authorization and semiotic inadequacy, so that *lo fren de l'arte*, "the brake of art," stopped him just short of heresy.

While for Dante apocalyptic textuality is thus a means for transcending history, for Langland it is finally an acknowledgment of the historical impossibility of transcendence. The ways these poets perceive and represent the limits of apocalypse illuminate crucial aspects of the relationship of eschatology to epistemology and suggest how that relationship may have shifted in the course of the fourteenth century.

Notes

Introduction

1. "Eschatology" is a modern coinage apparently first used by Karl Gottlieb Bretschneider in 1804; medieval thinkers spoke of *novissimi* or *res novissimae*. See G. Filoramo, "Eschatology," in *Encyclopedia of the Early Church*, ed. Angelo Di Bernardino, trans. Adrian Walford, 2 vols. (New York: Oxford University Press, 1992), 1: 284–86.

2. Philippe Ariès, *The Hour of Our Death*, trans. Helen Weaver (New York: Knopf, 1981); Oscar Cullman, *Christ and Time: The Primitive Christian Conception of Time and History*, trans. F. Filson, 3rd ed. (London: SCM, 1962); idem, *Unsterblichkeit der Seele oder Auferstehung der Toten?* (Stuttgart: Kreuz, 1964); Richard Heinzmann, *Die Unsterblichkeit der Seele und die Auferstehung des Leibes: eine problemgeschichtliche Untersuchung der frühscholastischen Sentenzen- und Summenliteratur von Anselm von Laon bis Wilhelm von Auxerre*, Beiträge zur Geschichte der Philosophie und Theologie des Mittelalters: Texte und Untersuchungen 40, 3 (Münster: Aschendorff, 1965); Gisbert Greshake and Jacob Kremer, *Resurrectio mortuorum: zum theologischen Verständnis der leiblichen Auferstehung* (Darmstadt: Wissenschaftliche Buchgesellschaft, 1986); Nikolaus Wicki, *Die Lehre von der himmlischen Seligkeit in der mittelalterlichen Scholastik von Petrus Lombardus bis Thomas von Aquin*, Studia Friburgensia, NF 9 (Freiburg: Universitätsverlag, 1954); Jacques Le Goff, *The Birth of Purgatory*, trans. Arthur Goldhammer (Chicago: University of Chicago Press, 1984; original publication Paris, 1981); Norman Cohn, *The Pursuit of the Millennium* (Fairlawn, N.J.: Essential Books, 1957); Simon Tugwell, *Human Immortality and the Redemption of Death* (London: Temple Gate, 1990); Caroline Walker Bynum, *The Resurrection of the Body in Western Christianity, 200–1336* (New York: Columbia University Press, 1995). See also the collection *Immortality and Resurrection: Four Essays*, ed. Krister Stendhal (New York: Macmillan, 1965).

3. Bernard McGinn, *The Calabrian Abbot: Joachim of Fiore in the History of Western Thought* (New York: Macmillan, 1985); Robert Lerner, *The Powers of Prophecy: The Cedar of Lebanon from the Mongol Onslaught to the Dawn of the Enlightenment* (Berkeley: University of California Press, 1983).

4. Richard K. Emmerson, *Antichrist in the Middle Ages: A Study of Medieval Apocalypticism, Art and Literature* (Seattle: University of Washington Press, 1981); Bernard McGinn, *Antichrist: Two Thousand Years of the Human Fascination with Evil* (San Francisco: Harper, 1994); Rosemary Muir Wright, *Art and Antichrist in Medieval Europe* (Manchester: Manchester University Press, 1995); L. J. Lietaert Peerbolte, *The Antecedents of Antichrist: A Traditio-Historical Study of the Earliest Christian Views on*

Eschatological Opponents (Leiden: E. J. Brill, 1996); and Curtis Bostick, *The Antichrist and the Lollards: Apocalypticism in Late Medieval and Reformation England* (Leiden: E. J. Brill, 1998).

5. Paul J. Alexander, *The Byzantine Apocalyptic Tradition* (Berkeley: University of California Press, 1984).

6. *The Encyclopedia of Apocalypticism*, 3 vols. (New York: Continuum, 1998). Several of the essays in volumes 1 and 2 cover in a synthetic way the topics discussed here in more detail.

7. Richard Landes, "Lest the Millennium Be Fulfilled: Apocalyptic Expectations and the Pattern of Western Chronography, 100–800 CE," in *The Use and Abuse of Eschatology in the Middle Ages*, ed. Werner Verbeke et al. (Leuven: Leuven University Press, 1988), pp. 137–211. See also Johannes Fried, "Endzeiterwartung um die Jahrtausendwende," *Deutsches Archiv für Erforschung des Mittelalters* 45, 2 (1989): 385–473.

8. Richard Landes, *Relics, Apocalypse, and the Deceits of History: Ademar of Chabannes, 989–1034* (Cambridge, Mass.: Harvard University Press, 1995); Derk Visser, *Apocalypse as Utopian Expectation (800–1500): The Apocalypse Commentary of Berengaudus of Ferrières and the Relationship Between Exegesis, Liturgy, and Iconography* (Leiden: E. J. Brill, 1996).

9. Richard Landes, "Between Aristocracy and Heresy: Popular Participation in the Limousin Peace of God, 994–1033" in *The Peace of God: Social Violence and Religious Response in France Around the Year 1000*, ed. Richard Landes and Thomas Head (Ithaca, N.Y.: Cornell University Press, 1992), pp. 184–218; idem, "La vie apostolique en Aquitaine en l'an mil: Paix de Dieu, culte des reliques, et communautés hérétiques," *Annales E. S. C.* 46, 3 (1991): 573–93.

10. Georges Duby, *The Three Orders: Feudal Society Imagined*, trans. Arthur Goldhammer (Chicago: University of Chicago Press, 1980), pp. 130–34; David Burr, *Olivi's Peaceable Kingdom: A Reading of the Apocalypse Commentary* (Philadelphia: University of Pennsylvania Press, 1993); idem, *Olivi and Franciscan Poverty: The Origins of the Usus Pauper Controversy* (Philadelphia: University of Pennsylvania Press, 1989); *Eschatologie und Hussitismus*, ed. Alexander Patchovsky and František Šmahel (Prague: Historisches Institut, 1996).

11. Andrew Colin Gow, *The Red Jews: Antisemitism in an Apocalyptic Age, 1200–1600* (Leiden: E. J. Brill, 1995).

12. See, for example, the essays collected in *The "Apocalypse" in the Middle Ages*, ed. Richard K. Emmerson and Bernard McGinn (Ithaca, N.Y.: Cornell University Press, 1992) as noted by Visser, *Apocalypse as Utopian Expectation*, pp. 2–3.

13. Frank Kermode, *The Sense of Ending: Studies in the Theory of Fiction* (London and New York: Oxford University Press, 1968).

14. Richard K. Emmerson and Ronald B. Herzman, *The Apocalyptic Imagination in Medieval Literature*, (Philadelphia: University of Pennsylvania Press, 1992); Katherine Kerby-Fulton, *Reformist Apocalypticism and Piers Plowman* (Cambridge: Cambridge University Press, 1990).

15. Guy Lobrichon, "L'ordre de ce temps et les désordres de la fin: Apocalypse et société, du IXe à la fin du XIe siècle," in Verbeke et al., eds., *Use and Abuse of Eschatology*, p. 221.

16. Ariès, *Hour of Our Death*; Paul Binski, *Medieval Death: Ritual and Repre-*

sentation (Ithaca, N.Y.: Cornell University Press, 1996); T. S. R. Boase, *Death in the Middle Ages: Mortality, Judgment, and Remembrance* (New York: McGraw-Hill, 1972); Aron Gurevich, "Perceptions of the Individual and the Hereafter in the Middle Ages," in Gurevich, *Historical Anthropology of the Middle Ages*, ed. Jana Howlett (Chicago: University of Chicago Press, 1992), 65–89; Jean Delumeau, *Sin and Fear: The Emergence of a Western Guilt Culture, 13th–18th Centuries*, trans. E. Nicholson (New York: St. Martin's Press, 1990); and H. Braet and W. Verbeke, eds., *Death in the Middle Ages*, Mediaevalia Lovaniensia ser. I, studia 9 (Leuven: Leuven University Press, 1983).

17. Damien Sicard, *La liturgie de la mort dans l'église latine des origines à la réforme carolingienne* (Münster: Aschendorff, 1978); Frederick Paxton, *Christianizing Death: The Creation of a Ritual Process in Early Medieval Europe* (Ithaca, N.Y.: Cornell University Press, 1990); Meghan McLaughlin, *Consorting with Saints: Prayer for the Dead in Early Medieval France* (Ithaca, N.Y.: Cornell University Press, 1994); Mary Catharine O'Connor, *The Art of Dying Well: The Development of the Ars Moriendi* (New York: Columbia University Press, 1942); Kathleen Cohen, *Metamorphosis of a Death Symbol: The Transi Tomb in the Late Middle Ages and the Renaissance* (Berkeley: University of California Press, 1973); Howard Montagu Colvin, *Architecture and the After-Life* (New Haven, Conn.: Yale University Press, 1991); Sybille Ebert-Schifferer and Theo Jülich, eds., *Gottesfurcht und Höllenangst: Ein Lesebuch zur mittelalterlichen Kunst* (Darmstadt: Hessisches Landesmuseum, 1993); and Barbara Harvey, *Living and Dying in England, 1100–1540: The Monastic Experience* (Oxford: Clarendon Press, 1993).

18. Aron Gurevich, "The *Tale of Thorstein Goose-Pimples*, the Underworld, and Icelandic Humour," in Gurevich, *Historical Anthropology*, 116–21; Claude Carozzi, *Le voyage de l'âme dans l'au-delà d'après la littérature latine (Ve–XIIIe siècle)* (Rome: Ecole Française de Rome, 1994); *Visions of Heaven and Hell Before Dante*, ed. Eileen Gardiner (New York: Italica Press, 1989); Alison Morgan, *Dante and the Medieval Other World* (Cambridge: Cambridge University Press, 1990); Peter Dinzelbacher, *Vision und Visionsliteratur im Mittelalter* (Stuttgart: Hiersemann, 1981); Ernst Benz, *Die Vision: Erfahrungsformen und Bilderwelt* (Stuttgart: Klett, 1969).

19. Colleen McDannell and Bernhard Lang, *Heaven: A History* (New Haven, Conn.: Yale University Press, 1988), 1–144; Jeffrey Burton Russell, *A History of Heaven: The Singing Silence* (Princeton, N.J.: Princeton University Press, 1997); Alan Bernstein, *The Formation of Hell: Death and Retribution in the Ancient and Early Christian Worlds* (Ithaca, N.Y.: Cornell University Press, 1993); Piero Camporesi, *The Fear of Hell: Images of Damnation and Salvation in Early Modern Europe*, trans. Lucinda Byatt (University Park: Pennsylvania State University Press, 1991); Georges Minois, *Histoire des enfers*, Nouvelles Etudes Historiques (Paris: Fayard, 1991). The lead article of *Time* for March 24, 1997 dealt with heaven. For art historical images of both heaven and hell, see Robert Hughes, *Heaven and Hell in Western Art* (London: Weidenfeld and Nicolson, 1968).

20. Le Goff, *Birth of Purgatory*; idem, *Your Money or Your Life: Economy and Religion in the Middle Ages*, trans. Patricia Ranum (New York: Zone Books, 1988). The most important recent work on the beatific vision, another "Last Thing," is Christian Trottman, *La vision béatifique: des disputes scholastiques à son définition par Benôit XII*, Bibliothèque des Ecoles Françaises d'Athènes et de Rome (Rome: Ecole Française de Rome, 1995).

21. Barbara J. Newman, "On the Threshold of the Dead: Purgatory, Hell, and

Religious Women," in *From Virile Woman to WomanChrist: Studies in Medieval Religion and Literature* (Philadelphia: University of Pennsylvania Press, 1995), 108–36.

22. McGinn, *Visions of the End*, argues that confidence in a coming millennial age was not necessarily correlated with social or political radicalism. On this point see also Ted Daniels, *Millennialism: An International Bibliography* (New York and Oxford: Oxford University Press, 1994); Stephen D. O'Leary, *Arguing the Apocalypse: A Theory of Millennial Rhetoric* (New York and London: Garland, 1992).

23. Rebillard's emphasis on the changing attitudes toward sin would put this shift to the personal earlier than Ariès. See Eric Rebillard, *In hora mortis: évolution de la pastorale chrétienne de la mort au IVe et Ve siècle* (Rome: Ecole Française de Rome, 1994).

24. See for example Jean Leclercq, *The Love of Learning and the Desire for God: A Study of Monastic Culture*, trans. Catharine Misrahi (New York: Fordham University Press, 1961), 65–86; Marie-Noël Bouchard, "La résurrection dans la spiritualité des premiers auteurs cisterciens," *Collectanea Cisterciensia* 37 (1975): 114–29.

25. See especially Richard Landes, "Lest the Millennium Be Fulfilled."

26. Cullman, *Christ and Time*; see also *Immortality and Resurrection* (above, note 1).

27. Bynum, *Resurrection of the Body*, 21–114.

28. See the essay by Anna Harrison in the present volume.

29. On this understanding of eschatological body and place generally, see Bynum, *Resurrection of the Body*, 279–343.

30. Alan Brinkley in a talk entitled "Imagining the Twentieth Century: Perspectives from Two Fins-de-Siècles," given at Columbia University in April 1998, notes how much more dramatic were the expectations of a century ago in contrast with the more restrained cynicism of contemporary times.

31. Lawrence Shainberg, *Memories of Amnesia* (New York: Paris Review Editions/British American Publishing, 1988); Nancy Weber, *Broken-Hearted* (New York: Dutton, 1989); Laurel Doud, *This Body* (Waltham, Mass.: Little Brown, 1998). For examples of such popular literature taken seriously by specialists in the philosophy of mind, see Peter A. French, ed., *Philosophers in Wonderland: Philosophy and Psychical Research* (St. Paul, Minn.: Llewellyn, 1975), Amelie O. Rorty, ed., *The Identities of Persons* (Berkeley: University of California Press, 1976), and Douglas R. Hofstadter and Daniel C. Dennett, eds., *The Mind's I: Fantasies and Reflections on Self and Soul* (New York: Basic Books, 1981).

32. Elizabeth Kübler-Ross, *On Death and Dying* (New York: Macmillan, 1969).

33. Frank J. Tipler, *The Physics of Immortality: Modern Cosmology, God, and the Resurrection of the Dead* (New York: Doubleday, 1994).

34. Toni Morrison, *Beloved: A Novel* (New York: Knopf, 1987).

35. Caroline Bynum, "Why All the Fuss About the Body? A Medievalist's Perspective," *Critical Inquiry* 22 (Autumn 1995): 1–33, esp. 8–12.

36. Carol Zaleski, *Otherworld Journeys: Accounts of Near-Death Experiences in Medieval and Modern Times* (New York: Oxford University Press, 1987); Jean-Claude Schmitt, *Ghosts in the Middle Ages: The Living and the Dead in Medieval Society*, trans. Teresa Lavender Fagan (Chicago: University of Chicago Press, 1998). The complex and far from anodyne use of the ghost theme in Toni Morrison's *Beloved* is the modern exception that proves the rule.

37. Two recent treatments of contemporary attitudes are David Dempsey, *The Way We Die: An Investigation of Death and Dying in America Today* (New York: Macmillan, 1975) and Douglas J. Davies, *Death, Ritual, and Belief: The Rhetoric of Funerary Rites* (London: Cassell, 1997). For crosscultural comparison, see Frank E. Reynolds and Earle H. Waugh, eds., *Religious Encounters with Death: Insights from the History and Anthropology of Religions* (University Park: Pennsylvania State University Press, 1977).

Settling Scores: Eschatology in the Church of the Martyrs

1. This essay is limited to discussion of the pre-Constantinian church, focusing on martyrs' passions and essays by ecclesiastical writers c. 100–310, e.g., Justin, Tatian, Athenagoras, Clement, Origen, Minucius Felix, and Tertullian. As this essay stems from a larger project on martyrdom in the early church, the bibliography here is highly selective. Condensed notations will be used throughout for classical and medieval works. Abbreviations for sources are supplied by the *Thesaurus Linguae Latinae* (Leipzig: Teubner, 1900–); Henry George Liddell and Robert Scott, *Greek-English Lexicon*, rev. ed. Henry Stuart Jones and Roderick McKenzie (Oxford: Clarendon Press, 1968; rep. 1990); G. W. H. Lampe, *Greek Patristic Lexicon* (Oxford: Clarendon Press, 1964). Most texts used for this chapter can be found in the Corpus Christianorum Series latina (=CCL), in the Corpus scriptorum ecclesiasticorum latinorum (=CSEL), in Herbert Musurillo, S.J., *The Acts of the Christian Martyrs* (Oxford: Clarendon Press, 1972) (=ACM), and in the Sources Chrétiennes (=SC). The last thorough study of eschatology of the church of the martyrs is that of Leonard Atzberger, *Geschichte der christlichen Eschatologie* (Freiburg im Breisgau: Herder, 1896; rep. Graz, Austria, 1970). See also A. J. Vissler, "A Bird's-Eye View of Ancient Christian Eschatology," *Numen* 14 (1967): 4–22; Brian E. Daley, S.J., *The Hope of the Early Church* (Cambridge: Cambridge University Press, 1991); G. W. H. Lampe, "Early Patristic Eschatology," *Scottish Journal of Theology* 2 (1953): 17–35; Frederick Grant, "Eschatology of the Second Century," *American Journal of Theology* 21 (1919): 193–211; G. Plorovosky, "Eschatology in the Patristic Age," *Studia Patristica* 2 (1957): 235–50; Henri Rondet, S.J., *Fins de l'homme et fin du monde* (Paris: Le Signe, Fayard, 1966); Marc van Uytfanghe, "Platonisme et eschatologie chrétienne: leur symbiose graduelle dans les passions et les panégyriques des martyrs et dans les biographies des martyrs spirituelles (IIe–VIe siècles)," in *De Tertullien aux Mozarabes: antiquité tardive et christianisme ancien (IIIe–VIe), mélanges offerts à Jacques Fontaine*, Collection des Etudes Augustiniennes, Séries Antiquité 132 (Paris: Institut d'Etudes Augustiniennes, 1992), 69–95.

2. Tert. *orat.* 5.3 (CCL 1, 260). See Jaroslav Pelikan, "The Eschatology of Tertullian," *CH* 21 (1952): 108–22; also Victor Saxer, *Mort, martyrs, reliques en Afrique chrétienne aux premiers siècles* (Paris: Editions Beauchesne, 1980), 36–83.

3. *M. Justin* 5.6 in Herbert Musurillo, *The Acts of the Christian Martyrs* (Oxford: Clarendon Press, 1972), 52; hereafter ACM.

4. *M. Carp.* 4.4 (ACM, 32); Tert. *orat.* 5.3 (CCL 1, 260).

5. Tert. *fug.* 7.2 (CCL 2, 1145), Min. Fel. *Oct.* 35.3 (CSEL 6, 50). See Iren. *haer.* 5 (SC 153) (entire), which is devoted to the Apocalypse.

6. Min. Fel. *Oct.* 37.1 (CSEL 2, 52).

7. *M. Poly.* 9.2 (ACM, 8).

8. *M. Poly.* 11.2 (ACM, 10). Of the extensive bibliography on hell and the beginnings of purgatory, see esp., Alan E. Bernstein, *The Formation of Hell: Death and Retribution in the Ancient and Early Christian Worlds* (Ithaca, N.Y.: Cornell University Press, 1993); Jacques le Goff, *The Birth of Purgatory*, trans. Arthur Goldhammer (Chicago: University of Chicago Press, 1981); A. Michel, "Feu de jugement," *Dictionnaire de théologie catholique* (Paris: Letouzey et Ané, 1909–50), 5:2239–46; Henri Crouzel, "L'Hadès et la Géhenne selon Origène," *Gregorianum* 59 (1978): 291–331; R. R. Atwell, "From Augustine to Gregory the Great: An Evaluation of the Emergence of the Doctrine of Purgatory," *Journal of Ecclesiastical History* 38 (1987): 173–86; Martha Himmelfarb, *Tours of Hell: An Apocalyptic Form in Jewish and Christian Literature* (Philadelphia: University of Pennsylvania Press, 1983).

9. *M. Perp.* 17.1 (ACM, 124); *M. Perp.* 18.8–9 (ACM, 126).

10. Tert. *adv. Marc.* 5.13.3 (CCL 1, 702). For the sake of clarity, I follow the distinction between revelation, from the verb ἀποκαλύπτω, with its roots of discernment, and the final revelation, or apocalypse, and ἀποκάλυψις, which entails a Last Judgment sifting the righteous from sinners and assigning them to appropriate fates. Eschatology is a more inclusive term, embracing the "Four Last Things": death, judgment, heaven, and hell—the quality of life after death. See note 18.

11. Tert. *orat.* 5.4 (CCL 1, 260).

12. E. R. Dodds uses the terms rather too broadly to explain change in his classic, *Pagan and Christian in an Age of Anxiety* (Cambridge: Cambridge University Press, 1965). A narrower usage may be justified by more specific definitions of thought patterns.

13. This philotimocratic culture is the subject of Peter Brown's *The Making of Late Antiquity* (Cambridge, Mass.: Harvard University Press, 1978). Love of honor and the culture of competition is addressed also by T. P. Wiseman, "Competition and Cooperation," in *Roman Political Life, 90 B.C.–A.D. 69* (Exeter: University of Exeter, 1985), 3–19; Nathan Rosenstein, *Imperatores Victi: Military Defeat and Aristocratic Competition in the Middle and Late Republic* (Berkeley: University of California Press, 1990); Walter Ong, *Fighting for Life: Contest, Sexuality and Consciousness* (Amherst: University of Massachusetts Press, 1981); Paul Plass, *The Game of Death in Ancient Rome* (Madison: University of Wisconsin Press, 1995). Carlin A. Barton examines honor in the nexus of competition; see *Roman Honor: The Fire in the Bones* (Berkeley: University of California Press, forthcoming).

14. A complementary "longue durée" perspective is supplied by Louis Dumont, "A Modified View of Our Origins: The Christian Beginnings of Modern Individualism," in *The Category of the Person*, ed. Michael Carrithers, Steven Collins, and Steven Lukes (Cambridge: Cambridge University Press, 1985), 93–122.

15. Political aims were operative on both sides. Michel Foucault's work has inspired a consideration of martyrdom as a public spectacle of celebrating the authority of the state and the values of the dominant class; see Kathleen Coleman, "Fatal Charades," *Journal of Roman Studies* 80 (1990): 44–73; Dennis Potter, "Martyrdom and Spectacle," in *Theater and Society in the Classical World*, ed. Ruth Scodel (Ann Arbor: University of Michigan Press, 1993). Ritual elements of martyrdom are addressed by Philippe Buc, "Martyre et ritualité dans l'antiquité tardive," *Annales HSS* 1 (1994): 63–

118. For the juxtaposition of gladiator and martyr in the arena, see Carlin A. Barton, "Savage Miracles: The Redemption of Lost Honor in Roman Society and the Sacrament of the Gladiator and the Martyr," *Representations* 45 (1994): 41–71.

16. Of the extensive literature on the pagan criticism of Christianity, see especially Stephen Benko, "Pagan Criticism of Christianity During the First Two Centuries A.D.," in *Aufstieg und Niedergang der römischen Welt* (Berlin: de Gruyter, 1980), 23: 2: 1055–1118; idem, *Pagan Rome and the Early Christians* (Bloomington: Indiana University Press, 1986); Anthony Meredith, "Porphyry and Julian Against the Christians," in *Aufstieg und Niedergang der römischen Welt* (Berlin: de Gruyter, 1980), 23: 2: 1056–1149; Pierre de Labriolle, *La réaction païenne: étude sur la polémique antichrétienne du Ier au VIe siècle* (Paris: L'Artisan du Livre, 1950); Richard Walzer, *Galen on Jews and Christians* (London: Oxford University Press, 1949); Robert Wilken, *Christians As the Romans Saw Them* (New Haven, Conn.: Yale University Press, 1984). Apologists such as Minucius Felix (Africa, second or third century), Tatian (Rome, c.160), and Justin Martyr (Ephesus, c.100–165) sought tolerance and defended Christianity against fantastic accusations—cannibalism, midnight love feasts, and the worship of the priest's *virilia*—but the very extravagance of these accusations was worrying; see Min. Fel. *Oct.* 9.2–7 (CSEL 2, 13–14). Christians were depicted as lower-class dregs hovering on the margins of social respectability: women, children, unskilled laborers, and hopeless slaves incapable of coherent thinking. A number of Christian beliefs were simply abhorrent to pagans who, to a greater or lesser degree, subscribed to a Platonic dualism that elevated the soul while considering body and physical matter lesser levels of existence. Consequently, the Incarnation of Christ was unthinkable, as was the resurrection of the body; even the creation of the world (rather than its eternity) implied a divine interest in the material that was by definition beneath the concerns of a "real god." Two articles of Henry Chadwick illustrate the quality of pagan and Christian debate: "Origen, Celsus, and the Resurrection of the Body," *Harvard Theological Studies* 41 (1948): 83–102, and "The Evidence of Christianity in the Apologetic of Origen," *Studia Patristica* 2 (1957): 337–39.

17. In this strategy, apologists argued that Christians "really" fulfilled the honorable values that Greeks had set as standards. With absolute proof of Christian claims postponed to the future, tolerance—at a minimum—was justified, and pagans should suspend disbelief. This however was difficult. According to Tertullian, pagans could not comprehend the magnanimity of Christ's patience in dying for humanity and so rejected faith; but for Christians this patience was the rational foundation of their faith; see Tert. *patient.* 3.11 (CCL 1, 302). At issue for Christians vis-à-vis pagans were the nature of truth itself and the ability of human beings to find or demonstrate truth. Celsus, Galen, and later Julian were offended by the "novelties" of Christianity, and Marcus Aurelius and Lucian of Samosata were repelled by Christian histrionics and the lack of philosophical rigor among these "desperate" people. Christians were accused of *superstitio*: irrationality, fear, and sheer nonsense; see Denise Grodzynski, "Superstitio," *Revue des Etudes Augustiniennes* 76 (1974): 36–60; and Pfaff, art. "Superstitio" in Pauly Wissowa, *Reallexikon* 2, 7 (1931): 937–39. Scholars believe that *superstitio* was one of the charges that led to the persecution of Christians; see W. H. C. Frend, *Martyrdom and Persecution in the Early Church* (New York: New York University Press, 1967), 122–23. Ironically, it is clear that pagan philosophers were similarly critical of their own cult beliefs as being irrational; cf. Harold W. Attridge, "The Philosophical Critique of

Religion under the Early Empire," *Aufstieg und Niedergang der römischen Welt* (Berlin: de Gruyter) 16, 1 (1978): 63–64. In essence, pagans argued that Christianity was based on undocumented and irrational beliefs. An Arab redaction of Galen of Peragmum is telling, asserting that Christians were "unable to follow any demonstrative argument consecutively"; cited by Benko, "Pagan Criticism," 1099. To vindicate Christianity necessitated hard "proof" of these beliefs: this was the role of the martyr.

18. The ideas of μαρτυρέω, μάρτυς, and μαρτύρια change from the classical Greek sense of bearing witness (equivalent to the Latin *testis*); see Liddell and Scott, *Greek-English Lexicon*, rev. ed., ed. Henry Stuart Jones and Roderick McKenzie (Oxford: Clarendon Press, 1990), 1081–82. Romans import the Greek μάρτυρ/martyr for one who bears witness by death; cf. Lewis and Short, *A Latin Dictionary* (Oxford: Clarendon Press, 1969), 1116. In patristic Greek the sense of witness has evolved to one who dies for the faith; see G. W. H. Lampe, *A Greek Patristic Lexicon* (Oxford: Clarendon Press, 1964), 828–32. As Giuliana Lanta argues in "Confessione o professione? il dossier degli atti dei martiri," the duty of the martyr was a more active profession of beliefs rather than passive confession; see *L'aveu: antiquité et moyen âge* (Rome: Ecole Française de Rome, 1986), 133–46. See esp. "μάρτυς" in *The Theological Dictionary of the New Testament*, ed. Gerhard Kittel, trans. and ed. Geoffrey W. Browmily (Grand Rapids, Mich.: Eerdmans, 1965; rep. 1984), 4: 474–514. See also, Bernard McGinn, "Early Apocalypticism: The Ongoing Debate," in *The Apocalypse in English Renaissance Thought and Literature*, ed. C. A. Patrides and Joseph Wittreich (Manchester: Manchester University Press, 1984)=Bernard McGinn, *Apocalypticism in the Western Tradition* (London: Variorum, 1994), 1; Morton Smith, "On the History of 'αποκαλύπτω and 'αποκάλυψις," in *Apocalypticism in the Mediterranean World and the Near East*, ed. David Hellholm (Tübingen: J.D.B. Mohr [Paul Siebeck], 1983), 10–30; Elisabeth Schüssler Fiorenza, "The Phenomenon of Early Christian Apocalyptic: Some Reflections on Method," ibid., 295–325; Lars Hartman, "Survey of the Problem of Apocalyptic Genre," ibid., 329–44.

19. Cypr. *ep.* 39.2.3 (CCL 3B, 188).

20. Cypr. *ep.* 31.3 (CCL 3B, 153–54). The emphasis is mine, to focus attention on the way the writers equated the act of testifying with the veracity itself of the truth witnessed, and the achievement itself with action. The entire passage is significant for this way of dialectical thinking that stresses the volition of the deeds:

> quid enim gloriosius quidue felicius ulli hominum poterit ex diuina dignatione contingere quam inter ipsos carnifices interritum confiteri dominum deum, quam inter saeuientis saecularis potestatis uaria et exquisita tormenta etiam extorto et excruciato et excarnificato corpore Christum dei filium etsi recedente, sed tamen libero spiritu confiteri, quam relicto mundo caelum petisse, quam desertis hominibus inter angelos stare, quam inpedimentis omnibus saecularibus ruptis in conspectu dei iam se liberum sistere, quam caeleste regnum sine ulla cunctatione retinere, quam collegam passionis cum Christo in Christi nomine factum fuisse, quam iudicis sui diuina dignatione iudicem factum fuisse, quam inmaculatam conscientiam de confessione nominis reportasse, quam humanis et sacrilegis legibus contra fidem non oboedisse, quam ueritatem uoce publica contestatum fuisse, quam ipsam quae ab omnibus metuatur moriendo mortem

subegisse, quam per ipsam mortem inmortalitatem consecutum fuisse, quam omnibus saeuitiae instrumentis excarnificatum et extortum ipsis tormentis tormenta superasse, quam omnibus dilaniati corporis doloribus robore animi reluctatum fuisse, quam sanguinem suum profluentem non horruisse, quam supplicia sua post fidem amare coepisse, quam detrimentum uitae suae putare uixisse?

21. Lact. *inst.* 5.22.17 (SC 204, 252).

22. Cypr. *Fort.* 11 (CCL 3, 206): "quam magna documenta fidei praebuerunt." Cyprian continues, "In [the Maccabees'] suffering" they bore "witness to themselves as the sons of God," Cypr. *Fort.* 11 (CCL 3, 206). The message extends to all Christians who "should continue through the same evidences of punishment, through the same testimonies of sufferings," finally receiving the "robes washed white in the blood of the lamb" (Apoc. 7: 14), Cypr. *Fort.* 11 (CCL 3, 210–11): "per eadam documenta poenarum, per eadem passionum martyria pergamus." Suffering itself was proof because the evidence was manifest publicly; this proved the quality of the witness whose bravery emanated from truth. "I don't think," the martyr Justin told the prefect Rusticus, "I am fully convinced." *M. Just.* Recension A 5.3 (ACM, 46).

23. See Tert. *orat.* 4.2 (CCL 1, 259), in which Tertullian stressed that Christ did not do his own will, but the will of his Father (cf. John 6: 38), and Christians are summoned to this model, that "we, too, may teach, work, and suffer even unto death." Mark 14: 36 reads, "Father, all things are possible with you; take this cup away from me. Yet not what I will, but what you will be done." The passage is key to describing the choice of martyrdom. Origen argued that Christ asked that this "cup" be removed because he preferred an even more difficult death; see *mart.* 29 (GCS 1, 25). See also Matt. 20: 20–30, where Christ asks if others can share his cup, and Luke 11: 44, where this cup is identified as the cup of the prophets of the Psalms; note also frequent echoes of Ps. 27: 1–3 (The Lord is my light and my salvation).

24. Tert. *scorp.* 10.9 (CCL 2, 1088).

25. See *M. Apollon.* 32 (ACM, 98).

26. Min Fel. *Oct.* 37.6 (CSEL 2, 52). We moderns are quite aware that willingness to die for a cause does not guarantee its truth or validity. Some pagans shared this conviction as well. Marcus Aurelius and Lucian of Samosata certainly thought Christians died for nothing. That the Christians' contempt for death could be viewed by pagans as folly is witnessed by Min. Fel. *Oct.* 8 (CSEL 6, 12). But one like Justin Martyr retorted wryly, "No one died for Socrates"; this proved the vacuousness of paganism, Just. *2 apol.* 10 (PG 6, 461).

27. Tertullian was aware that resurrection was a consolation for the fear of death, explaining Paul's treatment of the resurrection in 2 Cor. 4: 11–16: "He treats of this subject in order to offer consolation against the fear of death and of this mournful dissolution," *adv. Marc.* 5.12.1 (CCL 1, 700).

28. Some scholars have argued that the stance favorable to martyrdom is directed especially against Gnostics. The larger point is that the doctrines "proved" by the acts of martyrdom itself are precisely those rejected by heretics, pagans, and Jews. See W. H. C. Frend, "The Gnostic Sects and the Roman Empire," *Journal of Ecclesiastical History* 5 (1954): 25–37; Hans von Campenhausen, *Die Idee des Martyriums in der alten Kirche* (Göttingen: Vanderhoeck and Ruprecht, 1936), 94–95; B. A. G. M.

Dehandschutter, "Le martyre de Polycarpe et le développement de la conception du martyre aux deuxième siècle," *Studia Patristica* 17 (1982): 659–68, and his *Martyrium Polycarpi: een literair-kritische Studie*, B.E.T.L. 52 (Leuven: Universitaire Pers Leuven, 1979); and Elaine Pagels, "Gnostic and Orthodox View of Christ's Passion: Paradigms for the Christian's Response to Persecution?" in *The Rediscovery of Gnosticism* (Leiden: E. J. Brill, 1980), 1: 262–88. Tertullian's *Scorpiace* was written against the Gnostics, "opponents of martyrdom [who] bubble up" in time of persecution (see 1.5 [CCL 2, 1069]). Note that educated pagans and Jews also rejected notions of the Incarnation and suffering of the divinity in Christ.

29. Tert. *apol.* 50.13 (CCL 1, 171).

30. Lact. *inst.* 5.22.18–19 (SC 204, 254).

31. For example, Ignatius of Antioch fought to establish the authority of the bishop; Cyprian addressed the challenge confessors posed; Irenaeus, Lactantius, and Tertullian combated heresies that threatened to fragment the Christian community.

32. See several articles by Michele Pellegrino in his collected works, *Richerche Patristiche* (Turin: Bottega D'Erasmo, 1982): "Semen est sanguis Christianorum (Tertulliano," *Apologeticum*, 50, 13), 451–524; "Le sense ecclésial du martyr," 427–51; "Eucharistia e martirio in san Cipriano," 527–40. Also, Peter Brown, *The Body and Society* (New York: Columbia University Press, 1988), 190–209.

33. Individuals were more likely to see in the present the beginning of the final consummation. See Irwin R. Goodenough, *The Theology of Justin Martyr* (Jena: Frommannashe Buchhandlung [Walter Biedermann], 1923) notes inconsistencies in Justin's views of when the Second Coming was to arrive, 280–83. Others are more decisive, identifying present troubles with the beginning of the end; see Tert. *scorp.* 1.10 (CCL 2, 1070); *apol.* 32.1 (CCL 1, 143). Tertullian mentions the Antichrist in *anim.* 50.5 (CCL 2, 856); *resurr.* 25.1 (CCL 2, 953); *fug.* 12.9 (CCL 2, 1153). Equations of the present with the end are Iren. *haer.* 5.30.1–4 (SC 153.370–86); Cypr. *ep.* 58.2.1–2 (CCL 3C, 321–22); *Demetr.* 3–5 (CCL 3A, 36–37). While Origen conceded that Matt. 24: 3–44 could apply to his times, he does not stress this theme; cf. B. Daley, *Hope*, 47–60. In contrast, anonymous redactors of martyrs' passions seldom addressed the issue directly. Only three of the so-called "authentic" Acta make such equations, though again the use of apocalyptic passages and imagery is strong in all the passions: *M. Lyon.* 1.5 (ACM, 62); *M. Pion.* 4.14 (ACM, 140); *M. Perp.* 3 (ACM, 106). See L. Atzberger, *Eschatologie*, 163–71.

34. Especially important are John 16: 2–4 (to kill Christians will be a religious duty); and John 15: 18–27 ("I have chosen you out of the world and therefore the world hates you"); Matt. 24: 2–44 ("The end is still to come," "You know not what time the Son of Man will come"); Matt. 10: 22 and Luke 21: 12 ("You will be hated for my Name's sake"); Luke 19: 41–44 (destruction of the temple); Luke 21: 5–36 (general catastrophe: "They will set upon you and persecute you"; ". . . you will be brought before kings and governors for my name's sake. This will be a time for you to bear testimony.")

35. Cf. Tert. *spect.* 8.9 (CCL 1, 235).

36. Tert. *spect.* 26.4 (CCL 1, 249); see also Tert. *anim.* 16.7 (CCL 2, 803).

37. Tert. *orat.* 12.1 (CCL 1, 264).

38. This obstinate sense of identity is illustrated by Perpetua: just as a pitcher

can be nothing but a pitcher, so she could be nothing but a Christian; see *M. Perp.* 3.3.1–2 (ACM, 108).

39. See Antonio Quacquarelli, "La letteratura di preparazione al martirio e la convergenza iconologica nel III secolo," *Parola e spirito: studi in onore di Settimio Cipriani,* ed. Cesare Casale Marcheselli (Brescia: Paideia Editrice, 1982), 1:789–807; Colin Eisler, "The Athlete of Virtue: The Iconography of Asceticism," in *Essays in Honor of Erwin Panofsky,* ed. Millard Meiss (New York: New York University Press, 1961), 1:82–97; Adolf Harnack, *Militia Christi,* trans. David McInnes Gracie (1905; rep. Philadelphia: Fortress Press, 1973).

40. See Cypr. *ep.* 71.2.3 (CCL 3C, 519), *ep.* 59.20.1 (CCL 3A, 193), and *ep.* 69.1.2 (CCL 3A, 244), where this sharp opposition is with heretics.

41. See Cypr. *Demetr.* 20 (CCL 3A, 47).

42. Ign. *Magn.* 5.2 (SC 10, 98–99); see also Iren *haer.* 5.8.1 (SC 153, 92 and 94).

43. Tert. *scorp.* 8.8 (CCL 2, 1083–84); Cypr. *patient.* 10 (CCL 3A, 123–24); Cypr. *ep.* 58.5 (CCL 3C, 325).

44. Tert. *scorp.* 8.8 (CCL 2, 1083–84).

45. Cypr. *Fort.* 6 (CCL 3, 327).

46. *M. Fruct.* 4.1 (ACM, 180).

47. Lact. *instit.* 5.22.11–13 (SC 204, 252). Lactantius quotes Seneca instead of the usual "The Lord chastens the sons whom he receives" (see Heb. 12: 6).

48. See Cypr. *ep.* 6.1.1–6.2.1 (CCL 3B, 29–34).

49. Cypr. *mortal.* 24 (CCL 3, 30), an echo of John 15: 20: "because I have chosen you out of the world, therefore the world hates you."

50. See John 15: 18–20; John 16: 2–4; John 16: 20; John 16: 33; Matt. 24: 2–31.

51. Cypr. *Fort.* 11 (CCL 3, 202).

52. Tert. *mart.* 3.5 (CCL A, 6); see also Min. Fel. *Oct.* 36.9 (CSEL 2, 51–52).

53. Lact. *instit.* 5.22.17 (SC 204, 254).

54. Or. *mart.* 14 (GCS 1, 14).

55. *M. Pion.* 4.14 (ACM, 140); Iren. *haer.* 5.28.4 (SC 153, 360); Just. *dial.* 49 (PG 6, 584); Tert. *fug.* 1.4 (CCL 2, 2136).

56. *Pion.* 15–16 (ACM, 140); Cypr. *ep.* 11.4 (CCL 3B, 61).

57. See John T. Robinson, "The 'Parable' of the Sheep and the Goats," *New Testament Studies* 2 (1956): 225–37.

58. Tert. *fug.* 1.4 (CCL 2, 2136).

59. Tert. *fug.* 5.2 (CCL 2, 1141).

60. Tert. *spect.* 1.1.5 (CCL 1, 227).

61. Tert. *apol.* 46.14 (CCL 1, 162).

62. Ign. *Rom.* 3.1 (SC 10, 128).

63. Min. Fel. *Oct.* 37.1 (CSEL 2, 52).

64. Tert. *apol.* 30.5 (CCL 1, 141).

65. The significance of the Holy Spirit is often neglected in discussions of martyrdom, but it is key especially to understanding how Christians conceptualized motivation and their mimetic relationship with God. See William C. Weinrich, *Spirit and Martyrdom* (Washington, D.C.: University Press of America, 1981).

66. Ign. *Magn.* 5.2 (SC 10, 98).

67. Cypr. *ep.* 58.6.6 (CCL 3C, 328):

Quam uero grauis causa sit hominis christiani seruum pati nolle, cum passus sit
prior dominus, et pro peccatis nostris nos pati nolle, cum peccatum suum pro-
prium non habens passus sit ille pro nobis! Filius dei passus est ut nos filios dei
faceret, et filius hominis pati non uult ut esse dei filius perseueret!

See also *ep.* 76.4.1 (CCL 3C, 612):

Hoc est enim quod praecipue deo placeat, hoc est in quo maioribus meritis
ad promerendam uoluntatem dei opera nostra proueniant, hoc est quod solum
domino de beneficiis eius grandibus et salutaribus fidei ac deuotionis nostrae
obsequia retribuant praedicante in psalmis et contestante spiritu sancto, *quid
retribuam,* inquit, *domino de omnibus quae mihi tribuit? Calicem salutaris accipiam,
et nomen domini inuocabo. Pretiosa in conspectu domini mors iustorum eius.*

68. Or. *mart.* 19 (GCS 1, 18).

69. J. W. van Henten, ed., *Die Entstehung der jüdischen Martyrologie* (Leiden:
E. J. Brill, 1989). Dying for the name is mentioned also in *M. Carp.* 5 (ACM, 35);
M. Lyon. 35 (ACM, 73); *M. Mar. et Iac.* 4.10 (ACM, 199); *M. Mar. et Iac.* 7.6 (ACM,
204); *M. Iren.* 5.4 (ACM, 298 and 300).

70. Cyprian's *devotio* echoed pagan military tradition: the Christian was Christ's
soldier who fought to the death for the honor of Christ's name, whom Christ would
reward for his valor. Cypr. *ep.* 58.4.2 (CCL 3C, 325): "spectat militem suum Christus
ubicumque pugnantem et persecutionis causa pro nominis sui honore morienti prae-
mium reddit quod daturum se in resurrectione promisit." For the *devotio* and *sacramentum* in Cyprian, see also *eps.* 10.2; 15.1; 28.1–2; 54.1; 58.4; 60.2; 76.4; 76.6; 77.2.

71. In *M. Perp.* 10.5 (ADM, 130), the martyr Pudens dips his ring in his blood
and gives it to a soldier, who requests Pudens to "remember me, and remember the
faith."

72. Tert. *mart.* 3.1 (CCL 1, 5): "Vocati sumus ad militiam Dei uiui iam tunc,
cum in sacramenti uerba respondimus." For the *sacramentum,* see J. de Ghellinck,
S.J., *Pour l'histoire du mot "sacramentum"* (Louvain: Spicilegium Sacrum Lovaniense,
1924); F. Rütten, *Victorverehrung im christlichen Altertum* (Studien zur Geschichte
und Kultur des Altertums 20, 1936); W. Weismann, *Kirche und Schauspiele: die Schauspiele im Urteil der lateinischen Kirchenväter unter besonderer Berücksichtigung von Augustin* (1972), 62ff, esp. 111–18. Ignatius of Antioch's oath echoes that of the gladiator,
"Come fire, cross, battling with wild beast, wrenching of bones, mangling of limbs,
crushing of my whole body, cruel tortures of the devil—only let me get to Jesus
Christ." Ign. *Rom.* 3.3 (SC 10, 128); cf. *Smyrn.* 4.2. (SC 10, 158).

73. See Tert. *fug.* 12.2–3; Or. *mart.* 12 (GCS 1, 11–12). In Cyprian, sin is also
debt; see *domin. orat.* 22–23 (CCL 3A, 103–5), where good works are offered as sacrifices to God; *eleem.* 26 (CCL 3A, 72), where good works indebt God. The centrality
of Christ, the first martyr (see *M. Lyon.* 2.3 [ACM, 82]) and scapegoat (Just. *Dial* 13
[PG 6, 501 and 504]), to the martyr who must imitate him is addressed thoroughly
by Pellegrino in further articles from *Richerche Patristiche*: "Cristo negli atti dei martiri e nella letteratura sul martirio," 191–213; "L'imitation du Christ dans les actes des
martyrs," 38–54; and "Cristo e il martire nel pensiero di Origene," 541–67.

74. Cypr. *Fort.* 6 (CCL 3, 195).

75. This is not because the sacrifice of Christ was wanting but because Christians were bound to imitate Christ; see *M. Polyc.* 17.3 (ACM, 17); *M. Lyon.* 2.2 (ACM, 83); *M. Mar. et Iac.* 4.1 (ACM, 198); *M. Mont. et Luc.* 11.6 (ACM, 224); *M. Mont. et Luc.* 14.9 (ACM, 228); *M. Eupl.* Recensio Latina 1.5 (ACM, 314); *M. Mar. et Iac.* 4.1 (ACM, 198). Christians must share his sufferings; see *M. Perp.* 18.9 (ACM, 126); *M. Polyc.* 6.2 (ACM, 6); *M. Carp.* 41 (ACM, 26).

76. *Or. mart.* 30 (GCS 1, 26–27; see Hb 5:1; 7:21; 8:3; 10:12). Martyrs not only expiated their own sins, but might indeed "redeem" others "by [their] precious blood." *Or. mart.* 50 (GCS 1, 46–47).

77. Christ redeemed man once and for all, but his sacrificial death was repeated individually in the deaths of martyrs, much as the Eucharist continually replicated Christ's offering within the Church; see Ign. *Rom.* 4.1.; *Eph.* 8.1. See Pellegrino, "Eucharistia," 534–40. Martyrs were sacraments, so to speak, mediating between two worlds. As sacrifices themselves, some martyrs are scapegoats, dying for others; cf. *M. Polyc.* 14.1 (ACM, 12); Zachary, cf. *M. Lyon.* 10 (ACM, 64); Blandina, cf. *M. Lyon.* 41 (ACM, 75); Fructuosus died bearing in mind the "whole Church, East and West"; *M. Fruct.* 3.6 (ACM, 181); cf. *M. Conon.* 3.1 (ACM, 189).

78. *Or. mart.* 10 (GCS 1, 10).

79. *M. Just.* 5.7–8 (ACM, 52). I can do no better than Musurillo's translation here.

80. *M. Poly.* 2.25 (ACM, 2, 4). See also Tert. *coron.* 14.4 (CCL 2, 1064); Tertullian advises, "to escape [God's] severity or to invite his liberality one needs diligence in obeying as great as his severity menaces us or his generosity entices us." *patient.* 11.4.2 (CCL 1, 302).

81. Cf. *M. Mar. et Iac.* 8.7 (ACM, 207).

82. The martyrs' obedient death honored—"augmented" and "magnified"—God, bearing witness to his grandeur (*testimonium magnificientiae Dei*), *M. Mont. et Luc.* 1 (ACM, 214). Origen urged: "Let us, then, glorify God, exalting Him by our own death, since the martyr will glorify God by his own death," *Or. mart.* 50 (GCS 1, 47). Martyrs' "exalted death[s]" "glorify God" because their sacrificial offerings were forms of worship; see *Or. mart.* 50 (GCS 1, 74); *M. Lyon.* 41 (ACM, 74). See Antonius Johannes Vermeulen, *The Semantic Development of Gloria in Early-Christian Latin,* Latinitas Christianorum Primaeva (Nijmegen: Dekker & van de Vegt, 1956). Martyrs died for the "sanctification" of God's name, as in Hebraic tradition; cf. Cypr. *ep.* 58.2.2 (CCL 3C, 322): "si inproperatur uobis in nomine Christi, beati estis, quia maiestatis et uirtutis domini nomen in uobis requiescit, quod quidem secundum illos blasphematur, secundum nos autem honoratur." (1 Pet. 4: 14): "If you are upbraided for the name of Christ, you will be blessed, because the name of the majesty and the power of God rests upon you. What indeed is blasphemed among them, is honored among us." On this important letter, see Gennaro Lomiento, "Cipriano per la preparazione al martirio dei Tibaritani," *Annali Fac. di Magistero dell'Univ. di Bari* III (1962): 6–39. See note 68 above for dying for the name. Deaths of the martyrs were sacrificial offerings that honored the Lord: "precious in the sight of the Lord is the death of His saints" (Ps. 116: 13, 15). See also Polycarp, who was a sacrifice to God's glory: "ἐν οἷς προσδεχθείην ἐνώπιόν σου σήμερον ἐν θυσίᾳ πίονι καὶ προσδεκτῇ, καθὼς προητοίμασας καὶ προεφανέρωσας καὶ ἐπλήρωσας ὁ ἀψευδὴς καὶ ἀληθινὸς θεός. διὰ τοῦτο καὶ περὶ πάντων σὲ αἰνῶ, σὲ εὐλογῶ, σὲ δοξάζω διὰ τοῦ αἰωνίου καὶ ἐπουρανίου ἀρχιερέως Ἰησοῦ

Χριστοῦ ἀγαπητοῦ σου παιδός." *M. Polyc.* 14.2–3 (ACM, 12 and 14); Pampilius preferred to immolate himself to the living God, not idols, "A iuuentute mea deo seruio et simulacris uanissimis numquam immolaui. immolo me autem ipsum deo uiuo et uero, qui habet potestatem uniuersae carnis." *M. Carp.* Recensio Latina 4 (ACM, 30); Justin's stand is almost that of one seeking martyrdom: "Πολλῶν ἐν πείρᾳ γενόμενος ταύτην ἐξεῦρον ἀληθεστάτην οὖσαν καὶ μεγάλην τὴν πίστιν, ἧ δὴ καὶ στοιχῶ καὶ ῆ θανεῖν ἐθέλω διὰ Χριστόν." *M. Just.* 2.3 (ACM, 54 and 56); when Felix the bishop is to be beheaded, he extends his neck as a sacrifice to God: "tibi ceruicem meam ad uictimam flecto, qui permanes in aeternum," *M. Felix.* 30 (ACM, 270); Dasius chooses to be a sacrifice to God, not to Saturn: "Ἐπειδὴ ἐπὶ τὸ τοιοῦτον μυσαρὸν ἀναγκάζετέ με, κρεῖττόν μοί ἐστιν οἰκείᾳ προαιρέσει τᾶ δεσπότῃ χριστᾶ θυσία γενέσθαι ἢ τᾶ Κρόνῳ ὑμῶν τᾶ εἰδώλῳ ἐπιθῦσαι ἐμαυτόν." *M. Das.* 5.2 (ACM, 274); Euplus knocked on the door of the governor, announcing his readiness to die, "Christianus sum, et pro Christi nomine mori desidero," *M. Eupl. Recensio Latina* 1 (ACM, 314); later he insisted he be a sacrifice, "Sacrifico modo Christo Deo me ipsum: quid ultra faciam, non habeo," *M. Eupl. Recensio Latina* 6 (ACM, 316); Blandina is also offered in sacrifice, *M. Lyon.* 56 (ACM, 20). Conon was an offering to God and his glory, *M. Conon.* 6.7 (ACM, 192). Martyrs are consecrated to God, "illos Deo patri dicatos," *M. Mar. et Iac.* 6.4 (ACM, 200). Venues of execution were casually termed "the customary spot glorifying God," *M. Just.* 6.1 (ACM, 52). Christians must always take care that God be glorified, Tertullian said. Here reciprocity takes a mystical turn: "We are asking that it be sanctified in us who are in Him," Tert. *orat.* 3.4 (CCL 1, 259).

83. Suffering gained redemption, the expiation of sins, the liberation from death, and the new life of the resurrection. After death came the reward—the assimilation of the body to Christ, which was glorification.

84. Tert. *scorp.* 6.8 (CCL 2, 1080): "Porro et si fidei propterea congruebat sublimitati et claritatis aliqua prolatio, tale quid esse oportuerat illud emolumenti, quo magno constaret: labore, cruciatu, tormento, morte. Sed respice conpensationem, cum caro et anima dependitur—quibus in homine carius nihil est, alterum manus dei, alterum flatus,—ipsa dependi in profectum quorum est profectus, ipsa erogari quae lucri fiant, eadem pretia quae et merces."

85. The balanced opposition of the four elements in the Ionian philosophers is a legacy to Plato and Aristotle and thus to the educated Christian world; see Gregory Vlastos, "Equality and Justice in Early Greek Cosmologies," *Classical Philology* 52 (1947): 155–78. On a more instinctive level, reciprocity governs social relationships not only in gift-giving but within the family itself. In both Greece and Rome, the gift of a father's love indebted the son to repay that love when the father became dependent in old age. Love and gratitude meant obligation in the highest sense of *pietas* and *religio* for the Romans; Greek tradition also had a corresponding ethics of responsibility going back to Solon in the sixth century; see Fustel de Coulanges, *The Ancient City*, ed. A. Momigliano and S. Humphreys (Baltimore: Johns Hopkins University Press, 1980); George Dumézil, *La religion romaine archaïque* (Paris: Payot, 1974), 131–41. For patterns of equilibrium, see Claude Lévi-Strauss, *The Elementary Structure of Kinship*, rev. ed., trans. James Harle Bell and John Richard von Sturmer, ed. Rodney Needham (Boston: Beacon Press, 1969), who argues that ideas of reciprocity originate in systems of kinship, marriage, and economic (gift) exchange; see esp. 52–67 and 84–97. Similar arguments are made by Marcel Mauss, *The Gift*, trans. W. D. Halls

(New York: W. W. Norton, 1990). How reciprocity and gift exchange lie behind patterns of sacrifice is suggested in Henri Hubert and Marcel Mauss, *Sacrifice: Its Nature and Functions*, trans. W. E. Halls (Chicago: University of Chicago Press, 1964); see also J. Van Baal, "Offering, Sacrifice, and Gift," *Numen* 23 (1975): 11–179, who stresses the need to reciprocate the offering (sacrifice) given. The monistic universe of the Hebrews stressed the human obligation to honor God as well as one's parents (i.e., the first four commandments). Finally, the principle of reciprocity is manifest in the *communicatio idiomatum* unifying the two natures of Christ; see Alois Grillmeier, *Christ in Christian Tradition*, trans. John Bowden, 2nd ed. (Atlanta: John Knox Press, 1975).

86. Min. Fel. *Oct.* 17.11 (CSEL 2, 22–23); Tert. *apol.* 11.5 (CCL 1, 107–8); Lact. *opif.* 1.10–12 (SC 213, 108 and 110) (this whole work is devoted to the topic of divine providence as evidenced in creation, particularly of the soul and body); Iren. *haer.* 3.25.1–2 (PG 7, 968–69).

87. Apocalypticism can be found among certain philosophers of the early empire, e.g., Lucan's *Pharsalia*, Seneca's *Thyestes*.

88. Cf. Cypr. *ep.* 55.16.1 (CCL 3B, 274).

89. Cypr. *laps.* 27 (CCL 3, 236).

90. Most works on the problem of free will and determinism focus either on the classical period or the fourth century (Augustine and Pelagianism); exceptional is Dom David Armand, *Fatalisme et liberté dans l'antiquité grecque* (Louvain: Bibliothèque de l'Université, 1945). Late antiquity is treated briefly in Albrecht Dihle, *The Theory of Will in Classical Antiquity* (Berkeley: University of California Press, 1982). See also Pamela Huby, "The First Discovery of the Freewill Problem," *Philosophy* 42 (1967): 353–62, and Joseph P. Farrell, *Free Choice in St. Maximus the Confessor* (South Canaan, Pa.: St. Tikhon's Seminary Press, 1989).

91. Origen wrote with a hope characteristic of this heroic age: "man received the honor of the image of God (*imago dei*) in his first creation, whereas the perfection of God's likeness (*similitudo*) was reserved for him at the consummation. The purpose of this was that man should acquire it for himself by his own earnest efforts to imitate God (*propriae industriae studiis ex Dei imitatione*)." Or. *prin.* 2.6.1 (GCS 5, 509), an exegesis of Gen. 1:26–28: "Let us make man in the image and likeness of God." See also Or. *prin.* 3.6.1 (GCS 5, 280–81; Or. *hom. in Ex.* 6.5 (GCS 6, 196–97). See *Arché e telos*, ed. Ugo Bianchi and Henri Crouzel (Milan: Pubblicazioni della Università Cattolica del Sacro Cuore, 1981), 58–121. At the heart of heroic martyrdom lay a fundamental belief in human agency as the basis on which Christians are rewarded or punished. Predestination is viewed as little better than fate and determinism. This is an optimistic universe where humanity has an effective free will. Augustine will undermine this heroic ideal, presenting human beings as radically dependent on God. While earlier writers would not deny human dependence on divine grace, their exhortations assume human agency and an active cooperation with divine grace that earns them their crown. For Origen, this connection between free will, grace, and an optimistic end of the universe is presented in Constantine N. Tsirpanlis, "Origen on Free Will, Grace, Predestination, Apocatastasis, and Their Ecclesiological Implications," *The Patristic and Byzantine Review* 9 (1990): 95–121. In general, see Gerhard B. Ladner, *The Idea of Reform* (New York: Harper Torchbooks, 1967), 63–132; Joseph P. Farrell, *Free Choice in St. Maximus the Confessor* (South Canaan, Pa.; St. Tikhon's Seminary Press, 1989), 178–90, 195–228.

92. Ign. *Smyrn.* 11.3 (SC 10, 166).

93. Iren. *haer.* 3.20.1–2 (PG 7, 942–43).

94. Being created in the image of God, humanity could imitate the archetype and thus participate in the divine goodness. The end would be the assimilation of the image to the archetype, although personalities would remain distinct. In the East, this is the doctrine of **yévsiw**, in the west *deificatio*. See J. Gross, *La divinization du chrétien d'après les Pères grecs* (Paris, 1938); Gerhart B. Ladner, "The Concept of the Image in the Greek Fathers and the Byzantine Iconoclastic Controversy," *Dumbarton Oaks Studies* 6 (Cambridge, Mass.: Harvard University Press, 1953); idem, *The Idea of Reform* (New York: Harper Torchbooks, 1967); Henri Crouzel, *Théologie de l'image de Dieu chez Origène*, Théologie 34 (Paris: Aubier, Editions Montaigne, 1956); Régis Bernard, *L'image de Dieu d'après Saint Athanase*, Théologie 25 (Paris: Aubier, Editions Montaigne, 1952); Michel Aubineau, S.J., "Incorruptibilité et divinization selon saint Irénée," *Revue des Sciences Religieuses* 44 (1956): 25–52.

95. For example, Tertullian, Origen, and Irenaeus in the pre-Constantinian church. See Hans Urs vo Balthasar, "Apokatastasis," *Trier Theologische Zeitschrift* 97 (1988): 169–82; Brooks Otis, "Cappodocian Thought as a Coherent System," *Dumbarton Oaks Studies* 12 (Cambridge, Mass.: Harvard University Press, 1958); "Les fondaments cosmologiques de l'eschatologie d'Origène," *Revue des Sciences Philosophiques et Théologiques* 43 (1959): 32–80; A. Méhat, "Apocatastase, Origène, Clément d'Alexandrie, Act 3: 21," *Vigiliae Christianae* 10 (1956): 196–244; Paulo Siniscolo, "'apokatastasiw, apokayíothni nella tradizione della Grande Chiesa fino ad Ireneo," *Studia Patristica* 3 (1961): 380–96.

96. *M. Mar. et Iac.* 13.5 (ACM, 212).

97. Or. *mart.* 28 (GCS 1, 24). φιλότιμός τις ὁ ἅγιος ὢν καὶ ἀμείψασθαι θέλων τὰς φθασάσας εἰς αὐτὸν εὐεργεσίας ἀπὸ θεοῦ ζητεῖ, τί ἂν ποιήσαι τὰ κυρίῳ περὶ πάντων ὧν ἀπ' αὐτοῦ εἴληφε· καὶ οὐδὲν ἄλλο εὑρίσκει οἱονεὶ ἰσόρ 'ισορροπον ταῖς εὐεργεσίαις δυνάμενον ἀπὸ ἀνθρώπου εὐπροαιρέτου ἀποδοθῆναι θεᾷ, ὡς τὴν ἐν μαρτυρίῳ τελευτήν. See Gerard E. Caspary, *Politics and Exegesis: Origen and the Two Swords* (Berkeley: University of California Press, 1979), for an analysis of the structure of Origen's thought. See also Robert J. Daly, S.J., "Sacrificial Soteriology in Origen's Homilies on Leviticus," *Studia Patristica* 17 (1982): 872–78. See also Cypr. *ep.* 76 (CCL 3A, 612–13).

98. Cypr. *ad Donat.* 6 (CCL 3A, 6). On the violent tenor of life, see several articles from *Châtiment dans la cité: supplices corporeles et peine de mort dans le monde antique*, Collection de l'Ecole Française de Rome 79 (Rome: Ecole Française de Rome, 1984); François Hinard, "Le male mort: exécutions et statu du corps au moment de la prière proscription," 225–311; Jean-Pierre Callu, "Le jardin des supplices au Bas-Empire," 313–59; Denise Grodzynski, "Torture mortelles et catégories sociales: les *Summa Supplicia* dans le droit romain aux IIIe et IVe siècles," 361–403.

99. Hell is worse than any torture: *M. Polyc.* 11.2 (ACM, 10); *M. Ptol. et Luc.* 2 (ACM, 39); *M. Lyon.* 26 (ACM, 68); *M. Pion.* 24 (ACM, 142).

100. *M. Apollon.* 25 (ACM, 96).

101. *M. Lyon.* 26 (ACM, 68).

102. Tert. *resurr.* 40.8 (CCL 2, 974).

103. See Cypr. *laps.* 15 (CCL 3, 227–28); Cypr. *laps.* 25 (CCL 3, 234–35).

104. Tert. *coron.* 2.4 (CCL 2, 1042).

105. While the sources encourage that the Christian have a personal disposition of penitence to God, public penance for serious sins was limited to once in a lifetime; see Paul Galtier, *L'église et la rémission des péchés aux premiers siècles* (Paris: Gabriel Beauchesne et ses fils, 1932), 22–70; Cyril Vogel, *Le pécheur et la péntience dans l'église ancienne* (Paris: Editions du Cerf, n.d.), 1–25; Nathanel Marshall, *The Penitential Discipline of the Primitive Church*, Library of Anglo-Catholic Theology 13 (Oxford: John Henry Parker, 1844), 44–84.

106. Tert. *cult.fem.* 1.1.1–2 (CCL 1, 343–44).

107. See Tert. *coron.* 10.1–2 (CCL 2, 1053).

108. Tert. *cult.fem.* 1.8.5 (CCL 1, 350–51). Now one even witnessed sexual pleasure in killing; see Tert. *cult.fem.* 1.8.5 (CCL 1, 350–51); Cypr. *ad Donat.* 7 (CCL 3A, 6–7).

109. *M. Ptol.* (entire) (ACM, 38 and 40).

110. Tert. *cult.fem.* 1.4.2 (CCL 1, 347).

111. Tert. *cult.fem.* 2.2.5 (CCL 1, 355).

112. See Tert. *cult.fem.* 1.8.5 (CCL 1, 350–51); Tert. *spect.* 1.4 (CCL 2, 227).

113. Tert. *spect.* 2.7 (CCL 1, 228).

114. Or. *mart.* 9 (GCS 1, 9–10).

115. Two treatises (*De lapsis, De ecclesiae catholicae unitate*) address the disruption caused by penitential practices. The lapsed took advantage of privileges of penance given to confessors, and this undermined the power of the bishop. See also Cypr. *eps.* 15–19, 25, 27, 30, 33, 36, 39, 55, and 56.

116. The appearance of sin in this form was the result of the post-Constantinian monasticism, in which a prime vocation of monks of the desert was examination of conscience; this view of sin would raise the radical doubts about the depth of the moral dislocation caused by Original Sin that Augustine's writings would foster. See Régis Jolivet, *Le problème du mal d'après saint Augustin* (Paris: Editions Beauchesne, 1936); Stanislas Lyonnet, "Péché," *Dictionnaire de spiritualité ascétique et mystique: doctrine et histoire*, ed. Marcel Viller, et al. (Paris: Beauchesne, 1984), 12: 790–815; *Théologie du péché*, ed. Ph. Delhaye et al., Bibliothèque de Théologie 7 (Tournai: Desclée and Co., 1960), 293–514, esp. 456–474.

117. On this general change of sensibilities, see Robert Markus, *The End of Ancient Christianity* (Cambridge: Cambridge University Press, 1990); more specifically, see Joseph Ntedika, "Eschatologie et Pénitence," in *Message et Mission* (Louvain: Editions Nauwelaerts; Paris: Béatrice-Nauwelaerts, 1968), 109–27.

118. 1 Clem. 24.1 (Funk, 93).

119. 1 Clem. 36.2 (Funk, 107).

120. Tert. *scorp.* 6.10–11 (CCL 2, 1080–81). The first baptism gained forgiveness of sins but could not be repeated. This was why the baptism of martyrdom was given us, Or. *mart.* 30 (GCS 1, 26–27). Significantly, the martyrs' baptism by blood would cleanse many, not only themselves, Or. *mart.* 30 (GCS 1, 26–27): "As Christ brought cleansing into the world, perhaps baptism by martyrdom also served to cleanse many." Cf. Cypr. *Fort.* 4 (CCL 3, 185): "hoc esse baptisma in gratia maius, in potestate sublimius, in honore pretiosius, baptisma in quo angeli baptizant, baptisma in quo Deus et Christus eius exultant, baptisma post quod nemo iam peccat, baptisma quod fidei nostrae incrementa consummat, baptisma quod nos de mundo recedentes statim Deo copulat. In aquae baptismo accipitur peccatorum remissa, in sanguinis corona uir-

tutum. Amplectenda res et optanda et omnibus postulationum nostrarum praecibus expetenda, ut qui serui Dei fuimus simus et amici."

121. *M. Scill.* 15 (ACM, 88).

122. *M. Mont. et Luc.* 7.4 (ACM, 231).

123. *M. Fruct.* 3.2 (ACM, 178).

124. *M. Fruct.* 5.2 (ACM, 182).

125. *M. Pion.* 21.4 (ACM, 164).

126. Tert. *resurr.* 57.13 (CCL 2, 1005): "Permitte hanc et deo potestatem per uim illius demutationis condicionem, non naturam, reformandi, dum et passiones auferuntur et munitiones conferuntur. Ita manebit quidem caro etiam post resurrectionem eatenus passibilis, qua ipsa, qua eadem, et tamen inpassibilis, quia in hoc ipsum manumissa a domino, ne ultra pati possit."

127. Tert. *resurr.* 61–62 (CCL 2, 1009–11).

128. The "unjust and intemperate [would] be punished in eternal fire," while "the virtuous, that is those who live like Christ, [would] dwell in a state that is free from suffering," Just. *2 apol.* 1.1 (PG 6, 441).

129. Just. *1 apol.* 21.8, 21 (SQ 1, 18). See note 94 above for a bibliography on divinization and the reformed body.

130. Tert. *orat.* 28.2 (CCL 1, 273).

131. Daley, *Hope*, 236, argues that this was asserted by Origen's later critics, citing Justinian *Ep. ad Menam*, Anathema 5, ed. E. Schwarts, ACO III 213.25–26; Council of 553, Anathema Against the Origenists, ed. J. Straub, ACO IV, I, 249, 19–22, and argues that this stems from a misunderstanding of Origen's ideas. See A. M. Festugière, "Le Corps glorieux 'sphéroïde chez Origène," *Revue des Sciences Philosophiques et Théologiques* 43 (1959): 81–86.

132. Tert. *resurr.* 48.8 (CCL 2, 988); Tert. *adv. Marc.* 5.9.2–6 (CCL 1, 689), cf. 1 Cor. 15: 21; Tert. *adv. Marc.* 5.10.7–10 (CCL 1, 693), cf. 1 Cor. 15: 45–50.

133. Tert. *adv. Marc.* 5.9.5 (CCL 1, 689).

134. See Caroline Walker Bynum, *The Resurrection of the Body in Western Christianity, 200–1336* (New York: Columbia University Press, 1995), 19–58. Questions of the body and martyrdom have rightly drawn much interest; see, e.g., Maureen Tilley, "The Asçetic Body and the (Un)Making of the World of the Martyr," *Journal of the American Academy of Religion* 59 (1991): 467–79; Brent Shaw, "Body/Power/Identity: Passions of the Martyrs," *Journal of Early Christian Studies* 4 (1996): 269–312.

135. Ign. *Eph.* 3.1 (SC 10, 70); *Rom.* 2.1 (SC 10, 126); *Rom.* 4.1–3 (SC 10, 130); *Rom.* 5.3 (SC 10, 132). See Th. Preiss, "La mystique de l'imitation du Christ et de l'unité chez Ignace d'Antioche," *Revue de l'Histoire des Religions* 18 (1938): 197–421; Karin Bommes, *Weizen Gottes: Untersuchungen zur Theologie des Martyriums bei Ignatius von Antiochen* (Cologne: P. Han, 1976); Sergio Za-tartu, "Les concepts de vie et de mort chez Ignace d'Antioche," *Studia Patristica* 33 (1979): 324–41; Charles Munier, "La question d'Ignace d'Antioche, *Aufstieg und Niedergang der römischen Welt* (Berlin: de Gruyter, 1972–), 27: 1 (1993): esp. 424–27, 455–63; J. Van Eijk, *La résurrection*, 99–126.

136. Tert. *fug.* 14.2 (CCL 2, 1155).

137. Tert. *adv. Marc.* 5.11.15 (CCL 1, 699).

138. Tert. *resurr.* 40.10–11 (CCL 2, 974).

139. Ign. *Rom.* 4.3 (SC 10, 130).

140. Tert. *resurr.* 40.10–11 (CCL 2, 974); *resurr.* 40.14 (CCL 2, 975). See *M. Mont. et Luc.* 10.4 (ACM, 222); the body is the temple of and coheir with Christ in *M. Mar. et Iac.* 5.8 (ACM, 200). To "share the cup" or "chalice" of the Lord's suffering (see Luke 22: 42; Mark 10: 38) meant one would also share his glory; see *M. Polyc.* 14.2 (ACM, 12); "Seek to die a martyr," Tertullian advised, "so that he may be glorified in you who suffered for you." Tert. *fug.* 9.4 (CCL 2, 1147).

141. Tert. *scorp.* 6.8 (CCL 2, 1080): "Porro et si fidei propterea congruebat sublimitati et claritatis aliqua prolatio, tale quid esse oportuerat illud emolumenti, quod magno constaret: labore, cruciatu, tormento, morte. Sed respice conpensationem, cum caro et anima dependitur—quibus in homine carius nihil est, alterum manus dei, alterum flatus,—ipsa dependi in profectum quorum est profectus, ipsa erogari quae lucri fiant, eadem pretia quae et merces."

142. *M. Lyon.* 24 (ACM, 68): ἀλλ᾽ ἴασιν διὰ τῆς χάριτος τοῦ Χριστοῦ τὴν δευτέραν στρέβλωσιν αὐτὰ γενέσθαι. Quoting the sixth Maccabee brother, Origen wrote of the expiation of sin through willing self-sacrifice, "Since we are paying these penalties for our sins so that we may be cleansed by our suffering, we suffer them willingly," Or. *mart.* 25 (GCS 1, 22).

143. Tert. *scorp.* 11.1–3 (CCL 2, 1091–93); *scorp.* 5.7–10 (CCL 2, 1076–77).

144. Cypr. *ep.* 31.2.1 (CCL 3B, 153).

145. *M. Mont. et Luc.* 6.1 (ACM, 224).

146. *M. Mont. et Luc.* 22.2 (ACM, 236).

147. *M. Carp.* 7 (ACM, 22). *M. Carp.* (ACM, 24).

148. *M. Poly.* 2 (ACM, 5).

149. Cypr. *Fort.* 4 (CCL 3, 185); also Or. *mart.* 13 (GCS 1, 13).

150. The theme of "despising death" is a central point of comparison between the voluntary death of the martyr versus that of the classical hero and gladiator. See Christel Butterweck, *"Martyriumsucht" in der alten Kirche? Studien zur Darstellung und Deutung frühchristlicher Martyrien*, Beiträge zur historischen Theologie 87 (Tübingen: J.C.B. Mohr [Paul Siebeck], 1995); Theofried Baumeister, *Die Anfänge der Theologie des Martyriums*, Münsterische Beiträge zur Theologie 45 (Münster: Aschendorff, 1980); Arthur J. Droge and James D. Tabor, *A Noble Death: Suicide and Martyrdom Among Christians and Jews in Antiquity* (New York: HarperCollins, 1992); Carole Straw, "A Very Special Death: The Christian Martyr and Classical Tradition," *Martyrdom*, ed. Margaret Cormack (Missoula, Mont.: Scholar's Press, forthcoming).

151. See *M. Mar. et Iac.* 8.7 (ACM, 206); *M. Apollon.* 37 (ACM, 101).

152. See Tert. *spec.* 28.5–29.2 (103).

153. *M. Apollon.* 27–28 (ACM, 98).

154. *M. Apollon.* 27 (ACM, 98).

155. *M. Pion.* 21.9 (ACM, 164).

156. While by definition the martyr's death is volitional—an expression of free will—this language is especially strong in Or. *mart.* 22 (GCS 1, 19–20).

157. By sheer force of will, martyrs are able to convert pain into pleasure, defeat into triumph, humiliation into honor; see, e.g., *M. Lyon.* 24 (ACM, 68): for torture/cure; *M. Mar. et Iac.* 3.2 (ACM, 196): for penalty/glory; Tert. *adv. Marc.* 5.20 (CCL 1, 725): for humiliation/glory; Tert. *mart.* 2.4 (CCL 1, 4): for prison/safety; Tert. *patient.* 3.9 (CCL 1, 301): for suffering/joy.

158. Tert. *mart.* 2.10 (CCL 2, 5). Soul and body are both strongly connected because physical suffering affects the soul. But soul and body are also separated. The body is a house, temple, temporary lodging for the soul; and if it collapses, the soul leaves; see Tert. *anim.* 38.5 (CCL 2, 842). Death was the separation of soul from the body; Tert. *anim.* 51.1 (CCL 2, 857).

159. Cypr. *ep.* 58.5.2 (CCL 3C, 326).

160. *M. Perp.* 8 (ACM, 129): "in extasi fuerat."

161. *M. Perp.* 15.6 (ACM, 122 and 124).

162. Polycarp's countenance filled with grace at his confession, *M. Polyc.* 12.1 (ACM, 11). Pionius was "radiant," *Pion.* 4.2 (ACM, 138); "glowing red," *Pion.* 10.2 (ACM, 148) and 22.4 (ACM, 165). The association of light with divinity seems to be cross-cultural; see Jean Pierre Vernant, "Dim Body, Dazzling Body," in *Fragments for a History of the Human Body*, ed. Michel Feher, Ramona Naddaff, and Nadia Tazi (New York: Zone Books, 1989). Vernant mentions the association of grace with divinity and fire. I suspect a deeper chain of associations: sun-light-life-fire-divinity-grace-goodness. Such divine associations would be balanced by those of the devil and the underworld: darkness-death-evil. Here the conflagration, fire, can be regenerative through destruction; see Carl-Marin Edsman, *Ignis Divinus*, Skrifter Utgivna an Vetenskaps-Societeten 34 (Lund: G. W. F. Gleerup, 1949). While Stoics held such beliefs on a cosmic scale, an analogy exists in the fire of purgatory, which purifies, cleanses, and renews the Christian.

163. *M. Mont. et Luc.* 21.8 (ACM, 234).

164. *M. Mar. et Iac.* 9.2 (ACM, 206).

165. *M. Mar. et Iac.* 3 (ACM, 198): "Christus micante gratia de proxima passione fulgebat."

166. *M. Fruct.* 4.3 (ACM, 181).

167. *M. Perp.* 21.10 (ACM, 131).

168. *M. Carp.* 35 (ACM, 26).

169. *M. Lyon.* 20 (ACM, 68). Note also that Blandina simply would not die despite the scourges, the beasts, and the hot griddle; *M. Lyon.* 55–56 (ACM, 78).

170. *M. Pion.* 21.2 (ACM, 162).

171. *M. Lyon.* 23–24 (ACM, 68).

172. *M. Poly.* 15.2 (ACM, 15).

173. *Mar. et Iac.* 6.9 (ACM, 200).

174. *M. Lyon.* 57.1 (ACM, 82 and 84).

175. *M. Polyc.* 18 (ACM, 17).

176. *M. Cypr.* 5 (ACM, 175).

177. *M. Fruct.* 6.3 (ACM, 182 and 184).

178. Such is the gist of moral essays, particularly those of Tertullian and Cyprian. Tert. *orat.* 4.3 (CCL 1, 260) for suffer unto death; Tert. *patient.* 7.9 (CCL 1, 307) for endure loss, [endure loss]; Tert. *patient.* 14.5–7 (CCL 1, 315) [Job]; Cypr. *patient.* 5 (CCL 3A, 120–21) [be perfect and like God: imitate his patience]; Cypr. *domin.orat.* 15 (CCL 3A, 99) [humility and constancy].

179. *M. Mar. et Iac.* 12.4 (ACM, 210): "nullaé tamen aciem liberae mentis clausere tenebrae."

180. *M. Perp.* 4.3–5 (ACM, 110).

181. *M. Perp.* 10.1–5 (ACM, 116 and 118).

182. *M. Poly.* 5.2 (ACM, 6).

183. *M. Polyc.* 7.3 (ACM, 6).

184. *M. Mar. et Iac.* 12.7 (ACM, 211).

185. *M. Mont.* 7 (ACM, 218).

186. *M. Pota. et Bas.* 6 (ACM, 134).

187. *M. Mar. et Iac.* 11.3 (ACM, 208).

188. *Mont. et Luc.* 21.8 (ACM, 234).

189. *M. Mar. et Iac.* 6.10–14 (ACM, 202); *M. Mont.* 11.3 (ACM, 222).

190. *M. Poly.* 22.2 (ACM, 18).

191. On heaven, see Jeffrey Burton Russell, *A History of Heaven: The Singing Silence* (Princeton, N.J.: Princeton University Press, 1997); Jacquiline Amat, *Songes et visions: l'au-delà dans la littérature latin tardive* (Paris: Etudes Augustiniennes, 1985); Nancy Gauthier, "Les images de l'au-delà durant l'antiquité chrétienne," *Revue des Etudes Augustiniennes* 33 (1987): 3–22, who cites Alfons M. Schneider, *Refrigerium. I, Nach literarischen Quellen und Inschriften* (diss. Freiburg im Breisgau, 1928) as important. See also Alfred Stuiber, *Refrigerium interim, die Vorstellungen vom Zwischenzustand und die frühchristliche Grabeskunst* (Bonn: P. Hanstein, 1957); Claude Carozzi, *Le voyage de l'âme dans l'au-delà, d'après la littérature latine, Ve–XIIIe siècle* (Rome: Ecole Française de Rome, 1994); Malcom Davies, "Description by Negation: History of a Thought Pattern in Ancient Accounts of Blissful Life," *Prometheus* 13 (1987): 265–84; Aaron Gurevich, "Per un'antropologia delle visioni ultraterrene nella cultura occidentale del medioevo" in *La semiotica nei paesi slavi: programmi, problemi, analisi,* ed. Carlo Prevignano (Milan: Feltrinelli, 1979), 443–63; Herbert Schade, "Das Paradies und die 'Imago Dei,'" in *Wandlungen des Paradiesischen und Utopischen: Studien zum Bild eines Ideals* (Berlin: de Gruyter, 1966), 79–182.

192. *M. Perp.* 12.1–7 (ACM, 120).

193. *M. Mont. et Luc.* 8.4–7 (ACM, 220).

194. *M. Perp.* 9.8–9 (ACM, 118).

195. *M. Mar. et Iac.* 7.3–5 (ACM, 204).

196. *M. Mar. et Iac.* 6.1 (ACM, 202).

197. *M. Mont. et Luc.* 5 (ACM, 218).

198. Qur'an, Sutra 55, Mecca 58.

The Decline of the Empire of God: Amnesty, Penance, and the Afterlife from Late Antiquity to the Middle Ages

1. Jacob of Sarug, *On the Penitent Thief,* trans. P.S. Landersdorfer, *Ausgewählte Schriften der syrischen Dichter,* Bibliothek der Kichenväter 60 (Kempten/Munich: J. Kosel, 1912), 363.

2. *Ep.* 4⁸.4. 78, *Oeuvres de saint Augustin 46B: Lettres 1⁸–29⁸,* Bibliothèque Augustinienne (Paris: Etudes Augustiniennes 1987), 114; trans. Robert B. Eno, *Saint Augustine: Letters VI (1⁸–29⁸),* Fathers of the Church 81 (Washington, D.C.: Catholic University of America Press, 1989), 43.

3. Augustine, *Contra ii epistulas Pelagianorum* 3.5.14.

4. E.g., in the newly discovered sermons of Augustine, discovered at Mainz by François Dolbeau: *Sermon Mayence* 40/*Dolbeau* 11.14.284, ed. F. Dolbeau, *Revue Bénédictine* 102 (1992): 94, in *Vingt-six sermons au peuple d'Afrique* (Paris: Institut d'Etudes Augustiniennes, 1996), 67.

5. Augustine, *Enchiridion* 21.78; *Enarrationes in Ps.* 37.36 and 80.20.

6. Augustine, *Enchiridion* 29.110; see Heikki Kotila, *Memoria mortuorum: Commemoration of the Departed in Augustine*, Studia Ephemeridis Augustinianum 38 (Rome: Augustinianum, 1992), 138–41; and Claude Carozzi, *Le voyage de l'âme dans l'au-delà, d'après la littérature latine, Ve–XIIIe siècle*, Collection de l'Ecole Française de Rome 189 (Rome: Ecole Française de Rome, 1994), 22–33; with G. R. Edwards, "Purgatory: 'Birth' or 'Evolution'?" *Journal of Ecclesiastical History* 36 (1985): 634–46.

7. Eric Rebillard, *In hora mortis: évolution de la pastorale chrétienne de la mort aux IVe et Ve siècles, dans l'Occident latin*, Bibliothèque de l'Ecole Française d'Athènes et de Rome 283 (Rome: Ecole Française de Rome, 1994), 214.

8. Augustine, *Enarratio in Ps. 101*, serm. 1.10 and *Mayence* 44/ *Dolbeau* 14.6.120, ed. F. Dolbeau, *Revue Bénédictine* 103 (1993): 317, in *Vingt-six sermons*, 111.

9. Rebillard, *In hora mortis*, 160–67.

10. Augustine, *Enchiridion* 29.110.

11. E.g., the epitaph of the great Christian senator, Petronius Probus: Ernest Diehl, *Inscriptiones Latinae Christianae Veteres* no. 63.13–14 (Zurich: Weidmann, 1970), 1: 18–19.

12. Athanas Recheis, *Engel, Tod und Seelenreise* (Rome: Edizioni di Storia e Letteratura, 1958), 169–84.

13. Sulpicius Severus, *Ep.* 3.16: see A. C. Rush, "An Echo of Classical Antiquity in Saint Gregory the Great: Death as a Struggle with the Devil," *Traditio* 3 (1945): 369–80.

14. Gregory of Tours, *De virtutibus sancti Martini* 1.4, ed. B. Krusch, Monumenta Germaniae Historica: Scriptores rerum Merovingicarum 1.2 (Hanover: Hahn, 1885), 140, trans. in Raymond Van Dam, *Saints and Their Miracles in Late Antique Gaul* (Princeton, N.J.: Princeton University Press, 1993), 206.

15. Carozzi, *Voyage de l'âme*, 99–253. The texts are collected in M. P. Ciccarese, *Visioni dell'Aldilà in Occidente* (Florence: Nardini, 1989).

16. Claude Lévi-Strauss, *Social Anthropology* (Harmondsworth: Penguin, 1977), 179.

17. Rebillard, *In hora mortis*, 11–124.

18. Frederick S. Paxton, *Christianizing Death: The Creation of a Ritual Process in Early Medieval Europe* (Ithaca, N.Y.: Cornell University Press, 1990), 6; and P. A. Février, "La mort chrétienne," in *Segni e riti nella chiesa altomedievale occidentale*, Settimane di Studio sull'Alto Medio Evo 33 (Spoleto: Centro di Studi sull'Alto Medio Evo, 1987), 2: 881–942, at pp. 891, 915–19.

19. Carozzi, *Voyage de l'âme*, 23; 22–33, 296, and 640.

20. See esp. Carl-Martin Edsman, *Le baptême de feu*, Uppsala Universitet Nytestamentliga Seminar: Acta 9 (Uppsala: Almquist and Wiksells, 1940), 3–12.

21. Clement of Alexandria, *Eclogae propheticae* 25.4 and *Stromateis* 7.6; Origen, *Hom.3 in Ps.36* 1. See Henri Crouzel, "L'exégèse origénienne de 1 Cor. 3: 11–15 et la purification eschatologique," *Epektasis: mélanges patristiques offerts au cardinal Jean Danié-*

lou, ed. Jacques Fontaine and Charles Kannengiesser (Paris: Beauchesne, 1972), 273–83; W. C. van Unnik, "The 'Wise Fire' in a Gnostic Eschatological Vision," *Kyriakon: Festschrift Johannes Quasten*, ed. Patrick Granfield and Josef A. Jungmann (Münster: Aschendorff, 1970), 1:277–88; C. Carozzi, *Eschatologie et au-delà: recherches sur l'Apocalypse de Paul* (Aix-en-Provence: Université de Provence, 1994), 71–76.

22. Pierre Hadot, *Exercices spirituels et philosophie antique* (Paris: Etudes Augustiniennes, 1982), trans. and ed. A. I. Davidson, *Philosophy as a Way of Life: Spiritual Exercises from Socrates to Foucault* (Oxford: Oxford University Press, 1995), 81–125; Michel Foucault, *Le souci de soi* (Paris: Gallimard, 1984), trans. *The Care of the Self* (New York: Random House, 1986); see also P. Hadot, "Réflexions sur l'idée du 'souci de soi,'" in *Michel Foucault philosophe* (Paris: Le Seuil, 1989), 261–68, also in *Philosophy as a Way of Life*, 206–13.

23. Peter Brown, *Power and Persuasion in Late Antiquity: Towards a Christian Empire* (Madison: University of Wisconsin Press, 1992), 62–69; P. Hadot, *La citadelle intérieure: introduction aux Pensées de Marc Aurèle* (Paris: Fayard, 1992), 324.

24. E.g., Ignaz Ziegler, *Die Königsgleichnisse des Midrasch beleuchtet durch die römische Kaiserzeit* (Breslau: Schottlaender, 1903); N. Johansson, *Parakletoi* (Lund: Ohlsson, 1940).

25. Brown, *Power and Persuasion*, 55, 69.

26. *The Gelasian Sacramentary* 3.6, ed. H. A. Wilson (Oxford: Clarendon Press, 1894), 227.

27. Reprinted as Proper 21 (Collects: Traditional), *Book of Common Prayer . . . of the Episcopal Church* (Evanston, Ill.: Seabury Press, 1977), 281.

28. *Sacramentary of Gellone* 2895, ed. A. Dumas, Corpus Christianorum, Series latina 159 (Turnhout: Brepols, 1981), 462; V. D. Sicard, *La liturgie de la mort dans l'église latine des origines à la réforme carolingienne*, Liturgiewissenschaftliche Quellen und Forschungen 63 (Münster: Aschendorff, 1978), 261–345; Paxton, *Christianizing Death*, 62, 116–19.

29. Sicard, *La liturgie de la mort*, 399.

30. Peter Brown, *The Cult of the Saints: Its Rise and Function in Latin Christianity* (Chicago: University of Chicago Press, 1981), 62–68, and *Authority and the Sacred: Aspects of the Christianization of the Roman World* (Cambridge: Cambridge University Press, 1995), 73–74.

31. Augustine, *De civitate Dei* 21.18.1, ed. B. Dombart and A. Kalb, Corpus Christianorum 48 (Turnhout: Brepols, 1955), 784.

32. Augustine, *De civitate Dei* 18.9–11, p. 784.

33. Augustine, *De civitate Dei* 21.19–23, 21.21.13–20, pp. 785–789, 786.

34. Prudentius, *Cathemerinon* 5.125–36, ed. H. J. Thomson, Loeb Classical Library (Cambridge, Mass.: Harvard University Press, 1969), 1: 46.

35. *Codex Theodosianus* 9.38.3.

36. *Codex Theodosianus* 9.3.7.

37. Carozzi, *Eschatologie et au-delà*, 127–51.

38. Gregory of Tours, *De virtutibus sancti Martini* 2.60, p. 180; trans. Van Dam, *Saints and Their Miracles*, 259.

39. Gregory of Tours, *Liber historiarum* 4.21.

40. Gregory of Tours, *Liber historiarum* 5.14.

41. Gregory of Tours, *Liber historiarum* 9.8.

42. Gregory of Tours, *De virtutibus sancti Martini* 2.17, p. 164; trans. Van Dam, *Saints and Their Miracles*, 236.

43. Gregory of Tours, *Liber historiarum* 1, praef.: *qui adpropinquantem finem mundi disperant*. The reader should know that my interpretation of this phrase differs from the *communis opinio*. Lewis Thorpe, *Gregory of Tours: The History of the Franks* (Harmondsworth: Penguin, 1974), 67, translates the phrase as: "who are losing hope *as they see* the end of the world coming nearer." I would translate it as: "who do not expect the end of the world to come." *Disperare* can mean "not expect, lose hope of"; cf. *Liber historiarum* 4.12, citing Sidonius Apollinaris, *Letter* 2.1: *nec accipiebat instrumenta desperans*, trans. O. M. Dalton, *The Letters of Sidonius* (Oxford: Clarendon Press, 1915), 1: 35: "nor does he trouble to furnish himself with deeds, knowing it hopeless to prove a title." For the alternative adopted by most scholars, see Bruno Krusch, Monumenta Germaniae Historica: Scriptores rerum merovingicarum 1.1 (Hanover: Hahn, 1951), 142, n. 2. See also *Sortes Sangallenses* 33, R.8: *Habebis spem fidei, sed de disperato*, in Alban Dold, *Die Orakelsprüche im St. Galler Palimpsestcodex 908*, Österreichische Akademie der Wissenschaften: Sitzungsberichte 225: 4 (1948): 24, with note on p. 110: "from someone you do not expect." See A. H. B. Breukelaar, *Historiography and Episcopal Authority in Sixth-Century Gaul: The Histories of Gregory of Tours Interpreted in Historical Context*, Forschungen zur Kirchen- und Dogmengeschichte 57 (Göttingen: Vandenhoeck and Ruprecht, 1994): 300 and n. 23; and on Gregory's attitude to the approaching end of time, see pp. 52–55 and 169–74, with M. Heinzelmann, *Gregor von Tours (538–594). "Zehn Bücher der Geschichte.": Historiographie und Gesellschaftskonzept im 6. Jht.* (Darmstadt: Wissenschaftliche Buchgesellschaft, 1994), 69–101; both accept the conventional translation. By contrast to the insouciance castigated by Gregory, expectation of the coming end of the world was the attitude expected of religiously minded persons: e.g. the formula for a legacy to a pious foundation; see Marculf, *Formulae* 2.3, ed. A. Uddholm (Uppsala: Eranos, 1962): 178.

44. Carozzi, *Voyage de l'âme*, 99–138, with an edition of the *Visio Fursei* on pp. 679–92; Ciccarese, *Visioni*, 190–224.

45. *Visio Fursei* 9; Ciccarese, *Visioni*, 204; and Carozzi, *Voyage de l'âme*, 684.

46. R. Chapman Stacey, *The Road to Judgment: From Custom to Court in Medieval Ireland and Wales* (Philadelphia: University of Philadelphia Press, 1994), 111. See also N. B. Aitchison, "Kingship, Society, and Sacrality: Rank, Power, and Ideology in Early Medieval Ireland," *Traditio* 49 (1994): 45–75.

47. N. Patterson, *Cattle Lords and Clansmen: The Social Structure of Early Ireland* (Notre Dame, Ind.: Notre Dame University Press, 1994), 328–29.

48. Patterson, *Cattle Lords*, 348.

49. *Visio Fursei* 2–3, Ciccarese, *Visioni*, 194–96, and Carozzi, *Voyage de l'âme*, 679.

50. E.g., Leontius of Neapolis, *Life of John the Almsgiver* 27 and 44, trans. in Elizabeth Dawes and Norman H. Baynes, *Three Byzantine Saints* (Oxford: Blackwell, 1948), 239 and 255, and the material in Glenn Pears, "Approaching the Archangel Michael," *Byzantine and Modern Greek Studies* 20 (1996): 100–121.

51. Anastasius of Sinai, *Oratio in Ps. 6*, *Patrologia Graeca* 89: 1141C, records the

story of the death of a brigand chief; see also C. Farkas, "Räuberbehörde in Thrakien," *Byzantinische Zeitschrift* 86/87 (1993/1994): 462–70.

52. *Visio Fursei* 6, Ciccarese, *Visioni*, 198 and Carrozzi, *Voyage de l'âme*, 681.

53. *Visio Fursei* 7 and 9, Ciccarese, *Visioni*, 200, 204; Carozzi, *Voyage de l'âme*, 682, 684.

54. *Visio Fursei* 7, 9, Ciccarese, *Visioni*, 200, 204; Carozzi, *Voyage de l'âme*, 682, 684.

55. *Visio Fursei* 8, Ciccarese, *Visioni*, 202; Carozzi, *Voyage de l'âme*, 683. See Carozzi, *Voyage de l'ame*, 133–37, on the purificatory associations of fire in Celtic and northern folklore.

56. *Vita Geretrudis* 7, ed. B. Krusch, Monumenta Germaniae Historica: Scriptores rerum merovingicarum 2 (Hanover: Hahn, 1888): 462–63.

57. See esp. Carozzi, *Voyage de l'âme*, 112–20.

58. Jo Ann McNamara, "The Ordeal of Community: Hagiography and Discipline in Merovingian Convents," *Vox Benedictina* 2 (1986): 293–326.

59. [Waldebert], *Regula cuiusdam patris ad virgines* 5, *Patrologia latina* 88: 1059 D-1060 A.

60. Jonas of Bobbio, *Vita Columbani* 2.11, ed. B. Krusch, Monumenta Germaniae Historica: Scriptores rerum Merovingicarum 4 (Hanover: Hahn, 1902), 130; trans. in Jo Ann McNamara and John E. Hallborg, *Sainted Women of the Dark Ages* (Durham, N.C.: Duke University Press, 1992), 162–63.

61. Friedrich Nietzsche, *Die fröhliche Wissenschaft* 5 (358), Kroners Taschenbuch 74 (Stuttgart: Kroner, 1956), 268.

62. [Waldebert], *Regula cuiusdam patris* 7: 1060B; G. Muschiol, *Famula Dei. Zur Liturgie in merovingischen Frauenklöstern*, Beiträge zur Geschichte des alten Mönchtums und des Benediktinertums 41 (Münster: Aschendorff, 1994): 222–63.

63. Jonas, *Vita Columbani* 2.12, p. 132, trans. McNamara and Hallborg, 164.

64. Carozzi, *Voyage de l'âme*, 142–44; see now Yitzak Hen, "The Structure and Aim of the *Visio Baronti*," *Journal of Theological Studies* n.s. 47 (1996): 477–97, esp. 493–97.

65. *Visio Baronti* 12, ed. Wilhelm Levison, Monumenta Germaniae Historica: Scriptores rerum Merovingicarum 5 (Hanover: Hahn, 1910), 386; Ciccarese, *Visioni*, 254; trans. in J. N. Hillgarth, *Christianity and Paganism, 350–750: The Conversion of Western Europe* (Philadelphia: University of Pennsylvania Press, 1986), 199.

66. Carozzi, *Voyage de l'âme*, 638.

67. *Visio Baronti* 22, 354; Hillgarth, *Christianity and Paganism*, 204, citing Gregory, *Homilies on the Gospels* 2.8, 14.6, 32.8.

68. Arnold Angenendt, *Das Frühmittelalter: Die abendländische Christenheit von 400 bis 900* (Stuttgart: Kohlhammer, 1990), 147–58.

69. Muirchú, *Vita Patricii* 2.6.1, ed. Ludwig Bieler, *The Patrician Texts in the Book of Armagh* (Dublin: Institute of Advanced Studies, 1979), 116.

70. Aethelwulf, *De abbatibus*, line 6, ed. Alistair Campbell (Oxford: Clarendon Press, 1967), 3 and n.1.

71. *Landnámabók* S91/H79, ed. Jakob Benediktsson (Reykjavik: Islenzk Fornrit, 1968), 132–34.

72. Toshihiko Izutsu, *Ethico-Religious Concepts in the Qur'an* (Montreal: McGill University Press, 1966), 16.

73. Eva Riad, "*Safa'a* dans le Coran," *Orientalia Suecana* 30 (1981): 37–62, at pp. 37–42; and Taede Huitema, *De Voorspraak (Shafa'a) in den Islam* (Leiden: E. J. Brill, 1936), 45, 56.

74. Al-Bukhari, *Sahih* 76.19.476, ed. Muhammad Muhsin Khan (Beirut: Dar al-Arabia, 1985), 8: 316.

75. Al-Bukhari, *Sahih* 76.49.574, p. 374; Jane Idleman Smith and Yvonne Yazbeck Haddad, *Islamic Understanding of Death and Resurrection* (Albany, N.Y.: SUNY Press, 1981), 84.

76. Gregory, *Dialogi* 4.43.2, ed. Adalbert de Vogüé *Dialogues*, Sources chrétiennes 265 (Paris: Le Cerf, 1980), 154–55; see Carozzi, *Voyage de l'âme*, 187–89.

77. Eustratius, *De animis defunctorum*, 9, in Leo Allatius, *De utriusque ecclesiae occidentalis et orientalis perpetua in dogmate de purgatorio consensione* (Rome, 1655), 380–580, p. 373; see H. G. Beck, *Kirche und theologische Literatur im byzantinischen Reich* (Munich: C. H. Beck 1959), 411. On the background of such doubts, see Vincent Déroche, "Pourquoi écrivait-on des récueils des miracles?: l'exemple des miracles de saint Artémius," in *Les saints et leur sanctuaire à Byzance*, Byzantina Sorbonensia 11, ed. Catherine Jolivet-Lévy et al. (Paris: C.N.R.S., 1993), 95–116, esp. 113–16. See also L. S. B. MacCoull, "The Monophysite Angelology of John Philoponus," *Byzantion* 65 (1995): 388–95.

78. Eustratius, *De animis* 28, Allatius, 561–63.

79. Gregory, *Dialogi* 4.42.1–5, ed. de Vogüé, 150–54; compare the doublet *cultor pauperum et contemptor sui* used of Paschasius with Diehl, *Inscriptiones latinae christianae veteres*, no. 1195.10: *pauperibus dives sed sibi pauper erat* and 1778.6: *pauperibus locuples, sibi pauper.* See now A. Wirbelauer, *Zwei Päpste in Rom: Der Konflikt zwischen Laurentius und Symmachus (498–514)* (Munich: Tuduv, 1993).

80. Gregory, *Dialogi* 4.42.5, ed. de Vogüé, 154.

81. Angenendt, *Das Frühmittelalter*, 155.

82. Jacques Le Goff, *The Birth of Purgatory* (Chicago: University of Chicago Press, 1984), 96.

83. R. Meens, "Willibrords boeteboek?" *Tijdschrift voor Geschiedenis* 106 (1993): 163–78; "A Background to Augustine's Mission to Anglo-Saxon England," *Anglo-Saxon England* 23 (1994): 5–17; "Pollution in the Early Middle Ages: The Case of Food Regulations in the Penitentials," *Early Medieval Europe* 4 (1995): 3–19; now *Het tripartite boeteboek: overlevering en beteknis van vroegmiddeleeuwse biechtvoorschrfiten* (Hilversum: Verloren, 1994), 267–321, and now "Ritual Purity and the Influence of Gregory the Great in the Early Middle Ages," in *Unity and Diversity in the Church*, ed. R. N. Swanson, Studies in Church History 32 (Oxford: Blackwell, 1995), 31–43.

84. A. J. Festugière, *La révélation d'Hermès Trismégiste*, vol. 2, *Le Dieu cosmique* (Paris: Belles Lettres, 1981), 441–46 on the *Dream of Scipio*.

85. Boniface, *Epistula* 115, ed. Michael Tangl, in Monumenta Germaniae Historica: Epistulae selectae (Berlin: Weidmann, 1916), 248; Ciccarese, *Visioni*, 366, 370–72. See Carozzi, *Voyage de l'âme*, 200–222.

86. J. C. Schmitt, "Une histoire religieuse du Moyen-Age est-elle possible?" in *Il mestiere del storico del Medioevo* (Spoleto: Centro di Studi sull'Alto Medio Evo, 1994),

73–83, at p. 82: "Dieu n'est plus maître de toute l'espace et de tout le temps: c'est le sens de la nouvelle doctrine de purgatoire."

From Jericho to Jerusalem: The Violent Transformation
of Archbishop Engelbert of Cologne

This is a revised and expanded version of a paper presented at Columbia University's Seventh Annual Medieval Guild Conference in October 1996. It grew out of research conducted during a year-long seminar at Columbia with Caroline Walker Bynum, to whose many patient readings and incisive criticisms this essay owes a great debt and for whose generous enthusiasm and support I am immensely grateful. Many thanks also go to the other members of the seminar, especially Anna Harrison and Manuele Gragnolati, for the fruitful dialogues we carried on throughout the year and to Christopher Ranney for his insightful readings and comments.

1. The best edition of the text is the *Vita et miracula Engelberti*, ed. Fritz Zschaeck in Alfons Hilka, ed., *Die Wundergeschichten des Caesarius von Heisterbach*, Publikationen der Gesellschaft für Rheinische Geschichtskunde 43 (Bonn: Peter Hanstein Verlag, 1937), 3: 234–328; hereafter *VE* (all citations are from this edition and all translations are my own). A German translation was published by Karl Langosch as *Leben, Leiden und Wunder des heiligen Erzbischofs Engelbert von Köln* (*Die Geschichtsschreiber der deutschen Vorzeit* 100) (Münster/Cologne: Böhlau Verlag, 1955). On the place of the Vita within Caesarius's oeuvre, see Langosch's entry "Caesarius von Heisterbach" in *Die deutsche Literatur des Mittelalters: Verfasserlexikon* (Vol. I), ed. Kurt Ruh et al. Berlin: De Gruyter, 1978, cols. 1152–68; hereafter *DVL*.

2. For a valuable methodological discussion of the documentary value of saints' lives and related materials, see Friedrich Lotter, "Methodisches zur Gewinnung historischer Erkenntnisse aus hagiographischen Quellen," *Historische Zeitschrift* 229 (1979): 299–355.

3. Surius published a reworked Vita in his 1575 *De probatis Sanctorum historiis* VI, and that text provided the basis for Aegidius Gelenius's *Vindex libertatis ecclesiasticae et martyr S. Engelbertus . . . una cum brevi suae aetatis annalium . . . editione* (Cologne, 1633); see K. Langosch's introduction to the German translation (1955), 23. Surius' name appeared in the Martyrology for the first time in 1583: *Coloniae sancti Engelberti episcopi, qui pro defensione ecclesiasticae libertatis et romanae ecclesiae obedientia martyrium subire non dubitavit*. See Albert Poncelet, *Acta Sanctorum*, vol. 71 (November), Part III (Antwerp: Meursius, 1910), 643–44 (hereafter *AASS*); and Niccolo del Ré's entry in the *Bibliotheca Sanctorum* IV (Rome: Instituto Giovanni XXIII, 1964), cols. 1209–10.

4. The shrine, created in 1633 by the studio of Konrad Duisbergh, is discussed and reproduced in the exhibition catalogue *Erzbischöfe von Köln: Porträts—Insignien—Weihe*, ed. Rolf Lauer (Cologne: Erzbischöfliches Diözesanmuseum, 1989): 24–25 and plate 5.

5. See the entry in the exhibition catalogue *Bilder vom Menschen in der Kunst des Abendlandes: Jubiläumsausstellung der Preußischen Museen Berlin, 1830–1980* (Berlin: Gebr. Mann, 1980), 125.

6. The following account of Engelbert's reign is drawn from the *Vita*, Liber I

(*De vita et actibus domini Engilberti Coloniensis archiepiscopi et martiris*), 235–49; supplemented by Richard Knipping, ed., *Die Regesten der Erzbischöfe von Köln im Mittelalter* III: 1 (=Publikationen der Gesellschaft für Rheinische Geschichtskunde 21), (Bonn: Peter Hansteins Verlag, 1909), 26–88; and Julius Ficker's *Engelbert der Heilige: Erzbischof von Köln und Reichsverweser* (Cologne, 1853; rep. Aalen: Scientia Verlag, 1985), 53–144, which also contains documents pertaining to his career. A more concise but less complete account is Hans Foerster, *Engelbert von Berg der Heilige* (Elberfeld: Martini and Gruttefien, 1925).

7. On the family Berg, see Ficker, *Engelbert der Heilige* (1853), 14–16.

8. On the turbulent reigns of Archbishops Adolf I of Altena (1193–1205, 1212–16), Bruno IV of Sayn (1205–8), and Dietrich I of Hengebach (1208–12), see Knipping, *Regesten* (1909), 1–25; Ficker, *Engelbert der Heilige* (1853), 18–52; and *VE* I: 3, 238–40.

9. *VE* I: 6, 244–45.

10. On Engelbert's building activities and generosity in making donations to ecclesiastical establishments, *VE* I: 5, 241–44; on his assertion of control over secular lords, ibid. and *VE* I: 4, 240–41; on his welcoming of the mendicants in 1220 (Dominicans) and 1222 (Franciscans) in spite of public concerns that they represented the fulfillment of a frightening prophecy of Hildegard of Bingen, *VE* I: 7, 245–46. On Engelbert's relation to the mendicants, see J. Greven, "Engelbert der Heilige und die Bettelorden," *Bonner Zeitschrift für Theologie und Seelsorge* 2 (1925). On the oppressive state of affairs in the decades preceding Engelbert's reign, *VE* I: 3, 238–40, I: 4, 240–41.

11. Engelbert hears poor people's complaints, *VE* I: 7, 246; gives his glove as token of safe passage to a fearful merchant, *VE* I: 5, 242; allows a woman to bypass lawyers and state her case to him directly, *VE* I: 8, 246; orders on-the-spot hearing of a widow's complaint against him, overturns ruling in his favor, and pays her her debts, *VE* II: 5, 256–57.

12. See the Vita as translated by Dom Gerard Sitwell in *St. Odo of Cluny*, Makers of Christendom (London: Sheed and Ward, 1958), 89–180.

13. André Vauchez, *La sainteté en Occident aux derniers siècles du moyen âge d'après les procès de canonisation et les documents hagiographiques* (Rome: Ecole Française de Rome, 1981), 341, and note 26 below. See also the accounts in Stephanie Coué, "Acht Bischofsviten aus der Salierzeit—neu interpretiert," in Stefan Weinfurter, ed., *Die Salier und das Reich III: Gesellschaftlicher und ideengeschichtlicher Wandel im Reich der Salier* (Sigmaringen: Jan Thorbecke Verlag, 1991), 347–414; and Hatto Kallfelz, ed. and trans., *Lebensbeschreibungen einiger Bischöfe des 10.-12. Jahrhunderts* (Darmstadt: Wissenschaftliche Buchgesellschaft, 1973), where not all of the subjects were considered saints.

14. C. Stephen Jaeger, "The Courtier Bishop in *Vitae* from the Tenth to the Twelfth Century," *Speculum* 58, 2 (1983): 291–325, at 294.

15. Walther von der Vogelweide, "Kaiser Friedrichs-Ton 4: Engelbrechtspreis," in *Werke, Band I: Spruchlyrik*, ed. Günther Schweikle (Stuttgart: Philipp Reclam, 1994), 210–11.

16. The terms of the conflict and the various negotiations intended to solve the matter are described in *VE* II: 1, 249–52.

17. Wolfgang Kleist, "Der Tod des Erzbischofs Engelbert von Köln: Eine kritische Studie," *Zeitschrift für vaterländische Geschichte und Altertumskunde* 75 (1917):

182–249. This interpretation has been accepted by Karl Langosch; see his introduction to the German translation of the Vita (1955), 20–21.

18. See Appendix for a complete translation of Caesarius's Book II, Chapter 7, which relies in part on the account of Frederick of Isenberg's notary Tobias and from which all citations given here are taken. The excerpt is from Hilka, *Die Wundergeschichten* (see note 1), 259–66.

19. Annette von Droste-Hülshoff, *Gedichte*, ed. Siegfried Sudhof (Stuttgart: Philipp Reclam, 1974), 45–50.

20. Karl Morrison, *History as a Visual Art in the Twelfth-Century Renaissance* (Princeton, N.J.: Princeton University Press, 1990), 206. According to Morrison, the sense of "being there" would lead to heightened empathetic participation in the events described, allowing the reader imaginatively to reenact those events and thus bring portions of sacred history into his or her own life.

21. See *VE* II: 8, 264.

22. On the treatment of the corpse on its return to Cologne, *VE* II: 9, 266–67; on the widespread practice of the division of dead bodies and the theoretical problems it entailed, see Elizabeth A. R. Brown, "Death and the Human Body in the Later Middle Ages: The Legislation of Boniface VIII on the Division of the Corpse," *Viator* 12 (1981): 221–70.

23. The events leading up to the assassins' executions are described in *VE* II: 13, 270–72; Frederick's brutal punishment is described in detail in *VE* II: 17, 278–81. For further discussion of this, see below.

24. There is some disagreement as to Caesarius's position regarding the events. Michael Goodich cites Caesarius's "grudging tone" in the preface in order to argue that "this [work] was apparently less a labor of love than an obligation"; see his *Vita Perfecta: The Ideal of Sainthood in the Thirteenth Century* (=Monographien zur Geschichte des Mittelalters 25) (Stuttgart: Anton Hiersemann Verlag, 1982), 63. Karl Langosch, on the other hand, contends that "die Ermordung Engelberts hat C. tief getroffen" on the basis of other evidence such as the sermon and early plans for a Vita, which I will discuss below; see his entry in the *DVL*, col. 1163.

25. See Langosch, *DVL*, col. 1162. The sermon, to be discussed further below, appears in Poncelet, *AASS*, 639–40.

26. Aside from the biographical sketches provided by Karl Langosch in the *DVL* and in the introduction to his German translation of the Engelbert Vita, see the colorful depiction of Caesarius's life and cultural milieu by Alexander Kaufmann, *Caesarius von Heisterbach: Ein Beitrag zur Culturgeschichte des zwölften und dreizehnten Jahrhunderts* (Cologne: Verlag J. M. Heberle, 1862).

27. The letter was published by J. Braun in the *Zeitschrift für Philosophie und katholische Theologie* 6, 3: 7–11, and translated into German in Kaufmann, *Caesarius von Heisterbach* (1862), 89–90. The edition of the *Dialogue* to which I shall refer is Joseph Strange, ed., *Dialogus Miraculorum*, 2 vols. (Cologne, 1851; rep. Ridgewood, N.J.: Gregg Press, 1966); hereafter *DM*.

28. Langosch, *DVL*, col. 1164, especially in regard to Book II, Chapter 7 (the death scene).

29. See, for example, the judgments of Karl Langosch in his introduction to the German translation (1955), 19–20, and in the *DVL*, col. 1163. On the problem of

truth and fiction in medieval hagiography, see Hippolyte Delehaye, *The Legends of the Saints: An Introduction to Hagiography*, trans. V. M. Crawford (Notre Dame, Ind.: University of Notre Dame Press, 1961); and on working with and around that disparity, see Lotter, "Methodisches zur Gewinnung," note 2 above.

30. See below, pp. 66–67.

31. On episcopal biography as a genre, see Jaeger, "Courtier Bishop" (1983): 294–95; and Lotter, "Methodisches zur Gewinnung," 310–12.

32. See Vauchez, *La sainteté en Occident*, 303–6.

33. Ibid., 340–53.

34. See the edition by Poncelet *AASS*, 639–40.

35. Ibid., 640: "Et forte, sicut plures opinantur, Deus voluit delere culpam descensionis eius [Engelbert's] ab Hierusalem in Iericho. Per Hierusalem, in quo templum erat et religio, negotia designantur spiritualia: per Iericho mundana atque saecularia. Cum episcopus esset et dux, minus illis intendebat et ad ista nimis descendebat, ita ut quidam monachorum nostrorum illi diceret: 'Domine, vos estis bonus dux, sed non bonus episcopus.'"

36. *VE* I: 2, 238: "Nam mundane glorie deditus, totus illis multipliciter est irretitus."

37. Ibid.: "[Non opera iustitie hec neque salutis divitie, sed] retia demoniorum, instrumenta et laquei peccatorum, quos ipse evadere non potuit."

38. Engelbert appears at his memorial mass; *VE* II: 10, 268–69, Hermann of Lechenich is cured on his deathbed when Engelbert appears to him in a vision, see *VE* III: 24, 298–99.

39. The miracles of Engelbert comprise all of Book III of the Vita. They were no longer recorded, however, after the death of Caesarius in around 1240.

40. See below, pp. 72–73.

41. *VE* II: 14, 273: "Nequaquam credere possumus virum superbum, avarum et totum seculo deditum miracula posse facere." Having just related the story of one skeptic who had dared God to make him go insane and die if the rumors of Engelbert's miraculous activities were true, Caesarius proclaims that all those who are accustomed to make such cynical statements should consider his exemplum before voicing their doubts further.

42. *VE* III: Prologue, 282–83.

> Signa enim non sunt de substantia sanctitatis, sed quedam indicia sanctitatis. Nec fuisset necesse dominum episcopum Engelbertum miraculis claruisse post mortem, si vite perfectioris fuisset ante mortem. Beatus Evergislus et sanctus Agilolfus Coloniensis episcopi, ambo a nocentibus innocentes occisi, martirio coronati sunt; qui tamen post mortem paucis admodum signis claruerunt, quia non erat necesse, ut post mortem commendarent miracula, quos ante mortem commendarat vita sanctissima.

Klaus Schreiner has thoroughly explored medieval suspicions that attended both saints who lived good lives but did not perform miracles after death and those who worked wonders without having lived exceptionally well—both types sanctioned in this passage by Caesarius—in his studies "Discrimen veri ac falsi: Ansätze und Formen der

Kritik in der Heiligen- und Reliquienverehrung des Mittelalters," *Archiv für Kulturge-schichte* 48 (1965): 1–53 and "Zum Wahrheitsverständnis im Heiligen- und Reliquien-wesen des Mittelalters," *Saeculum* 17 (1966): 131–69. See also Eberhard Demm's impor-tant "Zur Rolle des Wunders in der Heiligkeitskonzeption des Mittelalters," *Archiv für Kulturgeschichte* 57 (1975): 300–344; and Michael Goodich, "Miracles and Disbelief in the Late Middle Ages," *Mediaevistik* 1 (1988): 23–38.

43. Pointed out in an editor's note, *VE* III: 282.

44. See his *DM*, dist. 10, cap. 1, 2:217. As the works of Klaus Schreiner (see note 42) and Benedicta Ward (see n. 45 below), make clear, miracles presented many problems to theologians trying to explain them, and their explanations tended to be at odds with the practices and beliefs of ordinary people. Many thanks to Caroline Walker Bynum for bringing this point up and for helping me to rethink and compli-cate my understanding of this rich issue.

45. See Benedicta Ward, *Miracles and the Medieval Mind: Theory, Record, and Event, 1000–1215*, rev. ed. (Philadelphia: University of Pennsylvania Press, 1987), 166–91.

46. Especially Schreiner, "Discrimen veri ac falsi," see note 42.

47. Ibid.

48. *VE* I: 1, 236: "Sanctitatem, que vite defuit, mors pretiosa supplevit, et si minus perfectus erat in conversatione, sanctus tamen effectus est in passione."

49. As Barbara Newman has pointed out, it was characteristic of holy women of the high Middle Ages to take on voluntarily the postmortem sufferings of others, as "apostles to the dead"; see her article "On the Threshold of the Dead: Purgatory, Hell, and Religious Women," in her *From Virile Woman to WomanChrist: Studies in Medieval Religion and Literature* (Philadelphia: University of Pennsylvania Press, 1995), 103–36, esp. 119ff. See also Jo Ann McNamara, "The Need to Give: Suffering and Female Sanctity in the Middle Ages," in *Images of Sainthood in Medieval Europe*, ed. Renate Blumenfeld-Kosinski and Timea Szell, (Ithaca, N.Y.: Cornell University Press, 1991), 199–211, on the replacement of penitential gift-giving by physical suffering among thirteenth-century women and Caroline Walker Bynum's discussion of the stress laid on the physicality of suffering, in *Holy Feast and Holy Fast: The Religious Significance of Food to Medieval Women* (Berkeley: University of California Press, 1987), 245–59.

50. *VE* II: 16, 276.

51. See *DM*, dist. VI, cap. 34, 386–87.

52. *VE* II: 16, 276: "[. . . t]empore moderniori in sancto Thoma episcopo Can-tuariensi occisus est propter libertatem ecclesie conservandam. Eadem causa mortis exstitit in presule nostro Engelberto."

53. Ibid., 276–77: "Occibuit ille pro libertate ecclesie Cantuariensis, iste vero pro defensione ecclesie Essendiensis. Liberavit ille ecclesiam Anglicanam sanguine suo de gravi iugo regis Henrici; liberavit iste eque morte sua ecclesiam sue defensioni commissam de intollerabili exactione comitis Friderici."

54. This is the first time the title "saint" is applied to Engelbert in the Vita.

55. *VE* II: 277:

Et licet beatus Thomas ante passionem multa sustinuerit incommoda, dampna et exilia, que non sustinuit Engelbertus, in ipsa tamen passione *plus doloris, angoris et confusionis* certum est eum Thoma tollerasse. Ille enim, sicut legimus, in capite uno ictu cesus a sacrilegis relictus est in templo; *iste vulneribus multis et a lictoribus plurimus toto corpore confossus*, nudus relictus est in sterquilinio. Sanctus Thomas occisus est ab eis qui eum aperte oderant; sanctus vero Engelbertus [*quod maiorem inferre solet dolorem et augere invidiam*] a cognatis et amicis, de quibus nichil mali presumebat et quos ipse sublimaverat (emphasis added).

56. See the passage in brackets in the preceding note.

57. Perhaps some earlier bishops, such as Otto of Bamberg, would have been envious of Engelbert's good fortune in having his sins cleared in this way. Compare Otto's response to an assault by pagan Slavs during a missionary expedition (as described by Morrison, *History as a Visual Art*, 146): "'With joyful spirit and cheerful countenance,' he had gone into the mêlée hoping to receive the crown of martyrdom. He had been struck down into the mire. When he pulled himself up, he raised his hands to heaven, giving thanks that, though he had not been slaughtered, he had at least been worthy to receive one blow in God's name."

58. The formulation is Caroline Walker Bynum's. On the complicated issues involved in the feeling or lack of feeling of pain during violent death, and its implications for the understanding of resurrection, see her discussion of early Christian martyrs in *The Resurrection of the Body in Western Christianity, 200–1336* (New York: Columbia University Press, 1995), 21–58.

59. *VE* I: 2, 238, on Engelbert's fall into sin as a young man: "Hec idcirco commemoro, ut cognoscat lector, de quali viro martirem sibi elegerit Dominus, de 'vase ire' faciens 'vas glorie.'" The citation is from Romans 9:22–23.

60. See the *Breviloquium*, Part IV, Chapter 9, in *The Works of Bonaventure* II, trans. José de Vinck (Paterson, N.J.: St. Anthony Guild Press, 1963), esp. 172. See also the essay by Manuele Gragnolati in this volume. I am grateful to Gragnolati for many illuminating discussions about these issues.

61. According to Caesarius, 40 is the number of penance, while 7 signifies the gifts of the Holy Spirit; see *VE* II: 8, 265.

62. *VE* II: 8, 265: "In omnibus siquidem membris, in quibus peccaverat, punitus est. Punitus est in capite multipliciter, sicut apparet in eius pillio, scilicet in vertice, in fronte et occipite, in tymporibus, labiis et dentibus, et tam graviter, ut rivuli sanguinis inundantes et decurrentes fossas oculorum, aurium, narium orisque influerunt et replerent. Punitus est etiam in gutture et collo, in humeris et dorso, in pectore et corde, in ventre et coxis, in cruribus et pedibus . . ."

63. Ibid., 265–66: "ut cognoscas, lector, quali baptismo Christus in martire suo diluere dignatus sit, quidquid culpe contraxerat superbiendo, videndo, audiendo, olfaciendo, gustando, cogitando, luxuriando, operando, tangendo, gradiendo sive aliis quibuscumque levitatibus, omissionibus et negligentiis circa disciplinam. . . . Certe, certe non sine causa ad gloriam martirii pervenit."

64. Frederick S. Paxton, *Christianizing Death: The Creation of a Ritual Process in Early Medieval Europe* (Ithaca, N.Y.: Cornell University Press, 1990), 181.

65. Arnold Angenendt, *Heilige und Reliquien: Die Geschichte ihres Kultes vom frühen Christentum bis zur Gegenwart*, 2nd rev. ed. (Munich: C. H. Beck, 1997), esp. 62–65; on 64–65 he includes the same passage from the Engelbert Vita that I discuss here. See also his "Sühne durch Blut," *Frühmittelalterliche Studien* 18 (1984): 437–67.

The quasi-supernatural powers associated with blood in the early modern period are treated by Piero Camporesi, *Juice of Life: The Symbolic and Magic Significance of Blood*, trans. Robert R. Barr (New York: Continuum Books, 1995).

66. *VE* II: 7, 263: "numquam aliquid horroris ex illius contactu, sicut de cadaveribus occisorum fieri assolet, passus est." Fear of cadavers—especially murdered ones —is treated by Ronald C. Finucane, *Appearances of the Dead: A Cultural History of Ghosts* (London: Junction Books, 1982); and Jean-Claude Schmitt, *Ghosts in the Middle Ages: The Living and the Dead in Medieval Society*, trans. Teresa Lavender Fagan (Chicago: University of Chicago Press, 1998).

67. *VE* II: 7, 263: "Haut dubium quin ex presentia sanctorum angelorum gratia hec, qui circa corpus martiris celestes excubias celebrabant. Fuerat enim idem Henricus ante conversionem miles et tanto fortassis ad huiusmodi opus expeditior et audacior quanto assuetior."

68. *VE* II: 8, 264: "Henricus vero, cum ob cruris sui infirmitatem in uno pede nutaret, cogitans beatum virum a nocentibus innocenter occisum, occisi brachium nudum nuda manu tetigit, et plena fide eandem benedictionem ad crus nudum transmittens, gradum pedis vacillantis roboravit.

69. *VE* II: 7, 263: "Quod Suelme perducentes, cum in ecclesia illud ponere decrevissent, non permisit sacerdos, contaminationem basilice pretendens, cum magis sanguine martiris dedicaretur. Propter quod et alia quedam, in quibus martiris gratiam demeruit, usque hodie graviter satis in suo corpore divinitus flagellatur." Fear of contaminating powers inherent in dead bodies is of course very ancient and widespread; among the Célí Dé in eighth-century Ireland, for example, a priest who was present at the moment of a sick person's death would not be allowed "to perform the sacrifice [of the Mass] until a bishop should consecrate him": see Paxton, *Christianizing Death*, 85.

70. *VE* II: 8, 264: "[Deinde cum vocibus lacrimosis corpus oratorio introferentes,] eadem nocte quibusdam fratribus quedam mirifice visiones de gloria martiris ostense sunt, in sompnis tamen."

71. Peter Brown, "The Decline of the Empire of God: Amnesty, Penance, and the Afterlife from Late Antiquity to the Middle Ages," this volume.

72. Ibid.

73. Ibid.

74. This cleansing process began with Engelbert's extraordinarily tearful confession to the bishop of Minden just prior to embarking on his final journey. It occurred immediately after he had brushed off rumors of Frederick's plot. See *VE* II: 4, 254–55.

75. On the complex issue of conversion to sanctity, which varied according to a person's social status, gender, and birthplace, see Donald Weinstein and Rudolph M. Bell, *Saints and Society: The Two Worlds of Western Christendom, 1000–1700* (Chicago: University of Chicago Press, 1982); on women's conversions as process or continuity rather than reversal, see Caroline Walker Bynum, "Women's Stories, Women's Symbols: A Critique of Victor Turner's Theory of Liminality," in her *Fragmentation and Redemption: Essays on Gender and the Human Body in Medieval Religion* (New York: Zone Books, 1992), 27–52; and eadem, *Holy Feast*, 277–302.

76. See the accounts of their lives in James of Voragine's *Golden Legend*, trans. Granger Ryan and Helmut Ripperger (New York: Longmans, Green, 1941), 597–609 (Francis) and 675–88 (Elizabeth); and André Vauchez, "Jacques de Voragine et les

saints du XIIIe siècle dans la *Légende dorée*," in *Legenda Aurea: sept siécles de diffusion* (Actes du Colloque International sur la Legenda Aurea), ed. Brenda Dunn-Lardeau (Paris: 1986), 27–56. Caesarius himself wrote a Vita of Elizabeth based on her canonization proceedings, as well as a fascinating account of her 1236 translation; they have been published by Albert Huyskens in A Hilka, *Die Wundergeschichten*, 345–90.

77. *VE* II: 6, 258:

> Sole properante ad occasum, hostia cum immolante properat ad aram, ut fieret Domino sacrificium vespertinum, quod dignius erat in lege. Passus est Christus sexta feria, hora sexta, scilicet in meridie, ut declararet se mediatorem Dei et hominum. Engelbertum vero pati voluit eadem feria, sed in fine diei, ut ostenderet eum per bonum finem, non per precedentem vitam coronatum. . . . Hostiam sine cauda offerre non licuit [in lege], neque Deo vita bona sine bono fine placebit.

Notice Caesarius's use of inversion in his very language to convey the notion that Engelbert's "good end" is literally a turning around of his life, in the *"vita bona . . . bono fine"* construction. Caesarius employs this grammatical maneuver elsewhere in the Vita, for example, in his description of Frederick of Isenberg's capture, torture, and execution; see below, pp. 76–78.

78. See below, p. 74.

79. *VE* II: 15, 274: " 'Quando oculi eius obducti sunt sanguine et involuti, anima nobis ablata est, et quo devenerit ignoro.' "

80. Surprisingly, this is not the first pronouncement of a Cologne archbishop's death to be given by a demon speaking through a nun. Thietmar of Merseburg's Chronicle reports of a certain Abbess Gerberga to whom the same thing happened; when she broke her promise to the demon to remain silent on the matter, however, the demon beat her to death. See the account in Walter Schlesinger, *Kirchengeschichte Sachsens im Mittelalter, 1. Band: Von den Anfängen kirchlicher Verkündigung bis zum Ende des Investiturstreites*, Mitteldeutsche Forschungen 27/I (Cologne: Böhlau Verlag, 1962), 227.

81. *VE* II: 16, 275. " 'Heu! heu! [Anima] subtracta est michi et sociis meis, qui illic conveneramus. Sic se ante mortem preparaverat, sic se laverat . . . ut nostri iuris nichil esset in illo.' "

82. Ibid.: " 'Quando voluntabatur in suo sanguine et iam moriturus erat, occisoribus suis ex toto corde ignovit, dicens hoc verbum: 'Pater, ignosce' et cetera [Luke 23: 34]. Propter hoc verbum tam potens est cum Altissimo, ut non ei negetur, quidquid petierit ab illo. Et hoc sciatis pro certo numquam aliquem episcopum sedisse Colonie in sede episcopali, qui ita possit cum Deo quomodo Engelbertus et tanti meriti sit apud Deum.' "

83. *VE* II: 10, 268: " 'Noveris pro certo, quod omnes qui me occiderunt vel quorum consilio occisus sum, male peribunt et citius quam credi possit.' "

84. See the many cases of ordinary murder victims appearing to the living to proclaim revenge on their killers in Schmitt, *Ghosts in the Middle Ages*.

85. *VE* II: 10, 268: " 'Frater, non est necesse, ut me inter mortuos nomines, quia cum Deo sum et in choro martirum gaudio fruens indicibili.' "

86. *VE* II: 1, 249: "quia qualis vel quanta sit nescimus."

87. See the seminal works by Bynum, *Holy Feast* and the essays in *Fragmentation and Redemption*; see also Elizabeth Alvida Petroff, *Body and Soul: Essays on Medieval Women and Mysticism* (Oxford: Oxford University Press, 1994); Elizabeth Robertson, "The Corporeality of Female Sanctity in the *Life of Saint Margaret*," in Blumenfeld-Kosinski and Szell, *Images of Sainthood*, 268–87; Brigitte Cazelles, *The Lady as Saint: A Collection of French Hagiographic Romances of the Thirteenth Century* (Philadelphia: University of Pennsylvania Press, 1991).

88. See note 12 above.

89. On changing patterns of sanctity in the twelfth and thirteenth centuries, see Vauchez, *La sainteté en Occident*, 329–478; idem, *The Laity in the Middle Ages: Religious Beliefs and Devotional Practices*, ed. Daniel E. Bornstein and trans. Margery J. Schneider (Notre Dame, Ind.: University of Notre Dame Press, 1993); and Weinstein and Bell, *Saints and Society*, 141–65.

90. On the theological background of *imitatio Christi*, see Giles Constable, "The Ideal of the Imitation of Christ" in *Three Studies in Medieval Religion and Social Thought* (Cambridge: Cambridge University Press, 1995), 145–93. On the practice of *imitatio* in the high Middle Ages, see Bynum, *Holy Feast*, esp. 255–59; and the general overview presented by Vauchez, "The Idea of God," in *The Laity*, 3–26.

91. See above, p. 73.

92. *VE* II: 17, 278–81. According to the commentators, this chapter was written and inserted into the Vita shortly after its presentation to the new archbishop Henry of Molenark in November 1226; the events described took place after his investiture. The much less painful atonement of another of the accused conspirators, Bishop Dietrich of Münster, is discussed by Theodor Rensing, "Die Ermordung Engelberts des Heiligen und die Ehrenrettung für Dietrich von Isenberg," *Westfalen* 33 (1955): 125–43.

93. On the semiotics of the tortured body in the Middle Ages, see Wolfgang Schild, "Der gequälte und entehrte Leib: Spekulative Vorbemerkungen zu einer noch zu schreibenden Geschichte des Strafrechts," in *Gepeinigt, begehrt, vergessen: Symbolik und Sozialbezug des Körpers im späten Mittelalter und in der frühen Neuzeit*, ed. Klaus Schreiner and Norbert Schnitzler (Munich: Wilhelm Fink, 1992), 147–68.

94. Walther von der Vogelweide, "Kaiser Friedrichs-Ton 5: Totenklage für Erzbischof Engelbrecht," in *Werke I* (see note 15 above), pp. 212–13.

95. According to this account, Frederick's punishment began on November 11 and ended with his death the following morning.

96. *VE* II: 17, 281:

Licet enim mala et turpi morte perierit in corpore Fridericus, speramus tamen eandem penam anime eius fuisse medicinam, eo quod bene contritus et diligenter atque frequenter tam privatim quam publice confessus se reum clamaverit et penam sibi illatam patienter sustinuerit, etiam ad confrigendum membra singula ultro offerens. Et cum in dorso eius fabricaret [Ps 128: 3] carnifex ille immisericors, ictus sedecim per securim ei infligendo, non emisit vocem, ita ut omnes mirarentur.

97. *VE* II: 17, 280:

At, Deo dispensante, eodem pene die anno revoluto, quo beatus martyr Engelbertus cum merore multorum civitati mortuus est illatus, Fridericus cum desiderio multorum per portam oppositam captivus est invectus. Qui die quarta, quando videlicet primum martiris septenarium celebriter agebatur, ipse nimis turpiter, revoluto anno, in rota tormentaliter levabatur.

98. On the circle—and in particular a wheel—as a paradigm of medieval hermeneutics, see Morrison, *History as a Visual Art*, 69ff.

99. The image of Engelbert blessing his enemies, which received much attention during his revival in the seventeenth century, does not appear in the primary account of the murder in the *VE* II: 7. In fact, prior to this statement it is only mentioned by the demon possessing the nun in Cologne (discussed above). While this justification is intriguing for what it reveals about the practice of *imitatio Christi*, it is noteworthy that Caesarius himself does not make use of it in his own explanation of Engelbert's miracles. Aside from the demonic account, the only time he evokes that scene is here, in his description of Frederick's last moments.

100. *VE* II: 17, 281: "[Postea usque ad matutinas in corpore durans, fertur tamen orasse et circumstantibus, ut pro se orarent, supplicasse.] Fortassis ex merito martiris Engelberti, qui moriens pro inimicis oravit, gratia hec Friderico."

101. Further information on specific persons and places mentioned in this text can be found in the footnotes to the Hilka edition.

102. *VE* II: 7, 261: "'Cedite latronem, cedite, qui et nobiles exheredat et nemini parcit.'" There is some discrepancy as to the translation of this crucial sentence. In the German edition, Karl Langosch has Frederick call explicitly for the murder rather than the seizure of Engelbert: "Tötet den Räuber, tötet ihn, der die Adligen enterbt und keinen schont!" (Langosch, *Leben*, 70).

From Decay to Splendor: Body and Pain in Bonvesin da la Riva's Book of the Three Scriptures

I would like to thank Caroline Walker Bynum for her constant help and generous support.

1. There are three twentieth-century editions of the *Libro delle tre scritture*: Bonvesin da la Riva, *Il libro delle tre scritture e il volgare delle vanità*, ed. V. De Bartholomaeis (Rome: Società Filologica Romana, 1901); Bonvesin da la Riva, *Il libro delle tre scritture e i volgari delle false scuse e delle vanità*, ed. L. Biadene (Pisa: E. Spoerri, 1902); and *Le opere volgari di Bonvesin da la Riva*, ed. G. Contini (Rome: Società Filologica Romana, 1941), in which the *Libro delle tre scritture* is found on pp. 101–76. Quotations from Bonvesin's poems will be from Contini's edition. For making sense of Bonvesin's often obscure dialect, one work proves very useful: Fabio Marri, *Glossario al milanese di Bonvesin* (Bologna: Patron, 1977). An English translation is available: Bonvesin da la Riva, *Volgari Scelti*, trans. Patrick S. Diehl and Ruggero Stefanini with commentary and notes by Stefanini and a biographical profile by Diehl (New York: Lang, 1987), 133–202. I will primarily use Diehl's and Stefanini's translation, indicating slight modifications with italics. On the one hand, Bonvesin has always been considered a simple

"precursor" of Dante, while on the other hand, there is no direct evidence that Dante knew his work. This is probably why such an interesting author has not been given the attention he deserves. A thorough knowledge of Bonvesin's work proves extremely useful for a precise understanding of Dante's intellectual background and spirituality. This is why, in the notes of this essay, I will give some hints on a few issues that the *Book of the Three Scriptures* helps one to understand and that are equally fundamental in Dante's *Commedia*. Quotations will be from Dante Alighieri, *The Divine Comedy*, trans. Charles S. Singleton (Princeton, N.J.: Princeton University Press, 1970–75; rep. 1977). I have considered these issues in the dissertation entitled "Identity, Pain, and Resurrection: Body and Soul in Bonvesin da la Riva's *Book of the Three Scriptures* and Dante's *Commedia*," which I have written at Columbia University.

2. Bonvesin da la Riva was a successful and wealthy teacher of Latin in a private capacity in both Legnano and Milan. He wrote works in Latin both in prose and verse and several poems in the vernacular of Milan. For a summary of his life, see Bonvesin, *Volgari scelti*, 1–4. For more detailed information about Bonvesin's life, see Luigi Zanoni, "Fra Bonvesin della Riva fu Umiliato o Terziario Francescano?," *Il Libro e la Stampa* 8 (1914): 141–48; Pio Pecchiai, "I documenti sulla biografia di Bonvicino della Riva," *Giornale Storico della Letteratura Italiana* 78 (1921): 96–127. For a general presentation of Bonvesin's work, see Francesco De Sanctis, *Storia della letteratura italiana dai primi secoli agli albori del Trecento*, ed. G. Lazzeri (Milan: Hoepli, 1950), 137–43, 240–66; Gianfranco Contini, *Poeti del duecento* (Milan and Naples: Ricciardi, 1960), 1: 667–70; Pietro Gallardo, "Bonvesin da la Riva," in *Letteratura italiana: I minori* (Milan: Marzorati, 1961), 1: 171–83; Aldo Rossi, "Poesia didattica e poesia popolare del nord," in *Storia della letteratura italiana* (Milano: Garzanti, 1965), 1: 470–486; D'Arco Silvio Avalle, "Bonvesin da la Riva," in *Dizionario biografico degli Italiani* (Rome: Istituto della Enciclopedia Italiana, 1970), 1: 465–69; Emilio Pasquini, "La letteratura didattica e allegorica," in *La letteratura italiana: storia e testi*, ed. C. Muscetta (Bari: Laterza, 1970), 1 ("Il Duecento"), part. 2: 3–111, esp. 32–54.

3. The meter employed is the monorhymed alexandrine quatrain (*aaaa, bbbb,* etc.), typical of contemporary didactic poetry in northern Italy. This oral genre comes from France and consists of the translation, or rather the vernacular adaptation of middle-Latin didactic and hagiographic literature. On the technical aspects of the meter, see Avalle, "L'origine della quartina monorima di alessandrini," in *Saggi e ricerche in onore di Ettore Li Gotti* (Palermo: Centro di Studi Filologici e Linguistici Siciliani, 1962), 119–60. For information about the audience and the genre of this well-developed didactic literature, see Esther I. May, *The "De Jerusalem celesti" and the "De Babilonia infernali" of Fra Giacomino da Verona* (Florence: Le Monnier, 1930), 30; Umberto Cianciolo, "Contributo allo studio dei cantari di argomento sacro," *Archivium Romanicum* 30 (1938): 180–83; Avalle, "Bonvesin da la Riva," 567–68. The strong commitment to the practical usefulness of the poem could also be connected with the kind of preaching typical of Humiliati: Raoul Manselli, addressing the preaching of the Humiliati, writes that "Tout en partant d'un passage de l'Evangile, on évitait les développements théologiques pour se limiter à une exhortation à la penitence, la prière, la vie de sainteté." "Italie: haut moyen âge: mouvements spirituels orthodoxes et hétérodoxes (11ᵉ et 12ᵉ siècles)," in *Dictionnaire de spiritualité, ascétique et mystique, doctrine et histoire* (Paris: Beauchesne, 1971), 7, part 2: cols. 2184–93; quotation col. 2190.

4. Sixten Ringbom, *Icon to Narrative: The Rise of the Dramatic Close-up in Fifteenth-Century Devotional Painting* (Åbo: Åbo Akademi, 1965), 12–13.

5. Jean Delumeau, *Sin and Fear: The Emergence of a Western Guilt Culture: 13th–18th Centuries*, trans. Eric Nicholson (New York: St. Martin's Press, 1990), 343.

6. For the allegorical comparison between Christ's wounded body and a book inscribed in red as a means to engage the mind in sustained attention to the sufferings of Christ, see Richard Kieckhefer, *Unquiet Souls: Fourteenth-Century Saints and Their Religious Milieu* (Chicago: University of Chicago Press, 1984), 91.

7. See Giles Constable, "The Ideal of the Imitation of Christ," in Constable, *Three Studies in Medieval Religious and Social Thought* (Cambridge: Cambridge University Press, 1995), 208–15. For the development of the empathic attitude in the late medieval devotion to the suffering Christ, see James H. Marrow, *Passion Iconography in Northern European Art of the Late Middle Ages and Early Renaissance: A Study of the Transformation of Sacred Metaphor into Descriptive Narrative* (Kortrijk: Van Ghemmert, 1979), 1–10; Kieckhefer, *Unquiet Souls*, 90–91.

8. For an excellent and concise study of the motifs of the contempt for the world, see Delumeau, *Sin and Fear*, 9–34. For a more detailed monograph, see Robert Bultot, *Christianisme et valeurs humaines: la doctrine du mépris du monde, en Occident, de S. Ambroise à Innocent III* (Louvain: Editions Nauwelaerts; Paris: Béatrice-Nauwelaerts, 1963–64), esp. vol. 4, parts 1 and 2. See also Caroline Walker Bynum, "Why All the Fuss About the Body? A Medievalist's Perspective," *Critical Inquiry* 22 (Autumn 1995): 14.

9. Philippe Ariès, *Western Attitudes Toward Death: From the Middle Ages to the Present*, trans. P. M. Ranum (Baltimore: Johns Hopkins University Press, 1974), 39–46.

10. For a thorough discussion of the theoretical problems that such a notion of identity would imply, see Caroline Walker Bynum, *The Resurrection of the Body in Western Christianity, 200–1336* (New York: Columbia University Press, 1995).

11. The discrepancy between the theory of theologians and the actual descriptions of the other-world was common in the eschatological narrations of the Middle Ages. Peter Dinzelbacher, "Il corpo nelle visioni dell'aldilà," *Micrologus: Natura, Scienze e Società Medievali* 1 (1993): 301–26, shows that the idea of the *anima exuta* as a completely spiritual being is true only in the texts of Scholastic theologians. Medieval visionary literature gives, on the contrary, clear evidence that in the common contemporary eschatological view the *anima exuta* (both of visionary men and of dead people "visited" by them) is generally represented by a strong insistence on its palpable and corporeal dimension. See also Claude Carozzi, "Structure et fonction de la vision de Tnugdal," in *Faire croire: modalités de la diffusion et de la réception des messages réligieux du XIIe au XVe siècle: Table Ronde organisée par l'Ecole Française de Rome, en collaboration avec l'Institut d'Histoire Médiévale de l'Université de Padoue, Rome, 22–23 juin 1979* (Rome: Ecole Française de Rome, 1981), 223–34; idem, *Le voyage de l'âme dans l'au-delà d'après la littérature latine* (Rome: Ecole Française de Rome; Paris: Diffusion de Boccard, 1994); Aaron Gurevich, "Au moyen âge: conscience individuelle et image de l'au-delà," *Annales* 37 (1982): 255–73. For a detailed analysis of the importance of the body as an essential component of the person, see Bynum, *The Resurrection of the Body*; eadem, "Material Continuity, Personal Survival and the Resurrection of the Body: A

Scholastic Discussion in Its Medieval and Modern Context," in *Fragmentation and Redemption: Essays on Gender and the Human Body in Medieval Religion* (New York: Zone Books, 1992), 239–97, esp. 265–97; eadem, "The Female Body and Religious Practice in the Later Middle Ages," in *Fragmentation and Redemption*, 181–238, esp. 222–38.

12. One of the most explicit passages is Hugh of St. Victor's *De sacramentis*, bk. 2, pt. 16, chap. 3 (PL 176, col. 584): "Quidam putant animas corporalibus poenis cruciari non posse, nisi per corpora et in corporibus manentes. Quapropter a corporibus exutas animas nullas alias poenas sustinere credunt. . . . Sed verissime auctoritate sacri eloquii et catholicae veritatis probatur testimonio, corporali et materiali igne animas etiam nunc ante susceptionem corporum cruciari." See Carozzi, "Structure et fonction," esp. 230–34. The proposition that the separated soul cannot be tormented by material fire was condemned in Paris in 1277. See Bynum, *Resurrection of the Body*, 280.

13. The senses of smell, sight, and hearing are highlighted respectively in the second, fifth, and sixth pains. These torments consist of the great stench that surrounds the sinner, of the sight of the miserable faces of the other damned and of the horrible faces of the devils, and of the doleful voices, the weeping, and the uproar that the damned are forced to bear. Insatiable hunger and thirst are the pains of the eighth "passion" where instead of bread the sinners eat burning coals and instead of water drink molten bronze.

14. See, for instance, the words of the angels to the soul of the blessed: "You will live forever there [in paradise] before your Lord in sweetest glory, in glorious sweetness. On the Last Day, your body will greatly thrive; here it will stand with the soul in joy and splendor" (*Golden Sc.*, ll. 69–71).

15. For a chart that contrasts them, see Bonvesin, *Volgari scelti*, 127–28.

16. Moreover, a reflection of the idea of the four gifts is present in a number of fourteenth-century mystics, such as Marguerite of Oingt, although they cease to be called "dowries" after around 1270. For the evolution of the doctrine of the dowries, see Joseph Goering, "The *De dotibus* of Robert Grosseteste," *Mediaeval Studies* 44 (1982): 83–101; Bynum, *Resurrection of the Body*, 131–32, and, for Marguerite of Oingt, 335–37; and eadem, "Why All the Fuss About the Body?" 21.

17. "Li corp de quatro cosse seran glorificai: / Plu firm ka adamanta e plu ka 'l sol smerrai / E plu ka omnia vox setí seran formai, / Plu prist han ess ka l'ogio e plu avïazai" (*Le opere volgari di Bonvesin da la Riva*, 209), my translation.

18. Special attention is given to impassibility and clarity, while the less corporeal qualities of agility and especially subtlety are stressed less. Bonvesin emphasizes clarity and impassibility probably because they are more palpable and represent an explicit counterpart to the limitations of the earthly body.

19. The eighth glory is one of the most interesting and consists of the celestial banquet with its "very sweet and genuine spiritual food." But, though defined as spiritual, this food is described in very physical terms and in a very peculiar way: it is "cib glorïoso" (l. 519), glorious food, a sort of resurrection food for resurrection bodies. Not only do these "glorios vivande" (l. 550) confer impassibility on the blessed, but they are also explicitly contrasted with the earthly food as described in the *Black Scripture*: "In that place, there is no spoiled or mouldy or nauseous food either, or any lack of it for all time; there is no bitter or nasty or poisonous morsel, nor does it spoil or

decay or disgust. Instead, it is always fresh, healthy, and perfect, exquisitely delicious, aromatic and well-seasoned, clean and pure and fair, attractive, tasty—its sweet sweet taste cannot be described" (*Golden Sc.*, ll. 501–8). In the same way, the garments of the blessed (which are described in the ninth glory as made of silk, purple, gold, and gems) never wear out or get old, but are durable, new, and always fresh (ll. 561–600).

20. For the doctrine of the resurrection body as victory over both fragmentation and the biological change that threatened the notion of identity, see Bynum, *Resurrection of the Body*, 135–37; eadem, "Why All the Fuss About the Body?" 19–25.

21. The same idea is in the *Commedia*. In the heaven of the sun, Solomon affirms that with the resurrection of the body, the vision of God will increase because the human person will be finally whole. (*Par.* 14: 43–45: "When the flesh, glorious and sanctified, shall be clothed on us again, our persons will be more acceptable for being all complete.") When the blessed hear Solomon talking about the resurrection of the body, they are so happy that they cry an "amen" of pure joy. These lines are among the most sublime of the *Commedia* and express the triumphant significance of the doctrine of the resurrection of the body as a victory against decay, aging, and loss: "So sudden and eager both the one and the other chorus seemed to me in saying 'Amen,' that truly they showed desire for their dead bodies—perhaps not only for themselves, but also for their mothers, for their fathers, and for the others who were dead before they became eternal flames" (*Par.* 14: 61–66).

22. What is immediately striking in Bonvesin—as in Giacomino of Verona, a member of the Franciscan Minorites who wrote two separate eschatological poems, a description of hell and a description of heaven—is the absence of purgatory. Jacques Le Goff speaks of Bonvesin and Giacomino as part of the "conservatives and traditionalists who preferred to stick to the old couple, Heaven and Hell, and to close their eyes to the newer Purgatory, the brainchild of theologian-intellectuals" (*The Birth of Purgatory*, trans. Arthur Goldhammer [Chicago: University of Chicago Press, 1984], 333). He is certainly right to distinguish their works from new theological concerns. Regarding Bonvesin's poem, however, some elements deserve further consideration. It is true that Christ's passion occupies the central part of the poem because, as we will see, it creates the possibility of heaven for humankind. Bonvesin repeatedly insists on this concept in the *Red Scripture*. Nonetheless, Bonvesin writes at the moment at which purgatory is going to be (or has just been) made official in the second Council of Lyons (1274). He writes at the end of thirteenth century when, according to Le Goff, purgatory is "ubiquitous" and mentioned in many kinds of texts (289). Recent scholarship has pointed out that as a conception, purgatory "had existed in inchoate form since the subapostolic age, and in a more or less rationalized form since Augustine" (Barbara Newman, "On the Threshold of the Dead: Purgatory, Hell, and Religious Women," in *From Virile Woman to WomanChrist: Studies in Medieval Religion and Literature* [Philadelphia: University of Pennsylvania Press, 1995], 109); and that, even later, purgatory was not necessarily conceived as a "third place" with a local habitation and a name, but could also be conceived as a condition of suffering both punitive and redemptive, as the very fact of suffering. Newman, "On the Threshold"; and Caroline Walker Bynum, *Holy Feast and Holy Fast: The Religious Significance of Food to Medieval Women* (Berkeley: University of California Press), 120–21, 183–86. See also Gurevich, "Au moyen âge," 70–71; and Brian McGuire, "Purgatory, the Communion of Saints,

and Medieval Change," *Viator* 20 (1989): 61–84. I would suggest that in Bonvesin's poem purgatory is present as the experience of physical suffering: the purifying power of pain is expressed primarily by Christ's passion that redeems humankind and is the ultimate example of the "characteristically Christian idea that the bodily suffering of one person can be substituted for the suffering of another"—an idea that is at the base of much of the purgatorial piety of the late Middle Ages (Bynum, *Holy Feast and Holy Fast*, 418). But purgatory is also expressed by the purifying and salvific valor that, especially through the figure of Mary, is accorded to human suffering throughout the whole poem. The *Red Scripture* helps one to better understand Dante's *Purgatorio* and the importance that it attributes to the purging role of physical suffering. I would argue that purgatorial punishments are presented by Dante as continual reenactments of Christ's passion and that their "efficacy" is a result of this identification. For instance, this connection is made clear in *Purg.* 23.70–75, in which the penitents of the circle of gluttony emphasize that the desire of purging themselves through physical pain is the same desire that led Christ to the sacrifice of the cross that saved humankind: "and not once only, as we circle this road, is our pain renewed—I say pain and ought to say solace: for that will leads us to the trees which led glad Christ to say '*Elì*,' when He delivered us with His blood." I have analyzed the concept of "productive pain" in both Dante and Bonvesin in my dissertation.

23. Kieckhefer, *Unquiet Souls*, 89, is clear and synthetic: "Atonement came not from charitable work, nor from prayer, nor from enlightenment, but from pain. God seemed to attach more weight to love manifested in suffering than to love displayed in other ways." For the redeeming power of pain, see Caroline Walker Bynum, "The Body of Christ in the Later Middle Ages: A Reply to Leo Steinberg," in *Fragmentation and Redemption*, 79–119; and Newman, "On the Threshold of the Dead," 108–36, esp. 119–22. The importance of suffering has been underlined also by Jeffrey Hamburger, " 'By Their Fruits You Shall Know Them': Image, Imitation, and the Reception of Suso's *Exemplar*," lecture, Columbia University, Branner Forum, April 21, 1996; idem, *Nuns as Artists: The Visual Culture of a Medieval Convent* (Berkeley: University of California Press, 1997).

24. The Milanese text of the two passages is found in *Le opere volgari di Bonvesin da la Riva*, respectively 52 and 233. The translation from the *De peccatore cum Virgine* is mine.

25. Twelfth- and thirteenth-century works emphasize that Christ is *impassibilis* before the Incarnation and after the resurrection. See Erich Auerbach, "*Excursus: Gloria Passionis*," in *Literary Language and Its Public in Late Latin Antiquity and in the Middle Ages*, trans. Ralph Manheim (Princeton, N.J.: Princeton University Press, 1993), 89, n. 3.

26. For an analysis of the complexity of this symbol, see Bynum, "Body of Christ," 86–92. On blood as suffering and on the intense devotion to Christ's blood that started in the twelfth century and increased in the centuries to follow, see Louis Gougaud, *Devotional and Ascetic Practices in the Middle Ages*, trans. G. C. Bateman (London: Burns, Oates, and Washbourne, 1927), 75–130; and Constable, "Ideal of the Imitation of Christ," 209–17.

27. The same idea was expressed in lines 65–68.

28. As Bynum points out (*Resurrection of the Body*, 251–52), Bonaventure's *Brevi-*

loquium (part 4, chap. 10, par. 1) expresses the idea that Christ's body on the cross suffered more exquisite pain than any other body because it was the most perfect of all the bodies. The same idea is present also in Thomas Aquinas's *Summa theologiae*, 3a, q. 46, art. 6. Question 46 concerns Christ's passion. Article 6 discusses whether Christ's passion was greater than all other pain. Thomas answers affirmatively for four reasons. The second reason is connected with the fact that Christ's is the most perfect body and therefore experiences the most. See St. Thomas Aquinas, *Summa theologiae*, trans. and ed. R. T. Murphy (Cambridge: Blackfriars; New York: McGraw-Hill, 1965), 54: 26–27: "Secundo, potest magnitudo doloris ejus considerari ex perceptibilitate patientis. Nam et secundum corpus erat optime complexionatus, cum corpus ejus fuerit formatum miraculose operatione Spiritus Sancti."

29. Auerbach shows that the ambivalence is expressed by the very term *passio*: "Those who stress the distinction between the two meanings 'suffering' and 'passion' have not understood the dialectical relation between them in the Christian use of the word—for God's love, which moved him to take upon himself the sufferings of men, is itself a *motus animi* without measure or limit" ("Excursus: *Gloria Passionis*," 70). For the ambivalence of the strong emotions that Christ's passion evoked in the later Middle Ages, see Kieckhefer, *Unquiet Souls*, 92.

30. The attention given to the face of Christ is connected to the importance of the Veronica in this period. See below, p. 96.

31. Bynum, *Holy Feast and Holy Fast*, 418, n. 54.

32. First appearing in the twelfth century, this new attitude toward Mary's compassion is defined more explicitly in the thirteenth century through the affective mysticism of St. Francis and his followers, especially Bonaventure, and progressively increases until the attribution of the role of co-redemptrix to Mary herself. For the evolution of the doctrine of Mary's compassion, see André Wilmart, *Auteurs spirituels et textes dévots du moyen âge latin: études d'histoire littéraire* (Paris: Bloud et Gay, 1932), 505–14; Otto Von Simson, "*Compassio* and *Co-redemptio* in Roger Van Der Weyden's *Descent from the Cross*," *Art Bulletin* 35 (1953): 9–16; Sandro Sticca, *Il Planctus Mariae nella tradizione drammatica del medio evo* (Sulmona: Teatro Club, 1984), 131–51; for bibliographical information, see Marrow, *Passion Iconography*, 252, n. 41.

33. See Donna Spivey Ellington, "Impassioned Mother or Passive Icon: The Virgin's Role in Late Medieval and Early Modern Passion Sermons," *Renaissance Quarterly* 48, n. 2 (Summer 1995): 227–41. In the *Red Scripture*, Mary's suffering is so intense that it is presented as similar to infernal punishments, like Christ's. Her invocation to death as a way to end her agony in lines 30–312 is identical to what the damned continuously said in the *Black Scripture*. Her last words, "Per gran dolor delenguo e tuta me desvenio" ("I droop in great suffering and pine away"), are identical to what the damned said in *Black Scripture*, 883.

34. Bynum points out that the concept of Mary as the flesh of Christ was so strong that it suggested that, as the Logos preexisted the Incarnation, so the humanity of Christ also preexisted the Incarnation in the sinless humanity of Mary ("Body of Christ," 100–101). The same idea is at the base of the doctrine of Mary's bodily assumption: Christ cannot be fully in heaven unless the body of Mary is also with him because otherwise his resurrection would be incomplete. See Rachel Fulton, "The

Virgin Mary and the Song of Songs in the High Middle Ages" (Ph.D. diss., Columbia University, 1994).

35. See Bynum, "Female Body and Religious Practice," 222–38. The conception that body was an essential part of the human person was common in contemporary philosophical discussions. In contrast with the Platonic definition of man as soul, beginning with the fathers of the Church, Christian thought conceived the human being as a union of body and soul. Even those like Hugh of St. Victor or Robert of Melun in the twelfth century who endorsed a more Platonic conception did not identify the human person with the soul but tended to treat it as an entity composed of body and soul. See Richard Heinzmann, *Die Unsterblichkeit der Seele und die Auferstehung des Leibes: Eine problemgeschichtliche Untersuchung der frühscholastichen Sentenzen- und Summenliteratur von Anselm von Laon bis Wilhelm von Auxerre* (Münster: Aschendorff, 1965); idem, "Was ist der Mensch? Zu einer Grundfrage des mittelalterlichen Denkens," *Theologie und Philosophie* 49 (1974): 542–47. With the increasing assimilation of Aristotelian philosophy, scholastic thinkers progressively strengthened the unitary character of the person. No theologian would have defined it as a soul using a body. What mattered was the human character of the composite, for which both elements were equally important. See Bynum, *Resurrection of the Body*, 135–36 (and n. 59 on p. 135 for bibliography).

36. In the same way as in the expressions referring to Christ's pain (ll. 70, 159, 179, 189), the prefix "stra" for the superlative suggests the intensity of Mary's love for Christ (ll. 269, 333–34) and of her pain (ll. 226, 252, 282, 290). In line 230 her "doler" is even "stradurissimo": not only is the prefix "stra" ungrammatically added to the superlative "durissimo" but the same expression "stradolere" defines the pain of Christ's hands when they are nailed to the cross (l. 159: "le man ge stradolevano") and his suffering limbs (l. 179: "In si no ha el membro ke tut no ge stradoia"). The same terms—"doia," "angustia," "angoxa," "pena," "dolor"—refer to both Christ's and Mary's sufferings. Moreover, often the very same phrases define both Mary and Christ: see, for instance, Christ's "dolur dexmesurai," his enormous suffering for the nailing of his feet and hands in line 154 and Mary's "doi dexmesurae" and "dolor dexmesurao" in lines 225 and 248; or Christ's "dolur angustïusi" in line 158 and Mary's "dolor angustievre" in line 142. In line 177 the expression "Oi tormentosa angustia, oi doia sover doia," which commonly described the infernal pains in the *Black Scripture*, refers to Christ's crucified body, while in line 289 "Oi dolorosa angustia, oi doia sover doia" defines Mary's tortured body.

37. One of the most famous examples is the fifteenth-century *Descent from the Cross* by Roger Van Der Weyden, now in the Prado. As Mary swoons, her body assumes a position almost identical to that of the dead Christ. Thus Mary in her compassion becomes nearly as important to the composition as the figure of Christ. See Von Simson, "*Compassio* and *Co-redemptio*," 10–11.

38. Bonaventure, *De assumptione B. Virginis Mariae*, sermo 2, in *S. Bonaventurae opera omnia* (Quaracchi: Collegium S. Bonaventurae, 1901), 9: 161.

39. In the almost contemporary *Meditations on the Life of Christ* of the Pseudo-Bonaventure, Mary's compassion under the cross is greatly highlighted (chaps. 74–80). In chap. 78, the identification of Christ's passion and Mary's compassion is acknowl-

edged by Christ himself, who speaks to the Father and says that Mary, too, is on the cross with him: "Pater mi, vides quomodo affligitur mater mea. Ego debeo crucifigi, non ipsa; sed mecum est in cruce. Sufficit crucifixio mea, qui totius populi porto peccata; ipsa nihil tale meretur." *S. Bonaventurae opera omnia*, ed. A. Peltier (Paris: Ludovicus Vives, 1868), 12: 606.

40. "To take the discipline" meant to take part in self-flagellation. For the extensive diffusion of this practice among both lay and religious people in the late Middle Ages, see Emile Bertaud, "Discipline," in *Dictionnaire de spiritualité, ascétique et mystique, doctrine et histoire* (Paris: Beauchesne, 1957), 3: cols. 1302–11. Since the last decades of twelfth century, the spirituality of Humiliati was characterized by a strong importance given to penitence, whose practices emphasized the valor of physical suffering and humiliation: according to André Vauchez, "Plus profondément, la pénitence comme état de vie se traduit par la recherche de la nudité, du dépouillement et de la souffrance physique." "Pénitents," in *Dictionnaire de spiritualité, ascétique et mystique, doctrine et histoire* (Paris: Beauchesne, 1984), 12, part 1: cols. 1010–23); quotation at col. 1020.

41. In the thirteenth century, belief in Mary's bodily assumption (which became dogma only in 1950) was very common and was followed by Bonaventure, among others, in his sermon *De assumptione B. Virginis Mariae*. In the passage from the *De peccatore cum Virgine* mentioned before, Bonvesin is explicit and says that Mary is in the court of heaven "with our flesh" (ll. 114–15). In the fifth glory of the *Golden Scripture*, the poet continuously stresses the beauty and the splendor of the faces of the "pure queen" and of Christ. The adjective "clarissima" in line 365 suggests that Bonvesin is referring to the splendor of their resurrection bodies because *claritas* was one of the four dowries of the glorified body. Through emphasis on Mary's clarity, Bonvesin is underlining not only her presence in heaven, but also her bodily assumption to it. For the doctrine of Mary's bodily assumption, see Fulton, "The Virgin Mary and the Songs of Songs," esp. chap. 3; and Martin Jugie, *La mort et l'assomption de la Sainte Vierge: étude historico-doctrinale* (Vatican City: Biblioteca Apostolica Vaticana, 1944), esp. 363–407. For Bonaventure's sermon, see Bynum, "Material Continuity," 257. See also Hilda Graef, *Mary: A History of Doctrine and Devotion*, 2 vols. (London: Sheed & Ward: 1963–65); and Mirella Levi-d'Ancona, *The Iconography of the Immaculate Conception in the Middle Ages and Early Renaissance*, Monographs on Archeology and the Fine Arts 7 (New York: College Art Association of America in conjunction with the Art Bulletin, 1957). Not only will Dante the poet explicitly affirm that Mary and Christ are in heaven with their glorified body, but he also imagines St. John telling the pilgrim to divulge the doctrine on earth: "With the two robes in the blessed cloister are those two lights only which ascended; and this you shall carry back into your world" (*Par.* 25: 126–29).

42. For an iconographic study of the doctrine of compassion, see von Simson, "*Compassio* and *Co-redemptio*"; and C. M. Schuler, "The Swords of Compassion: Images of the Sorrowing Virgin in Late Medieval and Renaissance Art" (Ph.D. diss., Columbia University, 1987).

43. See Hans Belting, *Likeness and Presence: A History of the Image Before the Era of Art*, trans. Edmund Jephcott (Chicago: University of Chicago Press, 1994), 208–24. For the deep emotional relationship between devotional image and beholder in

the later Middle Ages, see Hamburger, "The Visual and the Visionary: The Image in Late Medieval Monastic Devotion," *Viator* 20 (1989): 161–82.

44. Contemporary devotion to Mary was a way to move toward Christ. See Rosemary Hale, "*Imitatio Mariae*: Motherhood Motifs in Late Medieval German Spirituality" (Ph.D. diss., Harvard University, 1992), 33. For Mary as mediatrix between God and man, see Kieckhefer, *Unquiet Souls*, 106; Fulton, "Mimetic Devotion, Marian Exegesis, and the Historical Sense of the Song of Songs," *Viator* 27 (1996): 85–116, esp. 87–89; Spivey Ellington, "Impassioned Mother," 297.

45. In the *Golden Scripture*, at the end of several glories the blessed say what has the merit of their beatitude and therefore indicate correct behaviors to the listeners. Most behaviors are the same as in these final lines of the *Red Scripture*, such as penitence in the first and twelfth glories, fasting and affliction of the body in the first and eighth, poverty, humility, and misery in the first, third, and tenth.

Time Is Short: The Eschatology of the Early Gaelic Church

1. *Annals of Ulster*, ed. W. M. Hennessy and B. MacCarthy, 4 vols. (Dublin: HMSO, 1887–1901), ii, 56: *Uamon mór for feraibh Erenn ria feil Eoin na bliadhna-sa, co rothesairc Dia tria troisctibh comarba Patraic ocus cleirech n-Erenn archena.*

2. For discussions see Louis Gougaud, *Christianity in Celtic Lands* (London: Sheed and Ward, 1932), 271–76; Charles Darwin Wright, *The Irish Tradition in Old English Literature* (Cambridge: Cambridge University Press, 1993), esp. 23–37; and two works by St. John D. Seymour, who made the field his special interest: "The Eschatology of the Early Irish Church," *Zeitschrift für celtische Philologie* 14 (1923): 179–211, and *Irish Visions of the Other World* (London: SPCK, 1930).

3. James F. Kenney, *The Sources for the Early History of Ireland*, vol. 1, *Ecclesiastical*, ed. Ludwig Bieler (1929; rep. Dublin: Pádraic ó Táilliúir, 1979), 733.

4. R. E. McNally, "The Imagination and Early Irish Biblical Exegesis," *Annuale Medievale* 10 (1969): 5–27.

5. Some useful studies are St. John D. Seymour, "Notes on Apocrypha in Ireland," *Proceedings of the Royal Irish Academy* 26 (1926) C: 107–17; David N. Dumville, "Biblical Apocrypha and the Early Irish," *Proceedings of the Royal Irish Academy* 73 (1973) C: 299–338; Martin McNamara, *Apocrypha in the Irish Church* (Dublin: Dublin Institute for Advanced Studies, 1975); D. Greene, F. Kelly, and B. O. Murdach, *The Irish Adam and Eve Story*, 2 vols. (Dublin: Dublin Institute for Advanced Studies, 1976).

6. Rodulfus Glabrus, *Historiarum Libri Quinque* (Oxford: Oxford University Press, 1989), 52–54 (Bk II, Chap. 2), where Brendan becomes an Anglo-Saxon native of East Anglia.

7. Benedeit, *The Anglo-Norman Voyage of St. Brendan*, ed. Ian Short and Brian Merilees (Manchester: Manchester University Press, 1979), 4.

8. Irenaeus, *Contra Haereses Libri Quinque*, ed. J. P. Migne, *Patrologiae cursus completus Series graeca*, 166 vols. (Paris, 1857–66), 7, cols. 433–1223; Norman Cohn, *The Pursuit of the Millennium* (London: Paladin, 1970), 27.

9. *St. Patrick, His Writings and Muirchu's Life*, ed. A. B. E. Hood (Chichester: Phillimore, 1978), 23: "quem credimus et expectamus adventum ipsius mox futurum, iudex vivorum atque mortuorum."

10. Gildas, *The Ruin of Britain and other documents*, ed. Michael Winterbottom (Chichester: Phillimore, 1978), 143–44.

11. Leslie Hardinge, *The Celtic Church in Britain* (London: SPCK, 1972), 72; and *S. Columbani Opera*, ed. G. W. S. Walker (Dublin: Dublin Institute for Advanced Studies, 1957), 41.

12. Würzburg University Library MS M. th. f. 12, cited from Whitley Stokes and John Strachan, *Thesaurus Palaeohibernicus*, 2 vols. (Dublin: Dublin Institute for Advanced Studies, rep. 1975), 1: 559; after Hardinge, *The Celtic Church in Britain*, 72.

13. James Carney, *The Poems of Blathmac Son of Cú Brettan* (Dublin: Dublin Institute for Advanced Studies, 1964), 80–84; the verses are dated to the period 750–70.

14. Bede, *Historia Ecclesiastica* in Charles Plummer, ed., *Venerabilis Baedae Opera Historica*, 2 vols. (Oxford: Clarendon Press, 1896): Fursa at 1: 163–68, and Drythelm at 1: 303–10. The Vision of Fursa was popular and translated into Irish, see the edition by Whitley Stokes in *Revue Celtique* 25 (1904): 385–404.

15. Alan Orr Anderson and Marjorie Ogilvie Anderson, *Adomnán's Life of Columba* (Oxford: Clarendon Press, 1991), 188.

16. Nennius, *British History and Welsh Annals*, ed. John Morris (Chichester: Phillimore, 1980), 75.

17. Whitley Stokes, *The Tripartite Life of Patrick with Other Documents Relating to That Saint*, 2 vols. (London: Harrison and Sons, 1887), 1: 116: "muir mór do tuidecht tar hÉrinn secht mbliadna riambráth." The contemporary tract known as the Voyage of Snedgus and Mac Riagal (see n. 37) claims that St. Patrick and St. Martin were jointly responsible for preventing a lake of fire and a lake of water from engulfing Ireland.

18. Kenney, *Sources*, 376.

19. Whitley Stokes, ed., "Colloquy of the Two Sages" (*Immaccalam in dá Thuarad*), *Revue Celtique* 26 (1905): 4–64 (p. 48). The same seven years might be intended when later in the text, following the signs of the birth of the Antichrist, there are seven dark years when the lights of the heavens are not visible until the Final Judgment.

20. *Opera*, ed. Walker, 39 and 49, after H. P. A. Oskamp, *The Voyage of Máel Dúin* (Groningen: Walters-Nordhoff, 1970), 80–81.

21. A useful discussion of these voyage tales and their symbolism is in Alwyn Rees and Brinley Rees, *Celtic Heritage: Ancient Tradition in Ireland and Wales* (London: Thames and Hudson, 1961), 314–25.

22. An early study is by Alfred Nutt, "The Happy Otherworld in the Mythico-Romantic Literature of the Irish," in Kuno Meyer, ed., *The Voyage of Bran son of Febal to the Land of the Living*, 2 vols. (London: A. Nutt, 1895), 1: 101–331. See also Christa Löffler, *Voyage to the Otherworld Island in Early Irish Literature* (Salzburg: Institut für Anglistik und Amerikanistik, Universität Salzburg, 1983).

23. Canice Mooney, *The Church in Gaelic Ireland, 13th to 15th Centuries* (Dublin: Gill and Macmillan, 1969), 44.

24. Rees and Rees, *Celtic Heritage*, 325.

25. James Carney, *Studies in Irish Literature and History* (Dublin: Dublin Institute for Advanced Studies, 1955), 286.

26. Meyer, *Voyage of Bran*, 30. The text can be dated linguistically to the seventh or eighth century, but the language is archaic and is employed as the standard against which archaisms in other texts are measured; see Vernon Hull, "Two Tales About Finn," *Speculum* 16 (1941): 322–33, esp. 323.

27. Charles Plummer, *Irish Litanies* (London: Henry Bradshaw Society, 1925), litany no. 18, after Oskamp, *Voyage of Máel Dúin*, 82.

28. Carl Selmer, *Navigatio Sancti Brendani abbatis* (Notre Dame, Ind.: University of Notre Dame Press, 1959), 56.

29. Charles Plummer, *Vitae Sanctorum Hiberniae*, 2 vols. (Oxford: Clarendon Press, 1910), 1: 115; the name Ailbe is rendered phonetically as *Heluei*.

30. Whitley Stokes, ed., "The Voyage of the Húi Corra," *Revue Celtique* 14 (1893): 22–69 (p. 56). The date of the tale is uncertain. The extant text seems to be eleventh century, but the composition of the original might have been as early as the eighth century; a survey of opinions is given in Kenney, *Sources*, 740–41. More recently it has been suggested that the Ailbe episode should be dated prior to the Viking Age; see Oskamp, *Voyage of Máel Dúin*, 18.

31. Selmer, *Navigatio*, 78–80.

32. For example, the prophets Elias and Enoch linger in the Land of Promise according to the Voyage of Snedgus, but according to the Vision of Adomnán they are in Paradise.

33. The tract is preserved in Oxford, Bodleian MS Rawlinson B 512, f. 97r.b 14–23; it is noticed in Stokes, *Tripartite Life*, 1: xxix–xxx.

34. Stokes, "Colloquy of the Two Sages," 48.

35. Stokes, "Voyage of the Húi Corra," 60.

36. Oskamp, *Voyage of Máel Dúin*, 57, 172; Selmer, *Navigatio*, 70–76.

37. Whitley Stokes, "The Voyage of Snedgus and Mac Riagla," *Revue Celtique* 9 (1888): 14–25.

38. In *Lebor na Huidre*, ed. R. I. Best and Osborn Bergin (Dublin: Hodges for the Royal Irish Academy, 1929), 302–4; trans. T. P. Cross and C. H. Slover, *Ancient Irish Tales*, ed. C. W. Dunn (Totowa, N.J.: Rowman and Littlefield, 1981), 488–90. See also P. Mac Cana, "The Sinless Otherworld," *Ériu* 27 (1976): 95–115; and Carney, *Studies*, 287–88.

39. Nennius, *British History*, 75.

40. W. Stokes, "Voyage of Snedgus," 20.

41. W. Stokes, "Voyage of Húi Corra," 44.

42. This text has been edited several times, but not in works now conveniently available; the most accessible is the diplomatic edition by Best and Bergin in *Lebor na Huidre*, 67–76, (p. 69). A translation made by Whitley Stokes in *Fraser's Magazine* for February 1871, 184–94 is reprinted by his sister Margaret Stokes, *Three Months in the Forests of France: A Pilgrimage in Search of Vestiges of the Irish Saints in France* (London: G. Bell, 1895), 265–79 (p. 268). For a discussion see Kenney, *Sources*, 444–45.

43. Best and Bergin, *Lebor na Huidre*, 76; and M. Stokes, *Three Months*, 278.

44. Selmer, *Navigatio*, 18–19.

45. Eleanor Knott, ed., *Togail Bruidne Da Derga* (Dublin: Dublin Institute for Advanced Studies, 1975), 5.

46. *The Mabinogion*, trans. Gwyn Jones and Thomas Jones (London: J. M. Dent, rep. 1975), 61–63.

47. Whitley Stokes, "Tidings of the Resurrection," *Revue Celtique* 25 (1904): 232–59; Kenney, *Sources*, 738.

48. The so-called *Catechesis Celtica* is edited by André Wilmart in *Analecta Reginensia* (Rome: Vatican, 1933), 29–112.

49. Arguments for a Goidelic (Irish) background are presented by Paul Grosjean, "A propos du manuscrit 49 de la Reine Christine," *Analecta Bollandiana* 54 (1936): 113–36, esp. 118; and Martin McNamara, "Irish Affiliations of the Catechesis Celtica," *Celtica* 21 (1990): 291–334 (esp. 332–34 for a summary of his arguments).

50. Wilmart, *Analecta Reginensia*, 107.

51. Seymour, "Notes on Apocrypha in Ireland," 114. See also the same author's "The Bringing Forth of the Soul in Irish Literature," *Journal of Theological Studies* 22 (1920): 16–20.

52. Selmer, *Navigatio*, 65–68.

53. W. Stokes, "Voyage of the Húi Corra," 48.

54. Best and Bergin, *Lebor na Huidre*, 75; and M. Stokes, *Three Months*, 276.

55. Best and Bergin, *Lebor na Huidre*, xii.

56. Whitley Stokes, ed., *Saltair na Rann* (Oxford: Clarendon Press, 1883). The work has been studied as much for its grammatical and metrical forms as for its content, but see St. John D. Seymour, "The Signs of Doomsday in Saltair na Rann," *Proceedings of the Royal Irish Academy* 36 (1922) C, 154–63, and Kenney, *Sources*, 736–37.

57. A study of the legend of the fifteen signs, with an edition and translation of the relevant section from *Saltair na Rann* is in William W. Heist, *The Fifteen Signs Before Doomsday* (East Lansing: Michigan State College Press, 1952), 2–21.

58. Wilmart, *Analecta Reginensia*, 58.

59. [Pseudo-]Bede, *Excerptiones Patrum, Collectanea Flores ex Diversis, Quaestiones, et Parabolae*, ed. J. P. Migne in *Patrologiae cursus completus. series latina*, 217 vols. (Paris, 1844–55), 94, cols. 539–75 (col. 555).

60. Heist believed that the *Collectaneum* was a late work composed after *Saltair na Rann*; see *Fifteen Signs*, 95–96. An earlier date is argued by Robin Flower in Standish O'Grady and Robin Flower, eds., *Catalogue of Irish Manuscripts in the British Library (formerly the British Museum)*, 2 vols. (Dublin: Dublin Institute for Advanced Studies, 1992), 2: 487. Kenney, *Sources*, 680, dates its composition to the eighth century.

61. A transcript and translation of the relevant passage is in Heist, *Fifteen Signs*, 24–25.

62. Heist, *Fifteen Signs*, 115.

63. Margaret Enid Griffiths, *Early Vaticination in Welsh, with English Parallels* (Cardiff: University of Wales, 1937), 44–47.

64. J. O'Keefe, "A Poem on the Day of Judgement," *Ériu* 3 (1907): 29–33; Kenney, *Sources*, 737.

65. Best and Bergin, *Lebor na Huidre*, 74; and M. Stokes, *Three Months*, 274.

66. Fergus Kelly, *A Guide to Early Irish Law* (Dublin: Dublin Institute for Advanced Studies, 1988), 50; the law code cited is *Bretha Crólige*.

67. The main versions are edited by Georges Dottin, "Le Teanga Bithnua du

manuscrit de Rennes, 70a," *Revue Celtique* 24 (1903): 365–403; and Whitley Stokes, "The Evernew Tongue," *Ériu* 2 (1905): 96–162; a twelfth-century text is edited by U. Nic Énrí and G. Mac Niocaill, "The Second Recension of the Evernew Tongue," *Celtica* 9 (1971): 1–60. For a brief discussion see Kenney, *Sources*, 737–38; and Wright, *Irish Tradition*, 35.

68. Stokes, "Evernew Tongue," 102.

69. Ibid., 138.

70. Best and Bergin in *Lebor na Huidre*, 67–76. There is also a translation in C. S. Boswell, *An Irish Precursor of Dante* (London: D. Nutt, 1908).

71. For discussions see St. John D. Seymour, "The Vision of Adamnan," *Proceedings of the Royal Irish Academy* 37 (1927) C: 304–12; Boswell, *An Irish Precursor of Dante*; D. Dumville, "Towards an Interpretation of Fís Adomnán," *Studia Celtica* 12/13 (1977/78): 62–77; and Wright, *Irish Tradition*, 35.

72. Seymour, "Vision of Adamnan," 310.

73. The idea of thirty years as the perfect age is found also in the Irish Adam and Eve story, see Greene et al., *Irish Adam and Eve*, ii, 70.

74. W. Stokes, "Tidings of the Resurrection," 236.

75. For a brief discussion with references, see Benjamin T. Hudson, "Gaelic Princes and Gregorian Reform," in *Crossed Paths: Methodological Approaches to the Celtic Aspect of the European Middle Ages*, ed. Hudson and Vickie L. Ziegler (Lanham, Md.: University Press of America, 1990), 61–82 (65–66).

76. Whitley Stokes, "Tidings of Doomsday," *Revue Celtique* 4 (1880): 245–57; Kenney, *Sources*, 738.

77. Georges Dottin, "Les deux chagrins du royaume du ciel," *Revue Celtique* 21 (1900): 349–87.

78. Kenney, *Sources*, 738.

79. Seymour, "Eschatology of the Early Irish Church," 191–97.

80. This has been suggested for other theological works; see Milton McC. Gatch, *Preaching and Theology in Anglo-Saxon England* (Toronto: University of Toronto Press, 1977), 168, n. 11.

81. R. I. Best and H. J. Lawlor, *The Martyrology of Tallaght* (London: Harrison and Sons, 1931). The Life of Brendan in the Book of Lismore is a twelfth-century reworking of a probable ninth-century original; see Whitley Stokes, ed., *Lives of the Saints from the Book of Lismore* (Oxford: Clarendon Press, 1890), 99–115, 247–61, and 349–54.

82. Benjamin T. Hudson, *Prophecy of Berchán* (Westport, Conn.: Greenwood Press, 1996), 37–38.

83. Kuno Meyer, "Das Ende von Baile in Scáil," *Zeitschrift für celtische Philologie* 12 (1918): 371–82.

84. G. Murphy, "Two Sources in Thurneysen's Heldensage," *Ériu* 16 (1952): 145–51.

85. Kenney, *Sources*, 749–52.

86. The legend is preserved by Geoffrey Keating, *Foras Feasa ar Éirinn*, ed. David Comyn and Patrick S. Dineen, Irish Texts Society 6, 8–9 (Dublin: Irish Texts Society, 1914), 8, lines 3170–86.

87. *Félire Óengusso Céli Dé, The Martyrology of Oengus the Culdee*, ed. Whitley

Stokes (London, 1905; rep. Dublin: Dublin Institute for Advanced Studies, 1984), 190. Two studies by K. Müller-Lisowski are "Texte zur Mog Ruith Sage," *Zeitschrift für celtische Philologie* 14 (1923): 145–63, 422, esp. 154–56; and "La légende de St. Jean dans la tradition irlandaise et le druide Mog Ruith," *Etudes Celtiques* 3 (1938): 46–70.

88. Máire Herbert and Pádraig Ó Riain, *Betha Adamnáin* (London: Irish Texts Society, 1988), 60.

89. A most useful and succinct discussion of this chronology is given in the *Annals of Ulster*, 2: 56–57.

90. Whitley Stokes, "The Annals of Tigernach, the Continuation," *Revue Celtique* 18 (1897): 18.

91. *Annals of the Kingdom of Ireland by the Four Masters, from the Earliest Period to 1616*, ed. John O'Donovan, 7 vols. (Dublin: Hodges, Smith, 1851), 2: *sub anno* 1096.

92. Whitley Stokes, "Adomnan's Second Vision," *Revue Celtique* 12 (1891): 420–43. For an old but still useful discussion, see Eugene O'Curry, *Lectures on the Manuscript Materials of Ancient Irish History* (Dublin: J. Duffy, 1861; rep. 1878), 423–30.

93. Best and Bergin, *Lebor na Huidre*, 67.

94. For *scúap a Fánait, sirfes Érinn anairdhes draic lonn* and *roth ramach*, see the *Martyrology of Óengus*, 190; and the study by Paul Grosjean, "Le balai de Fánaid," *Etudes Celtiques* 2 (1937): 284–86.

95. Kenney, *Sources*, 751.

96. Bernard McGinn, *Apocalypticism in the Western Tradition* (Brookfield, Vt.: Variorum, 1994), 3: 277.

97. Hudson, "Gaelic Princes," 61–82.

98. For editions and references see Kenney, *Sources*, 741–42. A discussion appears in Carl Watkins, "Doctrine, Politics and Purgation: The Vision of Tnúthgal and the Vision of Owein at St. Patrick's Purgatory," *Journal of Medieval History* 22 (1996): 225–36.

99. McGinn, *Apocalypticism in the Western Tradition*, 3: 274.

100. Rodney Mearns, ed., *The Vision of Tundale* (Heidelberg: C. Winter, 1985), 8.

101. Whitley Stokes, "The Fifteen Tokens of Doomsday," *Revue Celtique* 28 (1907): 308–26, 432.

102. Oskamp, *Voyage of Máel Dúin*, 16.

103. Ibid., 61–63.

104. *Fragmentary Annals of Ireland*, ed. Joan Newlon Radner (Dublin: Dublin Institute for Advanced Studies, 1978), 104.

105. Kenney, *Sources*, 354–56.

106. Myles Dillon, "Literary Activity in the Pre-Norman Period," *Seven Centuries of Irish Learning, 1000–1700*, 2nd ed., ed. Brian Ó Cuív (Dublin: Mercier Press, 1971), 22–37, at 32.

Exodus and Exile: Joachim of Fiore's Apocalyptic Scenario

1. The words are taken from *Songs of Zion* (Nashville, Tenn.: Abingdon Press, 1981), no. 112. J. Jefferson Cleveland and William B. McClain in their introduction to the section of *Songs* on spirituals point out that "the Old Testament is much more

extensively represented in spiritual texts, for through its stories of the Hebrews in bondage, it immediately spoke to the slaves" (no. 73, 3rd unnumbered page).

2. Michael Walzer, *Exodus and Revolution* (New York: Basic Books, 1985), 149.

3. The translation is from the *New English Bible* (Oxford: Oxford University Press, Cambridge University Press, 1970).

4. My treatment of the origins of apocalypticism and the development of reformist apocalypticism is drawn from my manuscript in progress entitled "Bound for the Promised Land."

5. See Daniel, "Bound for the Promised Land." Bernard's *De consideratione* is edited in *Sancti Bernardi opera*, ed. J. Leclercq, H. M. Rochais, and C. H. Talbot, 8 vols. (Rome: Editiones Cistercienses, 1957–77), 3: 379–493, hereafter *Opera*. John D. Anderson and Elizabeth T. Kennan have translated it as *Five Books of Consideration: Advice to a Pope*, The Works of Bernard of Clairvaux, vol. 13, Cistercian Fathers Series 37 (Kalamazoo, Mich.: Cistercian Publications, 1976), hereafter *Consideration*.

6. Hildegard of Bingen, *The Letters of Hildegard of Bingen*, trans. Joseph L. Baird and Radd K. Ehrman, vol. 1 (Oxford: Oxford University Press, 1994), no. 8, 41–43; Lieven van Acker, ed., *Hildegardis Bingensis Epistolarium: Prima pars*, Corpus Christianorum Continuatio Mediaevalis (hereafter CCCM) 91 (Turnhout: Brepols, 1991), 19–22.

7. Gerhoch of Reichersberg, *Letter to Pope Hadrian About the Novelties of the Day* (*Liber de nouitatibus huius temporis*), prol., sect. 5, chap. 41, s. 9, ed. Nikolaus M. Häring, S.A.C. Studies and Texts 24 (Toronto: Pontifical Institute of Mediaeval Studies, 1974), 24, 105–6.

8. Gerhoch of Reichersberg, *De inuestigatione antichristi liber 1.*, ed. E. Sackur, Monumenta Germaniae Historica (hereafter MGH), Libelli de lite 3 (Hanover: Hahn, 1897), 304–95.

9. Gerhoch of Reichersberg, *De quarta uigilia noctis*, ed. E. Sackur, MGH, Libelli de lite, vol. 3 (Hanover: Hahn, 1897), 503–25.

10. Hildegard of Bingen, *Sciuias*, bk. 3, vision 11:1–6, ed. Adelgundis Führkötter OSB and Angela Carlevaris OSB, CCCM 43–43a (Turnhout: Brepols, 1977–78), 578–80, trans. Mother Columba Hart and Jane Bishop, Classics of Western Spirituality (New York and Mahwah: Paulist Press, 1990), 494–95. Robert Lerner, "The Refreshment of the Saints," *Traditio* 32 (1976): 97–144, traces the notion that a period of time will be left after the destruction of the final antichrist during which the saints will be at peace and rest. On Hildegard see pp. 112–13. Lerner's article has been printed in an Italian translation in *Refrigerio dei santi: Gioacchino da Fiore e l'escatologia medievale* (Rome: Viella, 1995), 19–66 (hereafter *Refrigerio*).

11. Hildegard of Bingen, *De operatione dei siue Liber diuinorum operum*, bk. 3, vision 10, sect. 15–38, PL 197, cols. 1017–38. Charles Czarski, *The Prophecies of St. Hildegard of Bingen*, Ph.D. diss., University of Kentucky, Lexington, Kentucky, 1983, is the fundamental work on Hildegard's apocalypticism. He first pointed out the significant differences between the *Sciuias* and the *Liber diuinorum operum* and suggested why Hildegard reinterpreted her vision. Kathryn Kerby-Fulton, *Reformist Apocalypticism and "Piers Plowman"*, Cambridge Studies in Medieval Literature 7 (Cambridge: Cambridge University Press, 1990), 26–75, first applied reformist apocalypticism to Hildegard.

12. The fundamental study is Herbert Grundmann, "Zur Biographie Joachims von Fiore und Rainer von Ponza," *Deutsches Archiv für Erforschung des Mittelalters* 16 (1960): 437–546. This was reprinted in Herbert Grundmann, *Ausgewählte Aufsätze*, Teil 2, *Joachim von Fiore*, MGH, Schriften 25.2 (Stuttgart: Anton Hiersemann, 1977), 255–360 (hereafter *Biographie*). Grundmann edited the anonymous *Vita b. Joachimi abbatis*, which was written by a companion who had been with Joachim since the abbot left Corazzo to become a hermit (pp. 528–38), and Luke of Cosenza's brief memorial (pp. 538–44). Luke was one of Joachim's scribes at Casamari and remained a friend and supporter. See also Joachim of Fiore, *Liber de concordia noui ac ueteris testamenti: Books 1–4*, ed. E. Randolph Daniel, Transactions of the American Philosophical Society, vol. 73, part 8 (Philadelphia: American Philosophical Society, 1983), xi–xxii (hereafter *Liber de concordia*).

13. Grundmann, *Biographie*, 528, where the anonymous *Vita* says: "Moises noster geminae reuelatione legis accepta de monte descendit et ad suos, quos pro desiderio terrenorum ima tenere nouerat, rediturus perambulare prius omnem terra, in qua uideri deus et cum hominibus conuersari dignatus est, uoluit et religiosos usquequaque degentes pia sollicitudine uisitare." Stephen E. Wessley, *Joachim of Fiore and Monastic Reform* (New York: Peter Lang, 1990), 29–31 (hereafter *Joachim*), interpreted this identification of Joachim with Moses to mean that the author of the *Vita* was a Florensian who saw the Florensians as part of a new exodus led by Joachim, the "new Moses." Joachim himself saw Bernard of Clairvaux as the new Moses. See below, p. 138.

14. Joachim, *Liber de concordia*, xii–xiii, xxvii. Most scholars have called these experiences visions, but I prefer "intuition" to distinguish Joachim's experiences from the visions of Hildegard of Bingen. Hildegard saw definite images and later described and interpreted them. Joachim had been thinking about a problem when a flash of insight solved the problem. Joachim, however, clearly believed that these insights came from God.

15. Grundmann, *Biographie*, 532: "Tunc cum esset in dicto monasterio Casamariae, reuelatum est ei misterium trinitatis et scripsit ibi primum librum Psalterii decem chordarum." The *Vita* refers to Joachim's *Psalterium decem chordarum* (Venice, 1527; rep. Frankfurt am Main: Minerva, 1965). Joachim described his Pentecost intuition on fol. 227rb–vb.

16. Grundmann, *Biographie*, 533: "Alexandro autem papa defuncto, cum omnia sub Siciliae rege Guiglermo secundo summa pace agerentur, tertio die post resurrectionis dominice festum, in quo sibi ueteris et noui testamenti fuerat concordia reuelata, uocauit." Joachim describes this intuition at length in his *Expositio in Apocalypsim* (Venice, 1527; rep. Frankfurt am Main: Minerva, 1964), fol. 39rb–va. Grundmann argued that the author must have meant Lucius III, who died on November 25, 1185, rather than Alexander III, who died in 1181. In Joachim, *Liber de concordia*, xvi–xviii, I have discussed the problem. Scholars disagree about both the number and the order of the intuitions. Marjorie Reeves argues that the Easter vision preceded the Pentecost vision. See her *The Influence of Prophecy: A Study in Joachimism* (Oxford: Clarendon Press, 1969; rep. South Bend, Ind.: University of Notre Dame Press, 1993), 21–24 (the reprinted edition differs from the original only in the bibliography), hereafter *Influence*; and her *Joachim of Fiore and the Prophetic Future* (New York: Harper and Row, 1977), 4–5. Robert Lerner, "Joachim of Fiore's Breakthrough to Chiliasm," *Cristianesimo nella storia* 6 (1985) 489–512; trans. into Italian in Lerner, *Refrigerio*, 97–116.

Lerner argues that the Easter vision came before the Pentecost one. Bernard McGinn, *The Calabrian Abbot: Joachim of Fiore in the History of Western Thought* (New York: Macmillan, 1985), 19–22, hereafter *Calabrian Abbot*, reversed the two later intuitions and argued that the Palestine one was unhistorical.

17. Delno C. West and Sandra Zimdars-Swartz, *Joachim of Fiore: A Study in Spiritual Perception and History* (Bloomington: Indiana University Press, 1983), 95–98, argue that the wheels of Ezekiel served Joachim as a means by which to integrate his thinking.

18. Joachim, *Liber de concordia*, xxii–xxvii.

19. For an edition of the *Testamentum*, see Joachim, *Liber de concordia*, 4–6.

20. Joachim of Fiore, *Tractatus super quatuor Euangelia*, ed. Ernesto Buonaiuti, Fonti per la storia d'Italia 67 (Rome: Istituto Storico Italiano, 1930). Henri Mottu, *La manifestation de l'Esprit selon Joachim de Fiore* (Neuchâtel and Paris: Delachaux and Niestlé Editeurs, 1977), argued that Joachim took a much more radical stance in the *Tractatus* than in his earlier writings and thus became the progenitor of modern notions of revolution. Mottu later retracted his arguments in two papers: "Joachim de Fiore et Hegel: apocalyptique biblique et philosophie de l'histoire," in *Storia e messaggio in Gioacchino da Fiore*: atti del I congresso internazionale di studi gioachimiti (San Giovanni in Fiore: Centro di Studi Gioachimiti, 1980), 151–94; and "La mémoire du futur: signification de l'ancien testament dans la pensée de Joachim de Fiore," in *L "Eta" dello spirito e la fine dei tempi in Gioacchino da Fiore e nel gioachimismo medievale*, Atti del II Congresso Internazionale di Studi Gioachimiti, ed. Antonio Crocco (San Giovanni in Fiore: Centro Internazionale di Studi Gioachimiti, 1986), 13–28.

21. Joachim, *Liber de concordia noui ac ueteris testamenti* (Venice, 1519: rep. Frankfurt am Main: Minerva, 1964), fols. 112vb–122va.

22. Wessley, *Joachim of Fiore*, 1–27; Cipriano Baraut, "Un tratado inédito de Joaquín de Fiore: *De uita sancti Benedicti et de officio diuino secundum eius doctrinam*," *Analecta Sacra Tarraconensia* 24 (1951): 33–122.

23. Joachim, *Liber figurarum*, ed. Leone Tondelli, Marjorie Reeves, and Beatrice Hirsch-Reich, *Il libro delle figure dell'abate Gioachino da Fiore*, 2nd ed., 2 vols. (Torino: Società Editrice Internazionale, 1953; rep. 1990), hereafter *Liber figurarum*. Marjorie Reeves and Beatrice Hirsch-Reich, *The* Figurae *of Joachim of Fiore* (Oxford: Clarendon Press, 1972), is an essential commentary on the figures (hereafter *Figurae*).

24. McGinn, *Calabrian Abbot*, 101–44. Jean Leclercq defined monastic theology in his *The Love of Learning and the Desire for God* (New York: Fordham University Press, 1982). Horst Dieter Rauh, *Das Bild des Antichrist im Mittelalter: Von Tyconius zum Deutschen Symbolismus*, 2d rev. ed., Beiträge zur Geschichte der Philosophie und Theologie des Mittelalters, Neue Folge 9 (Münster: Aschendorff, 1979), called monastic theology *deutsche Symbolismus*.

25. Joachim, *Liber de concordia*, xv–xvi; the *Vita* in Grundmann, *Biographie*, 532–33; Luke of Cosenza in Grundmann, *Biographie*, 539. Bernard McGinn edited the *De prophetia ignota* in his "Joachim and the Sibyl," *Cîteaux Com. Cist.* 2(1957): 97–138. Matthias Karp, De prophetia ignota: *Eine frühe Schrift Joachim von Fiore*, MGH Studien und Texte 19 (Hanover: Hahn, 1998), has provided a critical edition with commentary.

26. Joachim, *Liber de concordia*, xviii. Clement's letter is edited there on p. 3. See also Grundmann, *Biographie*, 492–93.

27. On this interview see E. R. Daniel, "Apocalyptic Conversion: the Joachite Alternative to the Crusades," *Traditio* 25 (1969): 128–54, esp. 134–35 (reprinted in Delno West, *Joachim of Fiore in Christian Thought*, 2 vols. [New York: Burt Franklin, 1975], 2:301–328, esp. 308–9, hereafter *Joachim of Fiore*). There are two accounts of the interview, both from the pen of Roger of Hoveden. The first is found in Ps. Benedict of Peterborough—Roger of Hoveden, *Gesta regis Henrici secundi Benedicti abbatis*, ed. William Stubbs, 2 vols., Rerum Britannicarum Medii Aevi Scriptores, Rolls Series (hereafter Rolls Series) 49 (London: HMSO, 1867), 2: 151–55. The second and somewhat different account is in Hoveden's later *Chronica*, ed. William Stubbs, 3 vols., Rolls Ser. 51 (London, 1870), 3: 75–78.

28. Joachim, *Liber de concordia*, xx; Grundmann, *Biographie*, 503.

29. Joachim, *Liber de concordia*, xx; Reeves, *Influence*, 12–14. The interview is recorded in Ralph of Coggeshall, *Chronicon anglicanum*, ed. J. Stephenson, Rolls Ser. 66 (London, 1875), 67–79.

30. Joachim, *Liber de concordia*, xviii–xix.

31. Bernard of Clairvaux, *De consideratione*, 5.7.15, *Opera*, 3:479; *On consideration*, 158.

32. Bernard of Clairvaux, *Sermones super Cantica canticorum*, 80.4.6–9, *Opera*, 2: 281–83. On this controversy, see Richard W. Southern, *Scholastic Humanism and the Unification of Europe*, vol. 1, *Foundations* (Oxford: Blackwell, 1995), 225–30.

33. Reeves, *Influence*, 28–36; Wessley, *Joachim of Fiore*, 90–92, 102–3. No copy of Joachim's treatise has been found, and the circumstances surrounding its composition are unknown.

34. Robert Moynihan, "The Development of the 'Pseudo-Joachim' Commentary 'Super Hieremiam': New Manuscript Evidence," *Mélanges de l'Ecole Française de Rome, Moyen Age—Temps Modernes* 98 (1986): 109–42, argues that three versions are extant among the manuscripts, of which the earliest may be Joachim's own work; the second is dated after 1215 and reflects the defense of Joachim by his disciples, and the third postdates the organization of the Order of Friars Minor and the Order of Preaching Friars. Moynihan has not yet published his promised edition.

35. E. R. Daniel, "A Re-Examination of the Origins of Franciscan Joachitism," *Speculum* 43 (1968): 671–76; reprinted in West, *Joachim of Fiore*, 2: 143–48.

36. Reeves, *Influence*, 59–70.

37. For scholarship prior to about 1955, see Morton Bloomfield, "Joachim of Flora: A Critical Survey of his Canon, Teachings, Sources, Biography, and Influence," *Traditio* 13 (1957): 249–311; reprinted in West, *Joachim of Fiore*, 29–91. E. R. Daniel, "Joachim of Fiore and Medieval Apocalypticism," *Medievel et Humanistica* n.s. 14 (1986): 173–88, surveys some of the later literature.

38. For Reeves, see note 16.

39. McGinn, *Calabrian Abbot*, 62–66, 190–91.

40. Joachim, *Liber de concordia*, bk. 2, pt. 1, chap. 9, pp. 74–76 (hereafter 2:1: 9:74–76), where Joachim compares the Son to the *uerbum dei* and the Spirit to the *amor dei*.

41. Augustine of Hippo, *Concerning the City of God Against the Pagans*, bk. 20, chap. 7; bk. 22, chap. 30, trans. by Henry Bettenson with an introduction by David Knowles (Harmondsworth: Penguin, 1972), 906–10, 1087–91. Joachim's most extended discussion of the *etates* is in his *De ultimis tribulationibus*, ed. E. R. Daniel,

"Abbot Joachim of Fiore: The *De ultimis tribulationibus*," in *Prophecy and Millenarianism: Essays in Honour of Marjorie Reeves*, ed. Ann Williams (Burnt Hill, Harlow, Essex: Longman, 1980), 165–89; ed. Kurt-Victor Selge, "Ein Traktat Joachims von Fiore über die Drangsale der Endzeit: *De ultimis tribulationibus*," *Florensia* 7 (1993): 7–35. On the widespread expectation of the seventh worldweek according to *anno mundi* dating, see Richard Landes, "Lest the Millennium Be Fulfilled: Apocalyptic Expectations and the Pattern of Western Chronography 100–800 C.E.," *The Use and Abuse of Eschatology in the Middle Ages*, ed. Werner Verbeke, Daniel Verhelst, and Andries Welkenhuysen, Medievalia Louvaniensia, ser. 1, studia xv (Leuven: Leuven University Press, 1988), 137–211.

42. Joachim, *Liber de concordia*, 4:1:2:62: "Concordia proprie esse dicimus similitudinem eque proportionis noui ac ueteris testamenti, eque dico quo ad numerum non quo ad dignitatem; cum uidelicet persona et persona, ordo et ordo, bellum et bellum ex parilitate quadam mutuis se uultibus intuentur."

43. Joachim, *Liber de concordia*, 2:1:4:66: "Intelligentia uero illa, que concordia dicitur, similis est uie continue, que a deserto porrigitur ad ciuitatem, interpositis locis humilioribus in quibus se uiator ambigat iter rectum adire, et nichilominus interpositis iugis montium a quibus possit posteriora et anteriora respicere et residui itineris rectitudinem ex retroacte uie contemplatione metiri."

44. John Bright, *A History of Israel* (Philadelphia: Westminster Press, 1959), 297–300 (hereafter *History of Israel*).

45. 2 Kings 23: 28–30; Bright, *History of Israel*, 302–3.

46. Joachim, *Liber de concordia*, 4:1:30–31:382–83.

47. See above.

48. Joachim, *Liber de concordia*, xxvi–xxvii.

49. Joachim, *Liber de concordia*, 2:1:11:80: "Prima diffinitio designatur in A quod est elementum triangulatum. Secunda designatur in w in quo una uirgula de medio duarum procedit." Chapters two through twelve of the *Liber de concordia* have been translated into English in Bernard McGinn, *Apocalyptic Spirituality* (New York: Paulist Press, 1979), 120–34 (hereafter *Apocalyptic Spirituality*).

50. Matthew only lists forty names, and because Abraham is counted by both Matthew and Luke, the total listed in the two gospels is fifty-nine. Joachim adds the remaining four generations, which are Ochozias, Ioas, Amasias, and Joachim (nos. 40–42, 50). Cf. *Liber de concordia*, Table Two, 88–92.

51. Joachim, *Liber de concordia*, 2:1: 25:108–9.

52. Joachim, *Liber figurarum*, tav. XIa, XIb, XIII. The first two of these are the tree circles, and in the upper left corner of each is a drawing of the alpha. Tav. XIII is a drawing of the ten-stringed psaltery.

53. Joachim, *Liber de concordia*, 2:1: 9:74–76; Table Seven, 173–77.

54. Joachim, *Liber de concordia*, 2:1:8: 72–73, 2:1:11:80; Joachim, *Liber figurarum*, tav. XIa, XIb. The *secunda diffinitio* is found on the lower left side.

55. E. R. Daniel, "The Double Procession of the Holy Spirit in Joachim of Fiore's Understanding of History," *Speculum* 55 (1980): 469–83, shows the similarities between the two schemes.

56. Joachim, *Liber de concordia*, xxxv–xlii; 2:2:10:185.

57. Joachim, *Liber de concordia*, 3:1:1:209–10; Joachim, *Liber figurarum*, tav. xv. See Ezekiel 1:15–28; Apocalypse 4:7–8. On this figure see Reeves and Hirsch-Reich, *Figure*, 224–31; and West and Zimdars-Swartz, *Joachim of Fiore*, 95–98.

58. Joachim, *Liber de concordia*, 3:1:1:210:

Porro generatio quadragesima prima sola ipsa una pro duplici est accipienda, ut iure dici possit bis sexta, nimirum quia duplex tribulatio sub sexta apertione futura est ad similitudinem parasceue, in quo, dupplicatis tenebris, passus est Christus. Sane quadragesima secunda, que erit in sabbatum, aperietur signaculum septimum, de quo dictum est in libro Apocalypsis: "Et cum aperuisset sigillum septimum, factum est silentium in celo quasi media hora."

59. This scheme is laid out graphically in Table Eight at the end of book two, part two. See Joachim, *Liber de concordia*, 193–95.

60. See above.

61. Joachim, *Liber de concordia*, 4:1:32–35:384: "Generatione quoque tricesima octaua, uenit rex Henricus in urbem, et cepit papam Paschalem in ecclesia sancti Petri; et tamdiu illum et alios multos cum eo tenuit in custodia, donec extorqueret ab eo priuilegium de inuestitura ecclesiarum."

62. Joachim, *Liber de concordia*, 4:1:29:380:

Fuit autem iste Sedechias, filius Iosie, homo pessimus et iniquus. Vbi et illud diligentius notari conuenit quod, instante tempore confusionis, confusum est regnum Iuda, ut non secundum ordinem et rationem generationum regnarent ipsi reges, sed tum frater, tum nepos, tum patruus, ueluti communiter duo et duo. Sic et in ecclesia confusio quedam facta est occasione principum mundi, de quorum uiribus scismatici homines presumpserunt; ita ut aliquando tam indecenter quam illicite duo et duo sub eodem tempore uiderentur conscendere ad papatum, de quibus stupefacti populi diutius dubitarent, et contrarie partes hominum contraria sentirent. Et quamuis unum duorum catholicum, alterum scismaticum fore constiterit, non ideo tamen quod sic accidit a concordia uacat.

63. Joachim, *Liber de concordia*, 4:1: 37:386: "Perseuerauit autem pax eadem reliquis diebus ipsius pape, que cepit iterum infringi in diebus pape Lucii maximeque Vrbani, ita ut in diebus eius supramodum et supra uires angustaretur ecclesia. Vtrum autem huiuscemodi occasione ammiserit aliquid ecclesia de libertate sua apud filios Babilonis noue, uideat ipsa que nouit melius quid patiatur."

64. Joachim, *Liber de concordia*, 4:1: 29:380–381.

Summa itaque concordie istarum generationum illa est, qua et ibi regem Babilonis pugnasse legimus contra Iherusalem, et hic Romanos imperatores contra libertatem ecclesie. Et quod ibi aliqui regum Iuda obedierunt ei, et rursum reniti et stare in libertate sua pristina regis Egypti uiribus usi sunt; aliquis absque bello egressus est ad eum, ducendus cum ipso in Babilonem; hic aliqui Romanorum pontificum aliquando inclinati sunt et assenserunt imperatoribus, aliquando uiribus aliquorum principum adiuti eisdem uiriliter restiterunt; aliqui omnino decreuerunt humiliari sub potenti manu eorum et agere pacifice dies suos.

65. Joachim, *Liber de concordia*, 4:1:38–39:388–94.
66. Joachim, *Liber de concordia*, 4:1:38:388:

Vsque ad presentem locum per experta, ut ita dicam, litora nauigantes securo remigio iter fecimus. A modo cautius est agendum, et hinc inde circumspecte reliquum itineris peragendum, utpote qui non per cognita nauigare incipimus, etsi uelut a uicino conspecta, quia nimirum aliud est audita referre, aliud uisa, quamuis eque ex deo sit utrumque possibile.

67. Joachim, *Liber de concordia*, 4:1:40–43:395–400. I will deal more completely with these two "antichrists" in my book "Bound for the Promised Land." Joachim's most succinct presentation of his thinking is in the *Liber figurarum*, tav. XIV, the dragon figure. McGinn, *Apocalyptic Spirituality*, 135–41, has a translation of this text.

68. Joachim, *Expositio*, pt. 6, fols. 195ra–202vb.

69. See above.

70. Joachim, *Liber de concordia*, 4:1:45:402:

In ecclesia incipiet generatio quadragesima secunda anno uel hora qua deus melius nouit. In qua, uidelicet, generatione, peracta prius tribulatione generali et purgato diligenter tritico ab uniuersis zizaniis, ascendet quasi nouus dux de Babilone, universalis scilicet pontifex noue Ierusalem, hoc est sancte matris ecclesie; in cuius typo scriptum est in Apocalipsi: 'Vidi angelum ascendentem ab ortu solis, habentem signum dei uiui;' et cum eo reliquie excussorum. Ascendet autem non gressu pedum aut immutatione locorum, sed quia dabitur ei plena libertas ad innouandam christianam religionem et ad predicandum uerbum dei, incipiente iam regnare domino exercituum super omnem terram.

71. Joachim, *Liber figurarum*, tav. XIa and XIb; Joachim, *Liber de concordia*, 2:2:6–7:162–72.

72. Joachim, *Liber de concordia*, 4:2:2:416.

73. Joachim, *Liber de concordia* 4:2:2:417:

Sed tamen gratie prerogatiua quasi dux omnium et magister, eo quod esset doctus a spiritu et manus domini esset cum eo, factus est etiam quasi alter Moyses, qui non tam filios suos quam fratres et filios fratrum suorum educeret de Egypto. . . . Nec defuit illi socius quasi alter Aaron, qui fuit summus sacerdos Eugenius papa Romanus.

74. Joachim, *Liber de concordia*, 4:2:2:417–19. The passage is from Bernard, *De consideratione*, bk 2:1–2, *Opera* 3:411–12.

75. Joachim, *Liber de concordia*, 4:2:2:411–16, 419–21.

76. Wessley, *Joachim of Fiore*, 1–70.

Arnau de Vilanova and the Body at the End of the World

1. The focus of most end-gazers was the arrival of Antichrist rather than the rearrival of Christ. For background see Bernard McGinn, *Visions of the End: Apocalyptic Traditions in the Middle Ages* (New York: Columbia University Press, 1979); idem, *Apocalypticism in the Western Tradition* (Aldershot: Variorum, 1994); idem, *Antichrist: Two Thousand Years of the Human Fascination with Evil* (San Francisco: Harper San

Francisco, 1994); McGinn and Richard K. Emmerson, *Antichrist in the Middle Ages: A Study of Medieval Apocalypticism, Art, and Literature* (Seattle: University of Washington Press, 1981). See also the essays collected in *The Apocalypse in the Middle Ages*, ed. Emmerson and McGinn (Ithaca, N.Y.: Cornell University Press, 1992). For the earliest Christian traditions, see Christopher Rowland, *The Open Heaven: A Study of Apocalyptic in Judaism and Early Christianity* (New York: Crossroad, 1982). For the Byzantine view, see Paul J. Alexander, *The Byzantine Apocalyptic Tradition*, ed. Dorothy DeF. Abrahamse (Berkeley: University of California Press, 1985).

2. A large literature exists, with studies of Arnau's scientific work vastly predominating, but a scholarly boomlet on his religious thought is now underway. The publication of critical editions of the religious writings is sorely needed, though, before further significant work is possible. The most impressive recent works in English are Robert E. Lerner, "Ecstatic Dissent," *Speculum* 67 (1992): 33–57; idem, "Writing and Resistance Among Beguins of Languedoc and Catalonia," in *Heresy and Literacy, 1000–1530*, ed. Peter Biller and Anne Hudson, Cambridge Studies in Medieval Literature 23 (Cambridge: Cambridge University Press, 1994), 186–204; John August Bollweg, "Sense of a Mission: Arnau de Vilanova on the Conversion of Muslims and Jews," in *Iberia and the Mediterranean World of the Middle Ages: Studies in Honor of Robert I. Burns, S.J.*, ed. Larry J. Simon (Leiden: E. J. Brill, 1995), 50–71. I have discussed aspects of Arnau's career in "Arnau de Vilanova and the Franciscan Spirituals in Sicily," *Franciscan Studies* ser. 2, 50 (1990): 3–29; "The Reception of Arnau de Vilanova's Religious Ideas," in *Christendom and Its Discontents: Exclusion, Persecution, and Rebellion, 1000–1500*, ed. Scott L. Waugh and Peter D. Diehl (Cambridge: Cambridge University Press, 1996), 112–31; and in chapter 5 of my *The Decline and Fall of Medieval Sicily: Politics, Religion, and Economy in the Reign of Frederick III, 1296–1337* (Cambridge: Cambridge University Press, 1995).

An exciting book by Joseph Ziegler, *Medicine and Religion c. 1300: The Case of Arnau de Vilanova* (Oxford: Oxford University Press, 1998), appeared too late for me to use in preparing this brief chapter.

3. See especially Michael McVaugh, *Medicine Before the Plague: Practitioners and Their Patients in the Crown of Aragon, 1285–1345* (New York: Cambridge University Press, 1993), with full bibliography. Together with Juan Antonio Paniagua Arellano and Luis García Ballester, McVaugh is coeditor of the ongoing *Opera medica omnia Arnaldi de Villanova* (Barcelona: Seminarium Historiae Medicae Cantabricense, 1975); six volumes have appeared to date.

4. Josep Perarnau, ed., "El text primitiu del *De mysterio cymbalorum ecclesiae* d'Arnau de Vilanova," *Arxiu de Textos Catalans Antics* 7/8 (1988–89): 7–22, see appendix 1.

5. Robert E. Lerner, "The Pope and the Doctor," *Yale Review* 78 (1988): 62–79, tells this tale exceptionally well.

6. Ramon d'Alós Moner, "Collecció de documents relatius a l'Arnau de Vilanova," *Estudis Universitaris Catalans* 3 (1909): 47–53, 140–48, 331–32, 447–49, 531–34; 4 (1910): 110–19, 496–98; 6 (1912): 98–103, doc. 22: "Sciat Regio Celsitudo, quod magnus rumor est in curia de verbis magistri Arnaldi de Villanova, etiam apud maiores. Dicunt enim, quod ipsius prenuntiationes iam incipiunt verificari, et timent, quod verba ipsius veniant ad effectum."

7. Ibid., doc. 20: "et dixerunt isti cardinales: Magister Arnaldus, utinam non venisset. Fama enim est hic—et est verum—quod iam papa fuiseet sepultus nisi magister."

8. *Protestatio facta Perusii*, in Heinrich Finke, *Aus den Tagen Bonifaz VIII: Funde und Forschungen* (Münster: Aschendorff, 1902; rep. Rome, 1964), 2:cxcvi; Vorreformationsgeschichtliche Forschungen: "ad detestationem evangelicam viciorum in catholicis statibus."

9. See Backman, "Reception," 120–21. See also the discussion in Manfred Gerwing, *Vom Ende der Zeit: Der Traktat des Arnald von Villanova über die Ankunft des Antichrist in der akademischen Auseinandersetzung zu Beginn des 14. Jahrhunderts* (Münster: Aschendorff, 1996).

10. Josep Perarnau, "L'*Allocutio christiani* d'Arnau de Vilanova: edició i estudi del text," *Arxiu de Textos Catalans Antics* 11 (1992): 7–135.

11. See Backman, "Arnau de Vilanova and the Franciscan Spirituals in Sicily."

12. *Expositio super Apocalypsi*, ed. Josep Carreras i Artau (Barcelona: Institut d'Estudis Catalans, 1971). This was intended as the first volume of a comprehensive edition of *Arnaldi de Villanova Scripta Spiritualia*, but nothing further came of the project.

13. Backman, "Reception," 118, nn. 16–17.

14. *Expositio in Apocalypsi*, prologue:

"Pertransibunt plurimi et multiplex erit scientia." Quamvis hoc dictum commune sit toti scripturae sacrae, quia tamen angelus qui dixit hoc Danieli tunc eum alloquebatur super intellectu visionis cuiusdam, idcirco specialius convenit eloquiis visionum: per omnia quidem eloquia sacra transierunt et adhuc transeunt, passibus meditationis et studii, multi expositores, et multiplicius exponunt secundum rationem scientiae mysticae sive spiritualis aut litteralis, sicut plenarie declaratur, ex his quae iam tradita sunt, in regulis expositionis eorum.

Sed, in eloquiis visionum, expositorum scientia multiplicius variatur, quoniam in illis valde occulta sunt ea quae proponuntur, ubi sunt eventus ignoti, vel quia iamdiu praeteriti, vel quia sunt omnino futuri; rursum etiam quoniam exprimuntur per figuras profundorum aenigmatum, quia per nomina rerum habentium quamplures proprietates et magna ex parte communiter ignotas etiam sapientibus; est etiam una de causis praedictae multiplicitatis diversitas finis vel intentionis, propter quam auctor visionum dictarum, scilicet Deus, dat intellectum earum: ipse enim qui claudit et aperit quando et quantum vult.

15. Ibid.:

Quandoque dat intellectum visionum ad certitudinem habendam de illis eventibus, quos praenuntiat per easdem; et hoc regulariter facit illo Ecclesiae tempore, quo scit expedire suis electis quod certam habeant illorum notitiam, et tunc principalem sensum aperit visionis cuiusque. . . . Cum autem Deus aperit intellectum visionum ad exercitium supradictum, tunc expositores ducit magis per sensus accessorios quam per principalem, praecise cum nondum advenit tempus in quo principalis debeat aperiri. Qualiter autem sensus principalis ab accessoriis discernatur, declaratum est sufficienter in regulis.

16. Caroline Walker Bynum, *The Resurrection of the Body in Western Christianity, 200–1336* (New York: Columbia University Press, 1995).

17. Backman, "Reception," 122–23, 126.

18. Paul Diepgen, *Die Theologie und der ärtzliche Stand* (Berlin: Rothschild Verlag, 1922), and Jacques LeGoff, "Body and Ideology in the Medieval West," in his *The Medieval Imagination* (Chicago: University of Chicago Press, 1985), pp. 83–85 give general background. On the Jewish tradition, see Joseph Shatzmiller, *Jews, Medicine, and Medieval Society* (Berkeley: University of California Press, 1994), and Gerrit Bos, "R. Moshe Narboni—Philosopher and Physician: A Critical Analysis of *Sefer Orah Hayyim*," *Medieval Encounters* 1 (1995): 219–51. On the Christian and Galenic traditions, see David L. D'Avray, "Some Franciscan Ideas About the Body," *Archivum Franciscanum Historicum* 75 (1991): 343–63, and Luis García Ballester, "Soul and Body: Diseases of the Soul and Diseases of the Body in Galen's Medical Thought," in *Le opere psicologiche di Galeno*, ed. Paola Manuli and Mario Vegetti (Naples: Bibliopolis, 1988), pp. 117–52.

19. Alós Moner, "Collecció," doc. 20.

20. Finke, *Aus den Tagen Bonifaz VIII*, clxxvii–cxcii.

21. The text appears in the collection of Arnau's writings compiled at Montpellier in 1305. See Vatican City, Vat. lat. 3824, fol. 226–30.

Of Earthquakes, Hail, Frogs, and Geography: Plague and the Investigation of the Apocalypse in the Later Middle Ages

I am indebted to the careful readings and suggestions of Philippe Buc, Thomas Kaiser, Maureen Miller, Amy Remensnyder, and Bruce Smoller.

1. Heinrich von Hervordia, *Liber de rebus memorabilioribus sive chronicon Henrici de Hervordia*, ed. August Potthast (Göttingen: Dieterich, 1859), 268–69: "Tricesimo primo anno Lodewici in conversione Pauli [January 25] et circa fuit terremotus in Carinthya tota et Cornicula, sevus in tantum, quod quilibet de vita desperavit. . . . Hec ex littera conventus Frisacensis ad priorem provincialem Theutonie. Item in eadem dicitur, quod hoc anno ignis de celo cadens terram Turchorum ad 16 dietas consumpsit. Item hoc anno pluit aliquot diebus bufones et serpentes. De quibus multi homines perierunt. Item hiis temporibus pestilentia jam invaluit in multis partibus mundi." Portions of Heinrich's descriptions of the plague are translated in Rosemary Horrox, *The Black Death*, Manchester Medieval Sources Series (Manchester: Manchester University Press, 1994), 127–30, 150–53.

2. *Annales Austriae, continuatio novimontensis*, ed. D. Wilhelmus Wattenbach, Monumenta Germaniae Historica, Scriptorum 9 (Hanover: Hahn, 1851), 674 (version in column 1, Codex episcopalis):

> In die conversionis beati Pauli universalis terremotus hora vesparum emersit, sed in aliquibus locis vehementior ac crudelior, quemadmodum in Villaco [Villach, in Carinthia] evidentius est ostensum. . . . Item eodem anno infinita disturbia in diversis regionibus apparuerunt, quemadmodum principaliter orta fuit seva pestilentia ultra in partibus orientalibus, et per diversos effectus imma-

nissime omnes ibidem interficiebat, ex maligna impressione superiorum causa efficiente. Nam sicut ex relatione veridica didicimus, homines et iumenta in illis temporibus quemadmodum erant in labore et loco qualicunque constituti, per validam aeris corruptionem in lapides transmutati sunt.

There is an English translation in Horrox, *Black Death*, 59–61, but she translates the version from the Codex novimontensis, p. 674, col. 2. The only significant differences here are that the Codex novimontensis has "in partibus transmarinis" for "in partibus orientalibus" and "ita in lapides transmutabantur" for "in lapides transmutati sunt."

    3. *Continuatio novimontensis*, 674, col. 1:

Insuper in partibus ubi cinciber nascitur, letalis pluvia roravit, mixta cum serpentibus pestiferis et vermibus diversis, cunctosque super quos inundavit, penitus extinxit. Non longe etiam ab illa regione accidit, quod terribilis ignis de celo fulminavit, et cuncta que erant in superficie terre consumpsit; lapides vero virtute illius ignis ita ardebant, ac si naturaliter in arida ligna fuissent transmutati; fumus etiam inde procedens fuit valde contagiosus, ita ut mercatores ipsum a longe intuentes continuo inficerentur, nonnulli etiam ex eis ibidem finierunt vitam. Qui autem fortuitu evaserunt, pestilentiam quam arripuerant, secum deportaverunt; et cuncta loca ad que cum mercimoniis applicuerunt, quemadmodum in Greciam, Italiam, Romam, infecerunt, et vicinas regiones per quas transierunt.

    4. *Breve Chronicon clerici anonymi ex MS Bibliotheca Regiae Bruxellis*, in J.-J. de Smet, ed., *Recueil des chroniques de Flandre/Corpus chronicorum flandriae* (Brussels: Hayez, 1856), 3: 14:

Eodem anno [1347], in mense septembri, incepit quaedam et maxima mortalitas et pestilentia, ut vidi in transcripto literarum cantoris et canonici Sancti Donatiani [namely, Louis Heyligen] contineri, qui eo tempore in curia Romana cum cardinali domino suo consistebat, quas literas sociis suis Brugis pro novis et trementibus transmiserat: videlicet quod circa Yndiam majorem in orientalibus partibus in quadam provincia terribilia quedam et tempestates inaudite totam illam provinciam tribus diebus oppressam tenuerunt. Primo quidem die ranas pluit, serpentes, lacertos, scorpiones et multa hujus generis venenatorum animalium; secundo vero die audita sunt tonitrua, et ceciderunt fulgura et choruscationes mixte cum grandinibus mire magnitudinis super terram, que occiderunt quasi omnes homines, a majori usque ad minimum; tercio die descendit ignis fetido fumo de celo, qui totum residuum hominum et animalium consumpsit, et omnes civitates et castra illarum partium combussit. Ex quibus tempestatibus tota illa provincia est infecta, et conjecturatur quod ex infectione illa, per fetidum flatum venti ex parte plage meridionalis venientis, totum litus maris et omnes vicine terre infecte sunt, et semper de die in diem plus inficiuntur, et jam venit circa partes marinas, voluntate Dei, per hunc modum, ut quidam suspicantur.

This letter also is translated in Horrox, 41–45, who identifies its author.

    5. There has been surprisingly little written about the apocalyptic interpretation of the plague. Many modern authors note that people living in the fourteenth

century viewed the plague as one of the Four Horsemen of the Apocalypse, but do not add much beyond that observation. For example, Robert S. Gottfried notes that "The Black Death was an ideal spur to millenarianism, and several natural disasters that occurred in 1348, including a number of earthquakes, seemed to provide physical evidence of the demise of the world." *The Black Death: Natural and Human Disaster in Medieval Europe* (New York: Free Press, 1983), 72. He devotes less than one paragraph to millennial movements and beliefs attendant on the plague, however. Plague figures not at all in Marjorie Reeves's magisterial *The Influence of Prophecy in the Later Middle Ages: A Study in Joachimism* (Oxford: Oxford University Press, 1969; rep. Notre Dame, Ind.: University of Notre Dame Press, 1993). Robert E. Lerner's work poses one significant exception to this rule. In an article devoted specifically to the plague's impact on European eschatology, Lerner argues that plague did little to change ideas about the apocalypse (as, say, the rise of papal monarchy had done), but rather fourteenth-century Europeans readily fit the plague into preexisting apocalyptic scenarios. Lerner discusses several ways in which apocalyptic prophecies were retooled to provide an explanation of plague in his "The Black Death and Western European Eschatological Mentalities," *American Historical Review* 86 (1981): 533–52; see also his *The Powers of Prophecy: The Cedar of Lebanon Vision from the Mongol Onslaught to the Dawn of the Enlightenment* (Berkeley: University of California Press, 1983), 114–22. See also Faye Marie Getz, "Black Death and the Silver Lining: Meaning, Continuity, and Revolutionary Change in Histories of Medieval Plague," *Journal of the History of Biology* 24 (1991): 265–89, esp. 267–74. Getz offers a brief analysis of the apocalyptic slant of several plague chronicles.

6. For a discussion of geography as conquest and possession, specifically within a medieval context, see Sylvia Tomasch and Sealy Gilles, eds., *Text and Territory: Geographical Imagination in the European Middle Ages* (Philadelphia: University of Pennsylvania Press, 1998), especially Sylvia Tomasch, "Introduction: Medieval Geographical Desire," 1–12.

7. The text appears in Robert Hoeniger, *Der schwarze Tod in Deutschland: Ein Beitrag zur Geschichte des vierzehnten Jahrhunderts* (Berlin: Eugen Grosser, 1882; rep. Wiesbaden: Martin Sändig, 1973), 155: "Coniunctiones enim et alie causa predicte partes istas [the south and the east] plus quam nostras respexerunt. Ista tamen cum indiciis [iudiciis?] astrologorum secundum dictum ptolemei inter necessarium et possibile sunt reponenda amplius quia uise fuerunt exalationes et inflammationes quam plurime, velut draco et sydera volantia." (Hereafter cited as *Opinion of the Paris Medical Faculty*.) There is an English translation in Horrox, *Black Death*, 158–63.

8. See Sylvia Tomasch, "Medieval Geographical Desire."

9. There is an enormous body of literature on the marvels of the east. See, e.g., John Block Friedman, *The Monstrous Races in Medieval Art and Thought* (Cambridge, Mass.: Harvard University Press, 1981); Mary B. Campbell, *The Witness and the Other World: Exotic European Travel Writing, 400–1600* (Ithaca, N.Y.: Cornell University Press, 1988); Anna-Dorothee von den Brincken, *Fines Terrae: Die Enden der Erde und der vierte Kontinent auf mittelalterlichen Weltkarten*, Monumenta Germaniae Historica, Schriften, 36 (Hanover: Hahn, 1992); and Iain Higgins, *Writing East: The Fourteenth-Century "Travels" of Sir John Mandeville* (Philadelphia: University of Pennsylvania Press, 1997). By the thirteenth century the marvels of the east were being naturalized in the writings of authors like Albertus Magnus and Roger Bacon, who

attributed the diversity of species and races in the east to the different influence of the stars on differing regions of the earth. See Katharine Park, "The Meanings of Natural Diversity: Marco Polo on the 'Division' of the World," in Edith Sylla and Michael McVaugh, eds., *Texts and Contexts in Ancient and Medieval Science: Studies on the Occasion of John E. Murdoch's Seventieth Birthday* (Leiden: Brill, 1997), esp. 140–43. Since I completed this chapter, there has also appeared Lorraine Daston and Katharine Park, *Wonders and the Order of Nature, 1150–1750* (New York: Zone Books, 1998).

10. For a discussion outside the *mappaemundi* of the far from universal medieval notion of Jerusalem as the world's center, see Iain Macleod Higgins, "Defining the Earth's Center in a Medieval 'Multi-Text': Jerusalem in *The Book of John Mandeville*," in Tomasch and Gilles, eds., *Text and Territory*, 29–53. On the *mappaemundi*, see David Woodward, "Medieval *Mappaemundi*," in J. B. Harley and David Woodward, eds., *The History of Cartography*, vol. 1, *Cartography in Prehistoric, Ancient, and Medieval Europe and the Mediterranean* (Chicago: University of Chicago Press, 1987), 286–370.

11. M. C. Seymour, ed., *Mandeville's Travels* (Oxford: Clarendon Press, 1967), 83.

12. See Seymour, *Mandeville's Travels*, ch. 13, 80–81. Adso Dervensis, *De Ortu et tempore Antichristi necnon et tractatus qui ab eo dependunt*, ed. D. Verhelst, Corpus Christianorum, Continuatio Mediaevalis 45 (Turnholt: Brepols, 1976), 24. An English translation appears in John Wright, trans., *The Play of Antichrist* (Toronto: Pontifical Institute of Mediaeval Studies, 1967), 100–110. On medieval Antichrist lore in general see Richard Kenneth Emmerson, *Antichrist in the Middle Ages: A Study of Medieval Apocalypticism, Art, and Literature* (Seattle: University of Washington Press, 1981); and Bernard McGinn, *Antichrist: Two Thousand Years of the Human Fascination with Evil* (San Francisco: Harper, 1994).

13. Quoting from Robert Lerner's composite edition of the prophecy as re-dated for 1347, ed. in Lerner, *Powers of Prophecy*, 226–31. Lerner's book remains the fundamental study of this prophecy.

14. On the expectation of this universal conversion and its relationship to geography, see Jacques Chocheyras, "Fin des terres et fin des temps d'Hésychius (Ve siècle) à Béatus (VIIIe siècle)," in Werner Verbeke, Daniel Verhelst, and Andries Welkenhuysen, eds., *The Use and Abuse of Eschatology in the Middle Ages*, Mediaevalia Lovaniensia, series 1, 15 (Leuven: Leuven University Press, 1988), 72–81; and Pauline Moffitt Watts, "Prophecy and Discovery: On the Spiritual Origins of Christopher Columbus's 'Enterprise of the Indies,'" *American Historical Review* 90 (1985): 73–102.

15. "Tunc passagium erit commune ab omnibus fidelibus ultra aquas congregatas ad terram sanctam, et vincentur. Et civitas Ierusalem glorificabitur, et sepulcrum Domini ab omnibus honorabitur" (ed. in Lerner, *Powers of Prophecy*, 230). There were some apocalyptic expectations centering on Rome as well, reflected, for example, in the belief in a final angelic pope and a papal Antichrist. See Bernard McGinn, "Angel Pope and Papal Antichrist," *Church History* 47 (1978): 155–73.

16. Hugh of St. Victor, *De arca Noe morali*, 4:9, in J.-P. Migne, ed., *Patrologiae cursus completus: series latina* (Paris: Garnier Fratres, 1854), 176, col. 677:

Ordo autem loci, et ordo temporis fere per omnia secundum rerum gestarum seriem concurrere videntur, et ita per divinam providentiam videtur esse dispositum, ut quae in principio temporum gerebantur in Oriente, quasi in principio mundi gererentur, ac deinde ad finem profluente tempore usque ad Occidentem rerum summa descenderet, ut ex ipso agnoscamus appropinquare finem saeculi, quia rerum cursus jam attigit finem mundi.

The Cedar of Lebanon vision is an example of a prophecy that was retooled to place the fall of Acre within an apocalyptic scenario. See Lerner, *Powers of Prophecy*, 622–83.

17. See Iain Higgins, "Imagining Christendom from Jerusalem to Paradise: Asia in *Mandeville's Travels*," in Scott D. Westrem, ed., *Discovering New Worlds: Essays on Medieval Exploration and Imagination* (New York: Garland, 1991), 91–114.

18. Henry Knighton, *Chronicon Henrici Knighton vel Cnitthon Monachi Leycestrensis*, ed. Joseph Rawson Lumby, 2 vols., Rerum Britannicarum Medii Aevi Scriptores, Rolls Series (hereafter Rolls Series) 92 (London: HMSO, 1895), 2: 58–59:

> Isto anno et anno sequenti [1348–49] erat generalis mortalitas hominum in universo mundo. Et primo incepit in India, deinde in Tharsis, deinde ad Saracenos, postremo ad Christianos et Judaeos. . . . Rex Tharsis videns tam subitam et inauditam stragem suorum, iter arripuit cum multitudine copiosa nobilium versus Avinoniam ad papam disponens se Christianum fieri et baptizari a papa, credens vindictam dei populum suum enervasse propter eorum malam incredulitatem. Igitur cum fecisset viginti dietas itinerando audivit quod lues mortaliter invaluit inter Christianos sicut inter alias nationes, verso calle ultra non progreditur in illo itinere, sed repatriare festinavit.

Thus for Knighton the potential convert is the king of Tharsis, the second place the plague strikes. For the Meaux abbey chronicler, it is the "Saracens" in whom the plague begins and who send messengers to Christendom to initiate their conversion to Christianity. *Chronica Monasterii de Melsa, a fundatione usque ad annum 1396, auctore Thoma de Burton, abbate: accedit continuatio ad annum 1406 a monacho quodam ipsius domus*, ed. Edward A. Bond, 3 vols., Rerum Britannicarum Medii Aevi Scriptores (Rolls Series), 43 (London: Longmans, 1868), 3:40:

> De ipsa autem pestilentia fertur, quod primo in Saracenismo nimium ingruebat. Unde Sarraceni residui adhuc superstites, sperantes vindictam Dei in eos propter fidem Christi non assumptam exarsisse, in Christum credere disponebant. Sed, primo missis nuntiis in Christianismum ad indagandum si dicta pestilentia ibidem sicut et inter ipsos inolevit, et ipsis regressis et pestilentiam generalem in Christianismo sicut et in Saracenismo renuntiantibus, in Christum credere iterum contemnebant.

(The story is repeated on p. 68.) There are translated excerpts from both chronicles in Horrox, *Black Death*, 75–80 (Henry Knighton) and 67–70 (Meaux).

19. Roger Bacon, *The "Opus Majus" of Roger Bacon*, ed. John Henry Bridges, 2 vols. (Oxford: Clarendon Press, 1897), 1: 303:

> Quando igitur hae nationes inclusae in locis certis mundi exibunt in desolationem regionem et obviabunt Antichristo, multum deberent Christiani et maxime eccle-

sia Romana considerare situm locorum, ut posset percipere hujusmodi gentium feritatem et per eos percipere tempus Antichristi, et originem; nam debent obedire ei: ergo si illi ex una parte mundi veniant, ipse ex contraria procedet.

20. See Andrew Runni Anderson, *Alexander's Gate, Gog and Magog, and the Inclosed Nations* (Cambridge, Mass.: Mediaeval Academy of America, 1932); Vincent DiMarco, "The Amazons and the End of the World," in Westrem, ed., *Discovering New Worlds*, 69–90; Scott D. Westrem, "Against Gog and Magog," in Tomasch and Gilles, eds., *Text and Territory*, 54–75 and Andrew Colin Gow, *The Red Jews: Antisemitism in an Apocalyptic Age, 1200–1600*, Studies in Medieval and Reformation Thought 55 (Leiden: E. J. Brill, 1995), 37–53, 65–89.

21. Westrem, "Against Gog and Magog," 57, 60–65; Anderson, *Alexander's Gate*, 3–7, 87–104; von den Brincken, *Fines Terrae*, 26, 61–62, 70, 93, 115, 118–19; and Andrew Gow, "Gog and Magog on *Mappaemundi* and Early Printed World Maps: Orientalizing Ethnography in the Apocalyptic Tradition," *Journal of Early Modern History* 2 (1998): 61–88.

22. This is particularly so given the rather loose connotations of "the East." As Mary Campbell has aptly put it, " 'The East' is a concept separable from any particular geographic area. It is essentially Elsewhere." Campbell, *Witness and the Other World*, 48.

23. Pseudo-Methodius, *Revelationes*, ed. in Ernst Sackur, *Sibyllinische Texte und Forschungen: Pseudomethodius, Adso und die Tiburtinische Sibylle* (Halle: Niemeyer, 1898), 91–92: "Tunc reserabuntur portae aquilonis et egredientur virtutes gentium illarum, quas conclusit intus Alexander . . . Gentes namque, que exient ab aquilone, comedent carnes hominum et bibent sanguinem bestiarum sicut aqua et commedent inmu[n]das serpentes et scorpiones et omnem sordissimum et abominabilem genus bestiarum et reptilia, que repunt super terra."

24. Seymour, ed., *Mandeville's Travels*, ch. 29, p. 193.

25. Roger Bacon, *Opus majus*, 1: 303: "O terra, mater draconum, nutrix scorpionum, fovea serpentum, lacus daemonum, facilius fuerat in te infernum esse quam tales gentes parturire. Vae terrae fructiferae et mellifluae, quando ingruent tot serpentes et bestiae in eam."

26. Westrem, "Against Gog and Magog," 68–70.

27. Westrem, "Against Gog and Magog," 69; see Seymour, ed., *Mandeville's Travels*, ch. 29, p. 193.

28. But many of the chroniclers cited in this paper—e.g., Heinrich of Herford—reject the notion of the Jews' guilt (Heinrich von Hervordia, *Liber de rebus memorabilioribus*, 280). Heinrich says the Jews were killed on account of their money, like the Templars. According to the confessions extracted from Jews in Chillon, the conspiracy had been directed from afar, by Jews in Toledo. *Urkunden und Akten der Stadt Strassburg: Urkundenbuch der Stadt Strassburg* (Strasbourg: K. J. Trübner, 1896), 5: 167–74; the confessions have been translated in Horrox, *Black Death*, 211–19. See also Carlo Ginzburg, *Ecstasies: Deciphering the Witches' Sabbath*, trans. Raymond Rosenthal (Harmondsworth: Penguin, 1991), 33–68. Ginzburg notes the parallels to the imagined leper conspiracy in 1321 that also linked up both external and internal enemies.

29. Horrox, *Black Death*, 73, translating from *Historia Roffensis*, in British Li-

brary, Cottonian MS, Faustina B V, fols. 96v–101. There are excerpts from this chronicle printed in Henry Wharton, *Anglia sacra, sive collectio historiarum, partim antiquitus, partim recenter scriptarum, de archiepiscopis et episcopis Angliae* (London: Richard Chiswel, 1691), part 1, 356–77. There the chronicle's author is identified as William Dene. Wharton omits the sections dealing with the plague, however.

30. Heinrich von Hervordia, *Liber de rebus memorabilioribus*, 269; *Chronica Monasterii de Melsa*, 35, 69.

31. It is perhaps not insignificant that Roger Bacon had proclaimed that the gates enclosing Gog and Magog "cannot be broken apart by . . . anything other than a mighty earthquake." Roger Bacon, *Opus majus*, 1: 304 ("nec igne nec ferro nec aqua nec aliqua re dissolvi potest, nisi solo terrae motu violento").

32. See, e.g., R. W. Southern, "Aspects of the European Tradition of Historical Writing: 3. History as Prophecy," *Royal Historical Association Transactions* 5th ser. 22 (1972): 159–80, esp. 170–73.

33. To be sure, many commentators read Revelation as presenting allegorically the whole course of the Church's history, so that, for example, in Nicolas of Lyra's commentary, all of the events described in the first sixteen books of Revelation have already been fulfilled (including all the earthquakes mentioned in Revelation, which Nicolas reads metaphorically anyway). See Philip D. W. Krey, trans., *Nicholas of Lyra's Apocalypse Commentary* (Kalamazoo, Mich.: Medieval Institute Publications, 1997), 214–16.

34. Gregory of Tours (Gregorius Episcopus Turonensis), *Libri historiarum X*, ed. Bruno Krusch and Wilhelm Levison, Monumenta Germaniae Historica, Scriptores rerum Merovingicarum, 1.1 (Hanover: Hahn, 1951), IX.5, p. 416: "Et multa alia signa apparuerunt, quae aut regis obitum adnunciare solent aut regiones excidium." See also V.33 (storms, a light traversing the sky, and an earthquake all precede the outbreak of an epidemic in V.34); VI.14 (fire and lights in sky and a rain of blood precede an epidemic of boils and tumors in the groin); IX.5–6 (a rain of snakes, flashes of lights, strange vessels bearing strange writing, floods, and odd growths all precede the appearance of a false Christ, Desiderius, whom Gregory specifically links to the false Christs of end times in Matthew 24:24). Gregory links the portents, plagues, and false prophets all together at the beginning of X.25 with apocalyptic quotations from Matt. 24: 7 ("And there shall be famines, and pestilences, and earthquakes") and Mark 13: 22 ("For false Christs and false prophets shall rise.").

35. Matthew Paris, *Chronica majora*, ed. Henry Richards Luard, 7 vols., Rerum Britannicarum Medii Aevi Scriptores (Rolls Series) 57 (London: Longmans, 1872–83), 5: 191–98:

> Notandum autem est, et non leviter attendendum, quod in nulla illarum quinquagenarum, scilicet viginti quatuor, sicut in ista ultima quinquagena, scilicet quae jam praeteriit, videlicet vicesima quinta, tot mirabilia et insolitae novitates evenerunt, ut in ultima. Et sunt quidam et multi historiarum scriptores et diligentes inspectores, qui dicunt, quod nec in omnibus aliis quinquagenis visa sunt tot prodigia et novitates admirandae, sicut in hac jam terminata. Et his tamen majora cum formidine expectantur. (191)

And at the chronicle's original end (he later changed his mind and continued the work up until his death in 1259), Matthew notes additionally, "It is thought to be not without significance that in this last year all the elements suffered unusual and improper degradation." ("Creditur quoque non vacare a significatione, quod omnia hoc ultimo anno elementa insolitum et irregulare passa sunt detrimentum" 5: 197). This reference to the four elements may be apocalyptic, too. In at least one enumeration of signs before Judgment Day, the author notes that "The natures will change/of each element, report that is most wondrous." The tenth-century Irish poem *Saltair na Rann*, strophe CLIX, as translated in William W. Heist, *The Fifteen Signs Before Doomsday* (East Lansing: Michigan State College Press, 1952), 12.

36. Matthew Paris, *Chronica majora*, 4:603: "quia, ut credebatur, significativus et insolitus in his partibus occidentalibus, necnon et innaturalis, cum soliditas Angliae cavernis terrestribus et profundis traconibus ac concavitatibus, in quibus secundum philosophos solet terraemotus generari, careat; nec inde ratio poterat indigari. Erat igitur, secundum minas Evangelii, [prope] finem mundi senescentis descriptus quasi per loca."

37. Matthew Paris, *Chronica majora*, 5: 192–93: "Una noctium visae sunt stellae infinitae cadere de caelo, ita quod simul et semel decem vel duodecim, hae in Oriente, hae in Occidente, Austro, et Aquilone, et in medio firmamenti, volitare viderentur, quae si essent verae stellae, nec una in caelo remansisset, nec potest inde in libro metheororum ratio reperiri manifesta, sed ut Christi comminatio mortalibus immineret, *Erunt signa in sole*, etc." (Luke 21: 25).

38. This is parallel to the scholastic redefinition of miracles as something *contra* or *praeter naturam*. In his commentary on book II of Lombard's *Sentences*, Thomas Aquinas classified miracles as *contra*, *supra*, or *praeter naturam*. *S. Thomae Aquinatis Opera Omnia*, vol. 1, *In Quattor Libros Sententiarum*, ed. Roberto Busa (Stuttgart: Frommann-Holzboog, 1980), bk. 2, dist. 18, ques. 1, art. 3: "[Miracula] autem quandoque sunt supra naturam, quandoque praeter naturam, quandoque contra naturam." See also Benedicta Ward, *Miracles and the Medieval Mind: Theory, Record, and Event, 1000–1215* (Philadelphia: University of Pennsylvania Press, 1982, 1987), 3–9; Laura Smoller, "Defining the Boundaries of the Natural in the Fifteenth Century: The Inquest into the Miracles of St. Vincent Ferrer (d. 1419)," *Viator* 28 (1997): 333–59; and Lorraine Daston, "Marvelous Facts and Miraculous Evidence in Early Modern Europe," *Critical Inquiry* 18 (1991): 93–124, which surveys definitions of the marvelous and the miraculous from Augustine through Francis Bacon. The eclipse at the crucifixion similarly was explained as not a natural event. See Laura Smoller, *History, Prophecy, and the Stars: The Christian Astrology of Pierre d'Ailly, 1350–1420* (Princeton, N.J.: Princeton University Press, 1994), 46, 160, n. 13. On the medieval "disenchantment of the world," see M.-D. Chenu, "Nature and Man: The Renaissance of the Twelfth Century," in Chenu, *Nature, Man, and Society in the Twelfth Century: Essays on New Theological Perspectives in the Latin West*, trans. Jerome Taylor and Lester K. Little (Chicago: University of Chicago Press, 1968), 11–18 (Chenu calls it a "desacralizing" of nature); Tullio Gregory, "La nouvelle idée de nature et de savoir scientifique au XIIe siècle," in John E. Murdoch and Edith D. Sylla, *The Cultural Context of Medieval Learning*, Boston Studies in the History and Philosophy of Science, 26 (Dordrecht

and Boston: D. Reidel, 1975), 193–218; and Daston and Park, *Wonders*, esp. 109–133. Later fourteenth-century authors extended this type of discussion, so that an author like Nicole Oresme could assert that all *mirabilia* can be explained by natural causes (even if these causes could not always be knowable by humans). Bert Hansen, *Nicole Oresme and the Marvels of Nature: The* De causis mirabilium (Toronto: Pontifical Institute of Mediaeval Studies, 1985), esp. 70–76.

39. The term "bleeding edge" refers to a technology that is so new—and therefore requires such a powerful system to use—that a company will actually lose customers by employing such technology in its web site. The term implies going too far too fast.

40. See the discussion of judicial astrology in part 4 of the *Opus maius*, in Roger Bacon, *Opus majus*, 1: 251–69. It has recently been argued that Bacon's condemnation by the Franciscan order in 1277 was because of the excessive claims he made for astrology's ability to predict religious change. See Paul Sidelko, "The Condemnation of Roger Bacon," *Journal of Medieval History* 22 (1996): 69–81. There is no contemporary evidence indicating what in Bacon's work was deemed offensive, however; Sidelko argues simply on the basis of Bacon's assertions about the stars' effects on religion.

41. Bacon, *Opus majus*, 1:269: "Scio quod si ecclesia vellet revolvere textum sacrum et prophetias sacras, atque prophetias Sibyllae, et Merlini et Aquilae, et Sestonis, Joachim et multorum aliorum, insuper historias et libros philosophorum, atque juberet considerari vias astronomiae, inveniretur sufficiens suspicio vel magis certitudo de tempore Antichristi."

42. See Smoller, *History, Prophecy, and the Stars*, 33, 152–53; S. J. Tester, *A History of Western Astrology* (Woodbridge, Suffolk: Boydell Press, 1987), 177; and Philippe Contamine, "Les prédictions annuelles astrologiques à la fin du Moyen Age: genre littéraire et témoin de leur temps," in *Histoire sociale, sensibilités collectives et mentalités: mélanges Robert Mandrou* (Paris: Presses Universitaires de France, 1985), 192 (listing twenty-seven condemned propositions dealing with astrology).

43. Arnau de Vilanova, *De tempore adventus Antichristi*, ed. Heinrich Finke, *Aus den Tagen Bonifaz VIII: Funde und Forschungen*, Vorreformationsgeschichtliche Forschungen 2 (Münster: Aschendorff, 1902), p. cxxxiv: "suam potentiam et sapientiam Deus non alligavit naturalibus causis. Set sicut in productione mundi fuit supernaturaliter operatus, sic et in consummatione huius seculi supernaturaliter operabitur."

44. John of Paris, *Tractatus de Antichristo*, ed. in Sara Beth Peters Clark, "The *Tractatus de Antichristo* of John of Paris: A Critical Edition, Translation, and Commentary," Ph.D. diss., Cornell University, 1981, 46–47, 59–62; John dismisses astrology's claims to offer any certainty about the time of Antichrist's arrival. See also Laura Smoller, "The Alfonsine Tables and the End of the World: Astrology and Apocalyptic Calculation in the Later Middle Ages," in Alberto Ferreiro, ed., *The Devil, Heresy and Witchcraft in the Middle Ages: Essays in Honor of Jeffrey B. Russell* (Leiden: E. J. Brill, 1998), 211–39.

45. Henry of Harclay, *Utrum astrologi vel quicumque calculatores possint probare secundum adventum Christi*, in Franz Pelster, ed., "Die Questio Heinrichs von Harclay über die zweite Ankunft Christi und die Erwartung des baldigen Weltendes zu Anfang des XIV Jahrhunderts," *Archivio Italiano per la Storia della Pietà* 1 (1951): 82.

46. Ibid., 82: "*Ad argumentum principale*, cum arguitur: in diebus ultimis post

tribulacionem sol contenebrabitur etc., dicendum quod tale signum erit miraculosum ante finem mundi, non naturalis eclipsis."

47. The astrologer was John of Aschenden (Joannis Eschuid). See Smoller, "Alfonsine Tables," 220–21, and the references therein.

48. John Clynn, *Annales hiberniae*, in Richard Butler, ed., *The Annals of Ireland by Friar John Clyn, of the Convent of Friars Minor, Kilkenny, and Thady Dowling, Chancellor of Leighlin, Together with the Annals of Ross* (Dublin: Irish Archaeological Society, 1849), 36: "De ista pestilencia facta est visio mirabilis (ut dicebatur) anno precedenti scilicet 1347, in claustro Cisterciensium Tripolis, sub hac forma; quidam monachus celebravit missam coram abbate suo, uno ministro presente, et inter ablucionem et communionem misse apparuit quedam manus scribens super corporale in quo predictus monachus confecerat. 'Cedrus alta Libani succendetur.'" Clynn's entry describing the plague has been translated in Horrox, *Black Death*, 82–84.

49. John Clynn, *Annales hiberniae*, 36: "Non est auditum a principio seculi tot homines pestilencia, fame aut quacunque infirmitate tanto tempore mortuos in orbe; nam terre motus, qui per miliaria multa se extendebat, civitates, villas, et castra subvertebat absorbuit et subversit; pestis ista villas, civitates, castra et oppida homine habitatore omnino privavit, ut vix esset qui in eis habitaret."

50. Ibid., 28–29.

> Item, die Martis, scilicet xv. Kal: Decembris, fuit maxima inundancia aque, qualis a xlta. annis ante non est visa; que pontes, molendina et edificia funditus evertit et asportavit; solum altare magnum et gradus altaris de tota abbacia Fratrum Minorum Kilkennie, aqua non attigit nec cooperuit. Hic annus fuit tempestuosus nimis et nocivus hominibus et animalibus; quia a festo Omnium Sanctorum usque Pascha, ut plurimum fuit pluvia, nix, aut gelu . . . Hoc anno boves et vacce moriebantur, et oves precipue, fere sunt desctructe . . . Item, in hoc anno in quadragesima, salices in Anglia rosas protulerunt, que ad diversas terras pro spectaculo sunt advecte.

Then Clynn lists a number of battles, duels, and murders, none of which is clearly said to be foreshadowed by these portents. Perhaps he simply enumerated these signs in the hopes that their meanings would become clear later.

51. Clynn, *Annales hiberniae*, 36: "Tunc passagium erit commune ab omnibus fidelibus ultra aquas congregatas ad Terram Sanctam." The consolatory power of such prophecies is a major theme of Lerner's in *Powers of Prophecy* and "Black Death and Eschatological Mentalities."

52. John of Winterthur, *Die Chronik Johanns von Winterthur*, ed. C. Brun and Friedrich Baethgen, Monumenta Germaniae Historica, Scriptores rerum germanicarum, nova series 3, pp. 275–76:

> Item eodem anno [1348] in fine Ianuarii in conversione sancti Pauli factus est terre motus magnus, qui in Longobardia multas turres deiecit, menia scidit vinaque in doliis turbulenta fecit. Villach quoque civitatem Karinthie subvertit. . . . Anno Domini MCCCXLVIII. tempore hyemali vel circa principium veris in partibus ultramarinis exorta est mortalitas seu pestilencia tam grandis, quod infinitam

et inestimabilem multitudinem infidelium absorbuit et absummpsit. . . . Predicta, scilicet terre motus et pestilencia, precurrencia mala sunt extreme voraginis et tempestatis secundum verbum salvatoris in ewangelio dicentis: "Erunt terre motus per loca et pestilencia et fames" et cetera.

John of Winterthur's chronicle ends in the year 1348; it is likely that he died in the plague.

53. *Historia Roffensis*, as translated in Horrox, *Black Death*, 73. The chronicle does note that the plague began in the east: "A great mortality of men began in India and, raging through the whole of infidel Syria and Egypt, and also through Greece, Italy, Provence and France, arrived in England, where the same mortality destroyed more than a third of the men, women and children" (Horrox, *Black Death*, 70).

54. Heinrich von Hervordia, *Liber de rebus memorabilioribus*, 268:

Sed et inter ecclesiasticos, seculares et religiosos eo tempore dissentiones, rebelliones, conspirationes, conjurationes et conventiones ubilibet et vallidissime sunt exorte, sicut predixerat apostolus II. Thim. 3. et 2. Cor. 12. Sed et alie tumultuationes, puerorum contra senes, ignobilium contra nobiles, in civitatibus, monasteriis et congregationibus plurimis seditiones et generales et particulares plurime temporibus hiis exstiterunt. Heresis etiam symoniaca tantum invaluit in clero et tam exuberanter inundavit, ut quilibet quanticumque status, maximus, mediocris et parvus, et qualiscumque, scilicet secularis vel religiosus, et quomodolibet etiam manifeste emeret et venderet spirituale quodcumque, nec verecundaretur, nec a quoquam corriperetur vel reprehendetur. . . . Prebendas etiam et personatus et dignitates ecclesiasticas alias omnes, ecclesias parrochyales, cappellas, vicarias et altaria pro pecunia, pro mulieribus et quandoque pro concubinis commutabant, in ludo taxillorum exponebant, perdebant et acquirebant. Tunc tumultuationes et decertationes pro regnis, principatibus, archiepiscopatibus, episcopatibus, prebendis et aliis hujusmodi plurimi plurimas habuerunt.

55. Ibid., 280: "Eodem anno gens sine capite, sui multitudine et adventus sui subitatione mirabilis universis, ex omnibus subito Theutonie partibus exsurgunt."

56. The prophecy reads, in part: "The high Cedar of Lebanon will be felled, and Tripoli will soon be destroyed and Acre captured. . . . Within fifteen years there will be one God and one faith. The other god will vanish. The sons of Israel will be liberated from captivity. A certain people (*gens*) who are called without a head will come." Translation quoted from Lerner, *Powers of Prophecy*, 74 (the version that began to circulate shortly after the fall of Acre in 1291).

57. Heinrich von Hervordia, *Liber de rebus memorabilioribus*, 277: "Gens sine capite flagellariorum adventum Anticristi prenuntiavit." The sense is that the flagellants were a sign of the approach of Antichrist, not that they themselves verbally proclaimed Antichrist's advent. Heinrich does not describe them as preaching about the apocalypse.

58. Ibid.: "Principium autem regni Karoli istius multum videtur memorabile propter monstra et portenta et singularia plurima, que tunc apparuerunt."

59. That is, in Robert Lerner's felicitous phrase, the "uncertainty principle" of Acts 1:7: "It is not for you to know the times or the seasons, which the Father hath

put in his own power." See Lerner, "Refreshment of the Saints: The Time After Antichrist as a Station for Earthly Progress in Medieval Thought," *Traditio* 32 (1976): 97–144 (p. 103).

60. Heinrich von Hervordia, *Liber de rebus memorabilioribus*, 289: "Et nota, quod annus iste Karoli regis, scilicet octavus, fuit annus ab origine mundi 5317., ab egressu Noe de archa 3661., a nativitate Abrahe 3369., a principio regni David 2427., ab exterminio regni Judeorum jam facto et principio etatis quinte 1944., ab incarnatione filii Dei 1355., . . ."

61. Richard Landes, "Lest the Millennium Be Fulfilled: Apocalyptic Expectations and the Pattern of Western Chronography, 100–800 c.e.," in *The Use and Abuse of Eschatology*, ed. Werner Verbeke, Daniel Verhelst, and Andries Welkenhuysen, 137–211. Such speculations could focus on the world's 6500th or 7000th year as well as on its completion of six millennia. See Smoller, *History, Prophecy, and the Stars*, 88.

62. Heinrich von Hervordia, *Liber de rebus memorabilioribus*, 289: "Residuum tempus etatis istius sexte soli Deo notum est. Non enim est hominis, nosse tempora vel momenta, que pater posuit in sua potestate."

63. Ibid., 290. Heinrich cites Augustine, *De civitate dei*, 22: 30: "Etas autem septima, que animarum quiescentium est et ab ascensione Domini, janua quietis aperta, initium habuit, usque in presens una cum etate sexta decurrit, sed et deinceps usque in finem mundi simul cum ista protenditur."

64. *Breve Chronicon clerici anonymi*, 14: "et ceciderunt fulgura et choruscationes mixte cum grandinibus mire magnitudinis super terram, que occiderunt quasi omnes hominis, a majori usque ad minimum."

65. Ibid., 22–23: "Eodem anno [1349], IIIo nonas junii, cum magna pluvia, choruscatione et tonitruo, Brugis et in territoriis ejus grando ad quantitatem ovorum cecidit, cum diversis faciebus, formis, oculis et caudis, que multis stupori fuit."

66. See Suzanne Lewis, *Reading Images: Narrative Discourse and Reception in the Thirteenth-Century Illuminated Apocalypse* (Cambridge and New York: Cambridge University Press, 1995), esp. 186–87.

67. See Lewis, *Reading Images*, 164.

68. The Neuberg chronicle for the year 1342 also reports that the four elements were confused (there was also an earthquake that year), *Continuatio novimontensis*, 672. The confusion of the four elements is also an apocalyptic sign. See note 35 above.

69. This was not really a triple conjunction, but a series of conjunctions of Mars and Jupiter (March 1), Mars and Saturn (March 4), and Jupiter and Saturn (March 21). See Bernard R. Goldstein and David Pingree, *Levi ben Gerson's Prognostication for the Conjunction of 1345*, Transactions of the American Philosophical Society 80, pt. 6 (Philadelphia: American Philosophical Society, 1990), 52.

70. *Opinion of the Paris Medical Faculty*, part 1, chap. 1, pp. 153–54.

71. Ibid., part 1, chap. 2, pp. 154–55.

72. Ibid., part 1, chap. 3, p. 155: "Idcirco si futura hyems fuerit pluuiosa multum et minus debito frigida epydimiam circa finem hyemis ut in tempore veris tememus futuram."

73. Ibid.:

quia non diximus futuram pestilentiam fore valde periculosam, nolumus intelligere quod sit adeo periculosa sicut in partibus meredionalibus [sic] vel orientalibus. coniunctiones enim et alie causa predicte partes istas plus quam nostras respexerunt. ista tamen cum indiciis [iudiciis?] astrologorum secundum dictum ptolomei inter necessarium et possible sunt reponenda amplius quia uise fuerunt exalationes et inflammationes quam plurime, veluti draco et sydera volantia.

(It is not entirely clear from the syntax here whether the doctors mean that these signs appeared only in the south and east or happened closer to home as well.) Horrox translates *draco* as comet, but the physicians must have in mind not a *cometa*, but rather the specific form of "fire in the sky" known as *Assub*, as described in Albertus Magnus's *De meteoris*, which can take the appearance of a flying dragon. Albertus Magnus, *De meteoris*, 1.4.8, in August Borgnet, ed., *B. Alberti Magni Ratisbonensis episcopi, ordinis praedicatorum, opera omnia*, 37 vols. (Paris: Vivès, 1890), 4: 514: "Quando autem materia est inaequaliter subtilis et simul elevata, anterior pars quae prius frigido tangitur, expellitur, quam sequitur alia grossior: et ideo apparet in modum trabis: trabs autem ista cum expellitur si obviat ei frigus, incurvatur, et apparet ad modum draconis flexuosi: et hoc est quidem quod quidam dicunt se vidisse dracones volantes per aerem." (See Horrox, *Black Death*, 162; she interprets the "comet" as a mysterious star seen over Paris in August 1348 and reported by Jean de Venette.)

74. *Opinion of the Paris Medical Faculty*, part 1, chap. 3, p. 155:

color eciam celi yctericius et aer subruens propter fumos adustos fequentius solito apparuit. fulgura etiam et choruscationis incense multe et frequentes, tonitrua et venti adeo impetuosi et validi ut puluerem multum terreum commouerent a partibus meridionalibus venientes, qui omnibus aliis deteriores existunt cito putrefactionis corpora magis disponentes, presertim terre motus fortes et multitudo piscium bestialium et aliorum mortuorum in litore maris, nec non in pluribus partibus arbores puluere cooperte. quidam et vidisse se fatentur ranarum et reptilium multitudinem que ex putrefactione generantur; que omnia magnam in aere et terra putrefactionem precedere videntur.

75. Ibid., p. 156: "nimirum igitur si epydimiam venire futuris temporibus timeamus."

76. See, e.g., Albertus Magnus, *De causis proprietatum elementorum*, 1.2.13, in Paul Hossfeld, ed., *Alberti Magni ordinis fratrum praedicatorum, episcopi, opera omnia* (Münster: Aschendorff, 1980), vol. 5, part 2, p. 86: "Similiter autem et in generatione animalium similium in corpore, sicut sunt serpentes et vermes et pisces; videmus enim quosdam lacus novos fieri, in quibus generantur per se et pisces et vermium multa genera. Et hoc ostendunt animalia nata ex putrefactione, quae generans univocum nullum omnino habent."

77. Martha R. Baldwin, "Toads and Plague: Amulet Therapy in Seventeenth-Century Medicine," *Bulletin for the History of Medicine* 67 (1993): 227–47. The toad amulet was attributed to Paracelsus.

78. Many of these signs also appear in lists of the fifteen signs before Doomsday. See the various versions in Heist, *Fifteen Signs*, 24–29.

79. *Utrum mortalitas, que fuit hijs annis, fit ab ultione divina propter iniquitates hominum vel a cursu quodam naturali*. The treatise appears in Erfurt, Amploniana, MS

Quart-Cod. 230, fol. 146v–148v. I am relying on the edition in Karl Sudhoff, "Pest-schriften aus den ersten 150 Jahren nach der Epidemie des 'schwarzen Todes' 1348, XI. Ausarbeitungen über die Pest vor Mitte des 15. Jahrhunderts entstanden im niederen Deutschland," *Archiv für Geschichte der Medizin* 11 (1918–19): 44–51.

80. This objection is not entirely astrologically correct because astrologers fre-quently attributed effects to conjunctions long after the fact and particularly argued that the slowest-moving planets, Jupiter and Saturn, had the longest-lasting effects. See Smoller, *History, Prophecy, and the Stars*, 20, 74.

81. *Utrum mortalitas fit ab ultione divina*, 47: "Qua propter quarta opinio, quam probabiliorem alijs credo, sit ista in sensu conditionis et locacionis Ypocratis videli-cet, quod si ex naturali cursu facta est mortalitas sepedicta, tunc eius tam per se et inmediata est exalacio terrestris corrupta et venenosa, que aerea in diuersis mundi partibus infecit, et inspirata hominibus ipsos suuffocauit subita quadam extinccione."

82. Ibid., 48:

> aer vaporosus et plenus fumo terrestri diu clausus et incarceratus in aliquo man-sorio terre adeo corrumpitur, ut venenum efficatiuum humane nature efficiatur et precipue in cauernis et ventribus terre, ubi per nouum et recentem aerem aduentari non poterit illud propter experientijs quam plurimis, sumptis a puteis longo tempore desertis et superius obstructis per plurimos annos. Nam quando tales putei aperiuntur et purgari debent, accidit nonnumquam, quod primus qui ingreditur suffocatur et quandoque mutuo sibi succedentes. Et vulgares tantum ignorantes basiliscum putant intus latitare.

(The basilisk is a mythical reptile whose very look was said to kill.)

83. Ibid.: "Certum fundamentum est, quod motus terre causatur ab exalatione terre suo fumo clauso in visceribus terre, qui quando pulsat cum impetu ad latera terre et ex illis non patet, terram quassat et mouet illam, ut patet ex philosophia naturali."

84. Ibid.:

> Tunc [?] dico, quod maximus vapor et aer corruptus, qui egressus est in terre motu purgandi, videlicet que accidit anno dominj M^0ccc^0 47 [1347] S. pauli et similiter aer corruptus in clausorijs terre, que preterea [?] in alijs motibus et eleua-cionibus terre egressus est, aerem super terram infecit, et homines in diuersis mundi partibus interfecit. . . . Mortalitas quantum ad partes Almanie primo in-cepit, in Carinthea post terre motum in eo loco.

Other authors give various dates for this earthquake on the Feast of the Conversion of St. Paul: Heinrich of Herford puts it in 1345 (Heinrich von Hervordia, *Liber de rebus memorabilioribus*, 268); the Neuberg chronicle puts it in 1348 (*Continuatio novimonten-sis*, 674); John of Winterthur places it in 1348 (John of Winterthur, *Die Chronik*, 275).

85. *Utrum mortalitas fit ab ultione divina*, 49: "Octaua ratio est, ut recitant Auicenna et Albertus, quod in aliquibus terre motibus homines in lapides trans-substanciati sunt et precipue in lapides salis propter fortem virtutem mineralem in vaporibus terrestribus existentem; igitur possibile est quod a uaporibus aliter dispo-sitis in terra infectos homines communiter moriuntur."

86. *Continuatio novimontensis*, 674.

87. Aristotle, *Meteorologica*, ed. and trans. H. D. P. Lee (Cambridge, Mass.: Harvard University Press, 1952), 2.7–2.8, pp. 198–223.

88. Albertus Magnus, *De meteoris*, 3.2.6, 3.2.9, 3.2.12. The explanation of the darkened sky and of pestilence comes in 3.2.12 (ed. Borgnet, 4:629):

> Scias etiam, quod frequenter pestilentia praecipue omnem sequitur terraemotum: vapor enim inclusus et privatus sic luce et aere libero grosso est habens quasi veneni naturam, et ideo animalia interficit, praecipue quae terrae quasi semper proximum os tenent, sicut oves: quia antequam totus erumpat vapor, per plures dies semper aliquid ejus paulatim per poros terrae evadit, et laedit animalia pastum in loco terraemotus accipientia, et continue os juxta terram habentia.

See note 121.

89. *Tractatus Petrus de Eliaco episcopi Cameracensis super libros Metheororum* (Strasbourg: Johann Prüs, 1504), fol. XIII:

> Sciendum quod vapores calidi et sicci pro magna parte includuntur infra terram . . . Istos autem vapores vocat Aristoteles spiritus propter eorum agitationem siue subtilitatem: qui quidem spiritus mouentur sum magno impetu infra terram et quando non potuerint habere liberum egressum exeuntes propter partes terrae circumstantes reuerberantur ad locum terrae: ex qua reverberatione agitatur terra siue mouetur motu tremulo.

> 90. Ibid., fol. XIIIIv.
> 91. Ibid.:

> Quandoque in terremotu (maxime quando mouent motu pulsus et non tremoris) elevantur vapores et lapides de terra per modum ebulitionis sicut corpora grauia ebulentia in caldarijs. Causa est: quia vapor infra terram inclusus successiue exiens de terra per unam partem eleuat lapides de terra: et de illis lapidibus sic descendentibus alios elevat per eos exeuntes de eodem et sic continui leuando lapides primus lapis videtur facere quandam ebulitionem.

92. Ibid., fol. XIIIv: "Huius terrae motus similitudo (secundum Aristotelem) in corporibus animalium habent. Videmus enim animalia moueri motu tremulo in paralisi: et in huiusmodi infirmitatibus." Tetanus and spasms are both motions of the wind, according to Aristotle, *Meteorology*, 2.8.

93. *Tractatus Petrus de Eliaco*, fol. XIII v.:

> Unde secondum Aristotelem huiusmodi tremor fit a quibusdam spiritibus supra-callefactis per naturam discurrentibus infra corpus animalium: et reuertuntur ad diuersas partes intrinsecas. Ex qua reuersione sequitur motus tremulus totius corporis. Aliquando fit etiam in hominibus post effusionem vrinae: quando per vias naturales vrinales subingrediuntur quidam spiritus, id est, vapores subtiles qui postea discurrunt per partes alias intrinsecas et faciunt tremorem totius corporis quousque per poros corporis exeunt.

94. Ibid., fol. XIIIIv–XV:

Item mouetur terra motu supradicto et huiusmodi terremotus saliendo sicut in febribus febres tertianae vel quartanae animalium: cum cessant febres iterum per alios dies reueniunt vt in quarto die: vel citra: vel quandoque post. Cuius causa est: quoniam prima cessatione febris non sufficienter fuit expulsa. sed derelinquebatur pars in corpore: quae non fuit sufficiens ad continuandum motum febrilem. sed huiusmodi multiplicatur a ratione male regiminis: iterum mouet corpus et facit paralisim.

95. Albertus Magnus's *De meteoris* also provides natural explanations for others of the portents that mark the outbreak of the Black Death, such as fire falling from the sky (1.1.4 and 1.1.5) and rains of stones (3.3.20).

96. Heinrich von Hervordia, *Liber de rebus memorabilioribus*, 277: "Principium autem regni Karoli istius multum videtur memorabile propter monstra et portenta et singularia plurima, que tunc apparuerunt."

97. Ibid., 268, 277, 280.

98. Ibid., 258:

Vicesimo tertio anno Lodewici pluvia sanguinis fuit in Erphordia Thuringie colore rubicundissimo. . . . Item hoc anno in Confluentia, ubi Mosella Renum influit, puella novem annorum a coco patris sui gravidatur et filium pulchrum peperit. Quod monstruosum est, sicut et illud, quod factum fuit in Sosato eodem anno. Ibi siquidem puella nascitur mamillis tumentibus, pilos et sub ascellis et in inguine habens, et fluxum menstruorum patiens, sicut esset 18 annorum. Cui per omnia simile ponit Albertus secundo phisicorum, tractatu tertio, cap. 3, dicens: Temporibus meis presentata fuit puella, que nata fuit dependentibus uberibus, cum pilis inguinis et ascellarum, et fatebatur mater ejus, quod etiam patiebatur resolutionem menstruorum. Quod absque dubio accidit propter fortitudinem caloris formantis et maturantis. Hec Albertus.

Quoting Albertus Magnus, *Physica*, 2.3.3, as in Paul Hossfeld, ed., *Alberti Magni ordinis fratrum praedicatorum, episcopi, opera omnia* (Münster: Aschendorff, 1987), vol. 4, part 1, p. 137.

99. Heinrich von Hervordia, *Liber de rebus memorabilioribus*, 258: "Cujus guttas in albo lineo panno receptas ego ipse vidi." Daston and Park remark that reports of prodigies are frequently accompanied by careful verification and location. *Wonders*, 52–57.

100. Heinrich von Hervordia, *Liber de rebus memorabilioribus*, 268–70.

101. Ibid., 270: "Item hoc anno [1346] in Sosato opido Westphalie natus est agnus cum duobus capitibus. Quorum caput inferius fuit sicut agni, superius autem sicut avis. Quod videtur et portentum fuisse et virtuti stellarum attribuendum." (Note that this prodigy occurs in the same town in which the sexually mature baby girl was born in 1337, according to Heinrich.) There is a two-headed human "monster" whose birth serves as a portent of plague in the chronicle of Matteo Villani, *Cronica di Matteo Villani*, ed. Gherardi Dragomanni, 2 vols. (Florence: Coen, 1846), 1: 14, and another

in the chronicle of the monastery of Meaux, *Chronica Monasterii de Melsa*, 69–70: "Et paulo quidem ante haec tempora [earthquake and plague of 1348–49], erat quoddam monstrum humanum in Anglia, ab umbilico et sursum divisum, masculus scilicet et foemina, et in inferiori parte connexum. . . . Solebant namque dulcissime simul cantare." Albertus Magnus says that such "monsters" are born (as are twins) when the mother takes excessive delight in the sexual act (*Physica*, 2.3.3, p. 137):

> Sunt enim quaedam mulieres et quaedem animalium, quae multum in coitu delectantur, et in delectatione illa movetur matrix, cum sperma infunditur nervis sensibilibus eius, et in motu illo dividitur sperma. Cum ergo divisio tota perficitur, tunc fiunt gemini, si coalescit semen in fetum. Si autem divisio non perficitur, sed sperma quasi ramificatur, tunc fiunt bicorporea animalia subtus vel supra vel etiam in medio secundum modum, per quem dividitur sperma.

102. Heinrich von Hervordia, *Liber de rebus memorabilioribus*, 270 (following Albertus Magnus, *Physica*, 2.3.3, p. 138):

> Porce quandoque pariunt porcellos cum capitibus humanis et hujusmodi. Quod ex seminum commixtione fieri non potest, quia semina valde diversa in specie se invicem corrumpunt, et nichil generatur ex eis. Sed potius fit hoc per constellationem moventem semen ad illam formam extra qualitatem suam; sicut est illud, quod dicit Ptolomeus in quadripartito, quod, in quadam parte arietis existentibus luminaribus et quibusdam planetis aliis, non potest fieri generatio humana.

See Igor Gorevich, *O kentavrah i rusalkah: raznovidnosti i granitsy* (Of Centaurs and Mermaids: Boundaries and Species), vol. 3 of his *O kritike antropologii zhivotnikh* (Toward a Critique of Animal Anthropology) (Kishinev: Kabul, 1987).

103. Heinrich von Hervordia, *Liber de rebus memorabilioribus* (following Albertus Magnus, *De meteoris*, 2.1.21, p. 536):

> Quia pluvia fit de vapore multum habente de terrestri, ideo, cum suavis est, aliquando cum pluvia generantur multa animalia aquatica, sicut ranunculi et pisces parvuli et vermes. Cujus causa est, quia calidum, quod est in nube, cum evaporare incipit, trahit secum humidum subtile, quod in si habet aliquid de subtili terreo bene commixto; et ideo est viscosum. Cum autem viscosum ducitur ad aerem, incipit durescere et in pellem constare. In qua continue pulsans calidum, efficit spiritum. Cui additur anima sensibilis virtute stellarum Et tunc fit animal. Fiunt autem hec ut plurimum aquatica, quia in tale pluvia vincit aqua.

104. Ibid. (following Albertus Magnus, *De meteoris*, 3.3.20, p. 663): "Corpora autem perfectorum animalium raro formantur in nube, licet hoc semel dicat Avicenna contigisse, quod corpus vituli de nube cecidit. Et hoc ipse maxime attribuit virtuti stellarum in tempore illo formam vituli imprimentium."

105. Ibid., 277: "Gens sine capite flagellariorum adventum Antichristi prenuntiavit."

106. Ibid., 281: "Vidi, cum se flagellarent, aliquando ferramenta dicta carni taliter infigi, quod uno tractu quandoque, quandoque duobus, non extrahebantur. . . . Cor lapideum esset, quod talia sine lacrimis posset aspicere."

107. Ibid., 282–84: "Ex tractatu de flagellariis hiis, quem edidit Gerhardus de Cosvelde, rector scolarium in civitate Monasteriensi Westphalie, cum secta ista cursum suum cepisset et potissime vigeret et non cito desitura putaretur." Because this passage is little known to modern scholars, it seems worth describing at length here. In his edition of Heinrich's chronicle, August Potthast was not able to identify either Gerhardus or his treatise (p. xx), nor was it known to Richard Kieckhefer (personal communication). Horrox mentions but does not translate this astrological section in her excerpts from Heinrich's chronicle (Horrox, *Black Death*, 150).

108. Heinrich von Hervordia, *Liber de rebus memorabilioribus*, 283: "Et sol fuit dominus anni in eadem significatione. Et aries erat domus tertia, cadens ab angulo medie noctis, qui appellatur domus terre. Et in eodem signo erat Saturnus combustus radio solis. Huic signo jungebatur pisces in eadem domo tertia, que erat cadens. In quo erat Mars et Mercurius, similiter cadentes cum piscibus." And 284: "Domus 3. cadens ab angulo noctis 6. gradu arietis. In hac domo sunt omnes significatores hujus secte, pro qua est questio facta, scil. Sol, Pisces, Mars, Merc., Saturnus." A horoscope divides the heavens into twelve artificial divisions called mundane houses (or places or sometimes simply houses); each of the twelve mundane houses was said to have significance for some different aspect of life. There is something wrong here, however, either in Heinrich's copying or in Gerhardus's calculations. In Heinrich's quotation of Gerhardus at least, the planets of Mars and Mercury are in the sign of Pisces, which would have to fall within the second house in his horoscope and not the third if the third house indeed begins with Aries 6°.

109. Ibid.: "Est ergo calculatio talis: Sol in ariete, que fuit domus tertie, multiplicat religionem et sectam. Nam domus tertia est fidei et religionis et mutationis, ut patet in Alkabitio, doctrina prima: de naturis domorum et earum significationibus." Alchabitius and most authors more commonly make the ninth mundane house the signifier of religion, but Gerhardus's interpretation is possible according to Alchabitius. See Alchabitius (al-Kabisi, al-Qabisi), *Alchabitius cum commento: noviter impresso* (Venice: Melchior Sessa, 1506), fol. 7: "Tertia domus est fratrum et sororum et propinquorum ac dilectorum fidei atque religionis mandatorum ac legatorum mutationum atque itinerum minorum et significat esse vite ante mortem."

110. Heinrich von Hervordia, *Liber de rebus memorabilioribus*, 283: "Et incipit hec religio ab oriente, quia aries est signum orientale, ut patet ibidem. Et respicit precipue Alemanniam, ut dicit glosator super Alkabitium in doctrina predicta. Quare hec secta precipue vigebat in Alemannia." See Alchabitius, *Alchabitius cum commento*, fol. 2v: "Aries ergo Leo et Sagittarius faciunt triplicitatem primam: quia unumquodque istorum signorum est igneum masculinum diurnum calidum scilicet et siccum colericum. sapore amarum est quoque et hec triplicitas orientalis. Cuius domini sunt in die sol et in nocte Jupiter et eorum particeps in die ac nocte est Saturnus." The assigning of various regions to various signs was not at all standard; there were many variations.

111. Heinrich von Hervordia, *Liber de rebus memorabilioribus*, 283: "Verumtamen, quia Mars conjunctus Mercurio, testatur super percussiones acuum et sanguinis effusionem, ut patet ibidem, doctrina secunda: de naturis planetarum cap. de Marte. Et Mercurius e converso testatur super percussiones flagellorum, ibidem cap. de Mercurio." Cf. Alchabitius, fol. 10: "Mars masculinus nocturnus malus . . . et natura eius colorica amari saporis et ex magisteriis omne magisterium igneum et quod fit per ferrum et ignem: sicut est percussio gladiorum cum martellis. Cumque ei complecti-

tur Saturnus significat percussionem ferri . . . Si mercurius percussionem acuum," and fol. IIv: "Si [Mercurio complectitur] Mars significat . . . numerum percussionum flagellorum atque clavarum."

112. Heinrich von Hervordia, *Liber de rebus memorabilioribus*, 283: "Et quia isti [Mars et Mercurius] erant in domo Jovis simul in predicto tempore in eadem domo tertia, cadente cum sole, induxerunt hominibus hujus secte penitentias per flagellationes acuum, et non sine ypocrisi, ut patet ibidem" (in addition to the mundane houses, each planet is assigned a particular sign that is its domus or domicile or mansion, in which it has particular strength). Cf. *Alchabitius cum commento*, fol. IIv: "Et significat ex sectis culturam unitatis et horum similia: et hoc secreto cum hypocrisia et simulatione."

113. Heinrich von Hervordia, *Liber de rebus memorabilioribus*, 283: "Et quia aries respicit caput, ut omnes concedunt, in quo fuit Saturnus cum sole, supponunt peregrini hujus secte pilleum griseum ante oculos, facientem Saturninum aspectum."

114. Ibid.: "Item hec secta horrendum facit casum ad terram. Cujus causa sine dubio est, quia sol et Saturnus et alii ejus significatores in predicto tempore ceciderunt ab angulo terre." The 3d, 6th, 9th, and 12th houses are considered "cadents"; the 2d, 5th, 8th, and 11th, succedents; while the 1st, 4th, 7th, and 10th mundane houses are the angles or *cardines*. Thus the sun and Saturn, in the third mundane house, are "cadent."

115. Ibid.: "Sed diceretur: que est causa nuditatis eorum? Dico, quod combustus Saturnus et ejus vilitas, quia sic adhuc est in domo sui casus. Sed Venus existens in domo Saturni addidit verendis, tybiis et cruribus ipsorum albam vestem. Nam testatur super vestes muliebres et pudibunda." Each planet has a particular degree of the zodiac in which it has an access of power, its exaltation; the opposite sign marks a low degree of influence, the planet's fall or dejection (*casus*).

116. Ibid.: "Dicunt ipsi, tabulam lapideam sectam hanc continentem per angelum de celo venisse. Quod teste Deo fingunt et mentiuntur. Sed causa fictionis et dicti eorum est Saturnus cadens, qui testatur super res graves, ut sunt lapides, et super oracula et super apparitores rerum secretarum." On the so-called Heavenly Letter, see Lerner, "Black Death and Eschatological Mentalities," 537; Richard Kieckhefer, "Radical Tendencies in the Flagellant Movement of the Mid-Fourteenth Century," *Journal of Medieval and Renaissance Studies* 4 (1974): 165–66; and (with caution) Norman Cohn, *The Pursuit of the Millennium*, rev. ed. (New York: Oxford University Press, 1961, 1970), 129–34.

117. Heinrich von Hervordia, *Liber de rebus memorabilioribus*, 283:

> Notandum etiam, quod scorpio, signum dolositatis et mendacii, in dicto tempore fuit in medio celi. Quapropter infinita mendacia sectam hanc precedunt et secuntur; immo major laus et gloria hujus secte est in mendaciis. Nam medium celi est domus Jovis et glorie et sublimationis, ut ibidem doctrina secunda: de naturis domorum. Hec tamen mendacia vulgus appellat miracula propter fidem Jovis. Item hec secta nullum habet fundamentum stabile, quia omnia signa rerum eam testantia sunt instabilia propter scorpionem.

See Alchabitius, *Alchabitius cum commento*, fol. 10r, on Jupiter: "et [Jupiter] significat fidem et appetitum in bonis." On the long tradition of beliefs about Scorpio's baleful influence, see Luigi Aurigemma, *Le signe zodiacal du Scorpion dans les traditions occiden-tales de l'Antiquité gréco-latine à la Renaissance* (Paris: La Haye, 1976). There are errors in the horoscope as printed in Potthast's edition (or as Heinrich copied it or Ger-hardus erected it). There is no indication of which sign begins the 10th house, but it must be Scorpio, given the reference in the text and the order of signs. That makes the horoscope in error as to the ascendant, which is given as Scorpio 14°, but which must be Capricorn 14°.

118. Heinrich von Hervordia, *Liber de rebus memorabilioribus*, 283–84: "Alia causa brevitatis pretermitto, sed dico, quod estimatione mea *secta hec pure naturalis est*, et quod agitantur quadam specie furie, que vocatur mania. Et possibile est, quod in ali-qua parte mundi fiat persecutio cleri ab hac secta. Et secta non diu durabit, sed cito et cum confusione et infamia finem habebit." (emphasis added)

119. Within a paragraph, however, Heinrich returns to the subject of the plague, which he describes through a lengthy quotation from Ovid's *Metamorphoses* (VIII, 523 seq.), in which the poet tells of a plague sent as punishment by Juno, which is lifted only after prayers and vows are made to Jupiter. If he means to imply similarly a divine origin for the Black Death, he does not spell this out for his readers. Heinrich von Hervordia, *Liber de rebus memorabilioribus*, 284–85.

120. Ibid., 285–86:

Quarto anno Karoli [1351] in opido Hamelen supra Mindam in metis West-phalie et Saxonie pestis quedam singularis oboritur. Siquidem fovea fodiebatur, purgabatur et eruderabatur in area civis cujusdam ibidem. Fossor existens in imo, subito, nescitur a quo tactus, corruit et exspiravit. Alius descendit ad extra-hendum primum jam frigidum, et ipse quoque mox extinctus est. . . . Tertius cautius agere volens, fune forti cingitur circa corpus, per quem de fovea, cum opus esset, extraheretur. Ad medium fovee descendens pervenit, totoque corpore stupidus esse cepit et rigere. Signum dat. Semivivus extrahitur, aliquamdiu sic permanens. . . . Quartus descendens in foveam similiter ut primi duo periclitatur. Quidam opinabatur, in aliqua cavernula fovee serpentem basiliscum habitare, qui visu et anhelitu suo, quidquid sibi propinquat, divitur vitiare; aliis putanti-bus, terram in fovea qualitatem aliquam venenosam contraxisse, quia prius et tempore multo latrina fuerit in eodem loco. Quid autem esset in veritate, peni-tus a nullo sciebatur. . . . Demum consilio casu transeuntis extranei decoctio in modum sorbitii ex aqua et farina silignis in quantitate tanta, quod fovea repleri posset, paratur, et de ipsa fortissime bulliente fovea totaliter ad summum usque velocius infunditur et impletur. . . . Quo facto et per decoctionem illam vel inter-fecto basilisco vel fovea a venenosa qualitate purgata et recentificata, Hamelenses peste dicta liberantur.

121. Albertus Magnus, *De meteoris*, 3.2.12, p. 629:

Ego autem vidi in Paduana civitate Lombardiae, quod puteus ab antiquo tem-pore clausus inventus fuit, qui cum aperiretur, et quidam intraret ad purgandum puteum, mortuus fuit ex vapore cavernae illius, et similiter mortuus est secun-dus: et tertius voluit scire quare duo moras agerent, inclinatus ad puteum adeo debilitatus est, quod spatio duorum dierum vix rediit ad seipsum: cum autem exspirasset vapor putrefactus in puteo, factus est bonus et potabilis.

122. See note 82 above. This is not the only parallel between the two texts; both mention the Carinthia earthquake, for example.

123. John Clynn, *Annales Hiberniae*, 37: "ne scriptura cum scriptore pereat, et opus simul cum operario deficiat, dimitto pergamenam pro opere continuando, si forte in futuro homo superstes remaneat, an aliquis de genere Ade hanc pestilenciam possit evadere et opus continuare inceptum."

124. *Opinion of the Paris Medical Faculty*, 156: "Amplius pretermittere nolumus quod epidemia aliquando a divina uoluntate procedit, in quo casu non est aliud consilium nisi quod ad ipsum humiliter recurratur, medicos tamen non deserendo."

125. *Utrum mortalitas fit ab ultione divina*, 51: "Deus non solum retrahere posset afflictionem supernaturaliter inflictam, sed etiam cursum nature in suis accidentibus retardandis." The question is posed in either/or terms: "Utrum mortalitas, que fuit hijs annis, fit ab ultione divina propter iniquitates hominum vel a cursu quodam naturali" (44).

126. *Continuatio novimontensis*, 674, col. 1: "Item eodem anno infinita disturbia in diversis regionibus apparuerunt, quemadmodum principaliter orta fuit seva pestilentia ultra in partibus orientalibus . . . ex maligna impressione superiorum causa efficiente."

127. See Smoller, *History, Prophecy, and the Stars*, esp. chaps. 2 and 6.

128. His prognostication appears in Paris, Bibliothèque Mazarine, MS 3893, fol. 65–99 (the sole Latin manuscript). There is an early printed edition: *Pronosticum, sive tractatus qui intitulatur de veritate astronomie, a principio mundi usque in ejus finem* (Antwerp: T. Martens, before 1503). There is also a French version, existing in two manuscripts: Paris, Bibliothèque Nationale, MS lat. 7335, fol. 115ra–131ra; Paris, Bibliothèque Ste. Geneviève, MS 2521, fol. 37–57v. There is a brief mention of Jean in the late fifteenth-century compilation of Simon de Phares, in Jean-Patrice Boudet, ed., *Le recueil des plus celebres astrologues de Simon de Phares* (Paris: Champion, 1997), 563–64. See also Lynn Thorndike, *A History of Magic and Experimental Science*, 8 vols. (New York: Columbia University Press, 1923–58), 4: 146–47; Jean-Patrice Boudet, *Lire dans le ciel: la bibliothèque de Simon de Phares, astrologue du XVe siècle* (Brussels: Centre d'Etude des Manuscrits, 1994), 80–83; and Smoller, "The Alfonsine Tables," 224–31.

129. For a more detailed description of medieval conjunction theory, see Smoller, *History, Prophecy, and the Stars*, 20–22, 70–71, 73–74; John D. North, *Chaucer's Universe* (Oxford: Clarendon Press, 1988), 370–74; and John D. North, "Astrology and the Fortunes of Churches," *Centaurus* 24 (1980): 181–211.

130. Bibliothèque Mazarine, MS 3893, fol. 94v: "Videtur ergo probabile cum naturali lumine per presentem triplicitatem aquatica antichristum et per futuram igneam diluvium per ignem naturaliter exspectandum." See Smoller, "Alfonsine Tables," 226–28.

131. E.g., the work of Pierre Turrell (published in 1531), described in Smoller, "Alfonsine Tables," 231–36; see also Denis Crouzet, *Les guerriers de Dieu: la violence au temps des troubles de religion, vers 1525–vers 1610*, 2 vols. (Seyssel: Champ Vallon, 1990), 1: 103–53; and Paola Zambelli, ed., *"Astrologi hallucinati": Stars and the End of the World in Luther's Time* (Berlin and New York: de Gruyter, 1986).

132. Watts, "Prophecy and Discovery," esp. 96. (But it must be noted that Columbus, like John of Paris, based his prediction on a calculation of the world's age and the belief that the world would endure only 7000 years.)

Community Among the Saintly Dead: Bernard of Clairvaux's Sermons for the Feast of All Saints

I gratefully acknowledge the generous help and encouragement of my teacher Caroline Walker Bynum and that of my classmates in the Eschatology seminar at Columbia University. I thank Nicole Randolph Rice for reading portions of this article before its publication.

1. Bernard of Clairvaux, *Sermones super cantica canticorum* 26.3.5, in *Sancti Bernardi opera*, ed. Jean Leclercq, C. H. Talbot, and H. M. Rochais, 8 vols. in 9 (Rome: Editiones Cistercienses, 1957– 77), 1: 173 (hereafter SC in SBO); trans. Kilian Walsh and Irene Edmonds in Bernard of Clairvaux, *On the Song of Songs*, Cistercian Fathers Series, 4 vols. (Kalamazoo, Mich.: Cistercian Publications, 1971–80), 2: 63 (hereafter *Song*). Abbreviations for the works of Bernard of Clairvaux in Latin are taken from "Commonly Used Abbreviations," *Cistercian Studies Quarterly* (Vina, Calif.: Abbey of Our Lady of New Clairvaux, 1994).

2. Bernard of Clairvaux, *Sermones in festivitate Omnium Sanctorum* 1–5, in SBO 5: 327–70 (hereafter OS in SBO); trans. a priest of Mount Melleray [Ailbe Luddy], *Sermons for the Feast of All Saints* in *St. Bernard's Sermons for the Seasons and Principal Festivals of the Year*, 3 vols. (Dublin: Brown and Nolan, 1921–25), 3: 330–96 (hereafter *All Saints,* in *Sermons for the Seasons*).

3. SC 26.3.5 in SBO 1: 173; trans. in *Song,* 2: 63.

4. I have not addressed this question directly here, but I believe that further investigation would show that the boundary between self and other is, for Bernard, lodged most fundamentally in memory and body.

5. OS 2.2 in OSB 5: 344. Bernard is thinking here of 1 Cor. 9: 26–27. Unless otherwise indicated, the translations are mine.

6. Bernard of Clairvaux, *Officium de sancto Victore*, in SBO 3: 501; trans. Robert Walton, *The Office of St. Victor* in *The Works of Bernard of Clairvaux*, Cistercian Fathers Series 1 (Spencer, Mass.: Cistercian Publications, 1970), 169.

7. OS 5.2 in SBO 5: 362; trans. in *All Saints*, in *Sermons for the Seasons* 3: 384.

8. In the twelfth century, as today, one of the Gospel readings for the Feast of All Saints was the Sermon on the Mount, and the bulk of Bernard's first sermon is a commentary on the Beatitudes, which he refers to as the "ladder on which the whole band [of saints] whom we honor today have climbed to glory"; OS 2.1 in SBO 5: 343.

9. Bernard McGinn, *The Growth of Mysticism*, vol. 2 of *The Presence of God: A History of Western Christian Mysticism* (New York: Crossroad, 1994), 212. The language of repose has a long history in monastic literature; see Jean Leclercq, *Etudes sur la vocabulaire monastique du moyen âge*, Studia Anselmiana Philosophica Theologica 48 (Rome: Herder, 1961), 67, 102–3; idem, *Otia monastica: études sur le vocabulaire de la contemplation au moyen âge* (Rome: Herder, 1963), 13–26, 119–21; Michael Casey, *Athirst for God: Spiritual Desire in Bernard of Clairvaux's Sermons on the Song of Songs*

(Kalamazoo, Mich.: Cistercian Publications, 1988), 229–30. In Bernard's own works, see, for example, SC 4.3.4 in OSB 1: 20; trans. in *Song*, 1: 23; *Liber de gradibus humilitatis et superbiae* 7.21, in OSB 3: 33–34 (hereafter Hum in OSB); trans. G. R. Evans in Bernard of Clairvaux, *On the Steps of Humility and Pride*, in *Selected Works*, Classics of Western Spirituality (New York: Paulist Press, 1987),117–18; for sleep as vital, watchful slumber, ecstasy, and embrace with Christ, see SC 52.2.3–3.6 in OSB 2: 91–93; trans. in *Song*, 3: 51–54. On the paradox of "waking sleep" and on the significance of *otium* in Bernard's writings and in writings of other medieval monastic authors, see Jean Leclercq, *The Love of Learning and the Desire for God: A Study of Monastic Culture*, trans. Catherine Misrahi, 3rd ed. (New York: Fordham University Press, 1982), 67; idem, *Vocabulaire de la contemplation*, 27–41, for the word's ancient, biblical, and patristic use.

10. OS 2.5 in OSB 5: 346; trans. in *All Saints*, in *Sermons for the Season*, 3: 359. Restlessness sometimes has a positive connotation, as, for example, when Bernard writes of the bride soul who "cannot rest . . . unless he [Christ] kisses me with the kiss of his mouth"; SC 9.2.2 in OSB 1: 43; trans. in *Song*, 1: 54. In this case, restlessness is desire and will be consummated in the "ecstatic repose" of the "kiss of his [Christ's] mouth"; SC 4.3.4 in OSB 1: 20; trans. in *Song*, 1: 23. Furthermore, Leclercq points out that "to desire Heaven is to want God and to love Him with a love that the monks sometimes call impatient. The greater the desire becomes, the more the soul rests in God"; Leclercq, *Love of Learning*, 68. Thus it is only *while* seeking that the soul can rest.

11. The tension between rest and labor is evident throughout Bernard's works. See, for example, SC 26.4.6 in OSB 1: 173–75. See also *Sermo in festivitate sancti Martini episcopi* 17, in OSB 5: 411–12.

12. OS 2.6 in OSB 5: 347. For some, there are moments of rest on this side: the person who, having eaten the food of good works and having drunk the beverage of prayer, falls asleep in the midst of prayer and dreams of God; SC 18.3.5–6 in OSB 1: 106–8.

13. OS 2.5 in OSB 5: 378.

14. Bernard of Clairvaux, *Sermones in dedicatione ecclesiae* 2.4, in OSB 5: 378 (hereafter Ded in OSB).

15. OS 3.2 in OSB 5: 350.

16. Bernard of Clairvaux, *Liber de diligendo Deo* 11.30, in OSB 3: 144–45 (hereafter Dil in OSB; trans. in *On Loving God*, in G. R. Evans, *Selected Works*, 197.

17. On the bed and bedroom, see Dil 3.8 in OSB 3: 125; Dil 3.10 in OSB 3: 126; SC 23.1.2 in OSB 1: 139; SC 23.2.3 in OSB 1: 140; SC 23.6.16 in OSB 1: 149–50; SC 84.1.3 in OSB 2: 304. On the bed as the location of encounter with God, see McGinn, *Growth*, 188–89. It is not surprising that the bed is also an image of the monastery; see SC 46.1.2. in OSB 2: 56–57.

18. SC 23.6.16 in OSB 1: 149–50; Hum 7.21 in OSB 3: 32–33. See also McGinn, *Growth*, 190.

19. In sermon twenty-three on the Song of Songs, Bernard suggests further the discreteness of each soul's union with God when he writes: "I feel that the King has not one bedroom only, but several. For he has more than one queen; his concubines are many, his maids beyond counting [Song 6: 7]. And each has her own secret rendezvous with the Bridegroom and says: 'My secret to myself, my secret to myself' [Isa. 24: 16]. All do not experience the delight of the Bridegroom's visit in the same

room"; SC 23.4.9 in OSB 1: 144–45; trans. in *Song*, 2: 33–34. Bernard's emphasis on the separateness of each soul's encounter with God from every other soul's encounter with God, his imagery of separate beds and separate bedrooms, raises interesting questions about privacy in the Middle Ages: the separate bedrooms in heaven contrast with the sleeping arrangements at Clairvaux, where, with the exception of the abbot, all monks slept in a single dormitory; Elphège Vacandard, *Vie de saint Bernard, abbé de Clairvaux* (Paris: J. Gabalda, 1894; rep. 1927), 70–71.

20. OS 5.4 in OSB 5: 364. The saints do seem to be aware of the damned; it is not clear if this awareness comes before or only after the resurrection; OS 3.3 in OSB 5: 351–52.

21. OS 1.3 in OSB 5: 329.

22. We find little concern for the communal aspect of eating when Bernard uses this image in a sermon for St. Victor. The conscience of St. Victor, resting from his conflicts, is seated at a table with Christ, the angels, apostles, and prophets. Bernard even names some of Victor's dining companions, it is true—Abraham, Isaac, and Jacob—but such identification simply underscores the saint's august company, rather than suggesting interaction among that company. Bernard of Clairvaux, *Sermones in natali sancti Victoris* 2, in OSB 6.1: 33–34 (hereafter Vict in OSB).

23. Thus, for example, no clear picture of the saints as particular, specific people emerges in these sermons, and neither emulation of individual saints nor their intercession is the connection between heaven and earth. If we want to know about the relationship between the living and the dead, we have to look elsewhere: indeed, it is in large part the monks' participation in the heavenly feast that joins heaven and earth. When, in the opening passages of his first sermon, Bernard labors to excite his monastic readers' (or listeners') desire for heaven (and not, it is worthwhile noting, their desire for the saints per se), he uses images of spiritual feasting and alludes also to the actual eating practices in the monastic community. Bernard describes himself and his monks as "beggars . . . lying before the door of a very rich king"; OS 1.2 in OSB 5: 328. Like hungry Lazarus, who pleaded with the rich man for scraps from his table, Bernard's monks, and Bernard himself, long to be sustained by the crumbs that fall from the table of the holy souls. God himself (not the saints) gives this food directly to Bernard, and it is through Bernard's sermon that his monks eat of these longed-for crumbs of Christ, tasting heaven by eating with their ears the words of Bernard's sermons. (That Bernard should talk about eating Christ's words and actions through hearing is not surprising. It is, after all, the flesh of the Incarnate *Word* that is eaten in communion.) By eating this food, the monk participates in the glory of the saints.

24. For eating as the occasion of union with others and on the eucharistic overtones of feasting in general in the Middle Ages, see Caroline Walker Bynum, *Holy Feast and Holy Fast: The Religious Significance of Food to Medieval Women* (Berkeley: University of California Press, 1987), 3–5; on the changing perceptions of fast and eucharist from late antiquity through the high Middle Ages, see ibid., 33–69. Miri Rubin analyzes the ways in which members of dominant as well as nondominant groups in the Middle Ages used the eucharist to circumvent local loyalties in an effort to achieve unity among those with widely differing social and political allegiances, as well as to buttress dominant ideology and to challenge it; *Corpus Christi: The Eucharist in Late Medieval Culture* (Cambridge: Cambridge University Press, 1991), esp. 347–49.

25. SC 71.2.5 in OSB 2: 217; trans. in *Song*, 4: 51–52.

26. SC 71.4.10 in OSB 2: 221.

27. SC 71.3.8 in OSB 2: 220. See McGinn, *Growth*, 213–15.

28. Dil 15.39 in OSB 3: 153; trans. in *On Loving God*, in *Selected Works*, 205.

29. Dil 10.28 in OSB 3: 143. For biblical and baptismal sources of water symbolism in medieval writings, see James C. Franklin, *Mystical Transformations: The Imagery of Liquids in the Work of Mechthild von Magdeburg* (Rutherford, N.J.: Associated University Press, 1978), 64–72.

30. "Pristina propriaque exutum forma"; Dil 10.28 in OSB 3: 143.

31. Dil 10.27–28 in OSB 3: 142–43.

32. Etienne Gilson, *The Mystical Theology of Bernard of Clairvaux*, trans. A. H. C. Downes (London: Sheed & Ward, 1940), 122.

33. Dil 10.28 in OSB 3: 143. Colin Morris argues (citing Dil 10.28 in OSB 3: 134) that, whereas Bernard spoke in *On Loving God* (written between 1125 and 1141 and perhaps in 1128) about deification as a loss of self in God, he spoke about deification as the fulfillment of self in his sermons *On the Song of Songs*, which he began in 1135 (see SC 71.4.10 in OSB 2: 221); Colin Morris, *The Discovery of the Individual, 1050–1200* (New York: Harper and Row, 1972), 154–55. Gilson, sensitive to charges of pantheism leveled against Bernard, is at pains to emphasize Bernard's insistence, throughout his writings, on the permanent distinction between God's substance and the substance of each soul; Gilson, *Mystical Theology*, 122–32.

34. See Gilson, *Mystical Theology*, 26–28, 128–29 and Morris, *Discovery*, 152–57. Bynum discusses this idea in the context of twelfth-century thought as a whole; Caroline Walker Bynum, "Did the Twelfth Century Discover the Individual?" in *Jesus as Mother: Studies in the Spirituality of the High Middle Ages* (Berkeley: University of California Press, 1982), esp. 87–88.

35. SC 82.3.5 in OSB 2: 295. See also Dil 11.32 in OSB 3: 146.

36. Gilson discusses this in *Mystical Theology*, esp. 28, 54. McGinn points out that, whereas Bernard argues in *On Grace and Free Choice* that the soul's likeness to God has not been lost through sin, he argues in his sermons on the Song of Songs that this likeness has been partly concealed; McGinn, *Growth*, 168–71.

37. Ded 1.7 in OSB 5: 374–75.

38. Ibid. Bernard believes that no created spirit can communicate with another created spirit without the use of bodily senses—God alone can act directly on the mind (OS 5.2.8–3.8 in OSB 1: 24–25), and neither human being nor angel can penetrate the secret intentions of another (*Sermones in Psalmum "Qui habitat"* 15.3.3–6, in OSB 4: 478). On Bernard's acceptance of the Augustinian principle of the "inviolability of spirits," see Adele Fiske, "St. Bernard and Friendship," parts 1 and 2, *Cîteaux: commentarii Cistercienses* 11 (1960): 5–25, 85–103 (quote at 6). This epistemology would militate against the notion of the union of souls' wills in heaven (and raise the question of how, before the resurrection, the bodiless souls of saints communicate with one another). But a different epistemology reigns in Bernard's heaven, if we take Ded 1.7 to mean that the thoughts of each are accessible to each without going through the medium of sense perception. And see Ded 2.4 in OSB 5: 378. The relation between the self—as image of God—and others is particularly intriguing in the light of the fact that the *imago Dei* is the same for all people. I have not been able to locate any text that

addresses this question directly. For the twelfth-century understanding of "the self" and for the soul as image of God, see Bynum, "Did the Twelfth Century Discover the Individual?" 85–88, Morris, *Discovery*, 64–95, and Robert Javelet, *Image et ressemblance au douzième siècle, de Saint Anselme à Alain de Lille*, 2 vols. (Paris: Editions Letouzey et Ané, 1967), esp. 1: 187–98. See M.-D. Chenu for a new sense of self in the twelfth century; M.-D. Chenu, "Nature and Man: The Renaissance of the Twelfth Century," in *Nature, Man, and Society in the Twelfth Century: Essays on New Theological Perspectives in the Latin West*, trans. Jerome Taylor and Lester K. Little (Chicago: University of Chicago Press, 1968), 23–37.

39. On the twelfth century's emphasis on the boundaries between people, see Bynum, "Did the Twelfth Century Discover the Individual?" 85–86.

40. SC 26 in OSB 1.

41. SC 26.6.9 in OSB 1: 177; trans. in *Song*, 2: 69.

42. SC 26.2.4 in OSB 1: 172; trans. in *Song*, 2: 61.

43. Ibid.

44. SC 26.2.4 in OSB 1: 172; trans. in *Song*, 2: 62.

45. Bernard of Clairvaux, Preface, *The Life of Saint Malachy*, in *The Life and Death of Saint Malachy the Irishman*, trans. Robert T. Meyer, Cistercian Fathers Series 10 (Kalamazoo, Mich.: Cistercian Publications, 1978), 13.

46. *The Life of Saint Malachy*, 93.

47. *Sermo in obitu domni Humberti* 1, in OSB 5: 440, (hereafter Humb in OSB); trans. in *Sermon for the Feast of Blessed Humbert*, in *Sermons for the Seasons*, 1: 61.

48. Jean Leclercq, "La joie de mourir selon saint Bernard de Clairvaux," in *Dies Illa: Death in the Middle Ages*, ed. Jane H. M. Taylor (Liverpool: Francis Cairns, 1984), 200–201.

49. Humb 6 in OSB 5: 445–46; trans. in *Blessed Humbert*, in *Sermons for the Seasons* 3: 68–69.

50. In these five sermons, Bernard expresses little interest in the complexity of the inner (or outer) life of the saints (on earth or in heaven), and he does not detail the diversity of the lives lived by the saints, of which we are given little if any sense at all: the saints remain, throughout, an anonymous, undifferentiated group. On the question of grouping, see "The Orders of Society," in Giles Constable, *Three Studies in Medieval Religious and Social Thought: An Interpretation of Mary and Martha, The Ideal of the Imitation of Christ, The Orders of Society* (Cambridge: Cambridge University Press, 1995).

51. SC 26.3.5 in OSB 1: 173; trans. in *Song*, 2: 63. It is important to note that I have not located traces of this preoccupation in other writings by Bernard. If we consider Bernard's own preference for withdrawing in union with the Word, it is not surprising that he should be fearful of being forgotten by Gerard. In sermon eighty-five on the Song of Songs, Bernard writes that in spiritual marriage the soul may give birth in two ways. On the one hand, she may give birth to others, in consideration of the joys of her neighbor; on the other hand, the soul may give birth to spiritual insight. It is this latter bringing to birth that Bernard relishes: "A mother is happy in her child; a bride is even happier in her bridegroom's embrace. The children are dear, they are the pledge of his love, but his kisses give her greater pleasure"; OS 85.4.13 in OBS 2: 316; trans. in *Song*, 4: 209. No wonder Bernard is worried. Fracheboud and Bynum

have drawn attention to the conflict Bernard felt over the competing claims of service and solitude, over preaching and prayer; M. André Fracheboud, "Je suis la chimère de mon siècle: le problème action-contemplation au coeur de saint Bernard," *Collectanea Cisterciensium Reformatorum* 16 (1954); Bynum, "The Cistercian Conception of Community," in *Jesus as Mother*, 71.

52. SC 26.2.4 in OSB 1: 172; trans. in *Song*, 2:61.

53. SC 26.3.5 in OSB 1: 173; trans. in *Song*, 2: 63. Bernard writes similarly about the love that Humbert, now in heaven, houses for those on earth; Humb 7 in OSB 5: 446–47.

54. Vict 3 in OSB 6.1: 33–35.

55. Bernard of Clairvaux, *De consideratione ad Eugenium papam* 5.7.26 in OSB 3: 488. It is interesting that (in at least some instances) it is Bernard's need to be remembered by the dead that prompts him to discuss the question of memory in heaven, indicating that the concern for the continuity of relationships established on earth is an impetus for his discussion of memory. See his sermon on St. Victor (Vict in OSB 6.1: 29–37), whom Bernard did not know, and his sermon on Gerard (SC 26 in OSB 1: 169–81).

56. The depth and ardor of Bernard's attachments triggered conflicting emotions in him. In sermon fourteen on the Song of Songs, he recounts the near despair by which he was several times overcome "in the beginning of his conversion," when he was unable to find and love the God whom he sought and when he could discover no friend who might loosen "the chilling winter that bound" his "inward senses (*sensus internos*)"; SC 14.4.6 in OSB 1: 79. But he also remembers that at a sudden and chance utterance, "or even at the sight of a spiritual and excellent man, and occasionally at the memory alone of someone dead or absent, the wind blew and the waters flowed [Ps. 147: 18]," and Bernard's tears fell almost day and night; ibid. Bernard acknowledges that he was disappointed not to have come to this experience of God without the mediation of fellow human beings and writes of the shame he feels at having been "moved more by the memory of a human being than by God"; ibid. As Fiske has remarked, a "friend can communicate to him [Bernard] what he cannot get for himself directly from God, even from the humanity of Christ"; "St. Bernard and Friendship,"13. Bernard has been singled out as a pivotal example of a twelfth-century person who placed an enormous value on friendship and cultivated friendships with energy and passion. On the importance of the twelfth century for the history of friendship, see Morris, *Discovery*, 96–107. For the role Bernard played in the subsequent identification of the twelfth century as "the age of friendship," see Brian Patrick McGuire, *Friendship & Community: The Monastic Experience c.350–c.1250*, Cistercian Studies Series 95 (Kalamazoo, Mich.: Cistercian Publications, 1988), 231–95. For the influence of Cicero's ideas about friendship on Bernard—and on the twelfth century as a whole—see Gilson, *Mystical Theology*, 8–13. Fiske shows the enormous importance of friendship to Bernard, considers the friendships Bernard had with William of St. Thierry and Peter the Venerable, and discusses the way in which Bernard's reflections on friendship figure into his theological reflections; Fiske, "St. Bernard and Friendship."

57. Hum 4.14 in OSB 3: 27; trans. in *Steps of Humility*, in *Selected Works*, 112–13.

58. Fiske has argued that Bernard held two different positions regarding love of others. First, Bernard expressed the belief that authentic love is grounded in a true

perception of the person whom one loves. Second, Bernard considered authentic love to be without proportion to the merit of the person loved; Fiske, "St. Bernard and Friendship," 21–23. Fiske's insight is important for my topic. To pursue it might very well shed further light on Bernard's understanding of whom and how we love in heaven.

59. OS 5.6 in OSB 5: 365.

60. Dil 10.28 in OSB 3: 143.

61. This "leveling" of all human beings may take place while we are alive, but with a different outcome; it creates a sort of solidarity among sinners. While we are alive, the ecstasy that the soul enjoys when she is carried away from herself and adheres to God ushers in the compassionate realization that all human beings are weak, wretched, and powerless. This realization causes the soul to cry out: "Every man is a liar"; Hum 4.16 in OSB 3: 28.

62. SC 26.3.6 in OSB 1: 173; trans. in *Song*, 2: 64.

63. SC 82.2.2–3.8 in OSB 2: 293–98. On the soul made in the image of God and the soul's likeness to God, see Javelet, *Image et ressemblance*, 1: 187–98.

64. OS 2.7 in OSB 5: 347–48.

65. OS 3.3 in OSB 5: 351.

66. OS 3 in OSB 5: 349–53. With their bodies back, the saints' love might spill outward into new sorts of relationships with others; after all, the return of their bodies to them frees them to love God fully for the first time. Moreover, there might be a connection between the establishment of the whole person and the nature of relationship with others. In addition, Fiske has drawn attention to Bernard's zest for the corporeal presence of his friends. Bernard expressed his preference for the corporeal presence of his friends, regarding it as "far more desirable than the spiritual bond alone"; Fiske, "St. Bernard and Friendship," 87–88. Finally, if embodiment more completely establishes the identity of each saint, might these new selves usher in a new kind of community?

67. *The Life of Saint Malachy*, 93.

68. SC 26.8.12 in OSB 1: 179; Humb 1 in OSB 5: 441.

69. OS 3.1 in OSB 5: 349–50. Simon Tugwell discusses Bernard's insistence on complete reward going only to complete people—not to bodiless souls; Simon Tugwell, *Human Immortality and the Redemption of Death* (London: Darton, Longman and Todd, 1990), 133.

70. Bynum has remarked on the rarity in the late Middle Ages of considerations of "the social implications of resurrection," and she has pointed to the lack of a communal dimension in the medieval discussions of the resurrection; Caroline Walker Bynum, *The Resurrection of the Body in Western Christianity, 200–1336* (New York: Columbia University Press, 1995), 249, 287.

71. OS 5.6 in OSB 5: 365.

72. Dil 11.30 in OSB 3: 144; trans. in *On Loving God*, in *Selected Works*, 197.

73. OS 1 in OSB 5: 350; OS 3.4 in OSB 5: 352; trans. in *All Saints*, in *Sermons for the Seasons*, 365, 369.

74. See Bynum, "Conception of Community," in *Jesus as Mother*, esp. 69–75, 80–81.

75. It is not clear whether there is a causal relationship between loving God

fully because desire for the body has been quieted and seeing God as he is. Bernard wants to insist that souls are at rest before the resurrection *and* that souls cannot be fully at rest—because not fully satisfied—until they get their bodies back. He does, nevertheless, seem to believe that bodies do add something, in addition to the cessation of distraction, to the soul's ability to experience in heaven; Dil 11.30 in OSB 3: 144–45. See Leclercq, *Vocabulaire de la contemplation*, 126 and Bynum, *Resurrection of the Body*, 163–66.

76. Bernard's thought was at the center of the controversy that erupted over the beatific vision in the 1330s. For that controversy, see Bynum, *Resurrection of the Body*, esp. 283–85. Tugwell discusses the controversy and points to the significance of Bernard's thought in it; Tugwell, *Human Immortality*, 130–55.

77. See M.-D. Chenu, "Monks, Canons, and Laymen in Search of the Apostolic Life," in *Nature, Man, and Society*, 202–38; Bynum "Did the Twelfth Century Discover the Individual?"; and, largely in response to Bynum's essay, Colin Morris, "Individualism in Twelfth-Century Religion: Some Further Reflections," *Journal of Ecclesiastical History* 3, 2 (April 1980): esp. 204–5.

Heaven in View: The Place of the Elect in an Illuminated Book of Hours

Versions of this paper were given at the Annual Meeting of the American Historical Association in January 1997 and a colloquium connected with the Paris exhibition *L'art au temps des rois maudits* in June 1998. I am grateful to many colleagues, both at these conferences and in correspondence, for their comments and suggestions.

1. Cambrai, Bibl. Mun., ms. 87 fols. 16v, 17v. Auguste Molinier, *Catalogue général des manuscrits des bibliothèques publiques de France* 17 (1891), 21–22. See National Gallery of Canada, *Art and the Courts: France and England from 1259 to 1328* (Ottawa: National Gallery of Canada, 1972), no. 18 (by M. Montpetit); Paris, Musée National du Moyen Age—Thermes de Cluny, and Cologne, Schnütgen-Museum der Städt Köln, *Un trésor gothique: la châsse de Nivelles* (Paris: Réunion des Musées Nationaux, 1996), no. 51 (by A. von Euw); Andreas Bräm, *Das Andachtsbuch der Marie de Gavre*, Paris, Bibliothèque Nationale, ms. nouv. acq. fr. 16251. *Buchmalerei in der Diözese Cambrai im letzten Viertel des 13. Jahrhunderts* (Wiesbaden: Ludwig Reichert Verlag, 1997), 177–80; and Paris, Galleries Nationales du Grand Palais, *L'art au temps des rois maudits: Philippe le Bel et ses fils 1285–1328* (Paris: Editions de la Réunion des Musées Nationaux, 1998), no. 210 (by François Avril).

2. In addition to the Hours of the Virgin, Office of the Dead, Canticles, and Creed, the manuscript contains a number of texts in French, including the Hours of the Cross, a short version of the story of Christ, and prayers in prose or verse to Mary and the guardian angel. See Jean Sonet, *Répertoire d'incipit des prières en ancien français* (Geneva: Droz, 1956), nos. 321, 330, 587, 588, 1100, 1278, 1599. On Sonet nos. 321, 330, 587, 1100, 1599, see Keith Val Sinclair, *Prières en ancien français* (Hamden, Conn.: Archon, 1978), and on nos. 588, 1278, R635, R1305, see Pierre Rézeau, *Répertoire d'incipit des prières françaises à la fin du Moyen Age: addenda et corrigenda aux répertoires de Sonet et Sinclair* (Geneva: Droz, 1986). See also Rézeau, *Les Prières aux saints en français à la fin du moyen âge* (Geneva: Droz, 1982–83), 515–18.

3. Molinier identified the arms as those of Mahaut d'Artois, wife first of Robert I d'Artois and then of Guy de Châtillon, count of St. Paul; because of his attribution, the manuscript is sometimes referred to as the Hours of Mahaut d'Artois. All subsequent writers, however, have followed Sydney C. Cockerell's suggestion in the catalogue of the Burlington Fine Arts Club *Exhibition of Illuminated Manuscripts* (London, 1908), no. 141 that the arms are those of Isabeau de Rumigny. Bräm, *Das Andachtsbuch der Marie de Gavre*, 178, citing Michel Pastoureau, seems to adhere to the earlier identification.

4. Avril, *L'art au temps des rois maudits*, 310.

5. Ibid.

6. Christ's nimbus is orange rather than gold, like the others in the miniature.

7. Beside the figure wearing a papal tiara are two men wearing bishop's mitres, and nearby is a priest with a chalice and the eucharist as well as a king in a plain blue robe. Only some of the figures in the rest of this all-male group are tonsured.

8. The men include St. John with his cup and possibly St. Paul with the sword; the others are presumably other apostles, martyrs, and confessors. Among the group of virgins and female martyrs are Margaret standing behind or in a small dragon, Ursula holding an arrow, and Katherine, who puts a sword in the mouth of the crowned Maxentius, as she does in illuminations accompanying the litany in the closely related Ruskin Hours, now in the J. Paul Getty Museum, Los Angeles, ms. 83. ML. 99; see Anton von Euw and Joachim Plotzek, *Die Handschriften der Sammlung Ludwig* (Cologne: Schnütgen-Museum, 1982), 2: 74–83, Fig. 39.

9. The armored figure wears a decorated helmet and carries a lance and shield. His shield and the horse coverings are decorated with his arms, which appear to be *argent a cross gueles*, the arms of St. George.

10. Florence, Bibl. Laurenziana ms. Plut. XII.17; C. M. Kauffmann, *Romanesque Manuscripts, 1066–1190*, Survey of Manuscripts Illuminated in the British Isles 3 (London: Harvey Miller, 1975), no. 19. For later manuscripts of the *City of God*, which follow another tradition, see Alexandre de Laborde, *Les manuscrits à peintures de la Cité de Dieu de Saint Augustin* (Paris: E. Rahir, 1909).

11. See Gertrude Schiller, *Ikonographie der christlichen Kunst*, vol. 4. 1 (Gütersloh: Gerd Mohr, 1976), 101. Marie-Louise Thérel, *Le triomphe de la Vierge-Eglise: sources historiques, littéraires et iconographiques* (Paris: CNRS, 1984), 180, notes that while the text would suggest that this figure is the Church in the midst of the elect, she connects the flowering scepter and its dove with Isaiah 11: 1–2 and thus sees here an allusion to the Mother of God.

12. Augustine, *De civitate Dei*, bk. 20, chap. 9, Corpus Christianorum Series Latina 43 (Turnholt: Brepols, 1955), 716.

13. Herrad of Hohenbourg, *Hortus Deliciarum*, ed. Rosalie B. Green et al., Studies of the Warburg Institute 36 (London, Warburg Institute, 1979), no. 302. The text identifies the figure as "Ecclesiam qui dicitur Virgo Mater." See also Herrad of Landsberg, *Hortus Deliciarum*, commentary and notes by A. Straub and G. Keller, ed. and trans. Aristide D. Caratzas (New Rochelle, N.Y.: Caratzas Bros., 1977), 205, pl. 59.

14. The diverse ranks we see here and in the Cambrai manuscript clearly reflect larger social structures, such as Peter Dinzelbacher has shown for textual descriptions of the next world. See his "Reflexionen irdischer Sozialstrukturen in mittelalterlichen

Jenseitsschilderungen," *Archiv für Kulturgeschichte* 61, 1 (1979): 16–34; and "Klassen und Hierarchien im Jenseits," in *Soziale Ordnungen im Selbstsverstandnis des Mittelalters*, Miscellanea Medievalia 12, (Berlin: de Gruyter, 1979), 20–40.

15. *Hortus Deliciarum*, 204 ("per obedientiam in suis ordinibus cottidie laborant et adventum sponsi, id est Christi, fideliter negociantes exspectant").

16. Munich, Bay. Staatsbibliothek, clm. 835; Nigel J. Morgan, *Early Gothic Manuscripts*, vol. 1, *1190–1250*, Survey of Manuscripts Illuminated in the British Isles 4 (London: Harvey Miller, 1982), no. 23 (attributed to Oxford).

17. They hold scrolls inscribed "Sanctus, sanctus, sanctus," "Gloria in excelsis deo," and the like; there is also a nonliturgical hymn, the *Laus deo*. See Reinhold Hammerstein, *Die Musik der Engel: Untersuchungen zur Musikanschauung* Bern: Francke, 1962), 221.

18. For Haimo, *Expositio in Apocalypsim*, PL 117 cols. 1169 A–D, 1170 B–C; for Richard, *In Apocalypsim Libri Septem*, PL 196 cols. 847C–848C. Also see Richard (PL 196 col. 759D–760C) and Rupert of Deutz (*Commentarium in Apocalypsim*, PL 169 col. 939A), who interpret the twenty-four elders of Revelation 19: 4 as the prelates and judges of the Church. The distinction in gender among the groups of saints in these miniatures may also be a function of the spousal imagery: see Berengaudus, *Expositio in Apocalypsim*, PL 17 (mistakenly attributed to Ambrose), col. 1010A, who discusses the marriage of Christ and the Church in terms of the joining of male and female into one flesh, as in Genesis 2.

19. Lionel J. Friedman, *Text and Iconography of Joinville's Credo* (Cambridge, Mass.: Medieval Academy of America, 1958), 48; and I. P. Mokretsova and V. L. Romanova, *Les manuscrits enluminés français du XIIIe siècle dans les collections soviétiques, 1270–1300* (Moscow: Isskusstvo, 1984), 194–231.

20. For the relation to contemporary apocalypse illustration, see Suzanne Lewis, *Reading Images: Narrative Discourse and Reception in the Thirteenth-Century Illuminated Apocalypse* (New York: Cambridge University Press, 1995), 176.

21. In the Munich Psalter the facing page represents the Last Judgment (fol. 30) and is followed by the related Torments of Hell (fol. 30v). The reading of this Credo page is unusual because the text of the eleventh article of faith (Carnis resurrectionem) and the Last Judgment are at the bottom of the page and the text of the twelfth article (Vitam eternam. Amen) and banquet scene are above. Because the previous texts and miniatures all read normally, from above to below, it is likely that the artist reversed the order so that the subjects illustrated would follow that of Revelation.

22. Thérel, *Le triomphe de la Vierge-Église*, 174–82 and passim.

23. New York, Metropolitan Museum of Art, acq. 1970.324.7a–b. See Peter Barnet, ed., *Images in Ivory: Precious Objects of the Gothic Age* (Princeton, N.J.: Princeton University Press, 1997), no. 9 (by C. Little); and Christian Heck, *L'échelle céleste dans l'art du moyen âge: une image de la quête du ciel* (Paris: Flammarion, 1997), 141.

24. Raymond Koechlin, *Les ivoires gothiques français* (Paris, A. Piccard, 1924), nos. 234, 348, 524.

25. See my "Narrative Structure and Content in Some Gothic Ivories of the Life of Christ," in Barnet, ed., *Images in Ivory*, 95–114.

26. Jacques Le Goff, *The Birth of Purgatory*, trans. Arthur Goldhammer (Chicago: University of Chicago Press, 1984), 309.

27. The theological issues have been recently surveyed and discussed in detail in Christian Trottmann, *La vision béatifique des disputes scolastiques à sa définition par Benoît XII*, Bibliothèque des Ecoles Françaises d'Athènes et de Rome 289 (Rome: Ecole Française de Rome, 1995). I have found especially useful the shorter discussions in Nikolaus Wicki, *Die Lehre von der himmlischen Seligkeit in der mittelalterlichen Scholastik von Petrus Lombardus bis Thomas von Aquin*, Studia Friburgensia n. f. 9 (Freiburg: Universitätsverlag, 1954); Caroline Walker Bynum, *The Resurrection of the Body in Western Christianity, 200–1336* (New York: Columbia University Press, 1995), esp. ch. 7; and Jeffrey Burton Russell, *A History of Heaven: The Singing Silence* (Princeton, N.J.: Princeton University Press, 1997), 122–46.

28. For example, Albertus Magnus, in Tract IV, Questo 1, Art. 9 sec. 3, distinguishes the *visio dei* in *patria* from lesser visions in *via*; see *De Resurrectione*, in *Opera omnia* (Cologne: Bernhard Geyer, 1958), 26: 330–31. For his discussion of "across the Jordan" as a metaphor for the interim of the blessed, see ibid., p. 270. For a similar discussion of the *sinus Abrahae*, see Alexander of Hales, *Glossa in quattuor libros sententiarum Petri Lombradi*, Bibliotheca Franciscana Scholastici Medii Aevi (Florence: Quaracchi, 1952), Liber IV, Distinctio I, 19. In contrast, Bonaventura, one of the strongest exponents of the beatific vision, leaves no doubt that souls are in heaven and of the "curia coelestis"; see Dist. XXI, part. I, art. III, quaest. II, in Saint Cardinal Bonaventura, *Opera omnia*, ed. A. C. Peltier (Paris: L. Vives, 1864), 6: 101–2. Elsewhere (Dist. XLV, quest. II, p. 512) he refers to this heavenly place of quietude and waiting as *Gloria* and likens it to the bosom of Abraham.

29. See Wicki, *Die Lehre*, esp. 209–12. For Mary as the ladder on which angels and, for that matter, the son of God and we ourselves ascend and descend, see Albertus Magnus, *Biblia Mariana*, in *Opera omnia*, ed. Augustus and Aemitius Borgent (Paris: L. Vives, 1890), 37: 369, on Genesis 23: 12–13 ("*Vidit Jacob in somnis scalam*, id est, Mariam. Per eam enim descendit Filius Dei ad nos, et nos per ad eam eum. . . . Ipsa etiam est porta regni, et nostrae ingressionis in regnum . . .").

30. Wicki, *Die Lehre*, and Bynum, *Resurrection of the Body*, 8, 235–47, and passim. See also Eileen C. Sweeny, "Individuation and the Body in Aquinas," in *Individuum und Individualität im Mittelalter*, ed. Jan Aertsen and Andreas Speer, Miscellanea Medievalia 24 (Berlin: de Gruyter 1996), 178–96.

31. PL 212 cols. 1059–60 ("Campus iste floridus locus est animarum sanctarum, quae in bonus operibus exierunt de corpore, et regnum Dei exspectant cum magna laetitia et exultatione."

32. See Giles Constable, "The Vision of Gunthelm and Other Visions Attributed to Peter the Venerable," *Revue Bénédictine* 56 (1956): 92–114, at p. 107. For the exempla of Stephen of Bourbon (c. 1260) describing visions in which Mary is the guide, see A. Lecoy de la Marche, ed., *Anecdotes historiques, légendes et apologues tirées du receuil inédit d'Etienne de Bourbon, dominicain du XIIIe siècle* (Paris: Librairie Renouard, 1877), nos. 115 (p. 99) and 125 (p. 107). Caesarius of Heisterbach (c. 1220) has numerous exempla in which Mary shows the living a vision of the *coelesti patria*, usually in which she presides, often in the company of saints; see *Dialogus Miraculorum*, ed. Josephus Strange (Cologne, 1858; rep. 1966), 2: 280–81, 351–53, 357–58, 360–61. For a similar situation seventy years later, see Anne-Marie Polo de Beaulieu, ed., *La scala coeli de Jean Gobi* (Paris: CNRS, 1991), no. 659, no. 445.

33. Erwin Panofsky, *Early Netherlandish Painting, Its Origins and Character* (Cambridge, Mass.: Harvard University Press, 1953), 1: 212–13.

34. For the former, see the All Saints window in the cathedral at Cologne, c. 1315, where the whole grouping is surmounted by Christ blessing Mary, both of whom are crowned, and there is a hierarchy of both saints and angels, in Herbert Rode, *Die mittelalterlichen Glasmalereien des Kölner Domes*, Corpus Vitrearum Medii Aevi, Deutschland IV, 1 (Berlin: Deutsches Verlag für Kunstwissenschaft, 1974), 65–68. For the latter, a striking example is the All Saints illumination from a *Laudario*, c. 1340 possibly made for the Company of Santa Maria del Carmine in Florence, now in the National Gallery of Art, Washington; see *Medieval and Renaissance Miniatures from the National Gallery of Art*, ed. Gary Vikan (Washington, D.C.: National Gallery of Art, 1975), 29–32, no. 8.

35. In the Ascension, Christ and Mary are enthroned together in a mandorla raised by angels, with Christ to Mary's right, possibly a reference to the bride and bridegroom of *Canticum Canticorum*, 2.6, 8.3; see I. Hueck, "Cimabue und das Bildprogramm der Oberkirche von S. Francesco in Assisi," *Mitteilungen des Kunsthistorischen Institut in Florenz* 25 (1981): 279–324, esp. 301–5. These themes are also stressed by J. Poeschke, *Die Kirche San Francesco in Assisi und ihre Wandmalereien* (Munich: Hirmer, 1985), 24, 73.

36. For example, the Clarisse Master's painting in Siena in James H. Stubblebine, *Guida da Siena* (Princeton, N.J.: Princeton University Press, 1964), 67–69, fig. 34; the panel in Santa Maria Novella reproduced in Richard Offner, *A Critical and Historical Corpus of Florentine Painting* (New York: College of Fine Arts, New York University, 1930), sec. III, vol. 2, pt. 1, 58–59, pl. XXV; or the painting attributed to Giovanni del Biondo in New Haven, reproduced in Lotte Brand Philip, *The Ghent Altarpiece and the Art of Jan van Eyck* (Princeton, N.J.: Princeton University Press, 1971), fig. 78. For Christ crowning Mary from her right, see the unusual drawing of the group in the gable of the Siena Baptistry in H. Keller, "Die Bauplastik des Sieneser Doms," *Kunstgeschichtliches Jahrbuch der Bibliotheca Hertziana* 1 (1937): 139–222, fig. 128. Such images are rarer in northern Europe; see, however, examples such as the Bonmont Psalter and others cited in Philippe Verdier, *Le couronnement de la Vierge: les origines et les premiers développements d'un thème iconographique* (Montreal: Institut d'Etudes Médiévales, 1980), 146–49.

37. See Francis Lee Pitts, *Nardo di Cione and the Strozzi Chapel Frescoes: Iconographic Problems in Mid-Trecento Florence*, Ph.D. diss., University of California, Berkeley, 1982, esp. 265–71.

38. Ibid., 256–61.

39. Ibid., 219–45, especially for the way the blessed and angels are ordered according to distinct physical and psychological qualities. The author sees the frescoes in part as a response to the continuing controversies surrounding Aquinas's teachings and recent canonization (141–56). The painting is usually referred to as the *Paradisio*; for the parallel to Dante's poem, canto XXXII, see Hans Belting, "Das Bild als Text: Wandmalerei und Literatur in Zeitalter Dantes," in Belting and Dieter Blume, *Malerei und Stadtkultur in der Dantezeit* (Munich: Hirmer, 1989), 23–64, esp. 52–53. For a discussion of Dante's poem in relation to the *visio dei*, see Bynum, *Resurrection of the*

Body, 298–305. Citing the angels sounding trumpets in the lower corners of the dark area below the enthroned Virgin and Christ, Bynum (306 n. 102, pl. 25) interprets the blessed as already resurrected and thus as " 'real' and paintable." However, Pitts, *Nardo di Cione*, 244–45, links the two trumpets to the two tambourines in the upper corners of this area and shows that both were used heraldically at the time and are part of an elaborate setting of musical instruments. Bynum's connection between what is resurrected and what is paintable raises the interesting question of whether it is possible, in a visual context in which the soul must always express itself in body, to distinguish between the resurrected and the unresurrected. Some distinctions are possible, I believe, such as between different levels of reality or of representation, as discussed below.

40. In this it naturally relates to other Marian themes, such as the Virgin enclosing the elect under her mantle. Like the subjects discussed here, the theme is found widely in devotional literature, especially in France in the mid-thirteenth century, and is especially widespread in Italy in the early fourteenth century; for this tradition, see Vera Sussman, "Maria mit Schutzmantel," *Marburger Jahrbuch für Kunstwissenschaft* 5 (1929): 285–351.

41. *Un trésor gothique*, no. 13, 300–303.

42. Bruno Boerner, "Interprétation du programme iconographique de la châsse de sainte Gertrude à Nivelles," in *Un trésor gothique*, 225–33.

43. In illumination too the new dispensation is shown by placing Sponsa or Ecclesia in structures with recognizably modern architectural details; see Reiner Haussherr, "Templum Salomonis und Ecclesia Christi: Zu einem Bildvergleich der Bible Moralisée," *Zeitschrift für Kunstgeschichte* 31 (1968): 101–21; and Véronique Germanier, "L'Ecclesia comme Sponsa Christi dans les Bibles Moralisées de la première moitié du XIIIème siècle," *Arte Cristiana* 84, 775 (1996): 243–52. At this time stained glass programs in architectural choirs increasingly assert ecclesiastical presence; see Peter Kurmann and Brigitte Kurmann-Schwarz, "Französische Bischöfe als Auftraggeber und Stifter von Glasmalereien: Das Kunstwerk als Geschichtsquelle," *Zeitschrift für Kunstgeschichte* 60 (1997): 429–50, who refer to the programs as creating an "église archiépiscopale" (440).

44. Cambrai, Bibl Mun., ms. 154; see *Un trésor gothique*, no. 53.

45. Philippe Verdier, "Les staurothèques mosanes et leur iconographie du Jugement Dernier," *Cahiers de Civilisation Médiévale* 16 (1973): 199–213.

46. It is unlikely that someone just wanted to include these subjects because several are already represented in the initials in the Hours of the Virgin.

47. Examples include the initials in the Bury Bible and Lothian Bible; see Kauffmann, *Romanesque Manuscripts*, no. 56, p. 89 and Morgan, *Early Gothic Manuscripts*, no. 32, p. 79.

48. The frame dimensions are approximately 17 × 10 cm.

49. The cycle of the Hours of the Cross shows the presumed patron in a series of temptations. For a detailed discussion, one looks forward to Adelaide Bennett, "A Woman's Power of Prayer Versus the Devil in a Book of Hours of ca. 1300," in *Image and Belief: Studies in Celebration of the Eightieth Anniversary of the Index of Christian Art*, ed. Colum Hourihane (Princeton, N.J.: Princeton University Press, 1998).

50. Published in Rezeau, *Le prières aux saints*, no. 217, pp. 515–18. The final

verses (lines 55–60) read: "Et quant m'arme ert del cors sevree, / faites que soit repre-sentee / devant la parmanaule joie, / la ou sans fin avec Diu soie, / ou jou le voie fache a fache. / Pryés ent Dieu et il le fache."

51. For a depiction of the *visio dei* of slightly later date, see Lucy Freeman Sandler, "Face to Face with God: A Pictorial Image of the Beatific Vision," in *England in the Fourteenth Century, Proceedings of the 1985 Harlaxton Symposium*, ed. W. M. Ormrod (Woodbridge, Suffolk: Boydell Press, 1986), 224–35. For devotional works, see Jeffrey F. Hamburger, *The Rothschild Canticles: Art and Mysticism in Flanders and the Rhineland circa 1300* (New Haven, Conn.: Yale University Press, 1990), ch. 4. An interesting analogy to the introductory role of the Cambrai miniature is the illumina-tion of Christ, Mary, and the saints in heaven which, along with the facing page of the Four Evangelists, introduce the Gospel Lessons (which precede the Hours in the Virgin) in a Flemish Horae of c. 1440, Morgan Library, M. 357; see Roger S. Wieck, *Painted Prayers: The Book of Hours in Medieval and Renaissance Art* (New York: George Braziller in association with the Pierpont Morgan Library, 1997), 49.

52. Philip, *Ghent Altarpiece*, chap. 1.

53. See Elisabeth Dhanens, "De Wijze Waarop het Lam Godsaltaar was op-gesteld," *Gentse Bijdragen tot de Kunstgeschiedenis en de Oudheidkunde* 22 (1969–72): 19–90, who proposes that the various panels were arranged into a large cabinetlike struc-ture. The analogy to a reliquary—in this case it would be a box reliquary—is still apt, all the more so because the central panels in her reconstruction enclose a tabernacle.

54. Philip, *Ghent Altarpiece*, 55–61. Various authors have argued for the influ-ence of specific theological works, especially Rupert of Deutz; see the summaries in H. Silvester, "Le retable de l'Agneau mystique et Rupert de Deutz," *Revue Bénédictine* 88 (1978): 274–86; Elisabeth Dhanens, *Van Eyck: The Ghent Altarpiece* (New York: Viking Press, 1973). For Berengaudus, see Derk Visser, *Apocalypse as Utopian Expecta-tion (800–1500)* (Leiden: E. J. Brill, 1996), 152–64.

55. See Carol J. Purtle, *The Marian Paintings of Jan van Eyck* (Princeton, N.J.: Princeton University Press, 1982), 17–39, esp. 35–38. The author also interprets the Annunciation on the exterior in terms of its spousal imagery and argues that the altarpiece was originally seen as a pairing of the Annunciation and Coronation of the Virgin, subjects linked in several contemporary works.

56. They may, however, have known similar works, as Jan and possibly Hubert may have worked as illuminators. Some of the altarpieces of their contemporary Robert Campin seem to have been influenced by the same True Cross triptychs discussed above. For Jan, see Anne van Buren, *Das Turin-Mailander Stundenbuch* (Lucerne: Faksimile Verlag, 1996), 303–6, 313–19; for Campin, see Barbara Lane, "'Depositio et Elevatio': The Symbolism of the Seilern Triptych," *Art Bulletin* 57 (1975): 21–30.

57. Trottmann, *La vision béatifique*, 357–60, 370–72, and passim.

The Limits of Apocalypse: Eschatology, Epistemology, and Textuality in the Commedia and Piers Plowman

1. Important recent work on Dante and apocalypse includes Guglielmo Gorni, "Spirito profetico duecentesco e Dante," *Letture classensi* (1984): 49–68; Dennis Costa, *Irenic Apocalypse: Some Uses of Apocalyptic in Dante, Petrarch and Rabelais* (Saratoga, Calif.: Anma Libri, 1981); Ronald Herzman, "Dante and Apocalypse" in *The Apocalypse in the Middle Ages*, ed. Richard K. Emmerson and Bernard McGinn (Ithaca, N.Y.: Cornell University Press, 1992); the chapter on "The *Commedia*: Apocalypse, Church, and Dante's Conversion" in Emmerson and Herzman's *The Apocalyptic Imagination in Medieval Literature* (Philadelphia: University of Pennsylvania Press, 1992); and Rebecca S. Beal, "Bonaventure, Dante, and the Apocalyptic Woman Clothed with the Sun," *Dante Studies* 114 (1996): 209–28. On Langland, see Morton W. Bloomfield, *Piers Plowman as a Fourteenth-Century Apocalypse* (New Brunswick, N.J.: Rutgers University Press, 1962); Mary Carruthers, "Time, Apocalypse, and the Plot of *Piers Plowman*" in *Acts of Interpretation: The Text and Its Contexts, 700–1600*, ed. Mary Carruthers and Elizabeth D. Kirk (Norman, Okla.: Pilgrim Books, 1982); Robert Adams, "Some Versions of Apocalypse: Learned and Popular Eschatology in *Piers Plowman*" in *The Popular Literature of Medieval England*, ed. Thomas J. Heffernan (Knoxville: University of Tennessee Press, 1985); and Kathryn Kerby-Fulton, *Reformist Apocalypticism and Piers Plowman* (Cambridge: Cambridge University Press, 1990). Richard Emmerson's "'Or Yernen to Rede Redels?' *Piers Plowman* and Prophecy," *Yearbook of Langland Studies* 7 (1993): 27–76, provides a comprehensive clarification of the critical confusion surrounding prophecy, apocalypse, and millennial expectation in Langland's poem and medieval culture more generally.

2. This definition and its derivation are more fully explained in the introduction to my "Fictions of Judgment: The Apocalyptic 'I' in the Fourteenth Century" (Ph.D. diss., Columbia University, 1996), in which I address the problem of apocalypse qua genre through the work of J. J. Collins in "Apocalypse: The Morphology of a Genre," *Semeia* 14 (1979); Bernard McGinn in *Apocalyptic Spirituality* (New York: Paulist Press, 1979), Lois Parkinson Zamora in *Writing the Apocalypse* (New York: Cambridge University Press, 1989), Frank Kermode in *The Sense of an Ending* (New York: Oxford University Press, 1967), Victor Turner in *Dramas, Fields, and Metaphors* (Ithaca, N.Y.: Cornell University Press, 1974), and Dennis Costa in *Irenic Apocalypse*. While apocalypse as a literary genre may not have existed in the fourteenth century, as Emmerson argues in "The Apocalypse in Medieval Culture" (*The Apocalypse in the Middle Ages*, pp. 295–300), the *Commedia* itself provides a generic template for the fiction of judgment, in light of which it is possible to consider Langland's negotiations with his own text.

3. Relevant comparisons of Dante and Langland can be found in Mary Carruthers, *The Search for St. Truth: A Study of Meaning in Piers Plowman* (Evanston, Ill.: Northwestern University Press, 1973); Anne Middleton, "Narration and the Invention of Experience: Episodic Form in *Piers Plowman*" in *The Wisdom of Poetry: Essays in Early English Literature in Honor of Morton W. Bloomfield*, ed. Larry D. Benson

and Siegfried Wenzel (Kalamazoo, Mich.: Medieval Institute Publications, 1982); and Pietro Cali, *Allegory and Vision in Dante and Langland* (Cork: Cork University Press, 1971).

4. Citations and quoted translations from the *Commedia* are from Charles Singleton's edition and translation, Dante Alighieri, *The Divine Comedy*, trans. and comm. Charles S. Singleton (Princeton, N.J.: Princeton University Press, 1970–75), with my bracketed emendations.

5. On post-*Commedia* representations of the otherworld as based on Dante's, see, e.g., Eugene Paul Nassar, "The Iconography of Hell: From the Baptistery Mosaic to the Michelangelo Fresco," *Dante Studies* III (1993): 53–105. See also Alison Morgan, *Dante and the Medieval Other World* (Cambridge: Cambridge University Press, 1990).

6. Robert Hollander has pointed out one moment when this claim is made explicit in "Dante's Book of the Dead: A Note on *Inferno* XXIX, 57," *Studi Danteschi* 54 (1981). The lines in question refer to the tenth bolgia of the *Inferno*, in which the falsifiers are punished:

> . . . là 've la ministra
> de l'alto Sire infallibil giustizia
> punisce i falsador che qui registra. (*Inf.*29: 55–57)

> . . . where the ministress of the High Lord, infallible
> Justice, punishes the falsifiers whom she registers here.

The claim that God's own justice (the same justice that punishes) registers itself, infallible, here in Dante's fiction makes it analogous, as Hollander notes, to the *libri* of life and death mentioned in the Apocalypse, the Book of Daniel, and the *Dies Irae*. See also Jesse Gellrich, "Dante's *Liber Occultorum* and the Structure of Allegory" in *The Idea of the Book in the Middle Ages* (Ithaca, N.Y.: Cornell University Press, 1985).

7. See Teodolinda Barolini, *The Undivine* Comedy: *Detheologizing Dante* (Princeton, N.J.: Princeton University Press, 1992) for a brilliant analysis of the narrative sleights of hand with which Dante achieves this effect and of how critics have for centuries allowed themselves to be fooled.

8. While Dante makes it clear (because only a few seats in the celestial rose remain to be filled) that the end of time, though imminent, has not yet arrived, he also says that he sees the blessed as they will appear at the end of time. See Caroline Walker Bynum, *The Resurrection of the Body in Western Christianity, 200–1336* (New York: Columbia University Press, 1995), esp. chapter 7, for the controversies surrounding the beatific vision and its precise eschatological significance (was it granted to the blessed at death or only at the end of time?) around the time of Dante's writing.

9. As Bloomfield points out: "the dream was a favorite [medieval] literary device because it bespoke a revelation, a higher form of truth. . . . A dream was or could be a vision, and the poet in reporting visions was only fulfilling his traditional role as seer" (11). Morning dreams were particularly endowed with truth in the Macrobian tradition on which the Middle Ages based their oneirology. However, Jacqueline T.

Miller amply demonstrates the limitations of authority in the dream convention with the chapter "Dream Visions of *Auctorite*," in her *Poetic License: Authority and Authorship in Medieval and Renaissance Contexts* (New York: Oxford University Press, 1986).

10. I will quote from the better-known B-text unless otherwise specified, using *The Vision of Piers Plowman*, ed. A.V.C. Schmidt (London: Everyman's, 1978) and J. F. Goodridge's prose translation in *Piers the Ploughman* (London: Penguin, 1959), with my bracketed emendations.

11. As Mary Carruthers has argued in *The Search for St. Truth*, *Piers Plowman* is basically "an epistemological poem, a poem about the problem of knowing truly," which is in large part, for Langland, a problem of language (see esp. 4–11).

12. In "Narration and the Invention of Experience" Middleton argues for the sense of inconclusiveness and indeterminacy present throughout *Piers* in the many "episodes" that move the poem forward without exactly giving it a plot, "units whose arrangement seems somehow reiterative rather than progressive" (92). These episodes each comprise "disputes" between competing authorities that inevitably remain unresolved: "While the purpose of this procedure may be, like that of scholastic disputation, to draw explicit discrepancies to the surface so as to show in what sense they may all point to the same truth, its narrative effect is quite different" (97–98)—it results rather in a sense of truth's fragmentation and multiplicity.

13. Carruthers asserts, regarding the poem's open ending, that "From the point of view of literary plot, Christian history refers both its beginning and end to an all-causative, all-significant middle [i.e., Christ]. Because of this, both beginning and end lose importance in relation to the midpoint. . . . *Piers Plowman* mirrors this distinctively Christian economy of time in its own plot. It neither has a decisive beginning nor builds toward a climactic ending. . . . From Langland's viewpoint . . . to tie up everything into a consonant whole as the classical canons of art would dictate would be to confirm the fictiveness of such an imposed design" ("Time, Apocalypse," 185–87). Interestingly, however, this view of the eschatological and epistemological limitations of Christian "plot" does not take into account the apocalyptic text's stance with respect to its own textuality, in which closure is traditionally definitive. While "the cry of St. John which ends Revelation exactly captures the eschatological expectation of ending, and is echoed in Conscience's cry after Grace at the end of *Piers Plowman*" (186), John's authorial ending, in which those who alter the text are cursed (Apoc. 22: 18–19) has no parallel in *Piers*.

14. Pietro Cali delineates other aspects of this allegorical parallel, *Allegory and Vision*, 109ff.

15. See Robert Hollander, "Dante and His Commentators" in *The Cambridge Companion to Dante*, ed. Rachel Jacoff (Cambridge: Cambridge University Press, 1993), 226–36, who asserts that "this poet behaves in such a way as to indicate that he is evidently in frequent search of a glossator" (227), and Barolini, who suggests the ways in which the poet then constrains the critics' exegesis, in *Undivine*, esp. 3–20.

16. See Robert Kaske, "The Seven *Status ecclesiae* in *Purgatorio* XXXII–XXXIII," in *Dante, Petrarch, Boccaccio: Studies in the Italian Trecento in Honor of Charles S. Singleton*, ed. Aldo Bernardo and Anthony Pellegrini (Binghamton, N.Y.: Medieval and Renaissance Texts and Studies, 1983).

17. See "Fictions of Judgment," chap. 1, for my argument that the major prophecies in the *Commedia* (the Veltro and the 515) are actually metatextual prophecies of the *Commedia* itself in its apocalyptic role.

18. For my discussion of the end of *Piers Plowman*, I will use the C-text, which I believe represents the most fully formed "fiction of judgment" among the versions of the poem (*Piers Plowman*, ed. Derek Pearsall [Berkeley: University of California Press, 1978], with my own translations of any differences from B). See "Fictions of Judgment" for an interpretation of the "apocalyptic" evolution of the three versions, and Theodore L. Steinberg's similar conclusions in Piers Plowman *and Prophecy: An Approach to the C-Text* (New York: Garland, 1991). See also the new verse translation of C by George Economou (Philadelphia: University of Pennsylvania Press, 1996). On Book, see Robert E. Kaske's "The Speech of 'Book' in *Piers Plowman*," *Anglia* 77 (1959): 117–44, in which a "Janus-like pattern of allusion" (124) is detected in Book's speech, where past *and* future are mirrored in the Word of the New Law (126).

19. My literal translation attempts to retain the ambiguities others have elided, particularly regarding the "Iewene ioye." Goodridge offers "and dash to pieces all the triumph of the Jews" (224), while Economou has "And all the joy of the Jews dissolve and despise" (189), and Pearsall glosses "they" (l. 267) as the Jews, adding "The conversion of the Jews to the New Law . . . was a traditional part of millennial prophecy" (331 n.267). More suggestively, Kaske interprets the grammatical difficulties of this passage by glossing the first line as "I, Book, will be burned, but Jesus (will) rise to life" ("Speech," 134–38), and reads the results in light of the tradition of the *Evangelium aeternum* in the writings of Joachim of Fiore, who conceived of this testament for the third age "not as a written document, but as the spiritual meaning or understanding of both Old and New Testaments. . . . According to Joachim, the *intellectus spiritualis* of the *Evangelium aeternum* will consume the letter of the Old and New Testaments like the fire which consumed the sacrifice of Elias" (139).

20. On the dangers of vernacular revelation in late-medieval England, see, e.g., Anne Hudson, *The Premature Reformation: Wycliffite Texts and Lollard History* (New York: Oxford University Press, 1988) and Nicholas Watson, "Censorship and Cultural Change in Late Medieval England: Vernacular Theology, the Oxford Translation Debate, and Arundel's Constitutions of 1409," *Speculum* 70, 4 (October 1995): 822–64.

21. These lines are an addition in the C-text that suggests Langland's heightened apocalyptic awareness in the final version of his poem, for the knowledge of good and evil is apocalyptic knowledge, rightly reserved only to God (my translation).

22. This triple vision suggests the "theology of history" of Joachim of Fiore, the influence of which on this part of the poem is considered by Kaske, who sees that "Langland seems to be clothing the Resurrection at least partly in the imagery of the third *status mundi*" ("Speech," 140). The role of Joachim in *Piers Plowman* is seen also by Bloomfield, Kerby-Fulton, and Robert Frank in *Piers Plowman and the Scheme of Salvation* (New Haven, Conn.: Yale University Press, 1957), and is considered briefly by Lawrence Clopper in *"Songes of Rechelesnesse": Langland and the Franciscans* (Ann Arbor: University of Michigan Press, 1997), chapter 7. See Emmerson, *"Piers Plowman* and Prophecy" for an overview of Joachimist interpretations of the poem, and Emmerson's rejection of them (41–49). In "Fictions of Judgment," I suggest a role for Joachim's thought in both Dante and Langland, but argue that both poets appropri-

ate elements of a Joachite "episteme" to their own visions, without their poems being subsumed by them.

23. Pearsall, 340 n.471.

24. Mary Carruthers, in *The Search for St. Truth* also argues for the epistemological turning point represented by this moment. On the figure of Antichrist in *Piers Plowman*, see Richard Emmerson, *Antichrist in the Middle Ages*, 193–203, and "*Piers Plowman* and Prophecy," 44–49, where he argues for a traditional reading of Langland's Antichrist as the Antichrist of the last days, rather than the more allegorical or polemical figure seen in Joachite and Lollard texts.

25. See, e.g., Leonard W. Cowie, *The Black Death and the Peasants' Revolt* (London: Wayland, 1972), which uses chronicles and other contemporary sources to explain the sociopolitical and religious ramifications of the plague, and their connections to the Rebellion of 1381, to which Langland's poem is also linked, as Steven Justice describes in *Writing and Rebellion: England in 1381* (Berkeley: University of California Press, 1994).

26. "The Black Death and Western European Eschatological Mentalities" in *The Black Death: The Impact of the Fourteenth-Century Plague*, ed. Daniel Williman (Binghamton, N.Y.: Medieval and Renaissance Texts and Studies, 1982), 77–95.

27. Robert Lerner uses these words to define chiliasm in "Medieval Prophecy and Religious Dissent," *Past and Present* 72 (1976): 3–24, 19.

28. See "Fictions of Judgment," chapter 2.

29. David Herlihy, *The Black Death and the Transformation of the West* (Cambridge, Mass.: Harvard University Press, 1997), 72.

30. Relevant work includes Nicholas Havely, "Poverty in Purgatory: From *Commercium* to *Commedia*," *Dante Studies* 114 (1996): 229–43; Charles T. Davis, "Poverty and Eschatology in the *Commedia*," *Yearbook of Italian Studies* 4 (1980): 59–86; Warren Lewis, *Peter John Olivi, Prophet of the Year 2000: Ecclesiology and Eschatology in the* Lectura super apocalipsim (Ph.D. diss., Tübingen University, 1972); Bruno Nardi, "Dante Profeta," in *Dante e la cultura medievale* (1941; rpt. Bari: Laterza, 1949), 336–416 and "Il punto sull' epistola a Cangrande" in *Lectura Dantis Scaligera* (Florence: Le Monnier, 1960); and Raoul Manselli, "Spirituali," *Enciclopedia Dantesca* (Rome: Istituto dell'Enciclopedia Italiana, 1970–78). I have addressed this influence in "*Fuggire* and *Coartare*: Dante and the Hermeneutics of the Spiritual Franciscan Controversies," presented at the Dante Society session of the International Congress on Medieval Studies (Kalamazoo, Mich.: 1996), as well as in "Fictions of Judgment," where I juxtapose the *Commedia* to the confession of Na Prous Boneta, a lay follower of the Spiritual Franciscans condemned as a heretic and apparently burned, with many others, for apocalyptic claims similar in many respects to Dante's.

Contributors

Clifford R. Backman is Associate Professor of History at Boston University. He is the author of *The Decline and Fall of Medieval Sicily: Politics, Religion, and the Economy in the Reign of Frederick III (1296–1337)* and is writing a biography of James II of Aragon-Catalonia and a study of the religious thought of Arnau de Vilanova.

Peter Brown is Rollins Professor of History at Princeton University. He is the author of ten books, including *Augustine of Hippo*, *The Body and Society*, and most recently *The Rise of Western Christendom: 200–1000 A.D.* He is currently working on the problem of wealth, poverty, and care of the poor in late antiquity.

E. Randolph Daniel is a Professor in the History Department at the University of Kentucky. His major interests are the history of religious movements and apocalypticism. He has written *The Franciscan Concept of Mission in the Middle Ages* and edited Books 1–4 of Joachim of Fiore's *Liber de concordia noui ac ueteris testamenti.*

Manuele Gragnolati is Assistant Professor in the Department of French and Italian at Dartmouth College. His recently completed dissertation explores the conception of human identity in Bonvesin da la Riva's *Book of Three Scriptures* and Dante's *Commedia*, focusing on the importance of the body, its relation to the soul, and the significance of pain. He has published articles on the poetry of Matteo Maria Boiardo, Giovanni Pascoli, and Filippo Tommaso Marinetti.

Anna Harrison is a Ph.D. candidate in the Department of Religion at Columbia University. Her dissertation concerns love of neighbor in twelfth- and thirteenth-century devotional literature. Her article " 'If one member glories . . . , if one member suffers': Bernard on Community Between the Living and the Saintly Dead" is forthcoming in *Cistercian Studies Quarterly.*

Benjamin Hudson is Associate Professor of History at Pennsylvania State University with an interest in the North Atlantic regions during the Middle Ages. He is the author of *Kings of Celtic Scotland* and *The Prophecy of Berchán: Irish and Scottish High Kings of the Early Middle Ages.*

Jacqueline E. Jung is completing her dissertation in the Department of Art History and Archaeology at Columbia University. Her research concerns the thirteenth-century sculptural program in the west choir of Naumburg Cathedral, focusing on the social implications of its style and content especially as triggers of emotional response. Her translations of two art history articles from German are forthcoming.

Claudia Rattazzi Papka received her Ph.D. in comparative literature at Columbia University and teaches at the University of Massachusetts, Amherst, in the Department of French and Italian Studies. She has published articles on medieval literature and culture in *The Chaucer Review* and *Annali d'Italianistica*. Her dissertation, "Fictions of Judgment: The Apocalyptic 'I' in the Fourteenth Century," defines the hermeneutic and rhetorical paradoxes inherent in apocalyptic literature.

Laura A. Smoller is Assistant Professor of History at the University of Arkansas at Little Rock. She is the author of *History, Prophecy, and the Stars: The Christian Astrology of Pierre d'Ailly, 1350–1420* as well as articles on late medieval astrology and miracles. She is working on a study of the canonization of St. Vincent Ferrer.

Harvey Stahl is Associate Professor of Medieval Art at the University of California, Berkeley. He has lectured and published on many medieval subjects, including French Gothic painting, reliquaries, and ivories. He is completing a book on the Psalter of Saint Louis.

Carole Straw is a professor at Mount Holyoke College, where she teaches ancient and medieval history. She is the author of *Gregory the Great: Perfection in Imperfection*, which won the John Nicholas Brown Prize from the Medieval Academy of America. She also wrote on Gregory in the Authors of the Middle Ages series for Ashgate/Variorum. She is completing a book on martyrdom in the early church.

Index

Page numbers in *italics* refer to illustrations.

Acknowledgments

This collection originated in two events: a panel organized by Paul Freedman for the American Historical Association meeting in New York in 1997 and a graduate seminar on eschatology taught by Caroline Walker Bynum at Columbia University during the academic year 1995–96. During a conversation in the spring of 1997, we saw that by combining the products of these two enterprises we might create a volume that brought together several understandings of "eschatology" pursued only in isolation from each other in recent scholarly literature.

In the end it did not prove possible to include all the papers from both events, but we were able to persuade several distinguished scholars to contribute additional essays that fill out the eschatological landscape we wish to depict. We thank those who participated in the American Historical Association panel and those who were part of Columbia University Seminar G9008–9009. Their conversation, insights, and questions helped both authors and editors of this volume craft what we hope is a coherent and wide-ranging collection. We also thank the two anonymous reviewers of the proposal and the manuscript for their very helpful comments and suggestions. We are grateful to Victoria Velsor for her hard work in editing and regularizing the citations and style of the different contributions and for preparing the index.